Tom Roberts

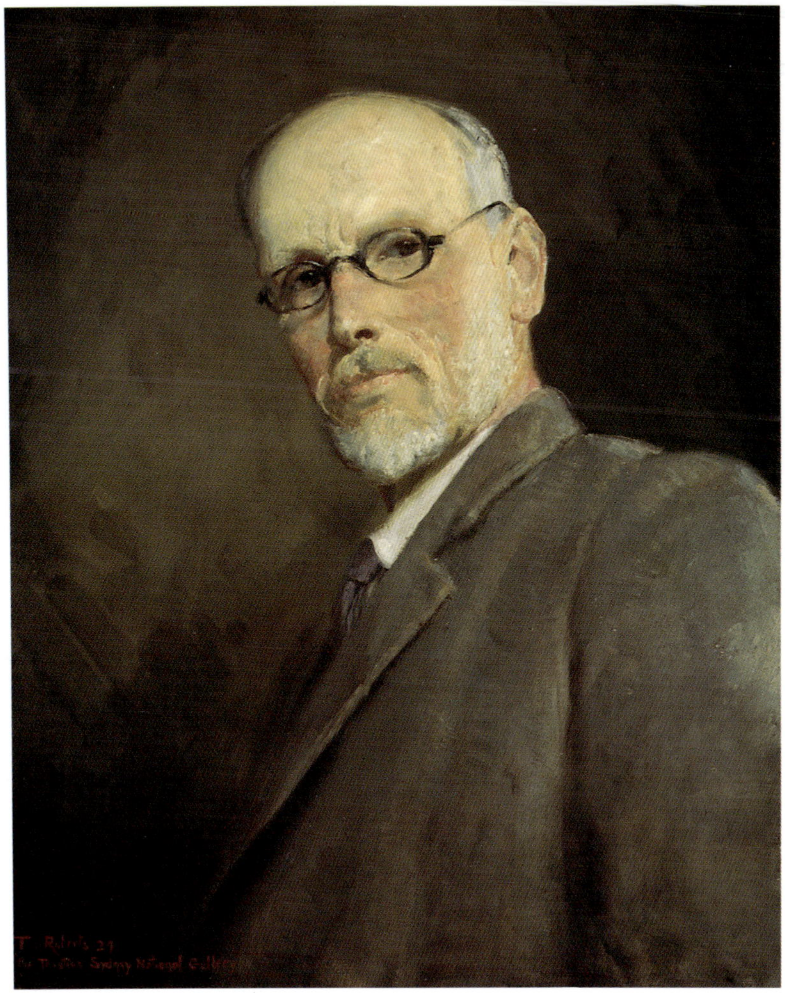

Selected and co-ordinated by
Ron Radford

Art Gallery of South Australia, Adelaide
Art Exhibitions Australia, Sydney

Art Exhibtions Australia is delighted to be associated with the Art Gallery of South Australia in bringing to the nation the first Tom Roberts retrospective for fifty years. Tom Roberts is considered Australia's most popular artist, one who has helped shape the Australian identity.

Art Exhibitions Australia, since its foundation in 1980, has established partnerships with public galleries, government agencies and corporate sponsors to bring major exhibitions to this country. No project of this scope is possible without corporate support and we are deeply grateful to the principal sponsor Mazda Australia for their generous sponsorship of this exhibition as well as Channel Seven, Triple M, Ansett Australia, Singapore Airlines and Hotel Sofitel/Novotel. We also acknowledge the invaluable involvement of the Commonwealth Government through the Department of Communications and the Arts in providing indemnification of the collection.

We would like to give special thanks to the Director, Ron Radford, Senior Curator of Australian Art, Jane Hylton and the staff of the Art Gallery of South Australia for curating this exhibition to tour to five Australian venues.

Michael Darling
Chairman
Art Exhibitions Australia Limited

Generously sponsored by

Mazda Australia Pty Limited

mazda

Channel Seven Triple M Ansett Australia Singapore Airlines Hotel Sofitel/Novotel

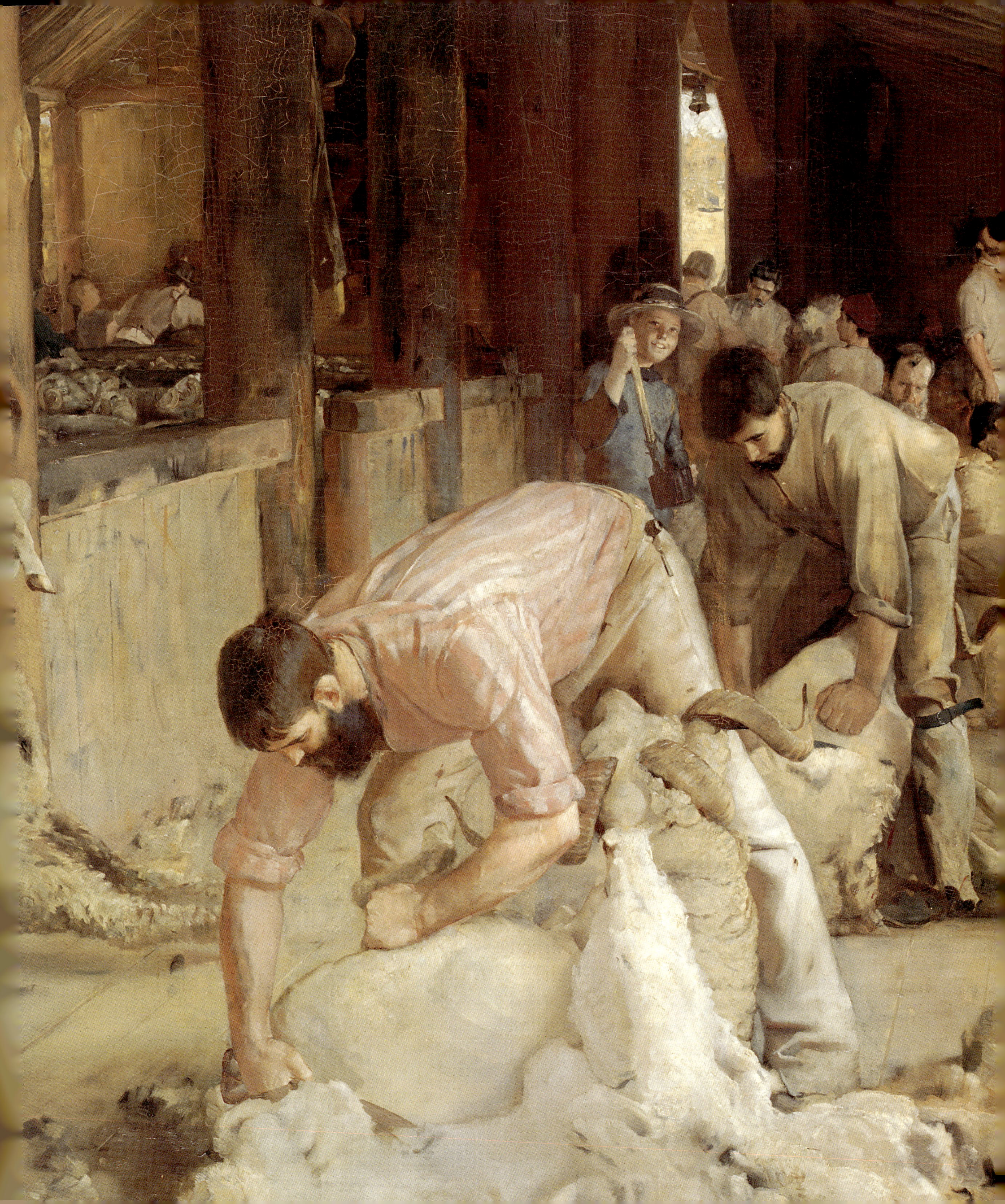

Acknowledgements

The success and magnitude of the exhibition which this publication accompanies is due to the good will of Australia's public art museums and libraries who generously agreed to lend key works from their collections, and to the support of private collectors who agreed to part temporarily with their paintings. Not all artists are loveable, but Australians have always loved the work of Tom Roberts. In our art museums Roberts's paintings are among the most popular; in private hands they are among the most treasured. Every loan to this exhibition therefore represents the kind of generosity usually reserved for old friends. For that we are deeply grateful.

On behalf of the Art Gallery of South Australia I would particularly like to thank Art Exhibitions Australia, especially its Chief Executive, Bob Edwards, for establishing this alliance with the Gallery of which this exhibition and publication are the happy results. They form a fitting climax to the inaugural year of the Gallery's new west wing, a splendid resource which has made it possible for us to mount a so-called 'blockbuster' exhibition. The Gallery's staff have risen to the organisational and intellectual challenge of producing a matching work of scholarship.

We are delighted that in partnership with Art Exhibitions Australia and Mazda Australia Pty Limited, our generous sponsor, the Art Gallery of South Australia can bring to cities across our vast continent this outstanding exhibition of paintings by one of the nation's most significant artists. The Adelaide showing of this exhibition has been supported by Santos Limited.

I would also like to express my appreciation to those colleagues who from its inception were committed to lend to this project and were unfailing in their support throughout its development; in particular, Betty Churcher, Director, and Mary Eagle, Senior Curator of Australian Art, National Gallery of Australia; Edmund Capon, Director, and Barry Pearce, Curator of Australian Art, The Art Gallery of New South Wales; Timothy Potts, Director, and Terence Lane, Senior Curator of Australian Art to 1900, National Gallery of Victoria; Stephen Gower, Director, and Lola Wilkins, Acting Senior Curator of Art, Australian War Memorial; Warren Horton, Director-General, National Library of Australia; Dagmar Schmidmaier, State Librarian of New South Wales; Margaret Rich, Director, and Paul Simmons, Registrar, Ballarat Fine Art Gallery; Peter Perry, Director, Castlemaine Art Gallery and Historical Museum; Michael Pursche, Director, Manly Art Gallery & Museum; Joseph Eisenberg, Director, and Belinda Cotton, Deputy Director, New England Regional Art Museum; and Janine Barrand, Director, and Sally Robins, Curator, Performing Arts Museum, Victorian Arts Centre Trust.

Charcoal burners, (detail), 1886, Melbourne, oil on canvas, 61.4 x 92.3 cm, Ballarat Fine Art Gallery; Bequest of J.R. Hartley 1961

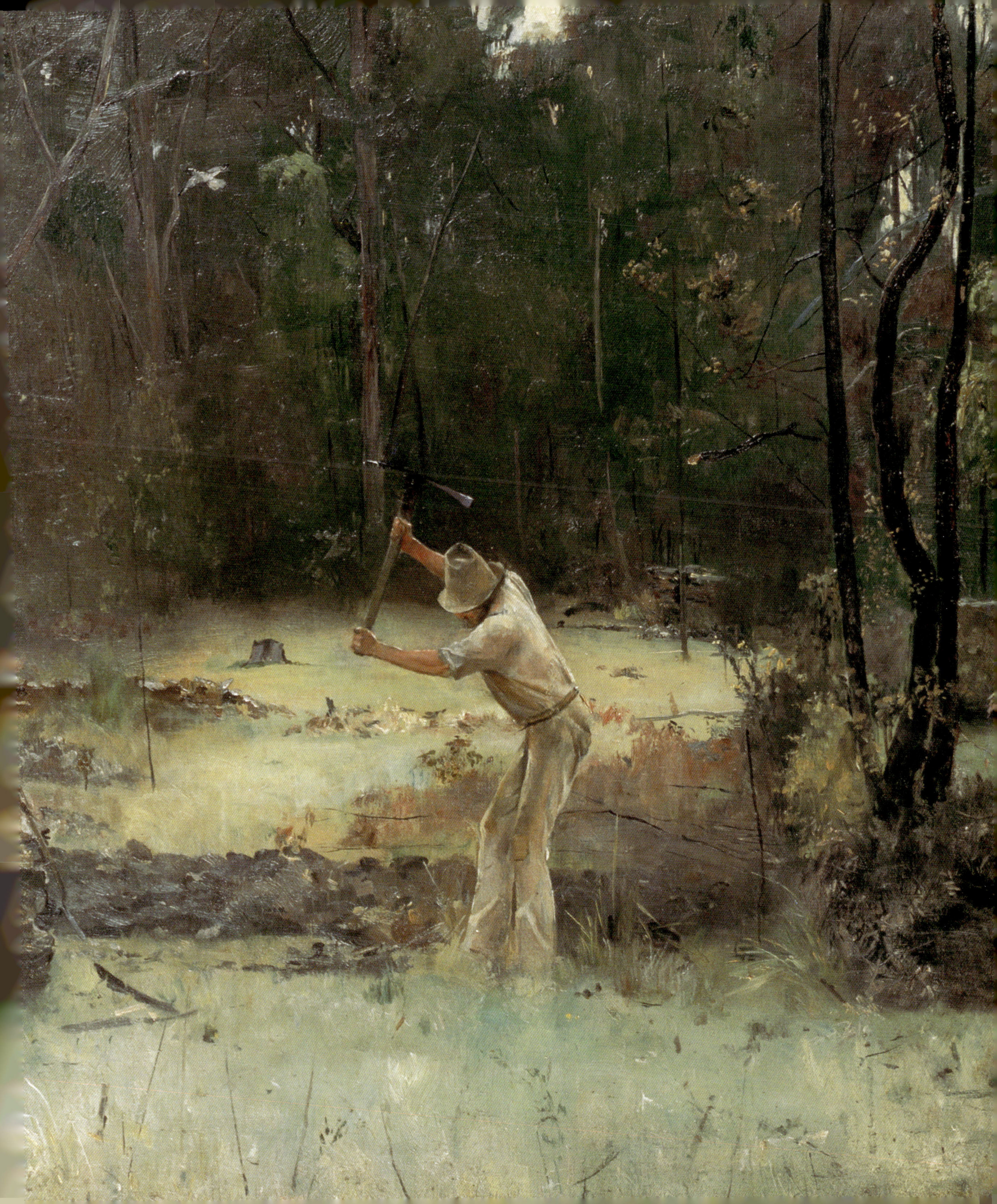

I am indebted to Helen Topliss for her extensively revised catalogue entries and essay. My warm thanks also go to several other Roberts scholars who have graciously committed time to this project and contributed original essays full of new information and interpretations: Leigh Astbury, Roger Butler, Mary Eagle, Jane Hylton, Humphrey McQueen, Barry Pearce, Virginia Spate and Daniel Thomas. I am particularly grateful to Daniel Thomas who shouldered the burden of editing this sizeable, collaborative publication.

I would like to thank Frank McDonald and Chris Deutscher for their kind assistance with negotiating some private loans; and of course the staff of the Art Gallery of South Australia for their unwavering support and proficiency, particularly Jane Hylton, Curator of Australian Art and Assistant Curator of the show; Tracey Lock-Weir, its Assistant Co-ordinator; Antonietta Itropico, Publications Manager, who designed and supervised the book; Georgia Hale, Photographic Services Officer; Kaj Lindstrom, Assistant Director; Nat Williams, Manager Public Programs; Judith Hamilton, Registrar; my secretary Lindsay Brookes and Heather Brooks, Curatorial Secretary.

The institutions who have generously lent works are: The Art Gallery of New South Wales, Sydney; Art Gallery of South Australia, including the M. J. M. Carter Collection, Adelaide; Australian War Memorial, Canberra; Ballarat Fine Art Gallery, Ballarat; Castlemaine Art Gallery and Historical Museum, Castlemaine; Manly Art Gallery & Museum, Sydney; Mitchell Library and Dixson Galleries, State Library of New South Wales, Sydney; National Gallery of Australia, Canberra; National Gallery of Victoria, Melbourne; National Library of Australia, Canberra; New England Regional Art Museum, Armidale; Performing Arts Museum, Victorian Arts Centre Trust, Melbourne.

I would also like to thank the generous private collectors, Joseph Brown, James Fairfax, ICI Australia, Tom Roberts (the artist's great-nephew), and twelve lenders who wish to remain anonymous.

Ron Radford
Co-ordinating Curator and
Director, Art Gallery of South Australia

Miss Minna Simpson, (detail), 1886, Melbourne, oil on canvas, 59.5 x 49.5 cm; Private collection, Canberra

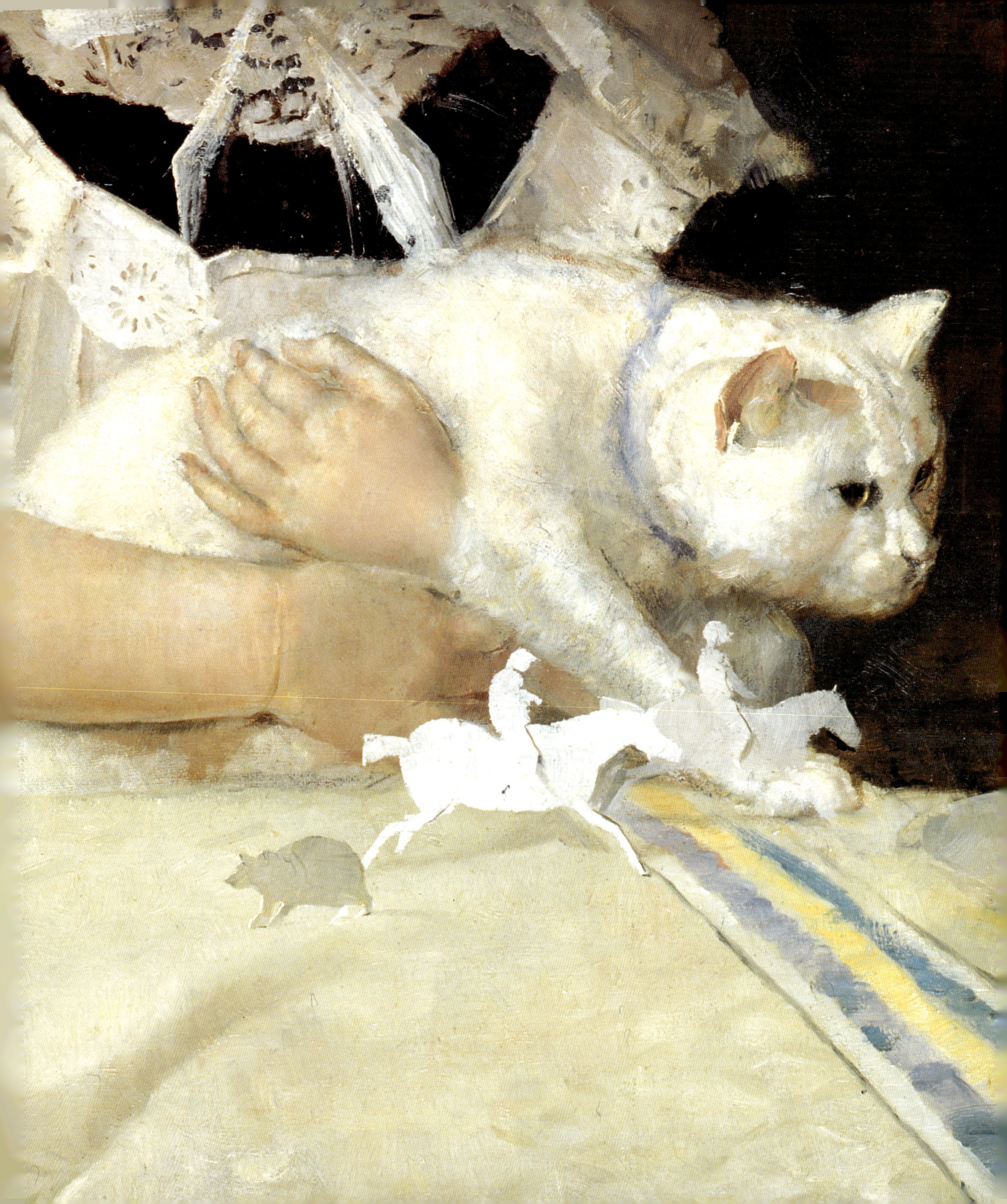

Tom Roberts is published on the occasion of the *Tom Roberts* retrospective, originated by the Art Gallery of South Australia, in conjunction with Art Exhibitions Australia touring to: Art Gallery of South Australia, Adelaide, 5 October – 17 November 1996; Tasmanian Museum and Art Gallery, Hobart, 30 November 1996 – 27 January 1997; National Gallery of Victoria, Melbourne, 12 February – 6 April 1997; The Art Gallery of New South Wales, Sydney, 19 April – 1 June 1997; Art Gallery of Western Australia, Perth 11 June – 27 July 1997.

Selected and co-ordinated by Ron Radford, assisted by Jane Hylton
Assistant co-ordinator Tracey Lock-Weir
Edited by Daniel Thomas

Designed and produced by Antonietta Itropico
Separations by Bartlett & van Gastel Graphics
Printing by Wallis Print

Cataloguing-in-Publication data National Library of Australia

Tom Roberts.

ISBN 0 7308 3049 7.

1. Roberts, Tom, 1856-1931. 2. Painters - Australia -
Biography. I. Roberts, Tom, 1856-1931. II. Radford, Ron, 1949-
III. Art Gallery of South Australia. IV. Art Exhibitions Australia.

759.994

Front cover: *A break away!*, (detail), 1891, Corowa, NSW and Melbourne, oil on canvas, 137.3 x 167.8 cm; Art Gallery of South Australia, Adelaide, Elder Bequest Fund 1899

Back cover: *A summer morning tiff*, 1886, Melbourne, oil on canvas mounted on board, 76.5 x 51.2 cm; Ballarat Fine Art Gallery, Martha K. Pinkerton Bequest Fund 1943

p. 1: *Self-portrait*, 1924, Kallista, Victoria, oil on canvas, 61.2 x 51.0 cm; The Art Gallery of New South Wales, Sydney, Gift of the artist 1924

p. 3: *Shearing the rams*, (detail), 1888-90, Brocklesby Station, Corowa, NSW, and Melbourne, oil on canvas mounted on board, 121.9 x 182.6 cm; National Gallery of Victoria, Melbourne, Felton Bequest Fund 1932

Art Gallery of South Australia, North Terrace, Adelaide, South Australia 5000 Australia.
Telephone (08) 8207 7000 Facsimile (08) 8207 7070

Contents

The Father of Australian Landscape Painting?

Ron Radford

Tom Roberts's paintings are now probably the best known and best loved of all Australian works of art. Yet, unlike his younger friend Arthur Streeton who became a living national hero, Roberts was comparatively neglected in the last decades of his life. And in his home town Melbourne, the National Gallery of Victoria acquired only one minor work during his lifetime. After his death in 1931 Roberts's reputation began to grow and by the mid 1960s Brian Finemore of the National Gallery of Victoria, and the nation's first Curator of Australian Art, began his lecture on Roberts at Melbourne University with the words, "Tom Roberts is the finest artist Australia has ever produced ...". Roberts's first biographer, R.H. Croll, entitled his 1935 book on the artist *Tom Roberts: Father of Australian landscape painting*, an oft-repeated description of Roberts's place in Australian art. Given that the history of Australian art has largely been written (although inaccurately) through the development of Australian landscape painting, this is high praise indeed. However it is a very warped view of Roberts and his place in the history of Australian art. He was both more than a landscapist and less than Australian landscape's father.

It is true that Roberts was probably the most influential figure in the development of open-air Australian *impressionist* landscape painting (or *naturalist*; the terminology is unsettled), the movement which in the 1880s so effectively captured typical Australian light, the bush, and the beach. But he was not the sole 'father' of that development. More significantly, he painted few ambitious Australian landscapes.

The poetic "*Evening, when the quiet east flushes faintly at the sun's last look*", c1887, could be described as his only pure landscape painting of major artistic significance. He did execute a number of similarly significant landscapes with figures, such as *The artists' camp*, 1886, *A summer morning tiff*, 1886, *Slumbering sea, Mentone*, 1887, *The Sunny South*, 1887, and *In a corner on the Macintyre*, 1895, but the figures provide a narrative element or theme in these paintings, and are as important to the composition as the landscape they inhabit. Even so there are, from the 1880s and 1890s, not many more than a dozen of these major but modest sized figure-in-landscape paintings.

Roberts is most famous, of course, for his large and deliberately nationalistic pre-Federation subject pictures. There are even fewer of these; the two woolshed pictures *Shearing the rams*, 1888-90, and *The Golden Fleece*, 1894, the dramatic sheep-droving picture *A break away!*, 1891, and the bushranging subject *Bailed up*, 1895. These four large paintings have long been in public art galleries, for which they were intended, and have become icons of Australian cultural identity. Without doubt these four are the best known and most reproduced of all Australian paintings. But none of them is the type of landscape painting of which Roberts has been claimed to be "the father".

"Evening, when the quiet east flushes faintly at the sun's last look", (detail), c1887, Melbourne, oil on canvas, 50.8 x 76.2 cm; National Gallery of Victoria, Melbourne, W.H. Short Bequest Fund 1944

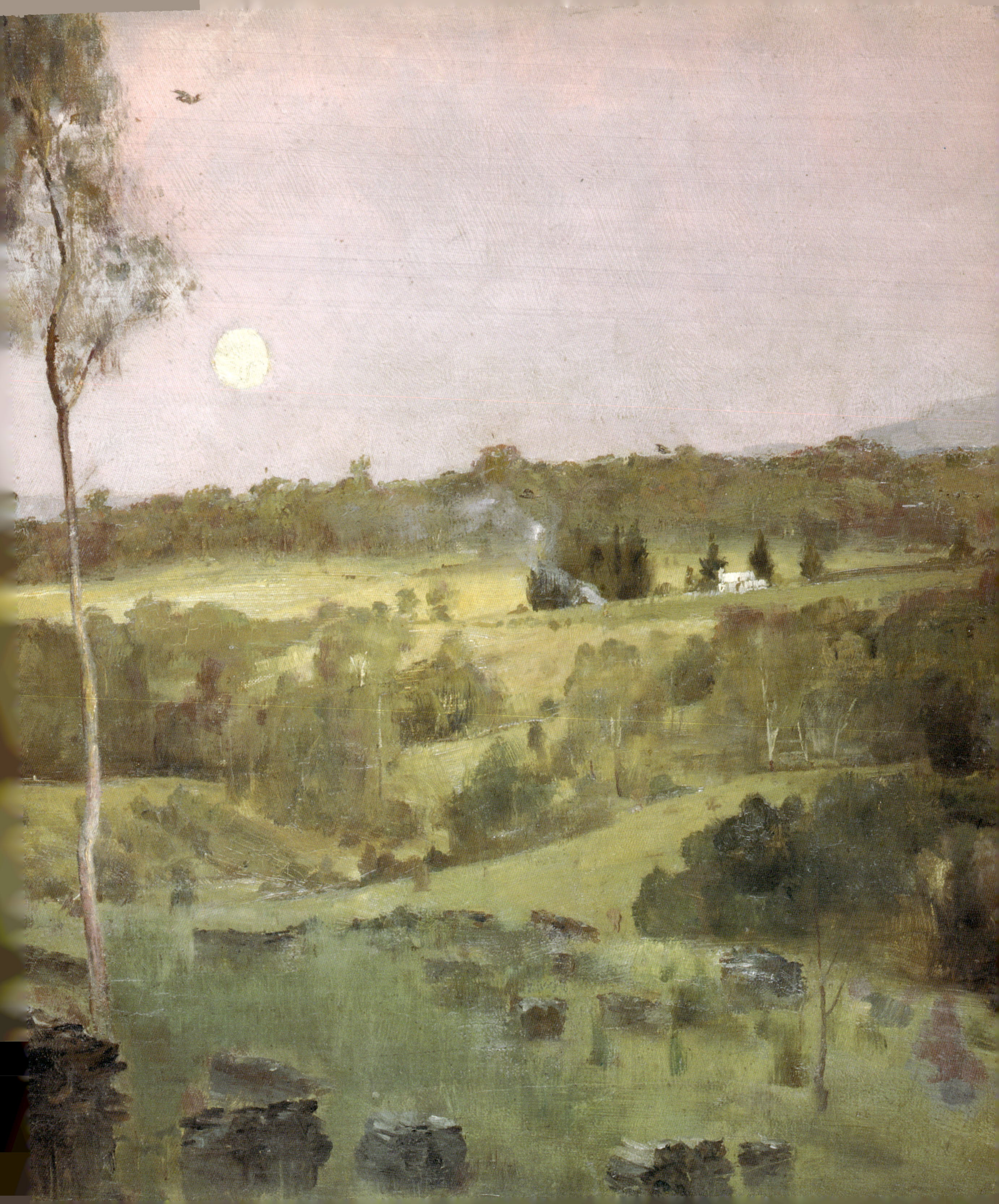

Tom Roberts

In fact Roberts painted more portraits than anything else in the 1880s and 1890s, the first two and most significant decades of his career, and he largely supported himself as a painter of commissioned portraits, in pastels as well as oils. Over a third of the entire output was devoted to portraiture. His finest portraits such as *Madame Pfund*, 1887, *Mrs L.A. Abrahams*, 1888, *Smike Streeton age 24*, 1891, *Eileen*, 1892, and *Florence Greaves*, 1898, are among the most interesting ever painted in Australia. Some would argue with much justification that Roberts is Australia's best portraitist of all time. He lobbied hard for a National Portrait Gallery to be established in Australia. Besides portraits, landscapes and subjects of bush life, Roberts also painted occasional mythological subjects, anecdotal subjects, city views and still-lives. He also made a few etchings.

Roberts can be accurately described as a landscape painter only after he left Australia for London. The majority of his landscapes were painted after 1903 in Britain and, after 1910, on visits to the Continent and then after 1923 when he returned permanently to Australia and finally became a comparatively prolific painter of Australian landscape. His output dwindled in the last couple of years of his life, so Roberts was a regular painter of the Australian landscape only for about six declining years of his long seventy-five-year life.

As Roberts's few large paintings of Australian national life and his smaller figures-in-landscape paintings have so captured the nation's imagination, it is best to define him not as the father of Australian landscape painting but as a creator of Australia's self-image.

A much travelled and well trained figure, portrait and landscape artist, he was by the mid 1880s uniquely qualified for his nation-building role. Having arrived from Britain aged thirteen, and having trained in Melbourne and then London, he could stand slightly aside and analyse Australia and its people somewhat as an outsider. He also travelled the Australian continent more extensively than any other major Australian artist of his generation. In the 1880s and 1890s he spent almost equal time in the country's two largest colonial capitals and art centres, Melbourne and Sydney. Because of family friends and relatives, he regularly visited and painted in Tasmania from the 1880s until his death in 1931; he is buried in Tasmania. He travelled to and painted in far north Queensland and he visited Adelaide and Perth several times during his career. And he painted his iconic bush-life pictures in inland New South Wales, far from the cities.

He knew and understood much of the vast continent of Australia. He painted portraits of a great range of its citizens: rural workers, pastoralist landowners, businessmen, fellow artists, musicians, actresses, society women, soldiers, politicians, Governors, and Aboriginal people. More significantly, Roberts painted the great themes of Australian life: immigration, shearing, stockriding, logging, threshing, bushranging, outdoor recreation and bustling city life. He painted the land itself, its pastures, mountains, forests and seacoasts. But he also painted an inner life, introspective interiors, domestic incidents, the intimacy of homes in which people read or play music.

Tom Roberts's ultimate nationalistic painting, his largest work and the one which took him the longest time to complete, was his historic Federation commission, *Opening of*

Slumbering sea, Mentone, (detail), 1887, Melbourne, oil on canvas, 51.0 x 76.5 cm; National Gallery of Victoria, Melbourne, Purchased with the assistance of a special grant from the Government of Victoria 1979

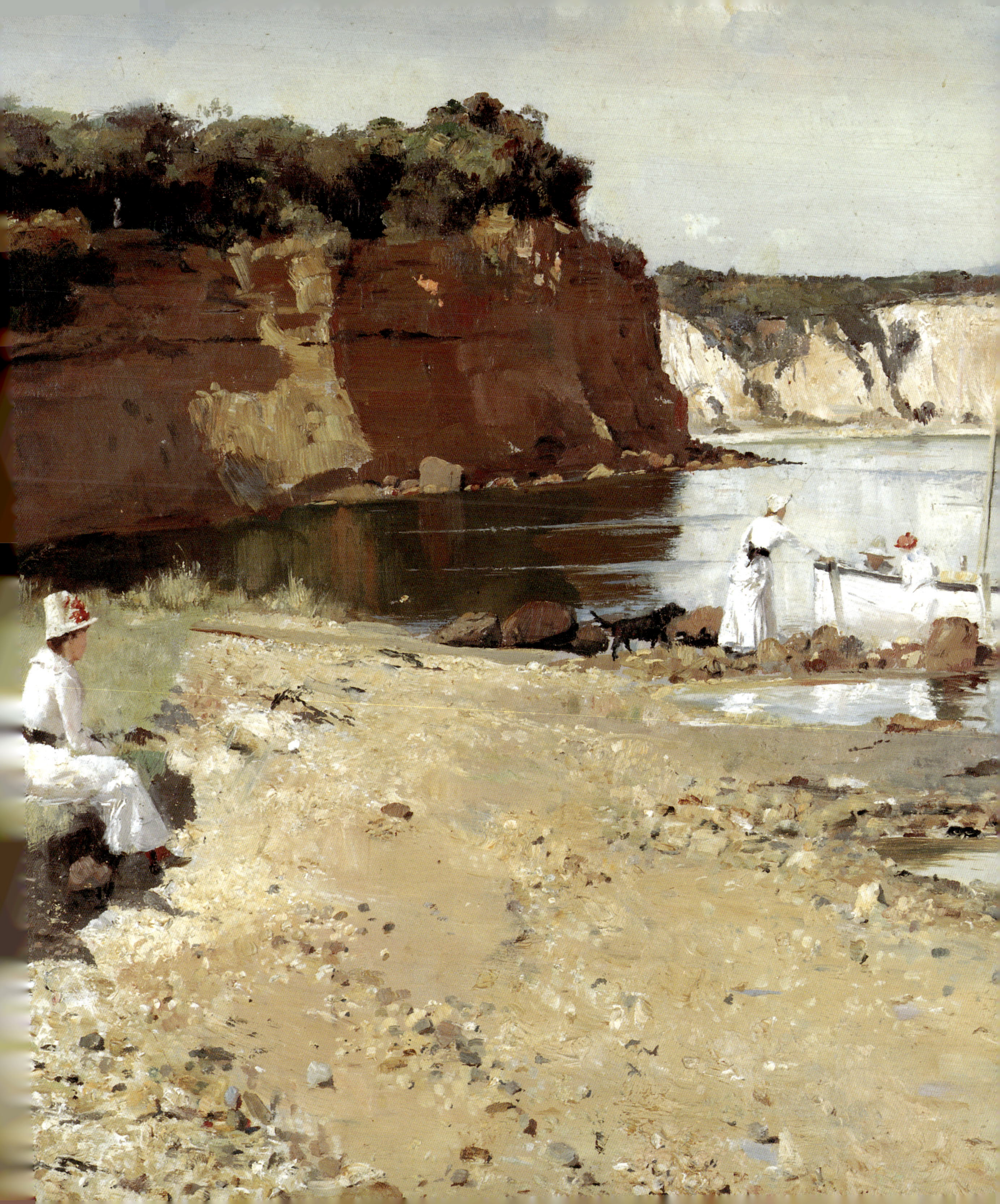

the First Parliament of the Commonwealth of Australia by H.R.H. The Duke of Cornwall and York, May 9, 1901, 1901-3, a vast "machine" which now hangs in Parliament House, Canberra, on loan from Her Majesty the Queen.

All this was Roberts's Australia, a mainly egalitarian place from which he remained slightly aloof but of which he was an integral part. He was also a painter of Empire: of London its imperial heart, of the English countryside, of British aristocracy and royalty. In Australia's eager claim of Roberts as the nation's great image-maker, it is convenient to forget his English birth, his training at London's Royal Academy and the fact that he spent, over three crucial periods, a total of thirty-six years – nearly half his life – in Britain. It was in London that he craved professional success, but the great city denied him and the centre of Empire destroyed his confidence. He retreated to his familiar outpost of Empire where in his last years he painted small, unambitious Australian landscapes.

Of those who emerged in the nineteenth century, Roberts seems to be the artist most aware of a previous tradition of Australian painting. He respected Aboriginal art. In late-colonial Melbourne he knew S.T. Gill and his lively early-colonial watercolours of workers in the Australian bush; art historians have long pointed to them as forerunners to the more substantial national-life figure subjects painted by Roberts. Both Roberts and Streeton were aware of Conrad Martens's light-filled early-colonial watercolours of Sydney Harbour. Their artist-critic friend Lionel Lindsay wrote the first significant monograph on an Australian artist when he published his book on Martens in 1920. In Melbourne, Roberts (like Frederick McCubbin) in his student days admired the painterly landscapes of Louis Buvelot and later encouraged other younger artists to use similar methods. Roberts befriended Buvelot in old age and as a tribute etched a striking portrait of him. Roberts was one of those who asserted during the 1880s that Buvelot was the father of Australian landscape painting.

Further, Roberts was the only artist of his time who was fully aware of the predecessor who had a far greater claim than either Buvelot or Roberts himself to the title "father of Australian landscape painting" – namely John Glover. Glover spent the last two decades of his life, the 1830s and 1840s, in Tasmania as a prolific painter of its scenery. On his numerous trips to Tasmania, Roberts must have seen many of Glover's landscape paintings in the museums and private collections there. (No Australian landscapes by Glover were held and displayed in public collections on the mainland until the 1950s.) When painting in northern Tasmania, Roberts acknowledged Glover's former sites; he titled one 1920s landscape *Glover's country*. He restored Glover's grave at Deddington and Roberts himself is buried in a country churchyard near Longford, only a few kilometres away.

* * *

Nearly all aspects of Roberts's varied artistic career covering more than half a century are represented in this retrospective exhibition. Although larger, more balanced and comprehensive than the two previous retrospectives, held in 1932 and 1947-48, this

Allegro con brio, Bourke Street west, (detail), c1885-86 and 1890, Melbourne, oil on canvas, 51.2 x 76.3 cm; National Library of Australia, Canberra, Purchased 1920 by Parliamentary Library Committee. On loan to the National Gallery of Australia, Canberra.

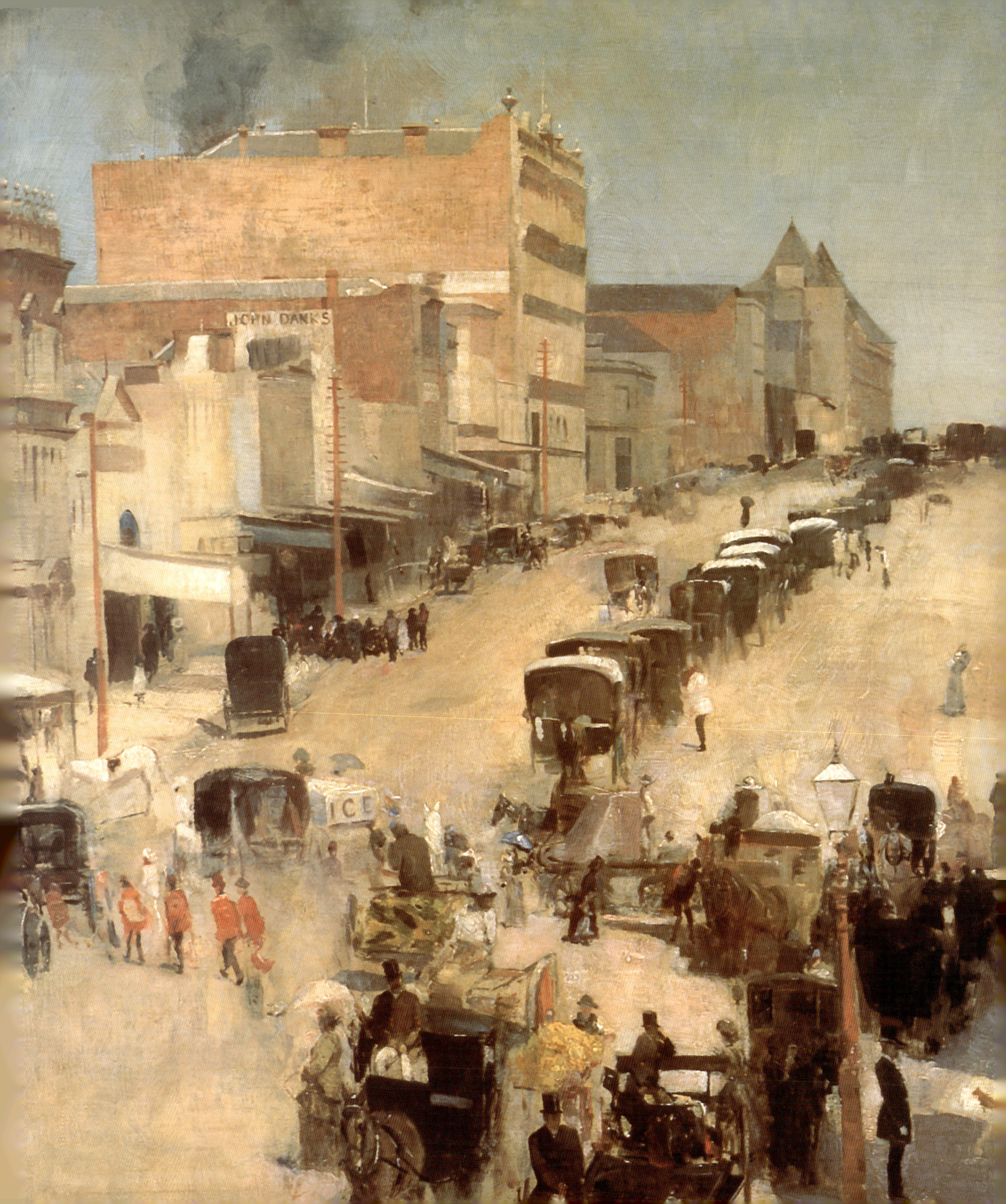
JOHN DANKS
ICE

exhibition has been deliberately restricted in size to just over eighty works. Although it includes all periods of his career and his various subjects, it omits his drawings, his few etchings (an essay on the etchings is included in this book) and his fewer sculptures. There is only one watercolour and for conservation reasons only three of his numerous pastel portraits.

More than those of any other Australian painter, Roberts's major works have now entered public collections, a further proof of the esteem in which his work is held. Over three quarters of the works in this exhibition come from art museums and libraries. Indeed, more than half the works in the exhibition come from three collections alone: the Art Gallery of South Australia, the Art Gallery of New South Wales (both of which were appreciative patrons of Roberts in his lifetime) and the National Gallery of Victoria.

To accompany a retrospective exhibition of such highly prized public property as Roberts's works have become, we determined to engage all the scholars on Roberts to offer new insights into his life and art. This book consequently has contributions from Virginia Spate who wrote the much admired 1972 monograph on Tom Roberts, Helen Topliss the author of the 1985 two-volume catalogue raisonné of Roberts's work, Leigh Astbury who has contextualised Roberts's work in *City Bushmen: The Heidelberg School and the rural mythology* (1985) and *Sunlight and Shadow: Australian impressionist painters 1890-1900* (1989), and Humphrey McQueen, author of the new biography of Tom Roberts published in 1996. Contributions have also been made by curators and former curators who have looked after and researched Roberts's works and have been responsible for acquiring many of them for art museums. They are Mary Eagle, Roger Butler, Barry Pearce, Daniel Thomas, Jane Hylton and myself.

This 1996-97 retrospective exhibition and its accompanying book are launched exactly 140 years after Tom Roberts's birth and sixty-five years after his death. It coincides with a similar-scaled 1995-96 retrospective exhibition of paintings by Arthur Streeton, his younger friend, one-time pupil and rival.

Since the late 1880s there has always been critical speculation as to which is the finer of these two Australian impressionist artists. Roberts and Streeton have both played an important part in developing an Australian national consciousness. In the years leading up to the 1901 Federation of the six Australian colonies, they made deliberately heroic paintings which have become national icons. This year affords the first opportunity to see the full range of both artists' work gathered together concurrently from private and public collections nationwide. The comparison is extraordinarily interesting.

The first and immediate conclusion one comes to in comparing their work, a conclusion which will surprise no one, is the limited range of subject matter of Streeton's output compared with Roberts's. Streeton seldom ventured beyond landscapes; he could not paint figures. Roberts on the other hand was not only a landscape painter, but also a subject painter and a portrait painter. There is a great variety of subjects in Roberts's œuvre; he was clearly a better trained draughtsman of the figure and that allowed his greater versatility.

Eileen, (detail), 1892, Sydney, oil on canvas, 49.0 x 36.0 cm; The Art Gallery of New South Wales, Sydney, Purchased 1892

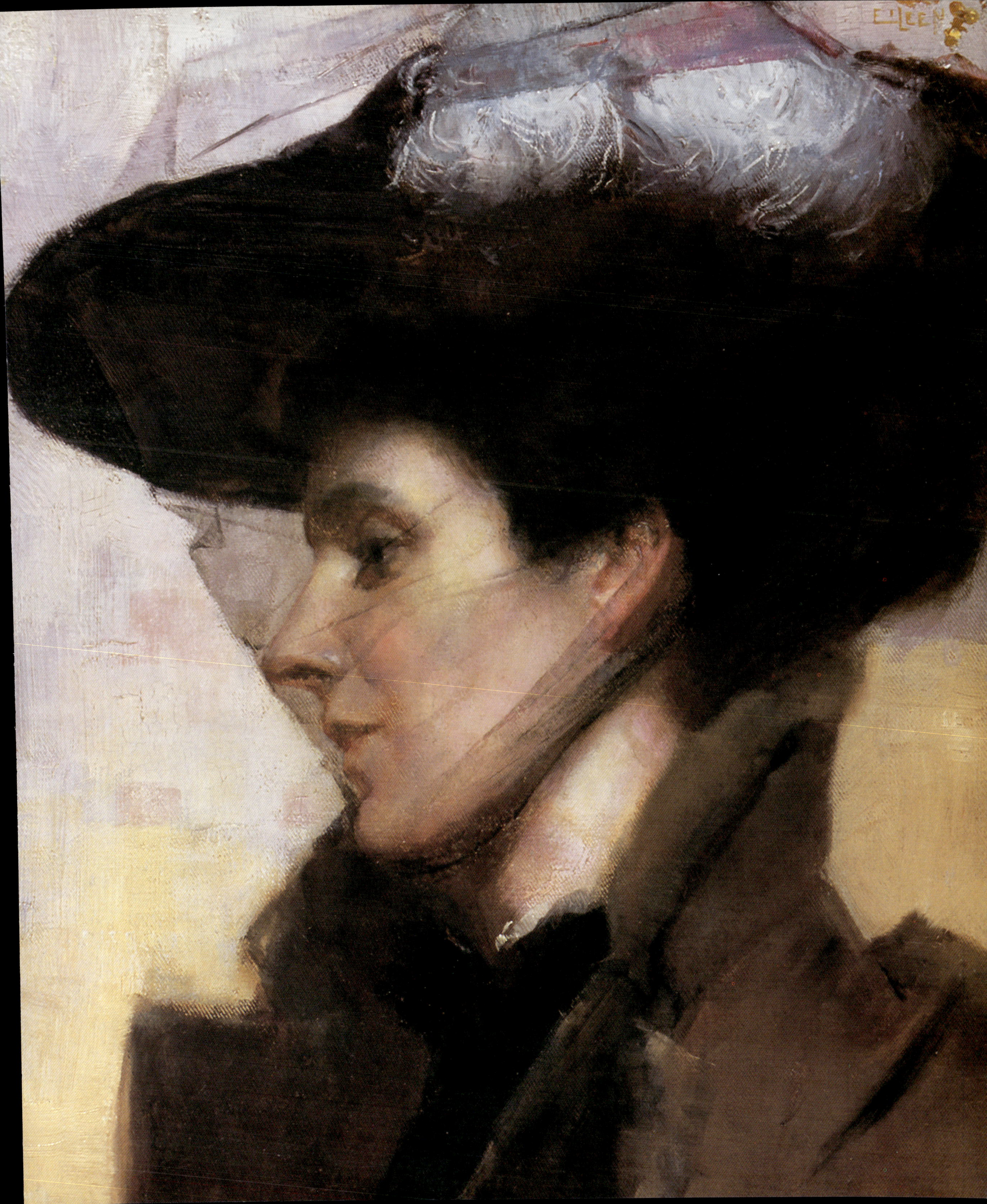
EILEEN

Nevertheless, the two retrospective exhibitions reveal that a number of Streeton's finest works painted between late 1888 and 1897, just before he left Australia for the first time, display what can only be described as a greater sense of magic. Australian-born and eleven years younger than Roberts his mentor, Streeton's youthful confidence – encouraged by both Roberts and Charles Conder – inspired him to a lyrical ecstasy when excited by a particular landscape motif. His was a spontaneously direct and emotive response to nature. Energy transferred from eye to hand with a deft impressionist's touch can be seen in Streeton's finest works like *Early summer - gorse in bloom*, 1888, and *Fire's on*, 1891, and in smaller works like *At Templestowe*, 1889, *The selector's hut: Whelan on the log*, 1890, *The railway station*, 1893, *Oncoming storm*, 1895, and *Summer noon, Hawkesbury River*, 1896. These inspired works are, however, very few. Streeton could not sustain this quality beyond his thirtieth year. They were created with the exuberance of youth.

Apart from Roberts's '9 by 5 Impressions' (which have firmer structure than Streeton's) his paintings generally do not have such an inspired and poetic 'impressionist' touch as Streeton's finest works. However, many more substantial pictures were produced by Roberts. His career developed more slowly, and his natural reticence may have held him back, but his better training and objectivity were a saving grace in the longer artistic haul. At the end of 1888 when Streeton began his best work he was only twenty-one; Roberts's best work began in 1885 by which time he was nearly thirty. Roberts's period of high-quality production, from 1885 to 1903, is twice as long as Streeton's which is confined to 1888 to 1897. The greater numbers of fine works and greater variety of subjects ultimately put Roberts ahead of Streeton.

The Streeton retrospective was intended to some extent to retrieve the reputation that his later (post-1897) works had suffered since his death. A handful of critics have welcomed this retrieval and reassessed the paintings as major contributions to twentieth-century Australian art. Nonetheless most critics and curators found that the Streeton retrospective reaffirmed the rather vacuous quality of most of his later landscapes. Most prefer Streeton's and Roberts's work produced in Australia in the two decades leading up to Federation. Thenceforth both Roberts and Streeton struggled to establish their reputations in the wider forum of Europe and both lost their way. Streeton had more confidence than Roberts and his work retains a bravado which continued to increase from his return to Australia in 1923 until his death in 1943. On the other hand, Roberts's later works are rarely as confident, large or showy as Streeton's. Nor are they as ambitious and are therefore, possibly, less likely to fail. Roberts's more modest – and more successful – late pictures also show a greater subtlety of tone and hue.

It is hoped that this retrospective exhibition of Tom Roberts's art will reveal some of the sustaining qualities of these quiet yet interesting later works. Whereas there are no major artists who followed Streeton's late work, Roberts has some major artistic successors in twentieth-century landscape art. Elioth Gruner, Lloyd Rees, Fred Williams and Arthur Boyd all have expressed their admiration for Roberts's late silvery paintings and have acknowledged an artistic debt to them. Arthur Boyd, who admired these and earlier works, is now Australia's senior landscape and figure painter and can be given a final word: "All Australian paintings are in some way a homage to Tom Roberts".

Sherbrooke Forest, (detail), 1924, Dandenong Ranges, Victoria, oil on canvas on paperboard, 48.0 x 68.4 cm; The Art Gallery of New South Wales, Sydney, Purchased 1946

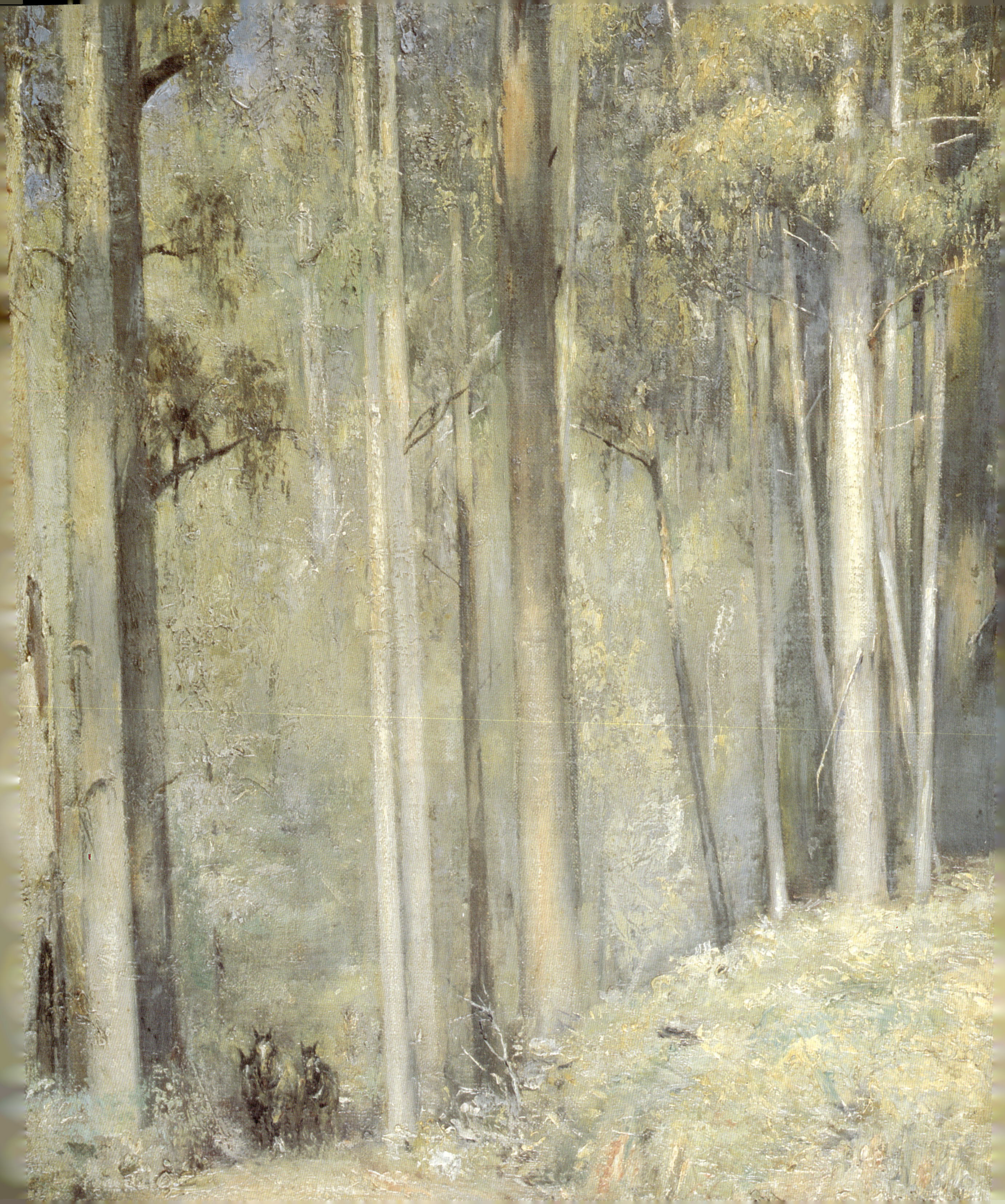

The Fortunes of Tom Roberts

Humphrey McQueen

Though grave-diggers' toil is long,
Sharp their spades, their muscles strong,
They but thrust their buried men
Back in the human mind again.

W. B. Yeats, Under Bul Bulben, 1938

The seventy-five years of Thomas William Roberts can be set down in as many words. Born in Dorchester in 1856 he emigrated in 1869 with his widowed mother from England to Melbourne. There he worked for photographers while studying fine art. He attended London's Royal Academy Schools 1881-85, and travelled through Spain. Back in Australia he painted portraits and sheep. He married in 1896 and fathered a son. After 1903 he lived in London until he retired in 1923 to the Dandenongs. Remarrying in 1928 he died three years later.

A list of Roberts's better-known images maps out his life as neatly as it limns his creativity. His immigrant status after two voyages to Australia is suggested in *Coming South*, 1885-86, where passengers wait tranquilly for the days to pass. The classical aspect of his schooling and of his art training is conveyed in *The sculptor's studio*, 1884-85, where a friend from the Royal Academy is shown at work on his prize-winning frieze *Socrates Teaching the People in the Agora.*

Woman on a balcony, 1884, Venice, oil on academy board, 21.7 x 13.1 cm; Private collection, Melbourne

The marvellousness of Melbourne during its 1880s land and building booms, from which Roberts benefited through portrait commissions and sales, is aflame in *Allegro con brio, Bourke Street west*, 1885-86/1890. Roberts's long stays in the Riverina and across northern New South Wales are represented in *Shearing the rams*, 1888-90, *A break away!*, 1891, and *The Golden Fleece*, 1894, in which he celebrated the pastoral industry. His large bushranger canvas *Bailed up*, 1897, followed from his acceptance that one function of the artist was to act as memorialist. Hence, Roberts campaigned for a National Portrait Gallery for Australia, hoping for a run of commissions though he received only one before the Great War. A group of Aboriginal heads was his ethnographic record of the dying race to whose abilities in drawing he paid respect. In 1926 the Commonwealth of Australia paid him £100 to work up a head-and-shoulders portrait of the colonial poet Henry Kendall from a photograph.

Roberts's circulation around the periphery of colonial politics is traced through the scores of portraits he made of public figures ranging from an ex-mayor of Melbourne to Henry Parkes, the 'Father of Federation'. Roberts's ambition in portraiture was to be another George Frederic Watts, esteemed as England's Michelangelo. Watts combined a fascination with mystical subjects with tireless depiction of Victorian worthies.

Still-life with pomegranates, c1883, Spain?, oil on canvas mounted on board, 31.1 x 64.3 cm; Private collection, Melbourne

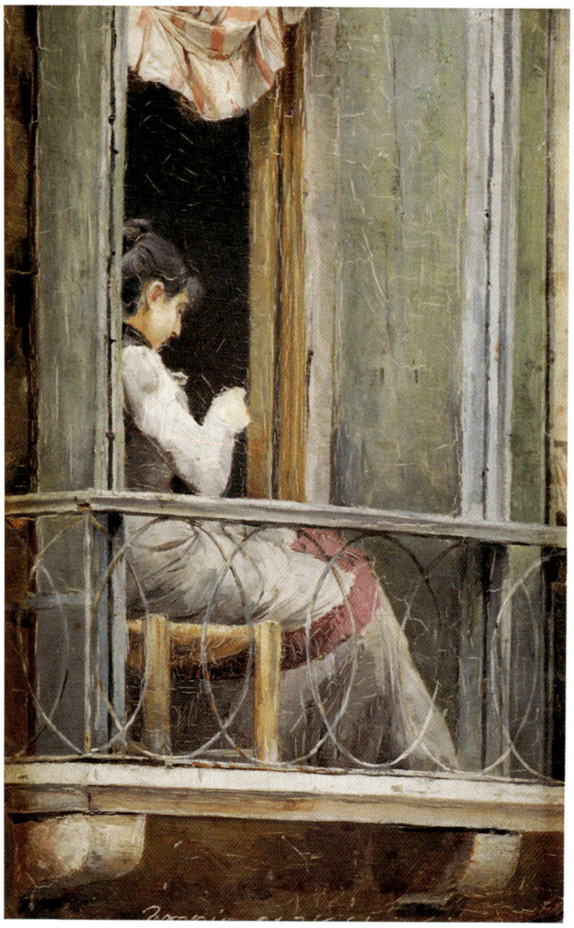

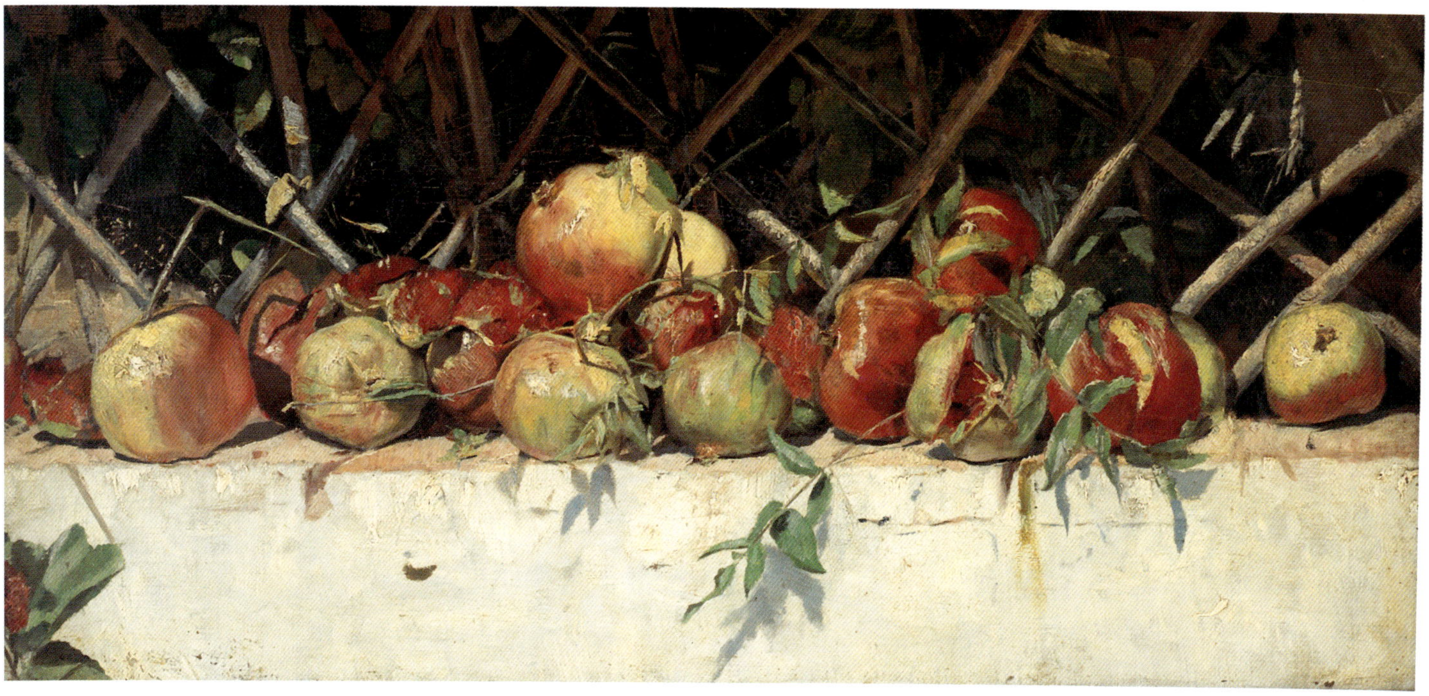

Tom Roberts

The commission for 'The Big Picture' of thc opening on 9 May 1901 of the Federal parliament in Melbourne's Exhibition Buildings promised to fulfil several of Roberts's ambitions. The subject and scale (more than five metres wide) were appropriate to a national project and promised a place of honour on the walls of the Royal Academy at one of its annual exhibitions. His social climbing reached its apogee through contact with the King-Emperor Edward VII. The rate of pay, measured in guineas, was worthy of a professional. The range of its identifiable faces displayed the compatibility of Roberts's twin public ideals of Australian democracy and British Empire.

Biographers are also gravediggers though we do not always exercise the discrimination of the one questioned by Hamlet. That fellow insisted that the grave he was digging was for neither man nor woman but for she who had been a woman. Hence, he would have quibbled that art is more than the reflection of a life just as a life encompasses more than a career. Yet both strands are crossed by the same currents.

Two views about what constitutes individuality are furthest apart when applied to artists. The Romantic notion is that the artist is born with a nugget of creativity which would blaze forth if only society got out of its light. The alternative starting point is to see that an artist's distinctiveness is established through a unique constellation of experiences with family, education and work. By adopting the second approach, we will appreciate why events and issues, which can seem to us now as mere backdrop, were in the foreground for Roberts.

For instance the late-nineteenth-century assumption that a painting should ennoble its viewers while telling them a story affected how Roberts crafted his ambitions. He acknowledged that aesthetic in three canvases: *A summer morning tiff*, 1886, *Reconciliation*, 1887, and *Jealousy*, 1889. He would come to recognise that a painting could not illustrate a poem because the latter moved through time whereas visual artists had difficulty even in suggesting movement, a lasting obstacle to his own success.

Wider changes buffeted his fortunes by challenging the dominance of an aesthetic secured on poise and peace. Born into the agricultural landscape of Dorset, Roberts lived through a mechanisation of everyday life. Revolutions in industry accelerated travel, communications and production just as rapidly as they overturned tastes in clothing and art. His first voyage from England to Australia in 1869 lasted ninety-four days whereas his fourth and last, in 1923, took forty-two. Roberts lived to see military and commercial aircraft, to ride in automobiles, to lecture over the wireless and to use electrical power at home. With notable exceptions such as *Allegro con brio* he did not depict these tumults. He also side-stepped them in his life, preferring to dwell as well as to paint in country districts. On retiring to Australia in 1923 the Robertses built at Kallista, in an orchard within the forested Dandenong Ranges, out of Melbourne. He gardened wherever he settled, to win more prizes for his flowers than for his canvases.

Churchyard at Shillingstone, 1884, England, oil on canvas, 30.5 x 45.5 cm; Private collection, Queensland

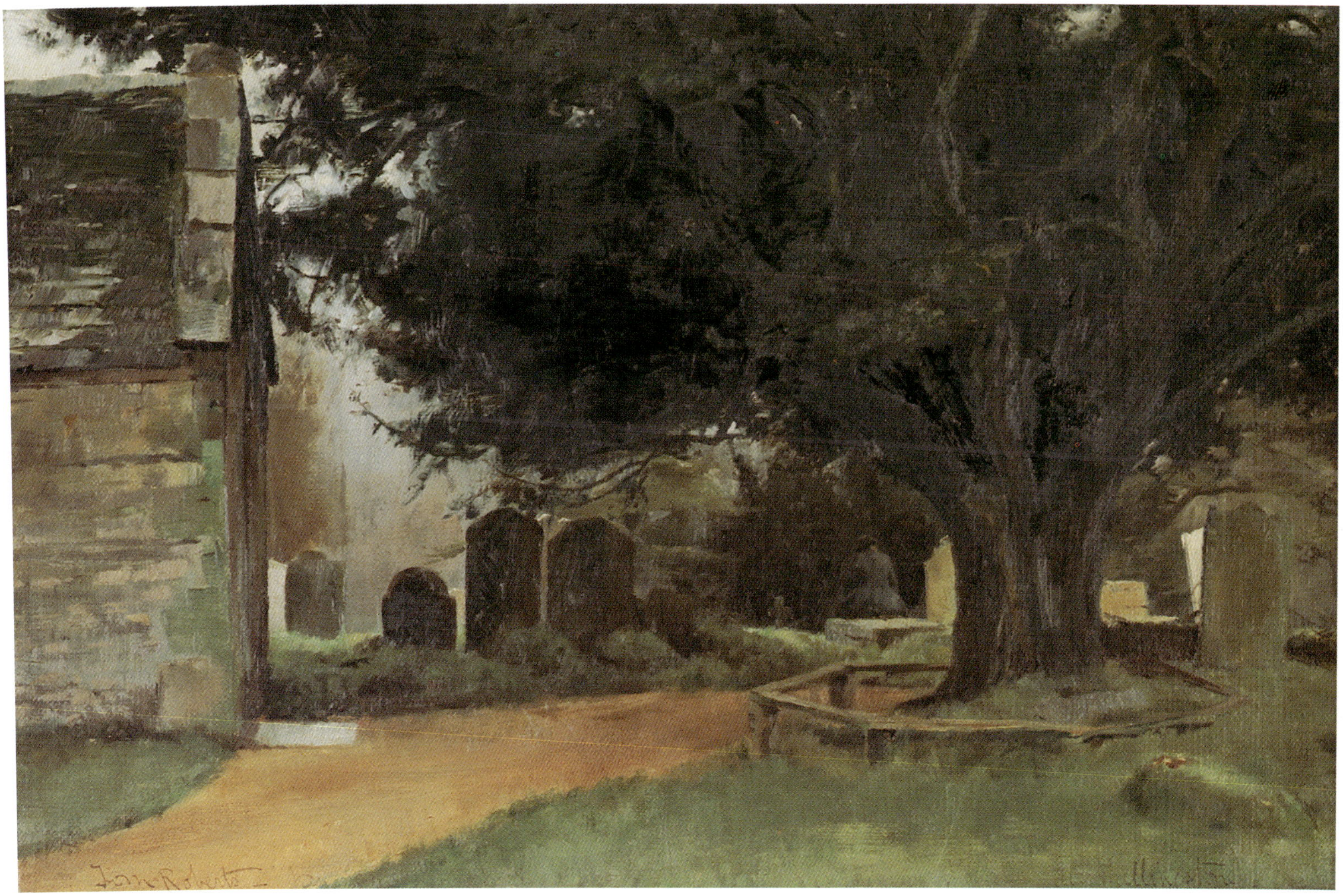

Tom Roberts

Similarly, the thread of militarism from the Zulu wars of the later 1870s, to the Sudan (1884-5), through the Boer War (1899-1902) and on to the Great European War connected with Roberts's reading about earlier deeds that had won the Empire in which he took pride. Those engagements provided subjects for pictures such as Alphonse de Neuville's *The Defense of Rorke's Drift*, an 1879 battle between the Zulu and the British, which Roberts praised for its Kiplingesque naturalism after seeing it at the National Art Gallery in Sydney. In 1895-96 in Sydney he painted portraits of soldiers and depicted an artillery exercise near Mosman. Throughout the Great War he slaved as an orderly at Wandsworth Military Hospital in London, reaching the rank of sergeant. Meanwhile his son Caleb trained as a military engineer and served in Egypt, France and Russia. Hence the tides of war were more than a context for Roberts's working life though he never made the battlefield a subject of his own art. Nor did he seek appointment as an official war artist but devoted himself to the care of the maimed. For as long as his boy was in danger he would do no less.

In surveying Roberts's career we must take care not to explain his choices by what we now know were the results. An outcome which can strike us today as a foregone conclusion presented itself to him as an opportunity or an obstacle. What is the past for us was still an undecided future to him. Consider 'The 9 by 5 Impression Exhibition', August 1889, which has been dressed up as Australia's most important art show in the nineteenth century. At the time, the 9 by 5s' organisers were looking forward to a commercial venture combined with a light-hearted diversion more than to a crusade to convert Melbourne's bourgeoisie towards the latest of aesthetic preferences. Some of the exhibitors' own gaiety was captured by the critic who supposed that *The Milky Way*, the title that Roberts had given to one of his nine-by-five-inch impressions, "is probably reminiscent of the condensed milk which the artist took with him along with the biscuits and billy".[1]

Admirers parted with a couple of guineas for one of Roberts's 'impressions' – or whatever those damned panels should be called. Those buyers indicate the range of his connections: the fashionable artist Carl Kahler, intellectuals such as professor of biology Baldwin Spencer, as well as Lady Clarke, a philanthropic holder of garden parties and costume balls. Portrait subjects such as Mme Pfund, proprietor of an academy for young ladies, would have guided Roberts on questions of etiquette.

Patrons paid good money for a speaking likeness, finished with varnish and mounted in a gilded frame. Although it matters little whether Roberts painted Henry Parkes once or thrice, the fact that 40 per cent of his surviving works are portraits is significant for an assessment of his place in Australian art history. In addition, the receipt of £2000 for the portrayal of 256 recognisable faces in his *Opening of the First Parliament of the Commonwealth of Australia* allowed him to live for a couple more years without worrying about where the money would come from next. A major commission a decade earlier would have given Roberts's career a different spin, though in which direction we can but speculate. He sought opportunities to publicise his face-making as in 1897 when he displayed his portrait of the singer Florence Schmidt in Nicholson's music shop in Sydney.[2]

The sculptor's studio, 1884-85, London, oil on canvas, 61.0 x 91.5 cm; National Gallery of Australia, Canberra, Purchased 1972

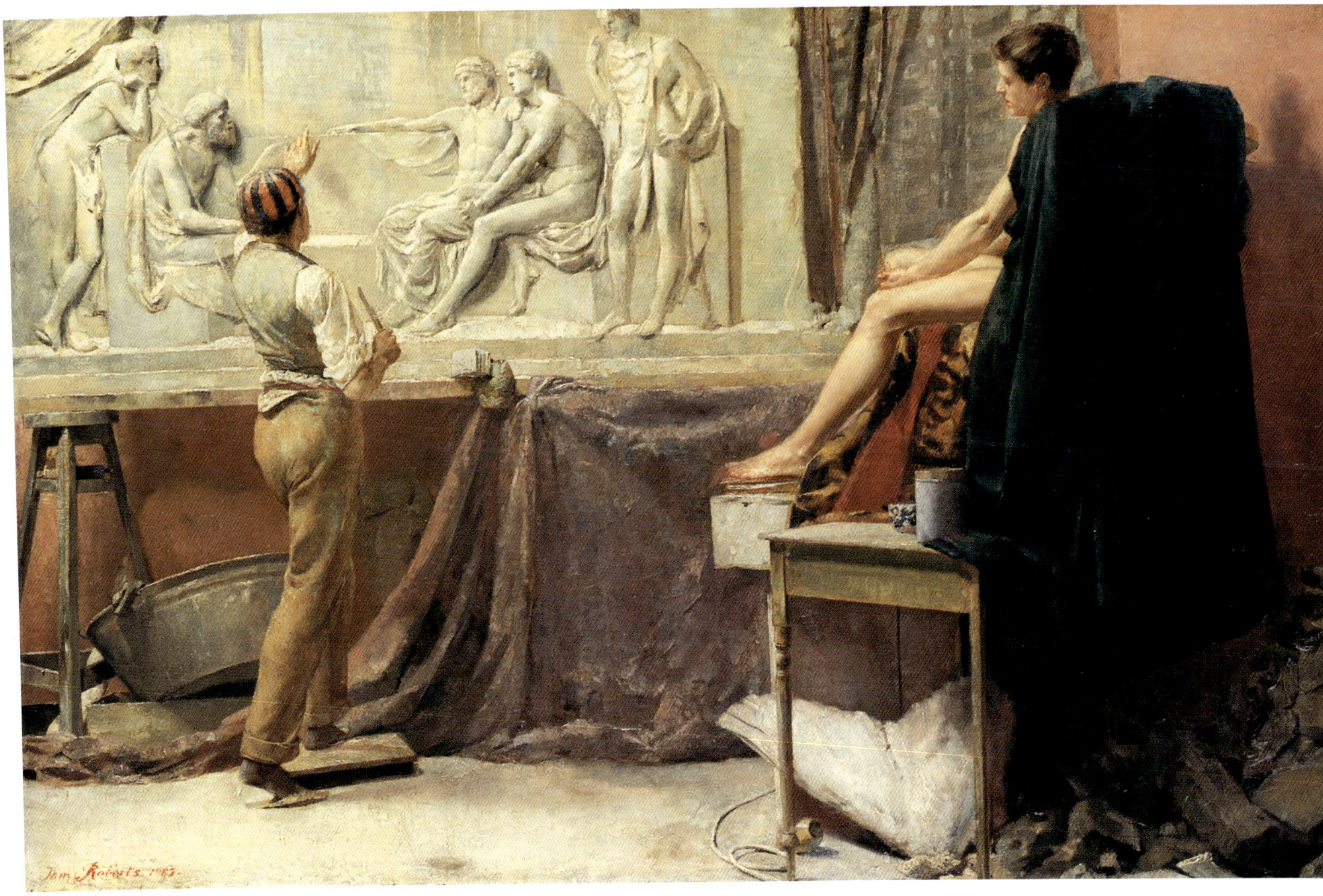
Tom Roberts

Tom Roberts

Portraits put jam on Roberts's bread-and-butter but he could refer to them as the bane of his creative life. As early as 1887 he was entertaining artists' smoke nights with a "pathetic ditty re 'High Art', [which] moved his hearers deeply".[3] The lyrics told how he had abandoned portrait commissions of "kids" in favour of the Higher Art. He took as his subject Joseph and his brothers in Egypt. Critics advised him to paint over ten of these thirteeen Biblical figures. Another critic then demanded the removal of one of the survivors. In the end he cut the huge canvas into sections until

> On little stretchers eight by ten
> I laid him and his Brethren.
> And all their classic mugs are hid
> By the smiling face of a little kid.

He was still singing these lines forty years on, a sign that he never fell victim to pomposity. Further, that skit breathes life into his showmanship, not to say showing off, and illuminates his power to lead his brother smudgers through his personality as much as with his painting.

Shakespeare's gravedigger possessed the absoluteness needed to divide personality from character. In drawing a distinction we can see character as a triumph of the will over the desires and impulses set loose by personality. Roberts's nickname of Bulldog might have applied to either his self-control or his instincts. His temper flared dogmatic. Equally, Roberts could have trained himself to persevere against the odds, rarely whingeing but instead presenting a demeanour ever hopeful no matter how desperate he felt. He would slip away from his friends when his mood became too grim.

An alternative way to ponder Roberts's personality is to see him in terms of protagonists from novels by his favourite author and fellow Dorsetman Thomas Hardy. In Roberts's determination to succeed he was like Henchard, the mayor of Casterbridge, who would box with one hand tied behind his back. Roberts's obsession to be taken up by the Royal Academy had much in common with the failure of that obscure stonemason Jude Frawley to enter Oxford University.

Roberts's favourite novel by Hardy was *Far from the Madding Crowd*, 1874. In the mid 1890s Roberts called his horse Black Bess after the one ridden by Hardy's dashing Sergeant Troy. The connections did not end there. For one of his 9 by 5s, Roberts painted how he imagined Gabriel Oak's cottage. He also acquired Oak's capacity for endurance. This preparedness to look "upon the horizon of circumstances without any special regard to his own standpoint" did not vanquish the vanity of Roberts's wishes until after the torments and courage of the wounded Great War troops had taught him not to "think quite so much of one's own importance".[4]

Roberts was a man's man and a lady's man who had, according to a close friend, a "wondrous soft way with women". One viewer of Roberts's *A Spanish Beauty*, c1885, offered to "give 5 years of his life to arrange the folds of her lace mantilla". A critic complained that in *Reconciliation* Mr Roberts had "painted a face without a single charm,

Twenty minutes past three, c1886, Melbourne, oil on canvas, mounted on composition board, 100.0 x 74.3 cm (sight); Private collection, Sydney

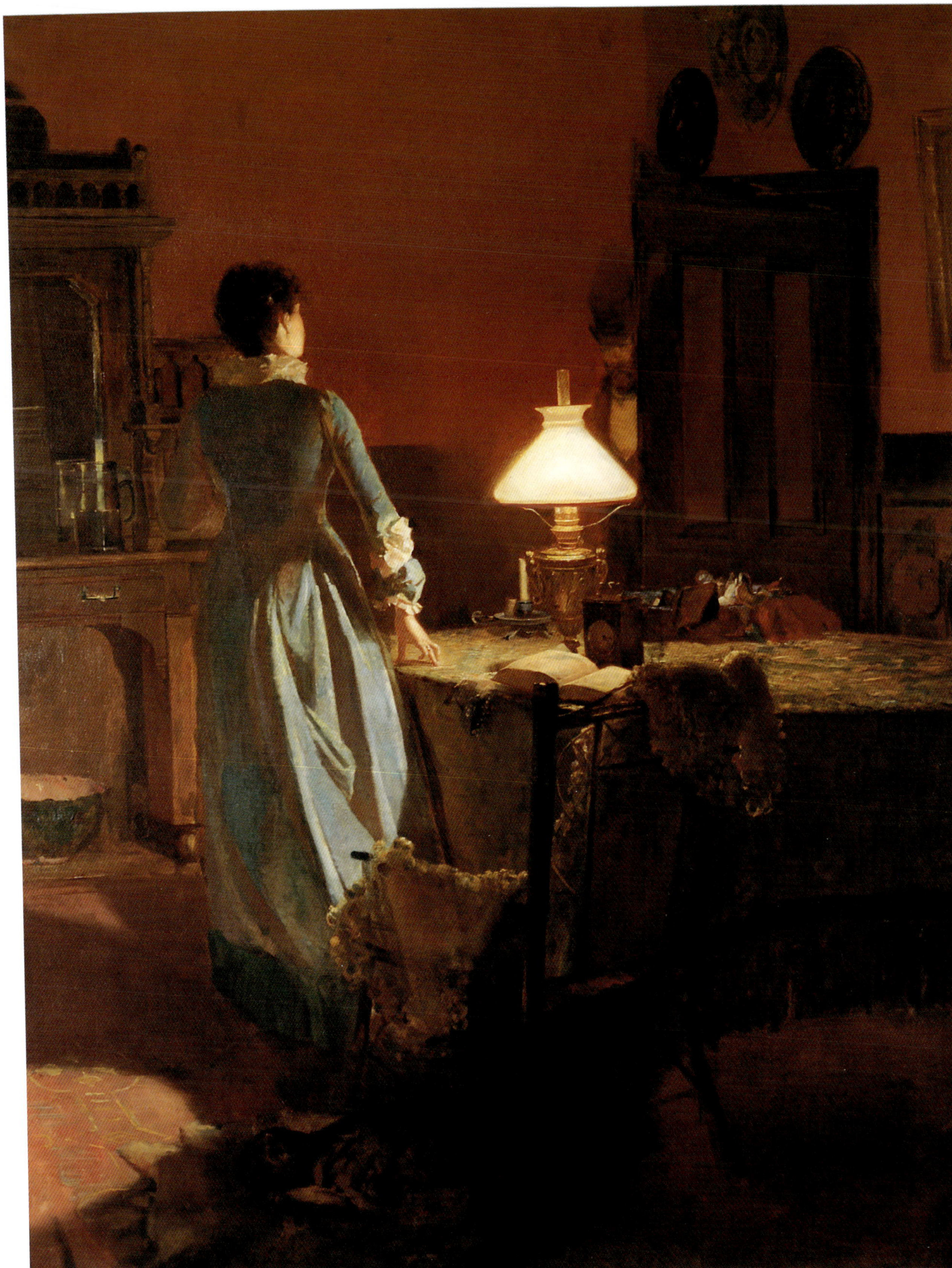

heavy, stolid, and uninteresting".[5] From his student days in the 1870s Roberts had wanted nude female models but complained that he could hardly ask young ladies to take off their clothes. Even in the Torres Strait in 1892 he did not take advantage of the Islander women to make nature studies. Not until 1915 in Dorset did he find a willing model as depicted in *The Mirror*.

Tales of his philandering, before and after marriage, lingered. One woman artist called him a "bounder".[6] Like many men of his generation, especially those who married as late as he did at forty, Roberts found it easier to act the father than stop thinking of himself as a bachelor. He was away from home and his wife Lillie so often that he merited the nickname Ulysses to her Penelope.

Roberts's appearance added to his attractiveness. His height was slightly under 180 centimetres. He kept his body trim with bicycling, gardening and tennis. Despite a prodigous appetite he never ran to fat or even developed a noticeable paunch. A fondness for beer and whisky was held in check by gout. The only physical oddity ever remarked upon was his spatula-shaped thumb which he used to lay in paint. Well before his thirtieth year he began to go bald which he offset with a beard. In later years his eyesight deteriorated so much that the lenses in his spectacles were as thick as the bottom of a bottle. When Streeton visited his old friend in the late 1920s he had to bellow to be heard.[7] Pipe-smoking contributed to the mouth cancer mentioned on his death certificate, alongside a carcinoma of the prostate. Roberts's grandsons remember him from those final years as a testy old man who warned them that the bunyip carried off naughty boys.

Roberts's courage and robustness were as ever-present as their manifestations were varied. He worked his passage on a pearling lugger from Sydney to Cooktown in 1892, rode a horse from the Clarence River coast across the Great Dividing Range to Inverell in 1894-95, pursued burglars in London in 1911, laboured mightily as a medical orderly while younger colleagues retreated tired and sick, and exercised with an axe during his last decade at Kallista.

Roberts's working habits of regular hours in a tidy studio matched the consolidation from the 1870s of professionalism among doctors and architects. He insisted that artists' organisations be controlled by practitioners, and no longer by the amateur or the friend of art. In Victoria from the mid 1880s he worked behind the scenes to form the Australian Artists' Association which he almost at once guided into the merger that set up the Victorian Artists' Society, which still exists. In Sydney, where he settled in 1891, others organised an 1895 breakaway Society of Artists before inviting Roberts in to be their president who, as the front-of-house swell, could approach Henry Parkes and the colonial Governor. So confident had Roberts become of his ability to manage vice-regal occasions that during a boat trip early in 1896 he pretended to isolated communities along the central coast of New South Wales that he was His Excellency.

Holiday sketch at Coogee, 1888 Sydney, oil on canvas , 40.3 x 55.9 cm; The Art Gallery of New South Wales, Sydney, Purchased 1954

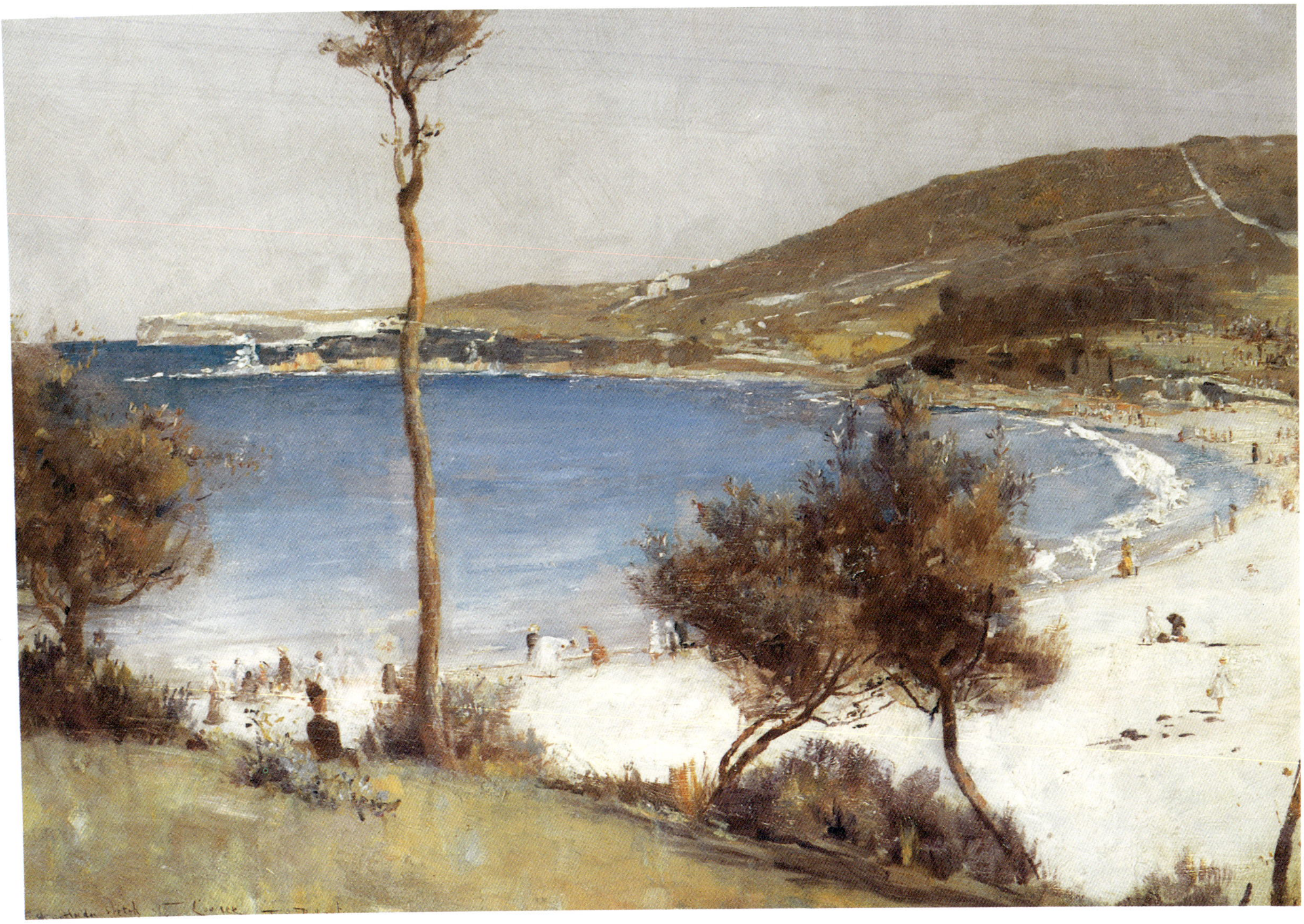

Tom Roberts

In London Roberts had learned from Frederic Leighton, president of the Royal Academy, and the American-born James McNeill Whistler how essential to sales was self-promotion through the cultivation of Society. Not long after Roberts's return to Melbourne, brother artists jostled each other in order to be the one to receive the Governor and his lady as they arrived at the opening of the Australian Artists' Association's spring exhibition.[8] He established studio afternoons to preview his works to a selected group before sending the canvases to public exhibition. Visitors were entertained with music and dainty cups of coffee, served by lady friends, often artists themselves.

Another aspect of professionalism was how an artist should dress. In particular, was masculinity compatible with the artistic life? Gilbert & Sullivan's satire in *Patience*, 1881, on the Aesthetic Movement of Whistler and Oscar Wilde in no way stopped Roberts from associating with Whistlerian 'Impressionism' and showmanship, culminating in the decor for the 9 by 5 exhibition. Usually with a flower in his buttonhole, though never a poppy or a lily in his hand, he flashed around Melbourne in an opera cape and the first spring top hat seen in the city. Roberts was not wedded to the artist's uniform of a velvet jacket.

Ridicule of Gilbert's "long-haired aesthetics" turned nastier with the 1895 prosecutions of Wilde, whom Roberts described as "one of the most disgusting and remarkable things in history ... The dismal joining of such depravity and such intellect".[9] Henceforth Roberts promoted himself in the terms he had used for his shearing pictures in which he had exalted "strong masculine labour". A decade of working up the country had hardened his body so that during a 1901 interview he affirmed his belief in "the muscular foundation of art".[10]

Roberts's progress as a landscape artist could be summarised as the Englishman who went into Melbourne's Studley Park and came out of the New England scrub. He recalled that he had passed several years in Australia as a youth before he could find beauty in the gum tree. Thereafter he cherished the eucalypt as "perhaps the most reflective object in the realm of art".[11]

Nonetheless after each absence he had to regain mastery of Australian effects. The tiny *Evening, Box Hill*, 1885, perhaps the first attempt upon his return, proved a mudpatch of olives and khaki. By the 1920s he no longer sought the high-keyed subjects of his vigorous manhood but washed English and northern Italian tints over genteel prospects of the Dandenongs and Tasmania, offering therapy to a shell-shocked society. Reviewing a 1926 exhibition Hugh McCrae had "no doubt that Mr Roberts's absorption in the analysis of English twilight problems has sapped some of his vitality as an interpreter of the Australian bush".[12]

The art that Roberts made in praise of Australia did not convince everyone that he was a dinky-di Australian. From John Longstaff in the 1880s through to Frederick McCubbin in the 1910s, the native painters resented their foreign-born rivals, even Britishers.

Saplings, c1889, Melbourne, oil on cedar cigar-box lid, 14.5 x 34.5 cm; Art Gallery of South Australia, Adelaide, Morgan Thomas Bequest Fund 1927

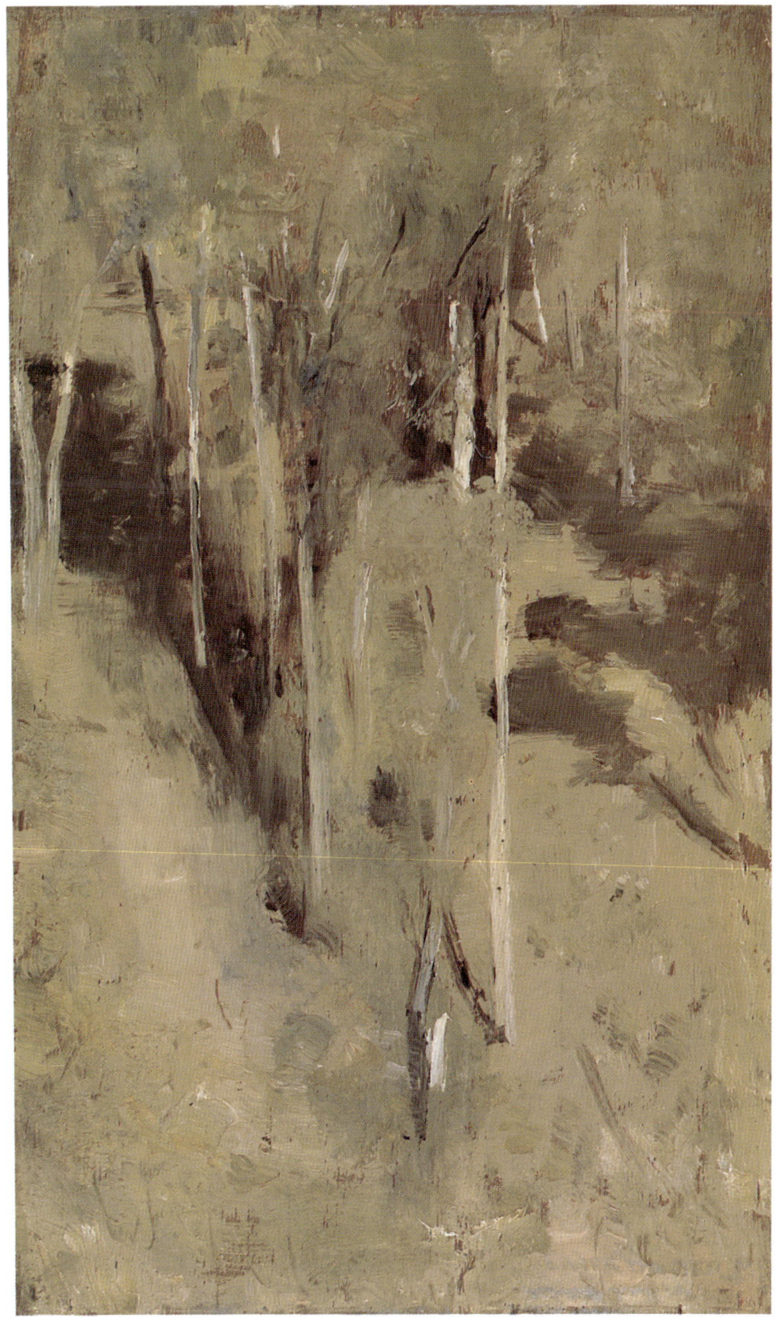

Tom Roberts

Roberts compounded the mistake of being born in the wrong country by passing twenty years among the 'absent Australians', the term of dismissal then used against expatriates. He joked about his British-raised son's being a pommy and in 1925 warned Caleb against coming the officer & gentleman when he had to oversee roadworkers used to a democratic temper.

As a student in London, Roberts was one of a group of Australians who pinched gumleaves from a small tree in St James's Park to burn in their studios,[13] a ritual he continued throughout his travels abroad. His accent retained a hint of a Dorset burr with its warm z-sounds though that inflection was but one of many which he could mimic, his most notable vocal trick being the power to throw his voice. In print he championed mateship as the distinctive feature of Australian life and he put that precept into practice through long friendships with McCubbin, Charles Douglas Richardson, Arthur Streeton, the musical clerk S. W. Pring and the cornet-playing pastoralist Duncan Anderson. However Roberts fell out in 1927 with his oldest friend, Walter Barnett, a reminder of the Bulldog's ferocious side.

Three – perhaps four – events in Roberts's life proved pivotal in the sense that if any one of them had not happened his career would have had a different shape.

The first nodal point was his father's death at the close of 1868 followed by his family's emigration ten weeks later. Had his father continued as editor of an ultra-Tory rural newspaper for a further decade Roberts probably never would have set foot on Australia. Indeed he might not have taken up painting as a profession. Instead he could have been apprenticed to an architect, as Thomas Hardy had been, or followed his father into journalism. His aptitude for words can be felt through the immediacy he conveyed in his newspaper articles and personal correspondence. In that case he would have dabbled in drawing and watercolours, as did Hardy.

The violin lesson, c1889, Melbourne, oil on cedar panel, 23.0 x 13.0 cm; Private collection, Melbourne

The death of Roberts's father at age forty-one demoted young Thomas William from Grammar School boy in Dorchester to a tearful floor-scrubber in Collingwood, Melbourne. That blow expelled him from the garden of southern England into the brickfielder blasts from Victoria's summers. This double dislocation underwrote a desire to reclaim his place up the English social scale. His own son would fulfil some of this ambition by winning a scholarship to one of England's Great Public Schools, St Paul's in London.

Before Roberts reached fifteen he had enrolled at the Collingwood branch of the Artisans' School of Design which the Victorian government had reformed in 1870 to advance local manufactures. For all we know the lad might have begun with the hope of becoming a draughtsman though he soon took up the Higher Art. Either way he showed a determination to improve himself, to assert his superiority over the larrikin push in his neighbourhood.

Adagio, 1899, Sydney, oil on paperboard, 25.6 x 51.0 cm; The Art Gallery of New South Wales, Sydney, Purchased 1947

Why did Roberts paint? His too ready answer was for money. He was not one of those artists who would rather paint than eat. Yet he kept on almost till his dying days. Such

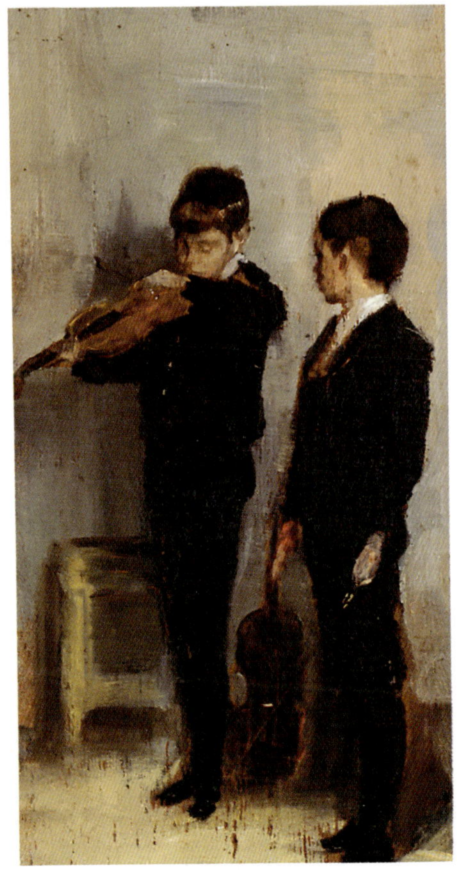

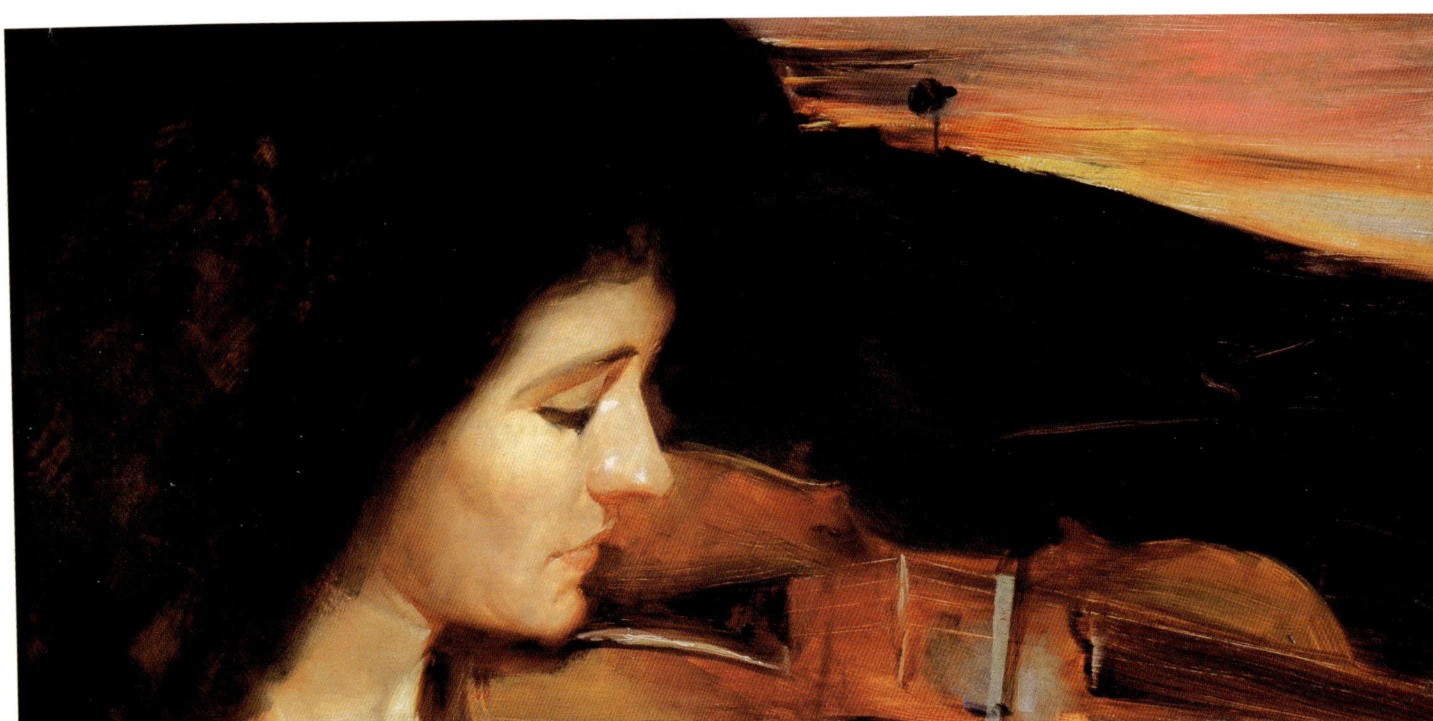

persistence welded an inner compulsion to a willed refusal to admit defeat. Freud had to admit that biographers could never "throw any light on the miraculous gift that makes an artist".[14]

Roberts set himself the goals of being accepted first as a student, then as an exhibitor and finally as an Associate, if not a full member, of the Royal Academy. The first stage he achieved in 1881. For reasons unknown he stayed for only half of the six-year course. A passion to be accepted at the Academy's annual exhibition lasted another thirty years. The Australian Parliament picture was admitted at the King's command in 1904, occasioning its creator little joy since critics ignored or damned it as just another municipal machine. His earliest success there had come in 1893 with a portrait of Henry Parkes, accepted because of its subject as much as because of its artistry. Roberts's wish to be hung at eye level ('on the line') was not met until he was fifty-four, in 1910, and then only with a society portrait.

Between 1903 and 1913 Roberts squandered his talents on "*The Sleeper Awakened*", a subject he had taken from the *Arabian Nights*. The Academy rejected one version in 1907 before accepting its reworked state in 1913. That canvas is lost. A black-and-white photograph suggests that at last he might have overcome his difficulties with figures in movement. His pursuit of its oriental subject tells us as much about Roberts's notion of his place in art as do his shearing pictures.

Nothing mattered more to Roberts and his generation than the judgement of London. When Streeton (born in Australia) went 'home' in 1897 Roberts praised his young friend for having made "perhaps the most distinctive mark in our circle" before adding that "Of course, we yet must wait for the result of critical opinion in Britain before we assume a complete success".[15] The following year London critics singled Roberts out for not being a distant imitator of British trends but as the creator of the "amazingly vigorous *A Break Away!* and his too [two?] brilliantly clever portraits."[16]

The second crucial event for Roberts's career was his marriage in April 1896 to Lillie Williamson (1860-1928), whose father was part-owner of a major drapery. Her own talents, at first as a flower painter and later as a wood-carver, meant that she accepted Roberts's art-making as a real job. They had known each other for at least a decade, perhaps nearly two. The uncertainty about when they first met extends to when they began their courtship and why they delayed so long in marrying. Her family fortune, although modest, was enough to underwrite Roberts's long decline after they ventured home to England in 1903. Had Roberts had to support a wife and child from his own pocket, he might have given up painting for commercial photography when, at the nadir of his hopes around 1909, his oldest friend proposed that solution. Roberts's youthful work with photographers had been as an arranger of backdrops and decor. He did not handle the camera or do any developing and printing and never mastered even the simplest Box Brownie equipment.

The third and related fate-filled decision was to stay in Europe after 1907, although he had not earned the footing for which he pined, neither with portrait commissions

Professor G.W.L. Marshall-Hall, 1899, Sydney, oil on pine panel, 61.0 x 33.7 cm; Performing Arts Museum, Victorian Arts Centre, Melbourne, Purchased 1980

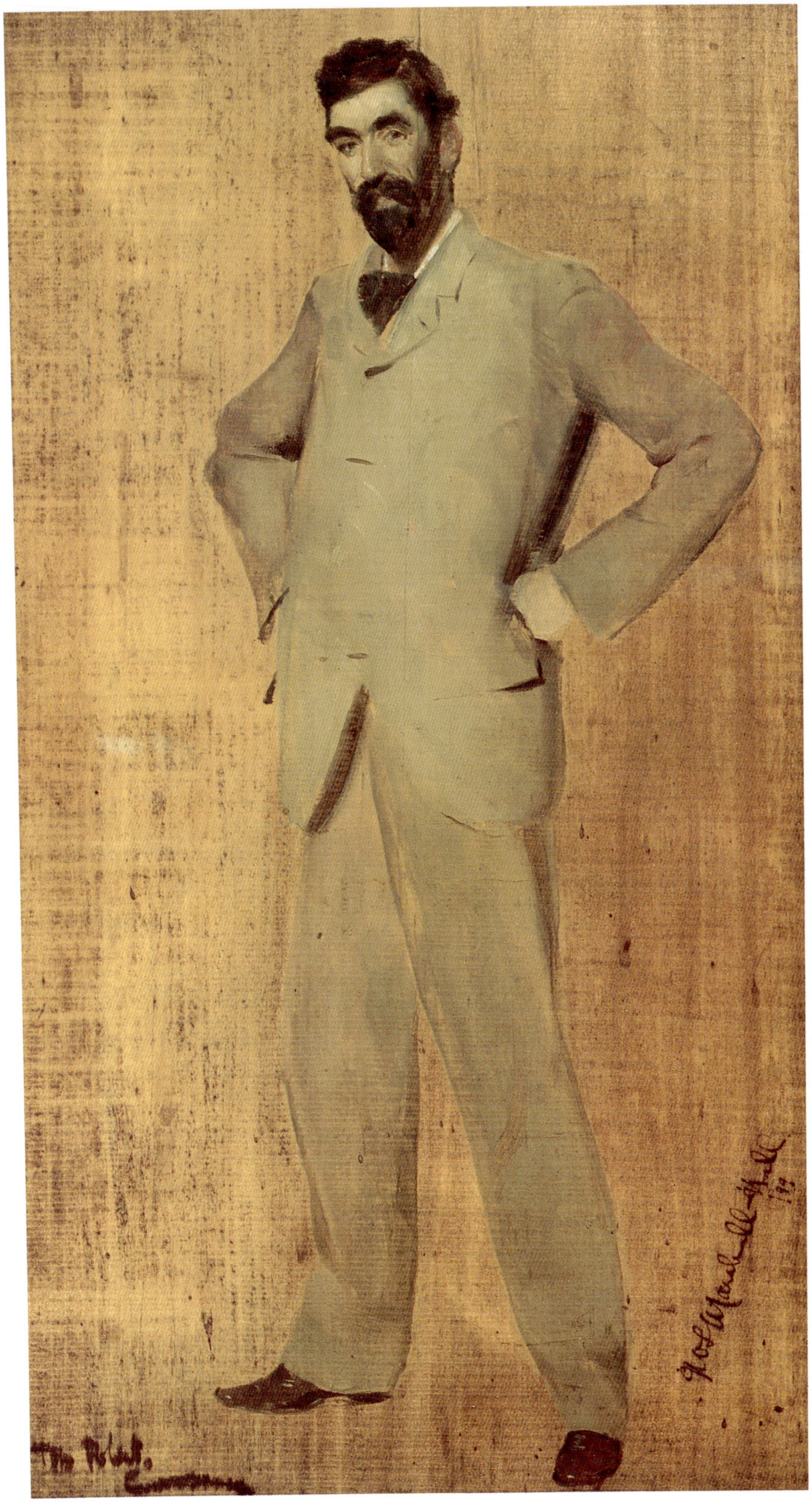

from Court or Society, nor with mythological subjects at the Royal Academy. For several years he had the excuse of eye troubles. His productivity became so slender and his successes so rare that he might have suffered from some form of nervous exhaustion, though not a complete nervous breakdown. The difficulty could have been psychosomatic. Without Lillie's inheritance he might well have cut his losses and reclaimed the post of "first court painter to the Commonwealth", as Prime Minister Alfred Deakin addressed him.[17]

Had Roberts come back to Australia around 1908 he could have expanded the handful of subject pictures upon which his reputation has rested. Instead, Lillie's fortune meant that he could afford to lounge round the Chelsea Arts Club, doing the occasional small English, Dutch or northern Italian landscape subdued into poeticism. Early in 1914 a collection of such canvases formed the only solo exhibition Roberts managed overseas. The gallery rent was guaranteed by a friend. The sales were modest. The highlight was an unannounced visit from Queen Mary whose portrait he had included in the big parliament picture. She had wondered whatever had become of him.

The fourth decisive step was Roberts's 1920 sojourn in Australia. That year of sentimental journeying combined with the success of his exhibitions in Melbourne and Sydney determined him to live out his days in his adopted land. His return to Australia in 1923 ignited his reputation. Had he died in England after a twenty-eight-year residence, no hagiography would have ennobled him in 1935 as 'The Father of Australian Landscape Painting', thereby usurping his mentor Louis Buvelot. Nor is it as likely that the National Art Gallery of New South Wales would have displayed *Bailed up* from 1928 or the National Gallery of Victoria would have purchased *Shearing the rams* in 1932. Without the network of friends and admirers that he re-established during those last eight years Roberts could have been as lost from sight as John Glover had been by 1928 when Roberts restored that early-colonial artist's grave in northern Tasmania. Professional gravediggers known as historians then could have interred Roberts between other colonial passers-by, such as William Strutt and Nicholas Chevalier who each worked in Australia for a dozen years.

Shortly before the end, Roberts told a Sydney journalist that

> ... a few dark patches in a life are valuable, because they serve a purpose similar to that produced very often by a sombre background in a picture ... I don't think any person who delights in sharp effects in Art should object to similar effects in real life ... and though I have gone through Winter days myself, extending over years of my life, I was always hopeful that I would live till Springtime came on, and I did, for I have been successful latterly, and hope to continue so.[18]

Portrait of a standing woman, c1898, Sydney, pastel on paper, 85.0 x 50.0 cm (sight); Private collection, Sydney

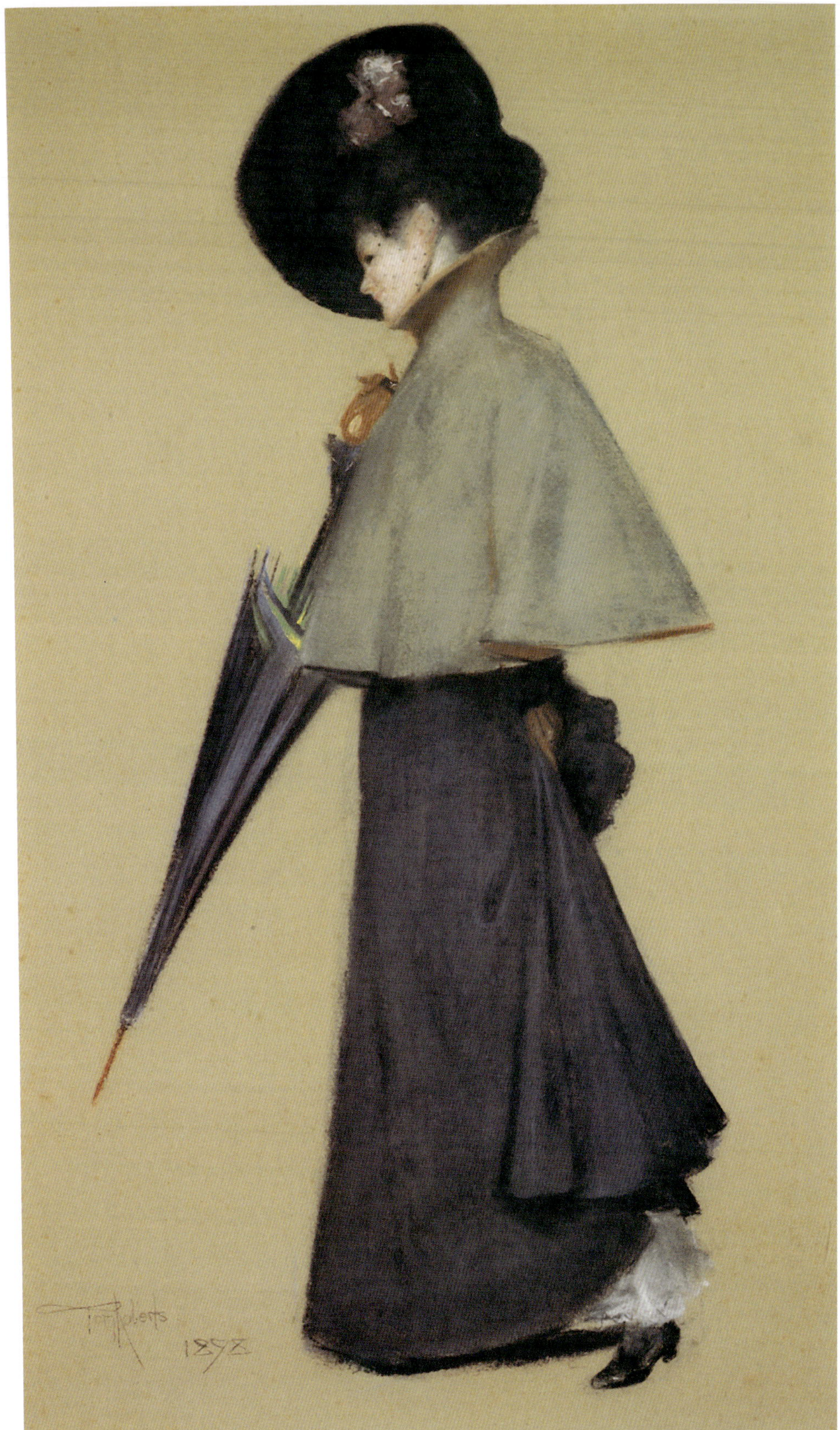

Tom Roberts

A Painter Making Himself

Mary Eagle

Tom Roberts was twenty-nine when he returned to Melbourne in April 1885 after some years at the Royal Academy Schools in London. Although he had been studying to be an artist since the mid 1870s he was still a beginner. Such a protracted apprenticeship, the rule for his generation of Australia-trained artists, was to be challenged very soon by the much younger flowering of Arthur Streeton, Charles Conder, Sydney Long, Alice Chapman, and others.

The dapper man who came off the ship at the railway pier, Williamstown, Melbourne, had definite notions about what he wanted to achieve in his paintings. It was this vision, shared with others of his circle, flowing into the art of the group and characterising their various personal styles, that mattered most in the creation of what would be nicknamed the Heidelberg School of Australian painting.[1] Without Roberts's guiding judgement, the events of the few years from 1885 would be without a connecting thread – the methodology of values, the subjects blending academic and topographical approaches with styles of contemporary European art, and the *plein-air* (open-air) philosophy of truth in outdoor light would be mere phenomena without sparkle. But vision was practically all his baggage. He had not developed a style to express what he wanted and probably had only a hazy idea about how to go about achieving his goal. Otherwise he brought back with him a few paintings and some practical tips about painting with the light and preserving the tonality of a work. Like most colonials, the scope of his ambition leapt beyond Australia. His vision was firmly centred on Europe – London in the main – and embraced the idea of a universal (read London) audience on the one hand and, on the other, the intimate texture of life at first hand.

The paintings Roberts produced in his first years back in Australia contain clues about the European paintings he had in mind as exemplars. His philosophy will be heard reflected in the words of others writing to him, in press reports, and his own few letters of the period. One of his guiding ideas (the deserted island idea) was to work towards realising his vision in beautiful isolation from all worldly distraction. Far from this being the reality, Roberts was too much of a club man to live without the stimulating company of a few good companions. When he went bush to spend the days working in quiet communion with nature he enjoyed the campfire conviviality, or homestead routine, of the evenings. Communing with nature meant in practice communing also with friends about nature and art.

With hindsight, Roberts was the "father of Australian landscape painting" through his teaching as well as his painting. In the early years the influence of his art was inseparable from the effect of his conversation; his intimates had to see one in relation to the

Moorish doorway, 1883, Granada, oil on canvas, 48.3 x 33.0 cm; Joseph Brown Collection

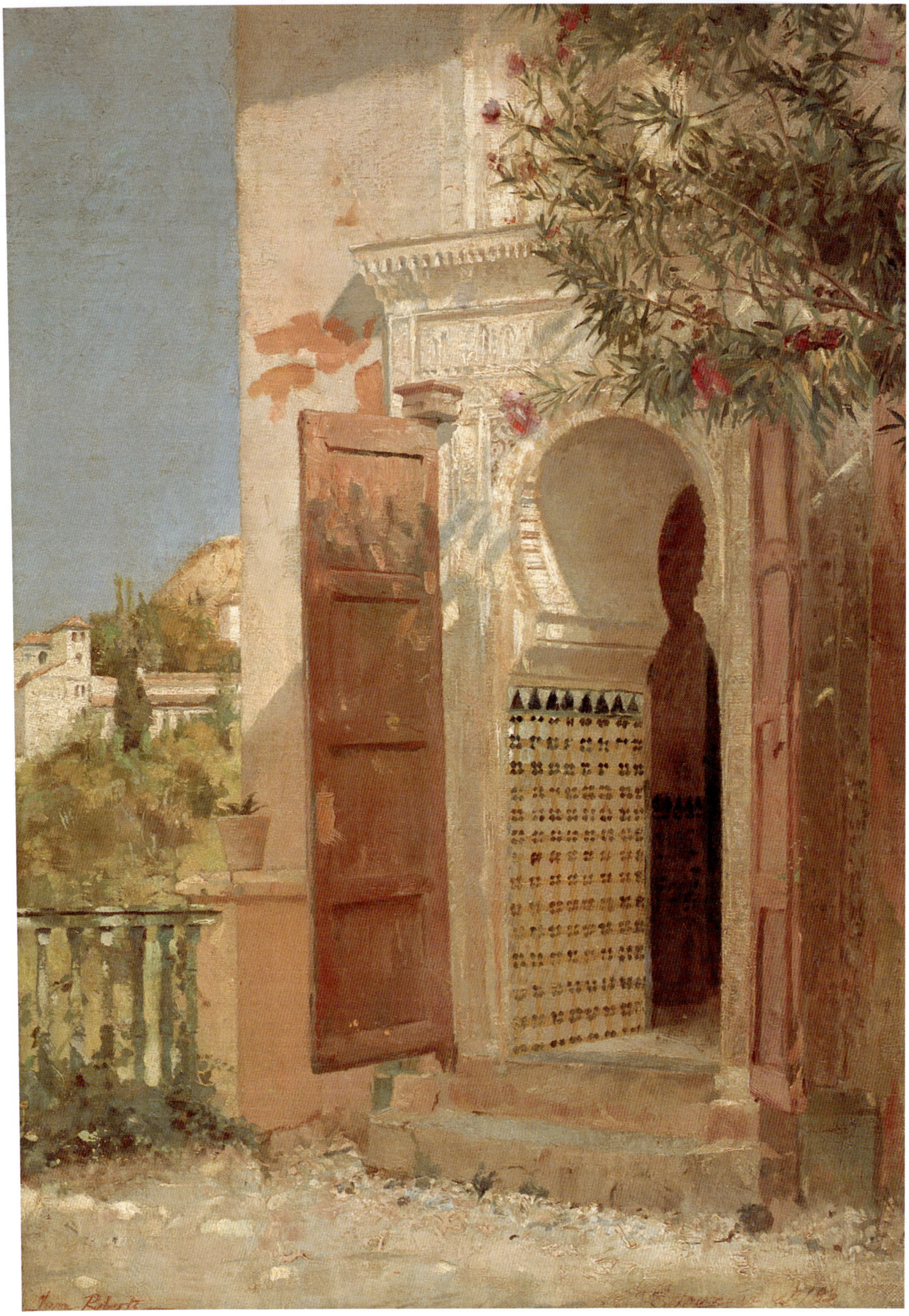

other, and the dialogue would be acute. Roberts, nervous, always conscious of appearances, did not allow himself the luxury of detachment. Between 1885 and 1887, as he sought for and developed a style of painting, he was observed by and in dialogue with a small group of other artists: friends of long standing Lillie Williamson, Louis Abrahams and Frederick McCubbin; companions of the Buonarotti Club such as Alice Brotherton, Rodney Cherry and Jane Sutherland; less intimate studio companions, John Mather and George Ashton; fellow members of the Australian Artists' Association; and younger National Gallery School students, with whom he had a leader-learner relationship, such as E. Phillips Fox, J. Llewellyn Jones, John Julian Gibbs, Nancy Elmhurst Goode and Arthur Streeton. From the summer of early 1887, Streeton was one of Roberts's close associates. Conder joined the circle in 1888, coming from Sydney to live in Melbourne.

The primary point of local reference and major challenge was James Smith, critic, whose opinions about art and culture had powerful effect in Melbourne through all the years of Roberts's youth. If Roberts, who knew his enemy, could wring his respect or break his rule, he had achieved at least part of his goal. He hoped on his return to be a fashionable success in wealthy and "Marvellous Melbourne", which meant winning Smith's recognition. The best colonial artist in Smith's reckoning was the elderly Louis Buvelot whose paintings revealed a larger vision than the usual topographic fare of colonial art. The true measure of Buvelot's achievement, claimed Smith, was not so much his wider scope of expression derived from knowing an older tradition, but that he had used it intelligently and lovingly to describe local circumstances. Smith honoured that uncondescending use of a sophisticated art tradition. Roberts paid homage to Buvelot for the same reason – he quite honestly shared Smith's opinion that great art required more sophistication than the narrowest colonial education could give. Needing to convince Smith of his own sophistication and individuality, he was at first conciliatory and then, in opposition, direct and provocative. In 1886 he defended the right of a student – Alice Chapman – to exhibit independently of the National Gallery School.[2] In 1889 he responded publicly to one of Smith's reviews. In 1892 he wrote tauntingly of the success in Paris of Streeton's *Golden Summer, Eaglemont*, which Smith had dismissed some years before. In Sydney in 1893, after reading a review by Smith, he took the boat to Melbourne to attack Smith's point of view.[3] The local, immediate contributions to the evolution of Roberts's style had to be as operative as the vision he brought from Europe.

Roberts's first year in Melbourne was spent preparing paintings for display in London. The only works he showed locally were monochrome illustrations. One group was in an exhibition that the Victorian Academy of Arts had organised to coincide with the display of eighty works on paper and a handful of oil paintings – including *A Note in Blue and Green* by Whistler – sent to Melbourne by the speculative, mis-named 'Anglo-Australian Society' of London artists.[4]

Winter morning after rain, Gardiner's Creek, 1885, Melbourne, oil on canvas, 47.0 x 66.0 cm; Art Gallery of South Australia, Adelaide, M.J.M. Carter Collection 1996

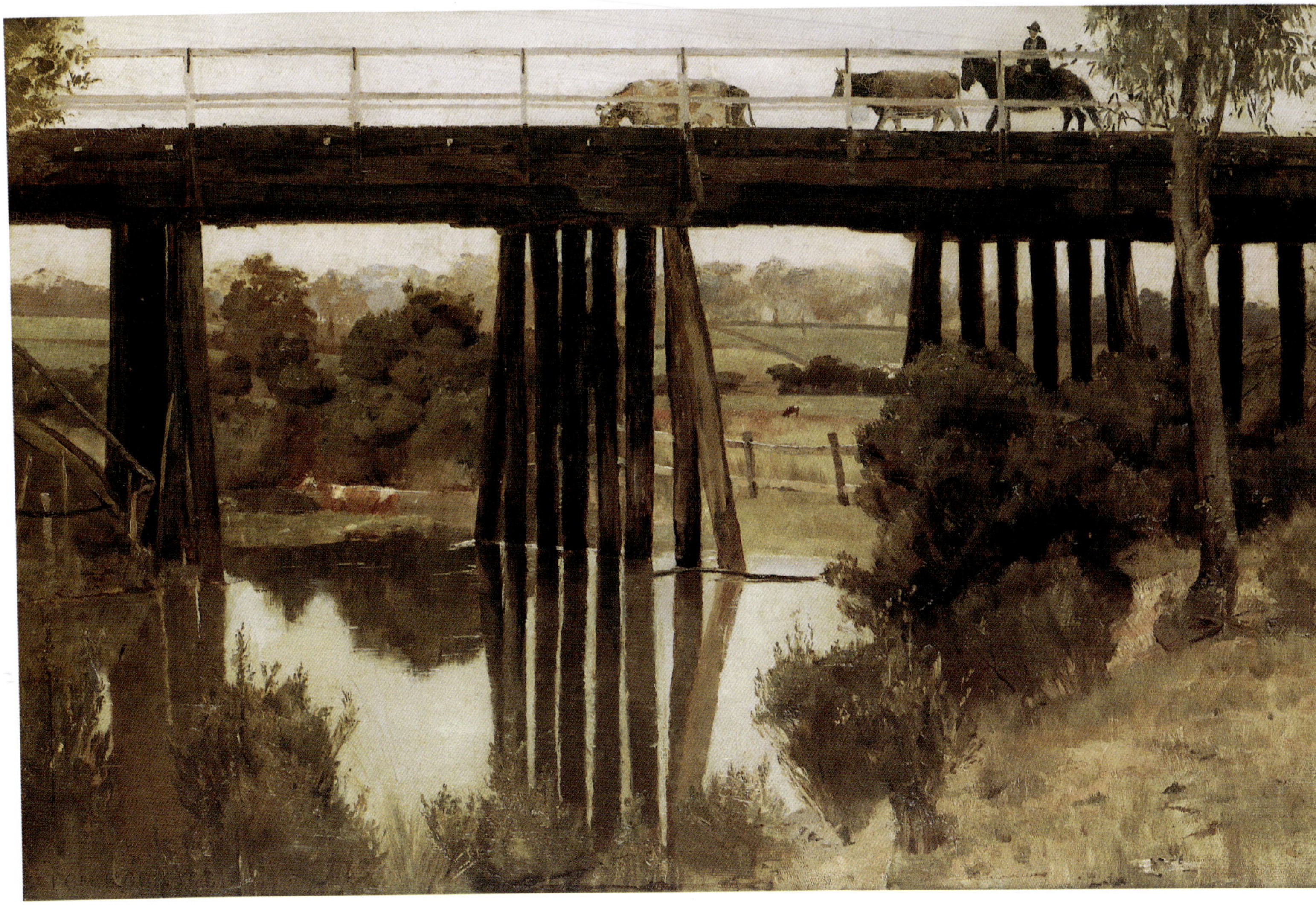

Tom Roberts

Three paintings in this late-twentieth-century retrospective of Tom Roberts's work were produced in 1885. Four were sent to the 'Colonial and Indian Exhibition' which opened in London on 4 May 1886: *A quiet day on Darebin Creek*; *Winter morning after rain, Gardiner's Creek*; *Coming South*, and a portrait of a demure young woman, *Mary* – McCubbin's sister. *Allegro con brio, Bourke Street west*, painted in the summer of December 1885-January 1886, almost certainly was begun as a work for that London exhibition; however the perspective and drawing were not resolved to academic standard and the work remained in Roberts's studio, unexhibited, until an art auction in December 1890. Except the portrait, here are four works that have been considered among the most important of Roberts's career.

The subject matter of *A quiet day on Darebin Creek* was outdoor painting – one painter at work (two, if we count Roberts) and another looking for something to paint. Near the Alphington station, the terminus of a new railway opened that year on the route to Heidelberg, the creek ran through the sort of nondescript, unemphatic country that had been made artistically desirable by the Barbizon School, having just the right broken texture of snub hills, bushes, boulders, varied grasses, creek and gravel scree. Plein-air sketching was not new in Melbourne. Alphington, accessible enough by coach or foot even before the train – ideal for a day or weekend excursion – had been to Melbourne outdoor painters what Barbizon and the Forest of Fontainebleau were to the landscape painters of Paris. In going there with his painter friends, Roberts was retracing the past rather than taking on new territory.[5] In such familiar context what was new about the painting stood out a mile – it was the light, the accommodating morning light, softening the surface of the landscape and described by Roberts in colour gradations of unexampled quietness.

Before Roberts, Melbourne's painters had been heavy-handed. Blue days had been rendered hard, sunrises and sunsets gaudy, twilight black and cloudy skies dull. One reason for the atmospheric softness of *A quiet day on Darebin Creek* is that it was painted with the morning light coming from behind and bathing the scene. Observed in the conventional way, sideways to the light, these many landscape details would appear in all their stringy complexity; a view into the light would heighten the tonal contrasts. Yet those had been the light conditions previously chosen by Melbourne's painters. Before Roberts, according to Streeton, artists had

> tried painting the sunset with somewhat conventional results. Roberts [looking with the light, not into it] pointed to the evening sky in the east and showed us the beauty of its subtle greys and the delicate flush of the afterglow when the shadow of the earth upon its atmosphere resembling a curved band of cool grey rises up and succeeds the rosy warmth as the sun descends further below the western horizon. He was the first artist in Australia to notice it and to point it out to the native-born.[6]

Roberts (like Buvelot before him) impressed his friends by seeing the nuances of light. In the craft of painting that meant mastering colour values – manipulating the image as

A quiet day on Darebin Creek, 1885, Melbourne, oil on pine wood panel, 26.6 x 35.2 cm; National Gallery of Australia, Canberra, Purchased 1969

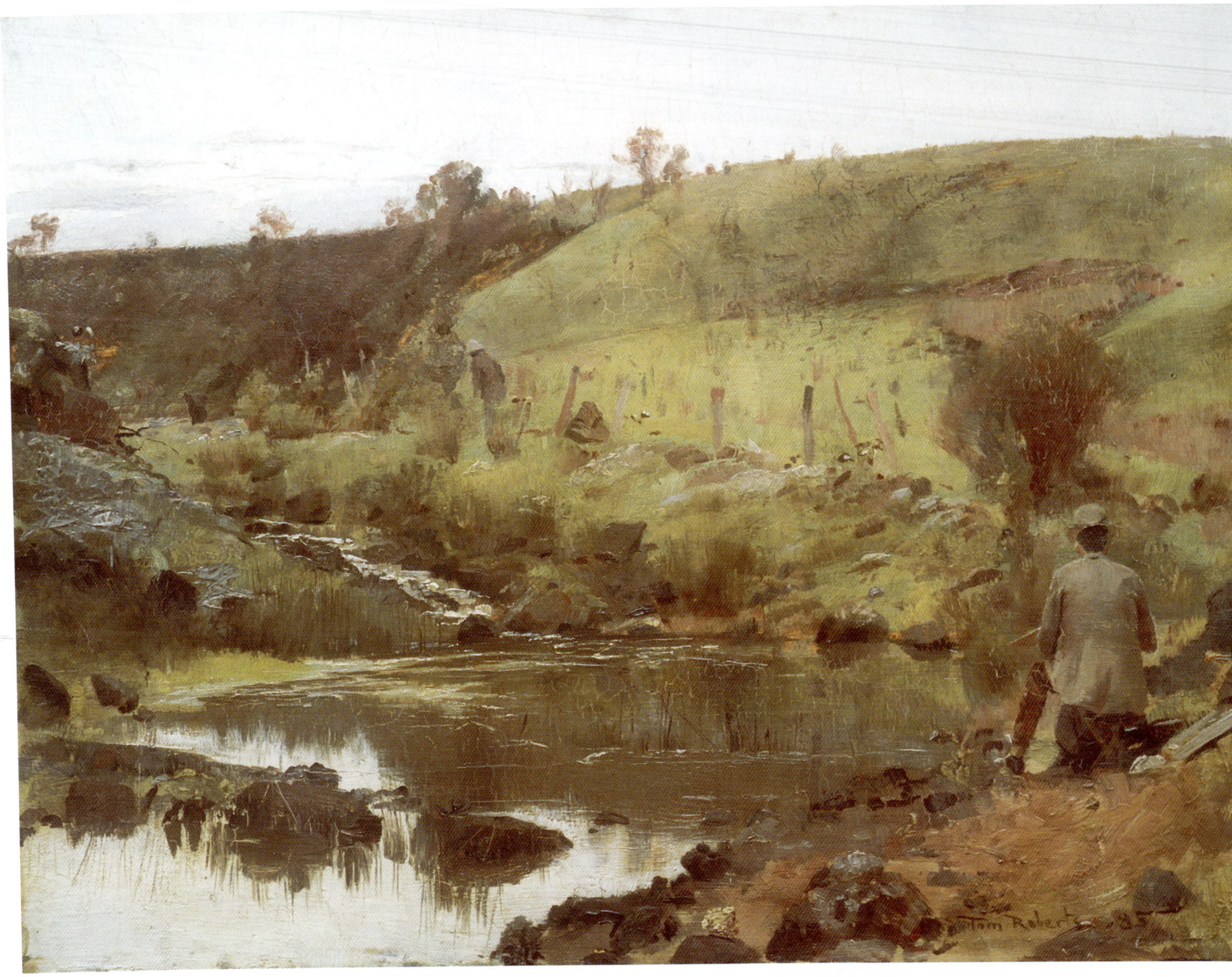
Tom Roberts 85

a whole according to the relative 'grey' of each touch of colour and, less easily managed, the volatile relations between hues. Another reason for the satisfying quiet of *Darebin Creek* is Roberts's mastery of tone: "The first sight of his pictures painted in the open air with all the grey of Nature was a revelation ... and the revolt against the Bitumen School began", said Streeton – referring to the students Llewellyn Jones, Phillips Fox and Julian Gibbs who in 1885 and 1886 accompanied Roberts on painting expeditions.[7] Roberts's companions at Darebin Creek in 1885 were most likely his friend McCubbin and the student Llewellyn Jones, who the following March showed a painting of the same region on Darebin Creek.

A quiet day on Darebin Creek was worked direct on the board, begun and probably largely completed on the spot. The vaporous grey morning light allowed Roberts to work at a comparatively slow speed. This early example of his plein-air work has a studied appearance without the wide, raw strokes and brusque pace associated with later impressionist sketches of momentary effects by Streeton, for example, or a few painted in 1889 by Roberts himself. In 1885 the steady method suited Roberts's inexperience. The tonal style he evolved for outdoor painting in 1885 and 1886 was a result of a long training in drawing and monochromatic modelling. The academic method could be employed outdoors or in the studio to approximate the shadowless light of a grey day outdoors. In Europe a new close-toned method, with modelling confined to the edges of forms and no shadows, was associated with open-air work by Jules Bastien-Lepage. The two figures of *A quiet day on Darebin Creek* merge into the background so well they are not at first visible: a blending of figure and ground within an overall tonality and colour which was to be a feature of later landscape paintings such as *Bailed up*, *In a corner on the Macintyre* and, from the end of his career, *The quarry, Maria Island.*

Another grey day in 1885, on a winter morning after rain, Roberts set his easel in a damp hollow under the bridge on Gardiner's Creek, Hawthorn, to paint one of the most stylish compositions of his career. His married sister, his aunt Burchill, his brother and McCubbin were all living in Hawthorn, so he knew the place well, and knew exactly what he wanted. Whereas many artists, including Louis Buvelot, had painted at Gardiner's Creek, none had chosen such a stark view looking up: *di sotto in su*, the Italians called it. Buvelot had preferred to draw attention to the foreground and middle distance, and other painters had been obedient to the older pictorial conventions he represented: a bit of creek, a modicum of screening trees, glimpses of receding ground, and a colour scheme of brown and olive tones tinged pink by the light of late afternoon. Roberts took his serene near-monochromatic colour from Buvelot, whose observation of the niceties of colour in the Australian landscape was often praised by James Smith; he even incorporated the brown cows which were familiar staffage from Buvelot's many images of the Yarra valley. However the Buvelot-style landscape was the background of Roberts's otherwise contrary image, dominated by the dark vertical and horizontal silhouette of the wooden bridge in the near foreground. Roberts's reference would have been Whistler's bridge etchings such as *Under Old Battersea Bridge*, 1877, or the lithotint *The tall bridge*, 1878, and possibly some of Hiroshige's Japanese woodcuts

Slumbering sea, Mentone, 1887, Melbourne, oil on canvas, 51.0 x 76.5 cm; National Gallery of Victoria, Melbourne, Purchased with the assistance of a special grant from the Government of Victoria 1979

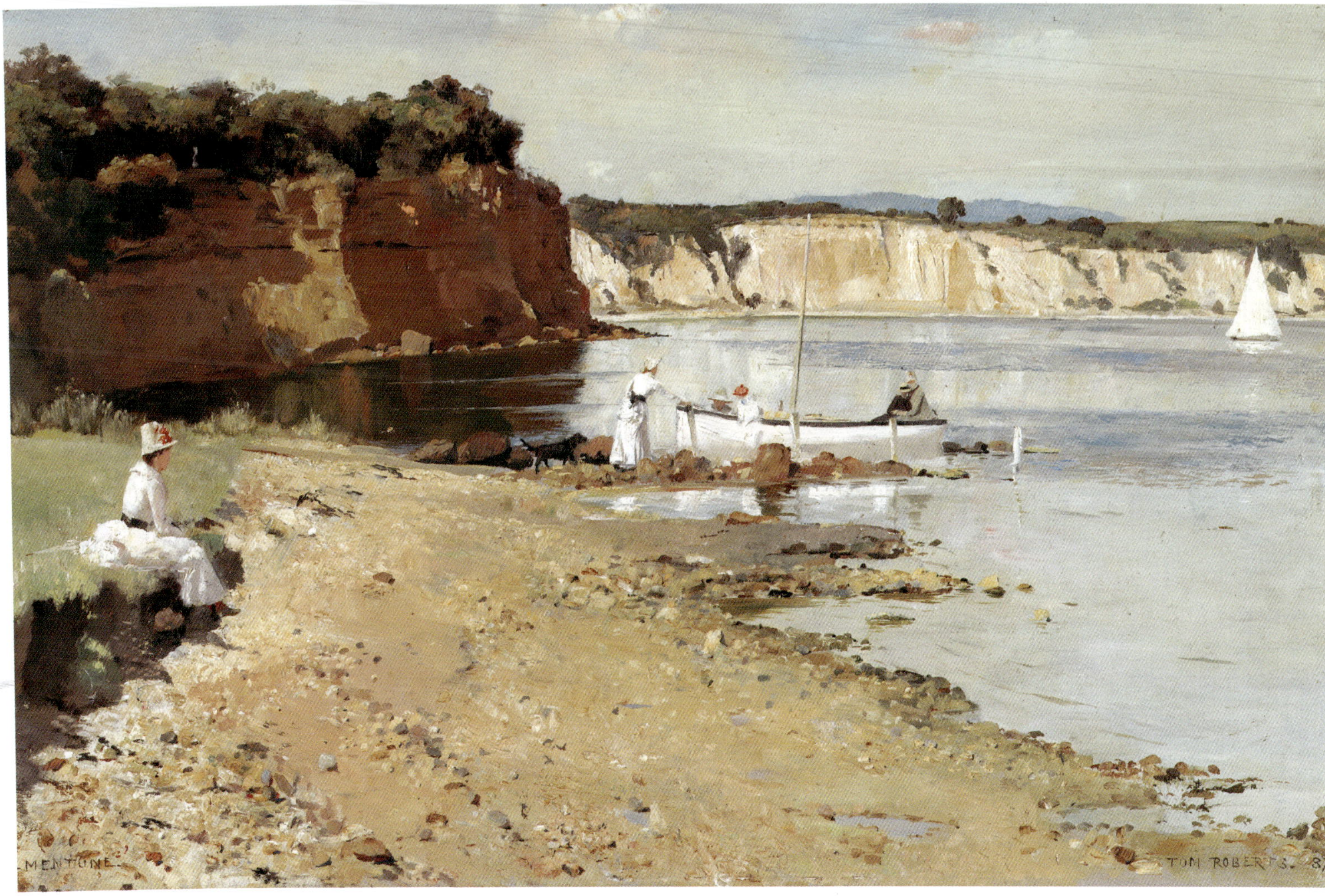
MENTONE
TOM ROBERTS. 87

dominated by great wooden bridges.[8] *Winter morning after rain, Gardiner's Creek* was in Roberts's studio when Charles Conder came to Melbourne in October 1888. Inspired by its mixture of Whistler and the Japanese, Conder immediately painted a work of around the same size, *A holiday at Mentone*, 1888, a blue-and-white image of Japanese flatness and clarity, dominated by another high bridge.

In *Winter morning after rain* Roberts made the statement for anyone (such as Smith) who cared to see it that he could paint like Buvelot but he chose a more engaged view of the landscape and its people. Some years later in a letter to James Smith's newspaper – The Argus – Roberts gave his reason for challenging safe art conventions:

> it is better to give our own idea than to get a merely superficial effect, which is apt to be a repetition of what others have done before us ... which, while it will not attract condemnation, could never help towards the development of what we believe will be a great school of painting in Australia.[9]

The two paintings *A quiet day on Darebin Creek* and *Winter morning after rain, Gardiner's Creek* set new terms for Australian landscape painting. The claims were made bluntly, within the familiar context of established older practice.

The other works intended for the Colonial and Indian exhibition, *Coming South* and (by inference) *Allegro con brio*, had the unreal pink and blond palette of Roberts's Royal Academy style, to be seen in *The sculptor's studio*, 1885. Because their streetscape and shipboard subjects were common in the illustrative rather than the high-art practice of the colonies, Roberts may have chosen that palette to put his high-art accomplishments forward. At any rate the bright, pale colours spoke of a classicising academic mode fashionable in London. Whereas Roberts adapted the blond tonality well to describe the hot summer atmosphere of Bourke Street – the effect of dusty heat is that painting's great strength – in *Coming South* the same colours are merely decorative.

Roberts's creed of "relative values" was to his friends a message as well as an example: a sign synonymous with achieving poetic empathy, a technique meeting the high standards of modern French tonal painting, and soon to be identified as a means of describing high-keyed Australian sunlight. Roberts emphasised the importance of unity in one's impression of a scene. He told McCubbin who showed him his 1885 painting of the Melbourne Gaol from the Library Gardens, "You have the drawing and colour, but you've got no values".[10] For all its faults of drawing, his own painting of Bourke Street had successfully captured the atmosphere of a hot summer's day with a brickfielder blowing the red sand of the inland into the blue sky, and colouring the sunlight pink.

James Smith in late October 1885 was drawn to a small display of illustrations in the George Ashton-John Mather-Tom Roberts group of studios at 95 Collins Street east, led there by the promise of seeing works by Louis Buvelot. He was *not* to be coaxed into reviewing Roberts's group of works for the Colonial and Indian exhibition, neither when they were on display in the Exhibition Buildings in early December nor in Roberts's studio in January; seemingly all the newspapers reviewed them except his. Smith was

Allegro con brio, Bourke Street west, c1885-86 and 1890, Melbourne, oil on canvas, 51.2 x 76.3 cm; National Library of Australia, Canberra, Purchased 1920 by Parliamentary Library Committee. On loan to the National Gallery of Australia, Canberra

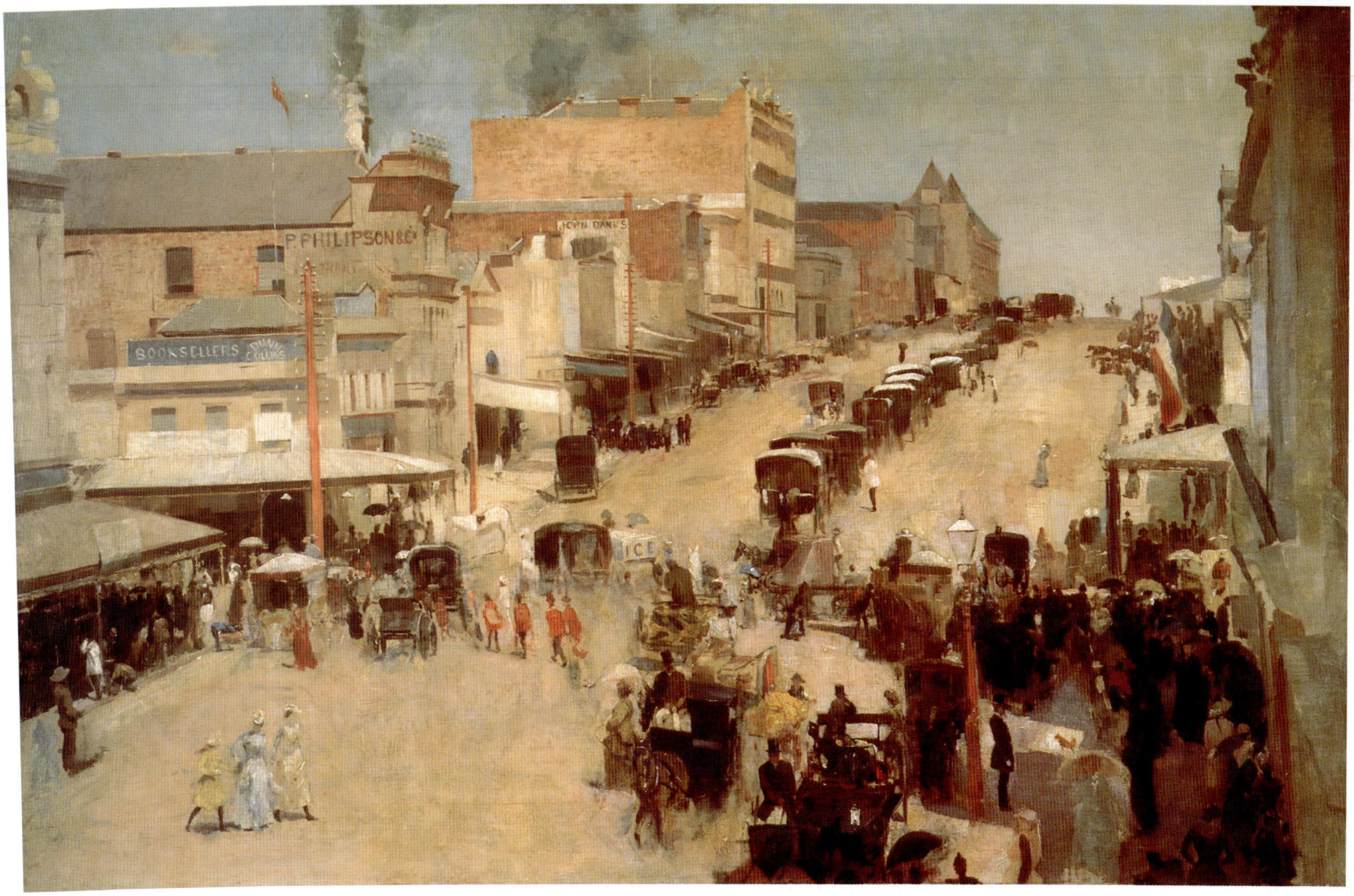
BOOKSELLERS
ICE

one of those imported intellectuals who believed the younger Melbourne-trained colonials were inferior by virtue of their background. After tempered praise of Roberts's work for almost two years, Smith's judgement came down against him in April 1888 when he saw signs of a national school forming around the artist. He decided that the paintings lacked good drawing, were painted coarsely in the French manner, showed no appreciation of intimate detail (his implication was that Roberts did not know his subjects well enough); in total, the younger man's accomplishment was considerably less than ideal despite his evident good intentions.[11] And five months later:

> Mr. Tom Roberts, Mr. F. McCubbin and Mr. Arthur Streeton, who may be grouped together on account of the similarity of their procedure in landscape painting, seem to be falling more and more under the influence of the French impressionists; leaving so much unexpressed in their representations of nature and avoiding lucidity of statement, and delineation of detail, as if both of these were aims against the canon of art.[12]

A haughty disinclination to recognise the achievements of the native-born, coupled with Smith's own taste for the older style exemplified by Buvelot, had led him to block the ambitions of Tom Roberts. He was adamant in opposition even though he shared Roberts's belief that a successful painting was an expression of the artist's intimate knowledge and feeling for the subject.

In London, R. A. M. Stevenson appraised the paintings in the Colonial and Indian Exhibition for the Magazine of Art. As one of the most discerning critics of modern, French-influenced painting, he looked for paintings that had the unaffected stance, comprehensive simplicity and understanding that his taste preferred. He found few signs that Australian art extended beyond mere natural-history record though some painters, among them Roberts, were on the right track. But he saw definite faults in Roberts: in particular his drawing which in *Coming South* was too detailed, in places even mean, and in the portrait of *Mary* was downright wrong in places – criticisms which Smith echoed.[13] Letters from Roberts's friends in Europe confirmed Stevenson's more important endorsement, John Buxton Knight writing, "Your work looked genuine"[14] and E. Phillips Fox relaying the opinion of an American painter Birge Harrison, "Surely work like that is not recognised yet out there".[15]

* * *

After sending his pictures to London, Roberts returned to the project of painting in the country in direct response to Australian nature. "You remember I was going out to Box Hill camping & sketching. I have one or two things fairly well on now. McCubbin's sister stands for us in sunlight amongst some exquisite young white gum saplings. She, a little downcast – up the hill a youth in some state about to let his horse through the slip panel – title not yet decided – 'a tiff' has been done before – suppose 'another tiff' – what do you think?", he wrote to Lillie Williamson in early April 1886.[16] *A summer morning tiff*, painted in the late summer or early autumn (March-April) of 1886 at Box Hill, with McCubbin sharing the same model, was Roberts's first real attempt to paint

Coming South, 1885-86, Melbourne, oil on canvas, 63.8 x 50.5 cm; National Gallery of Victoria, Melbourne, Gift of Colonel Aubrey Gibson in memory of John and Anne Gibson, settlers (1887), 1967

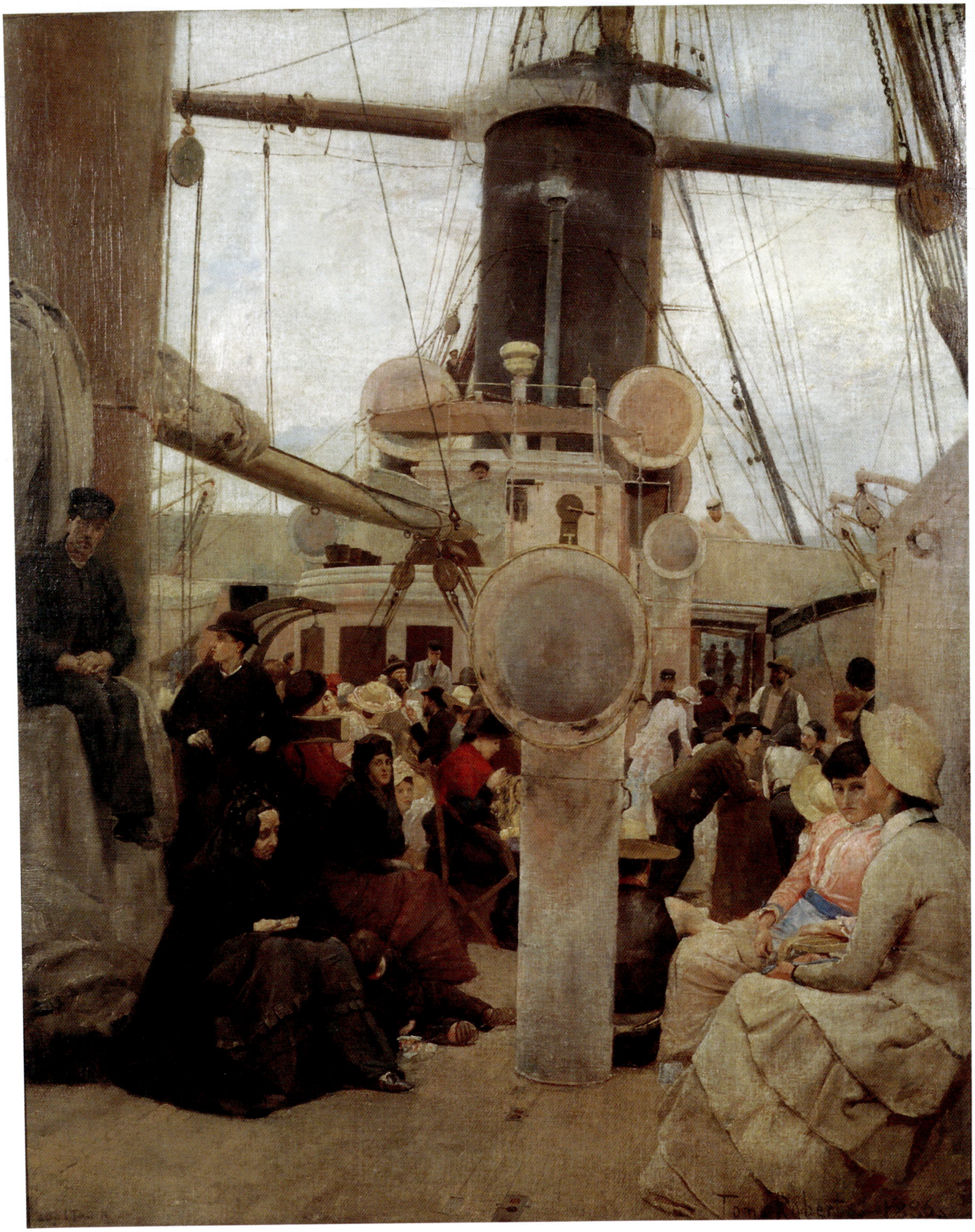

sunlight outdoors. The Granada sunlight of his *Moorish doorway*, 1883, and the Melbourne Bourke Street sunlight had been studio approximations, a matter of controlled tones rather than of direct observation. The broken sunlight and shade at Box Hill could not be described the same way. It had to be painted, as seen, in contrasting colours and abrupt changes of tone. The success of *A summer morning tiff* (and the comparative failure of its later companion picturc *Reconciliation*, c1887) is that it was an unprogrammed, first-hand report of sunlight in open woodland country. McCubbin in his painting from the same model, *Gathering mistletoe*, 1886, relied on the details of grass, bark and leaves and a telescoped view to capture the dry texture of sunlit bush enveloping a young girl. Roberts painted a deeper landscape and an overall impression, his treatment of grass and trees more cursory and his manner of describing dark shadows in sharp juxtaposition with areas of yellow grass much more peremptory. By comparison with McCubbin's twiggy scrub, the saplings against the hillside in *A summer morning tiff* have the spare, vertical grace of similar saplings in France in paintings by Bastien-Lepage, a special hero of those such as Roberts who wanted to paint country people engaged with the landscape. Since all McCubbin's sisters were in their twenties in 1886, Roberts was more realistic in painting a young woman than McCubbin in portraying a child, although the courting subject, if from real life, may have referred to Rodney Cherry and Alice Brotherton of the Buonarotti Club (who married the following year). The story of "the tiff", which Tom debated with Lillie Williamson (whom he would eventually marry ten years later), was resolved when Roberts showed the finished painting at a Buonarotti Club meeting on 29 May and Alice Brotherton wrote a poem:

> *"Under the saplings. (For Mr Roberts' Sketch)"*
> Only a word at the splitter's track.
>   A thoughtless blunder.
> She is fair and haughty, and answers back,
>   So they part asunder.
> With a jerk he loosens the fastening rein,
> And she turns her back with a fine disdain,
> And the saplings murmur a sad refrain
>   As she passes under.
>
> But I certainly think if we only wait
>   We shall soon discover
> That a patient horse will be tied to the gate,
>   And a penitent lover
> Will coo-ee once more from the trysting place
> And the blue gum boughs in that possible case
> Will serve as a screen for her blushing face
>   As she passes under.
>
> (6.6.86)[17]

A summer morning tiff, 1886, Melbourne, oil on canvas mounted on board, 76.5 x 51.2 cm; Ballarat Fine Art Gallery, Martha K. Pinkerton Bequest Fund 1943

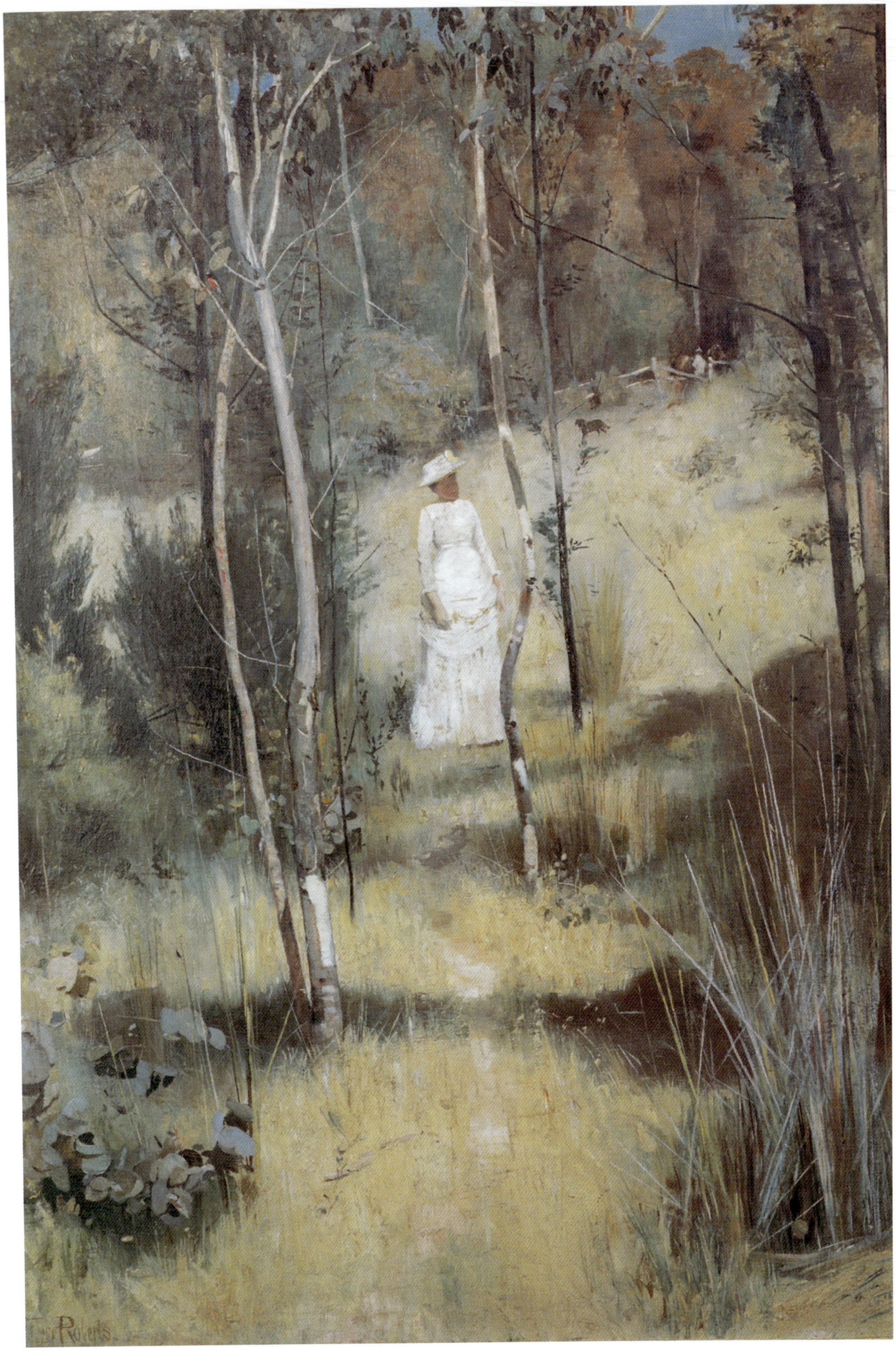

Roberts at Box Hill wanted to paint images of a rustic way of life. Box Hill, fourteen kilometres from Melbourne, was in 1870 the first country he had seen as a boy arriving in Australia with his family from England. Studying in London, reading the novels of Thomas Hardy and discussing with his painter friends how to emulate Hardy's empathetic depiction of people at home in their landscape, he had remembered Box Hill. The country of Hardy's novels had counterparts at Box Hill in the wood-carters, the pervasive eucalypt smoke from the charcoal-burners' fires and the acres of apple orchards. In the 1880s, camping on the sunny side of a small creek at Box Hill, Tom Roberts and his companions cultivated the acquaintance of the pioneer settler David Houston who lived in an old bark-roofed cottage on the rise above the creek. They delighted in the authentic details: the old man's pipe, his yarning Scottish voice delivering a tough homespun philosophy – "wummen's queer cattle";[18] and his wife Minnie who once frightened Streeton by taking a waddy to her drunken husband.[19] Houston may have been the model for a lost painting *End to a career – an old scrub-cutter* that was reviewed unkindly by James Smith: "an elderly man, with closed eyes and small hands evidently unused to labour, holding an axe suspended in the air as if hesitating whether he should cut another notch in the sapling before him, or lie down and have a nap by the side of it".[20] A painting showing charcoal-burners at work in a bush clearing (given the misleading title of *Woodsplitters* by its first owner – a timber merchant) and an open landscape foregrounded with stacks of well-cut wood, *"Evening, when the quiet east flushes faintly at the sun's last look"*, c1887, were Roberts's most considered images in the Hardy mode, one industrious, the other afterwork elegiac. Smith chose sarcastically to paraphrase the title of the second, "the full moon rising in a sky of warm pink over a landscape of considerable extent, which has apparently been parched by a hot summer". In doing so he merely described its success.[21] At Box Hill, Roberts reconciled the disparate ingredients of his early style. As a present-day curator has observed of this painting, "the harmony of muted pinks is primarily the result of careful observation of changing light rather than a calculated aesthetic ploy".[22]

The spirit in which they were painted, a mixture of humility before Nature and ambition to create an art that commanded attention, was debated by McCubbin in letters to Roberts a few years later. On the one hand, "Nature is so consoling [–] to get away for a couple of days a week from the circumambient office ... out in the wild woods ... no trains ... just away ... I am feeling this place more every time, it just suggests enough to let me feel my pictures ... I have a small photo of a 'Landscape' by Leparge, a hillside. It is so lovely. The hill is just so that you might walk over it".[23] And on the other hand there was the urge to create for oneself: "We are all trying for the same thing, power. I feel that we must give in a day what we fumble over for years [–] too timid & ... serious & earnest & conscientious etc etc ... all too conscious. So we do not begin till we forget".[24]

To hold 'The 9 by 5 Impression Exhibition', of many little nine-by-five inch paintings by several young artists, was Roberts's idea.[25] Roberts may have had it in mind some time before the exhibition was finally proposed, inspired, most probably, by a talk about Robert Browning's poetry given on 31 May 1889 to the Victorian Artists' Society

Charcoal burners, 1886, Melbourne, oil on canvas, 61.4 x 92.3 cm; Ballarat Fine Art Gallery, Bequest of J.R. Hartley 1961

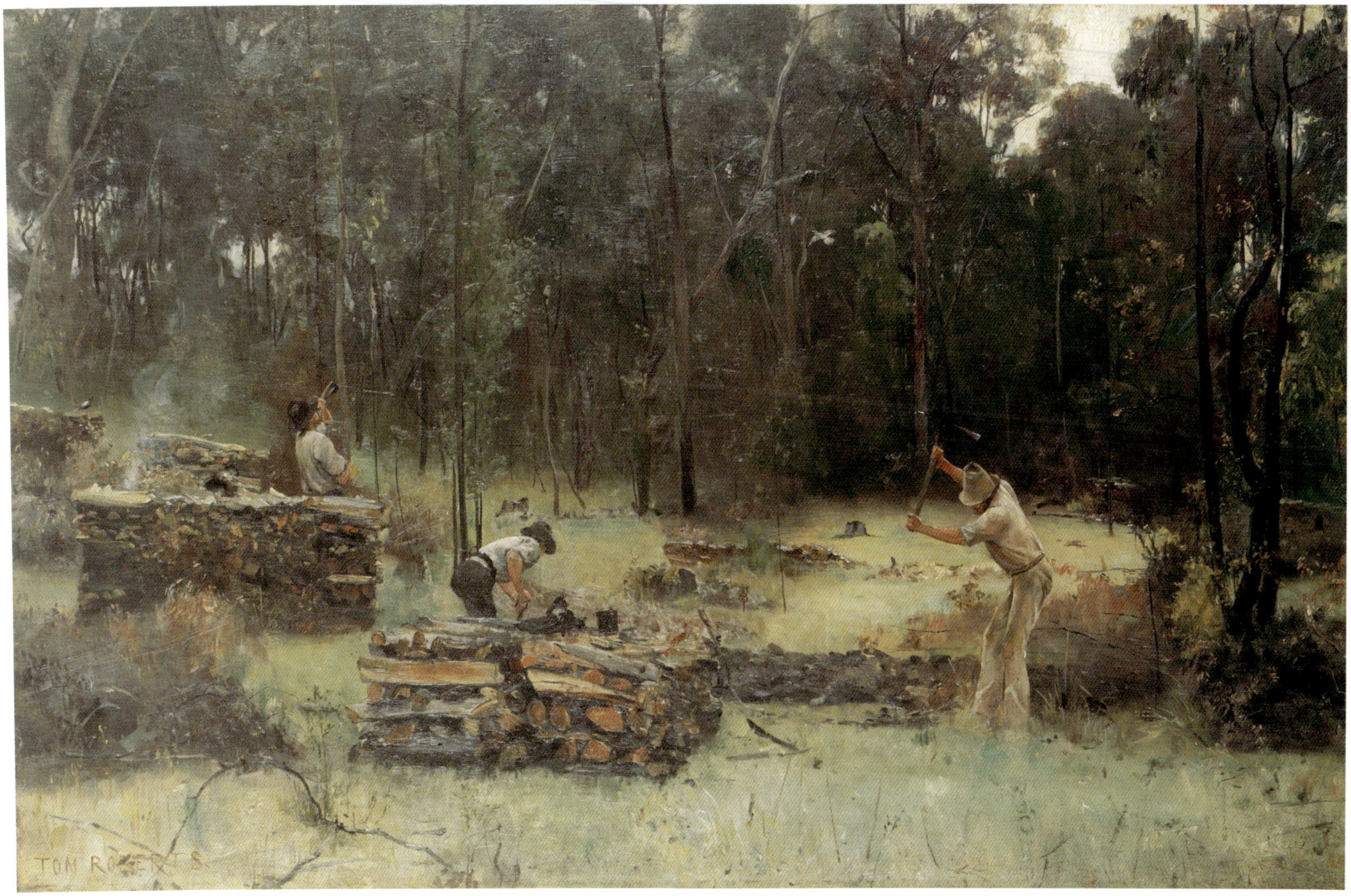

by Professor Henry Laurie of the University of Melbourne. Roberts had known Laurie some time, and had painted his portrait in 1887. Laurie's philosophy of inductive inquiry encouraged independent perception, of which the poet Browning (about whom he wrote some important essays) was a famous exemplar. Browning's style, as interpreted by Laurie, clarified Roberts's thinking about impressionism in painting when, for example, he commented in May 1889, "they are honestly searching for the truth"[26] and, in August, defended his, Streeton's and Conder's desire

> to put only the truth down, and only as much as we can feel sure of seeing ... It is here we have our great difficulty. For the question arises, how much do we see, and how much are our ideas and judgment of works made up by comparing with those we have already known, cared for, and are familiar with.[27]

There was a useful comparison to be drawn between the impressionist style in Browning's poetry and in painting: both were characterised by the first-person form of address, the casual disregard of formality, an unconventional entrance into the subject without preliminaries, the assumption of a shared familiarity with the subject, and the choice of artistically new yet commonplace situations, phrasing and rhythms.

In one sense the 9 by 5 exhibition was a natural conclusion to Roberts's program of plein-air painting, a summation of his effort to learn to paint directly from nature without recourse of drawings, composition studies and the like. It held the excitement of testing the validity of Laurie's version of impressionism. And it challenged James Smith's position as taste-maker in Melbourne.

The exhibition was successful on all those counts. Smith, outraged, wrote a vituperative review, which the artists nailed to the door leading to the display in Buxton's Rooms. Melbourne's social set visited in droves, buying many of the impressions, some even before the opening, and the bulk of the remainder went under the hammer when the exhibition ended. Roberts's sales (excluding payment in kind) amounted to seventy-four guineas, not bad for sketches priced at one to three guineas. Under the spur of preparing for the show Roberts acquired – temporarily – a sketch style of stylish verve. His, and his friends', exploration of impressionism produced not only their written definitions of what it meant to them, but the few months of working through a series of impressions directed them further towards a school style. Why, then, was Roberts so miserable immediately afterwards that he took to his bed? According to Table Talk on 30 August, he had "a severe injury to his foot" – evidently his Achilles heel! By mid September he had left Melbourne for the bush, the shearing season at Corowa in the New South Wales Riverina. He was away for months, returned for Christmas, went away again, returned in May – a pattern that continued. The exhibition marked a break in his practice as he turned to up-country subjects. It also marked the end of Roberts's commitment to Melbourne.

Assuming that his unhappiness was connected with 'The 9 by 5 Impression Exhibition', there are several possibilities. The exhibition was the first to show his work in bulk – sixty-two works – an opportunity to review his success. He may have been wounded by

A Sunday afternoon picnic at Box Hill, c1887, Melbourne, oil on canvas, 38.6 x 28.7 cm; National Gallery of Australia, Canberra, Purchased 1984

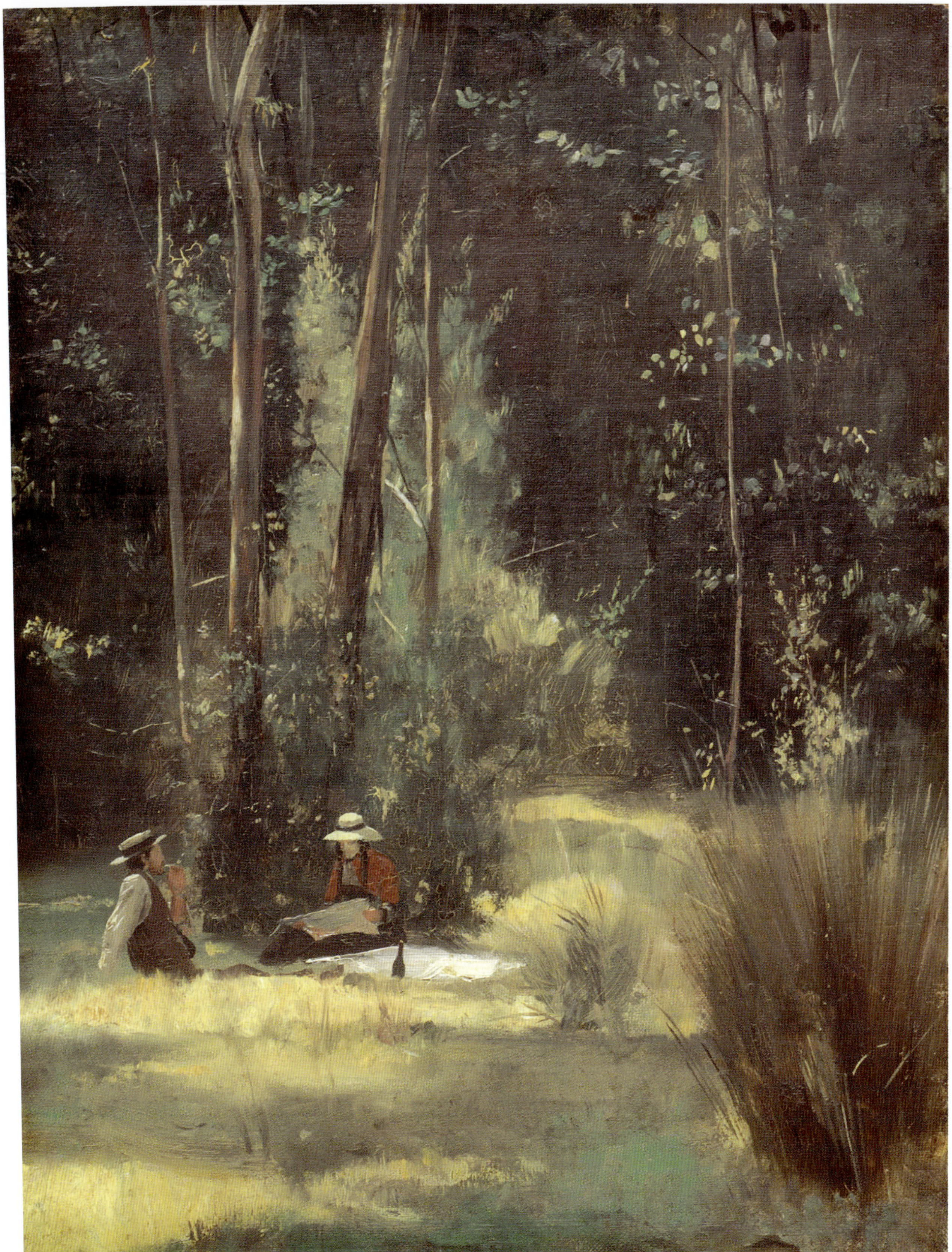

James Smith's review; certainly he bothered to write a response. He may privately have decided that his work was weaker than Streeton's and Conder's, though it was not an assessment others shared. Or he may have drawn back from the style they had evolved with its mixture of city slick and country plain. At a guess his friend McCubbin would not have approved the threesome's jaunty, streetwise attitude of the *flâneur*.[28]

The obvious model for such an exhibition was Whistler's carefully stage-managed and enormously well publicised 1884 exhibition of small impressions – called 'Notes, Harmonies, Nocturnes' – which Roberts had seen in London. The Melbourne exhibition, opening at Buxton's Rooms on 17 August 1889, was presented as a social event for an audience that purported to be not only wealthy but also interested in getting the best experience of European culture. The fastidiousness exemplified by Whistler informed the display, a drawing-room aesthetic to be seen both in the swagger decor of draped muslins and Asian knick-knacks and in many of Roberts's impressions, as well as those by Conder and some by Streeton. The subjects and the style of Roberts's sketches would suggest that the roles of aesthete and city flâneur had often displaced his romantic desire for a Thomas Hardy-like unity between humanity and rural nature. A dark sketch distinguished by a few spots of colour, identified by the title *The Milky Way*, evidently referred to Whistler. *Going home*, an image of lovers walking a city street, was painted after Conder's *The Gray and Gold* rather than from nature. Modern city life was the inspiration for three sketches of a busker at Scott's Hotel, two impressions the titles of which referred to the cigar-box lids on which they were painted, and a number of street and transport themes like *By the Treasury*, *The tram signal*, *Evening train to Hawthorn* and *The first tram*. Roberts's drawing-room scenes mostly had reading or music as their subject: *Quiet study*, *Easy chair and a book*, *The violin lesson*, *Lieder ohne Worte*, *Andante* and *Harper's Weekly*. Roberts's rural impressions in the exhibition (so far as they are identified) were relatively straightforward descriptions without the serious poetry that was his ideal.

Impression, 1888, Melbourne, oil on cedar panel, 11.4 x 19.0 cm; National Gallery of Victoria, Melbourne, Purchased 1955

* * *

In 1893 Tom Roberts, then resident in Sydney, incensed by James Smith's condescending review of 'The Loan Collection of Victorian Artists' decided to go to Melbourne and review the exhibition himself. In his article he stated the credentials of the younger generation and confronted the colonial men of affairs (of Smith's generation) who had created Australian cities which looked anything but Australian,

> Happily there is something better here [in the visual arts], and it is a pleasure to turn to the works of those who, in all the fret and fume of the last eight years, have tried to look into the deep quiet face of Nature, lingering where the winding, almost silent river bathes the feathery wattle branches; sometimes on a hillside watching the sun setting over range and valley, the cool shadows rising on the soft pile of the tree-clothed slopes, while the far-off hills go distant and more distant in the grey dusk until the moon rises in the quiet east; finding beauty in some odd corners of some country shanty, or by some lagoon which palely reflects the banks all bathed in a great shimmer of trembling brilliant sunlight:

The mailman to Omeo (Snow shoes), c1888, Melbourne, oil on cedar cigar-box lid , 22.0 x 30.0 cm; Private collection, Canberra

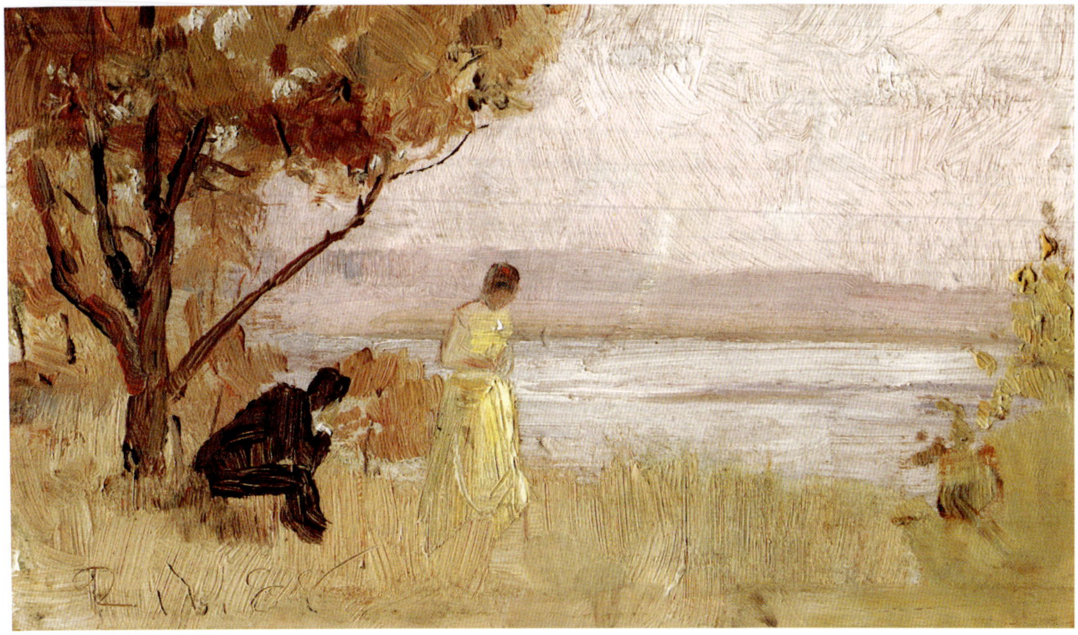

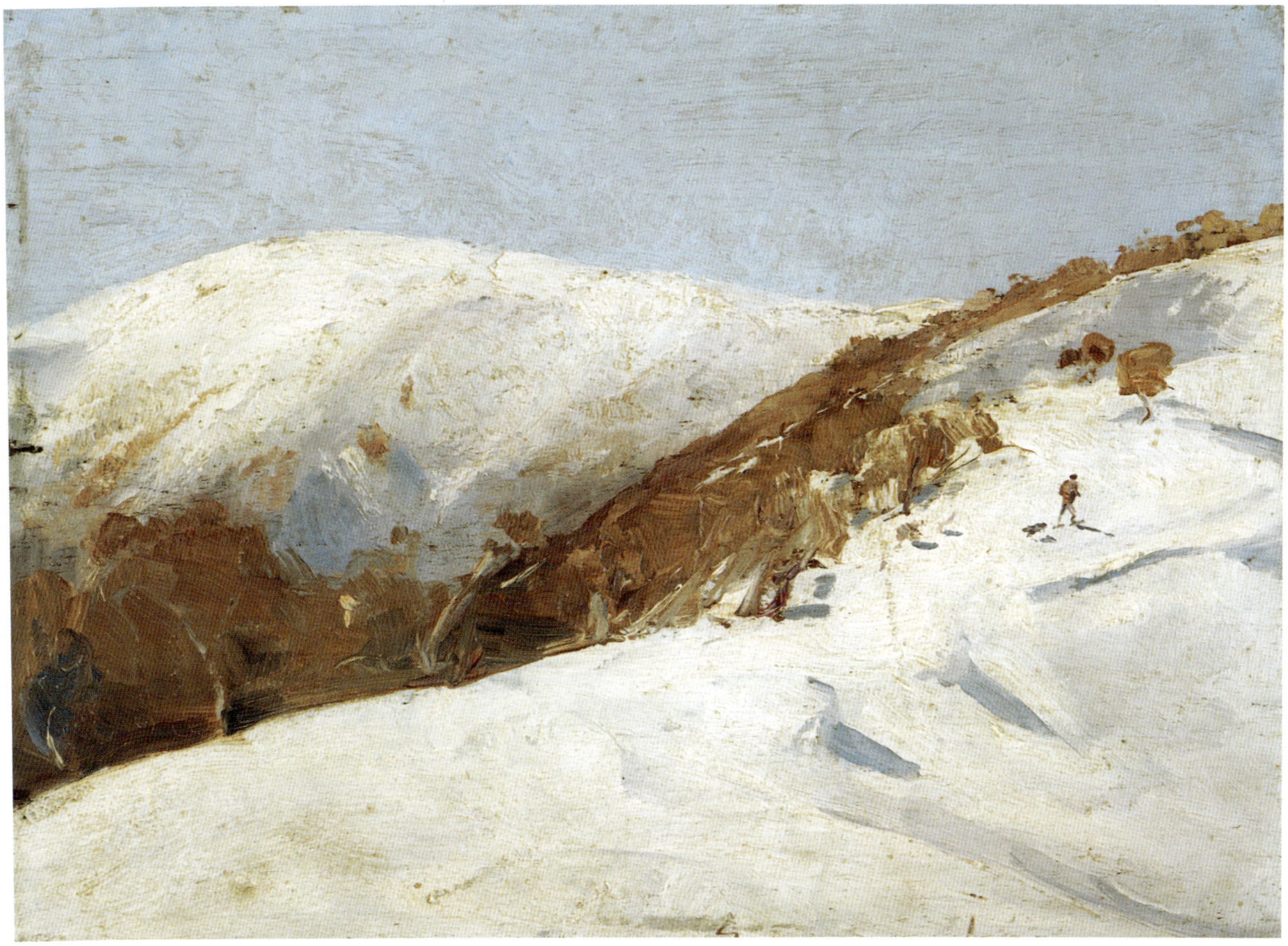

> and again, in the studio, away from the hustling of the street, where on the quiet wall will hang a head from Velasquez or Rembrandt, or a gentle pure work in plaster of Donatello, have studied the line and strength of the human form.[29]

A quality of make-believe in Roberts's images of country workers did not apply either to his images of artists camping at Box Hill – *The artists' camp*, 1886, and *A Sunday afternoon picnic at Box Hill*, c1887 – or to *The Sunny South*, 1887. The last painting had an expansive universality as well as a piercing immediacy of specific reference. Late afternoon sun glitters on the sea and gleams ruddily on the sinuous trunks of Australian banksia trees and the strong limbs of nude bathers. The beach would have been immediately recognisable to a Melbourne audience as near Ricketts Point, Sandringham. Two of the nude bathers were in classical poses: one seated faun-like on the ground and the other standing with arms linked behind his neck in a pose much favoured by art schools. The identity of these two was given away by the third, lily-white and peering shyly from a screen of tree-trunks. He was the boy Streeton, and therefore the older men were McCubbin (standing) and Abrahams (the faun). Roberts shared a house with them by the beach that summer. McCubbin reminded Roberts years later, "Do you remember looking at the Tea tree at Sandringham that evening long ago when you first came back from England. The Don [Louis Abrahams] you and I and you showed us its glorious colour. I have never forgotten it".[30] Streeton revisited the spot on a return visit to Australia in December 1906, "Spencer took me to Mentone & after lunch we went all over the spots & I felt sad at missing the row of large Banksias (Honeysuckle) you painted with figures".[31] To any audience it was a Nietzschean image of virile Aryans. In terms of the soon-to-be-federated Australia it was an image of the indigenous people of a new country dubbed "the sunny south".

The Sunny South, c1887, Melbourne, oil on canvas , 30.8 x 61.2 cm; National Gallery of Victoria, Melbourne, Felton Bequest Fund 1940

p. 60 left: *Woman at the piano*, c1889, Melbourne, oil on cedar panel, 26.0 x 13.1 cm; Art Gallery of South Australia, Adelaide, M.J.M. Carter Collection

p. 60 right: *Harper's Weekly*, c1889, Melbourne, oil on cedar panel, 23.8 x 14.2 cm; National Gallery of Victoria, Melbourne, Purchased 1958

p. 61 top: *Across to the Dandenongs*, 1889, Melbourne, oil on cedar cigar-box lid, 13.7 x 22.9 cm; National Gallery of Victoria, Melbourne, Purchased 1962

p. 61 bottom: *Sunrise*, c1929, oil on panel, 10.0 x 24.5 cm; Art Gallery of South Australia, Adelaide, Gift of the Friends of the Art Gallery of South Australia 1996

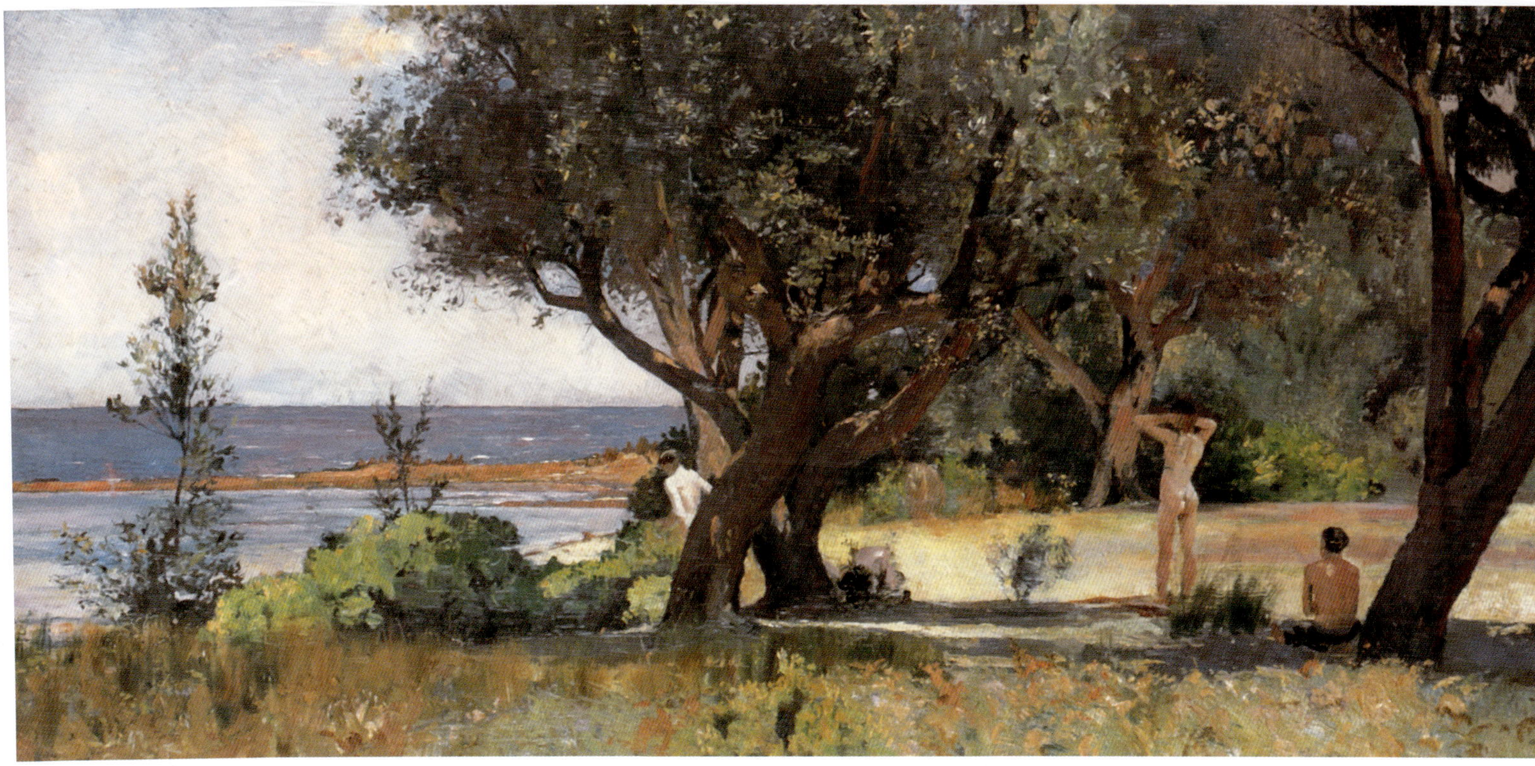

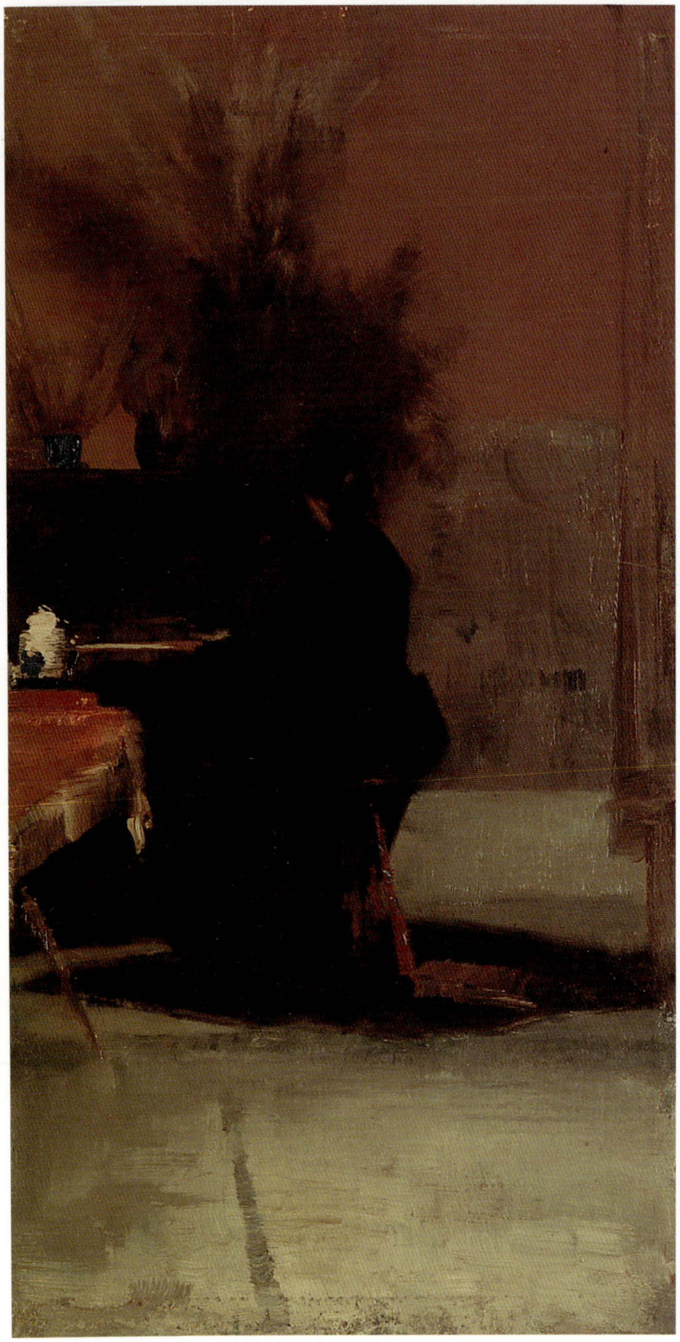

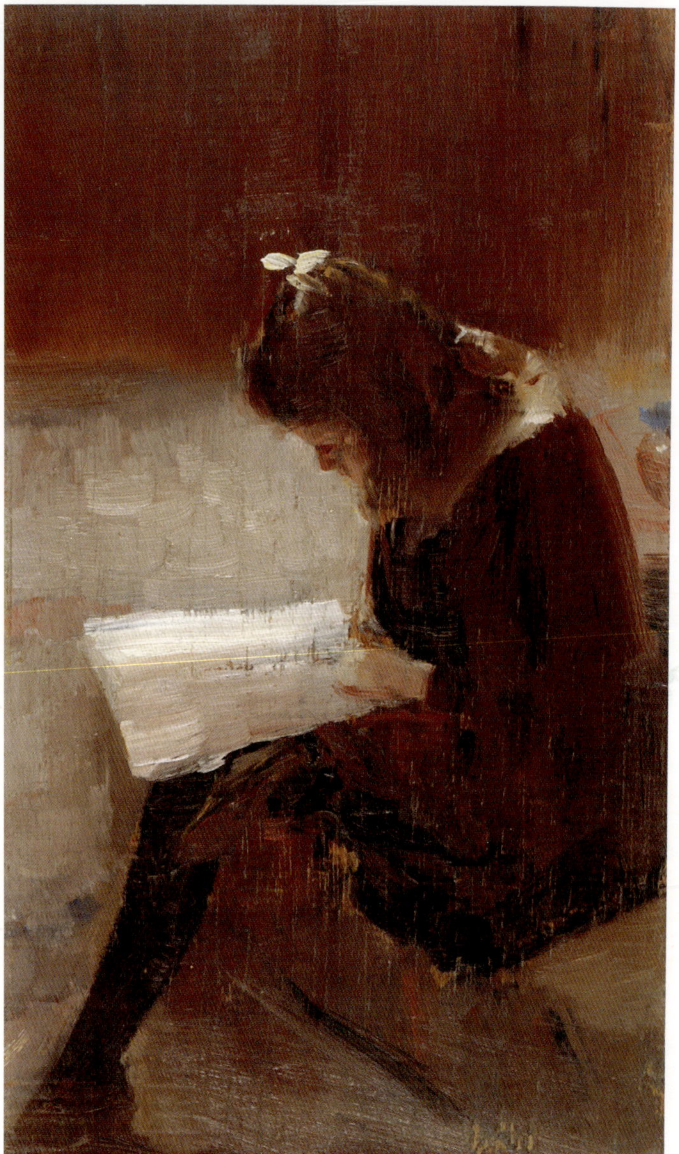

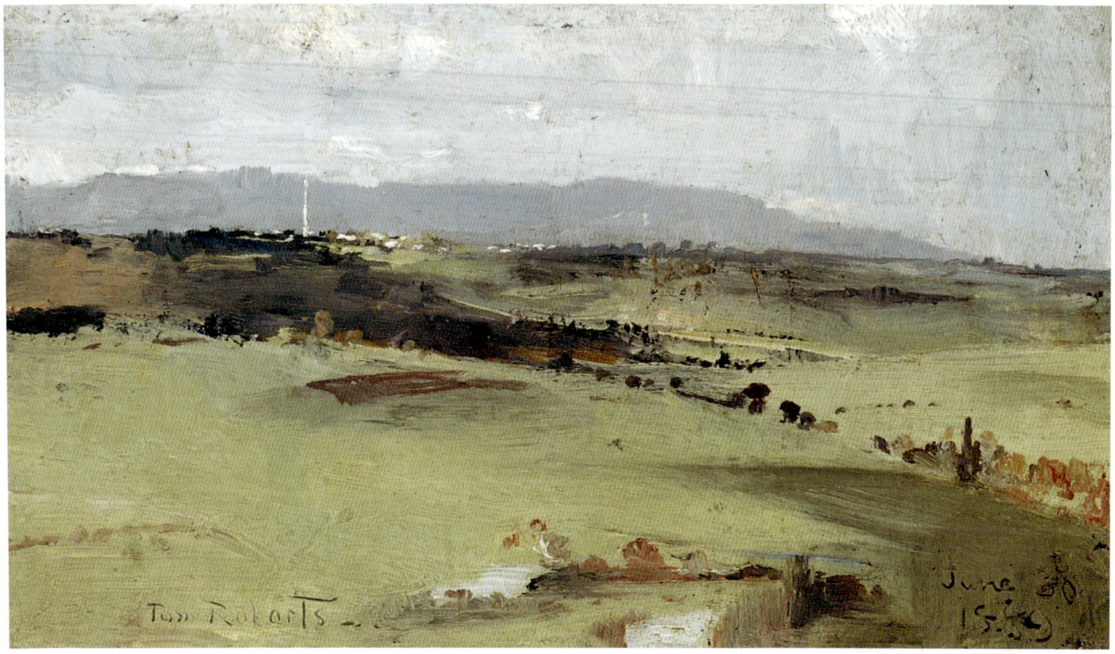
Tom Roberts

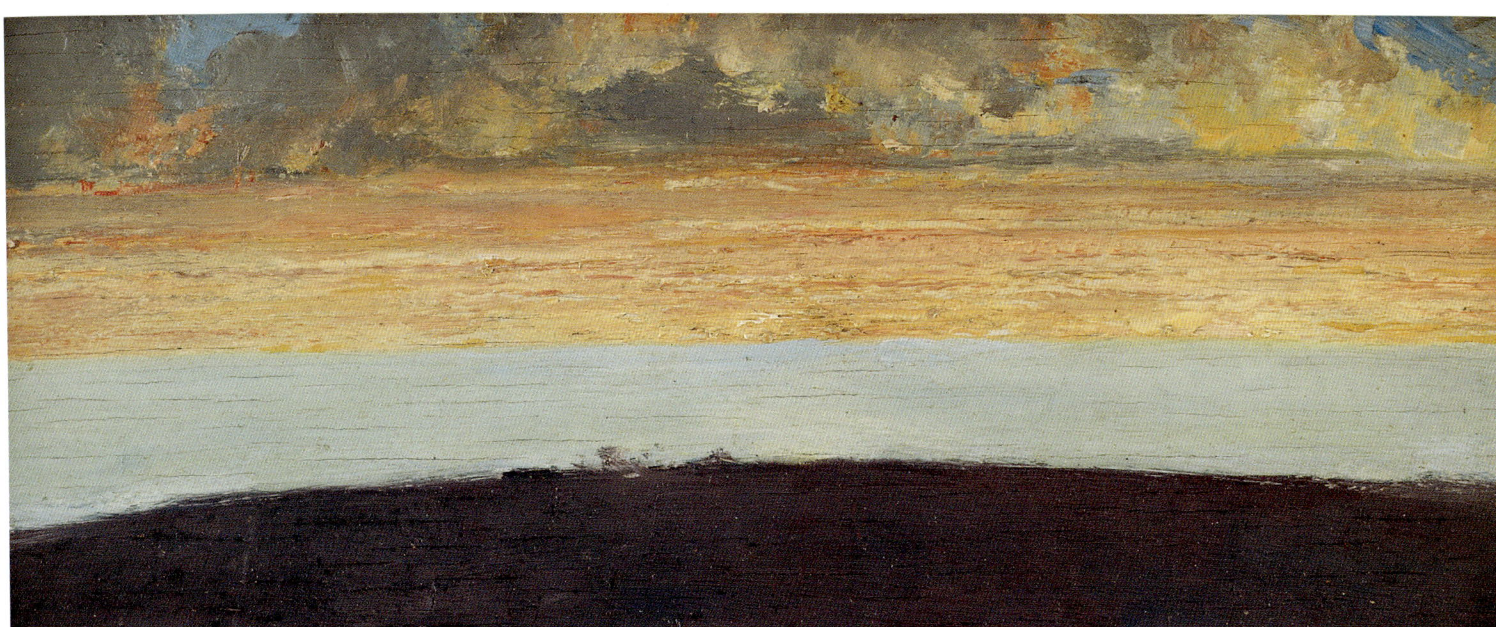

Where The Sun Never Set. Tom Roberts and the British Empire

Virginia Spate

If ever, my son, you go away from the centre of our race for a long time, you will know what a sensation it is to come back. I had longed and longed, and it was up to all of my longing.

[Return to Australia] had the sensation that as a child you thought it would be going to heaven. I don't exaggerate.[1]

The confidence of Tom Roberts's assertion that, "by making art the perfect expression of one time and one place, it becomes art for all times and all places" was inspired less by commitment to universal ideas than by his faith in the British Empire.[2] This was the Empire on which the sun never set because its colonies ringed the globe. Roberts could thus believe that around the world everyone could see in the way he saw, understand what he wished to say. 'Everyone' meant, of course, men like himself: the white man, the conqueror of empty spaces, the shaper of a feminine Nature (which he once referred to as a "mistress"), the civiliser of the savage, and the bringer of the Law.[3] His triptych, *Church, State and the Law*, 1892, exemplifies such beliefs. It consisted of three separate portraits representing Cardinal Moran, Sir Henry Parkes and Sir William Windeyer, Judge of the Supreme Court of New South Wales.[4] The portraits of the judge in his wig and gown and the cardinal in red robes flanked that of Parkes who was depicted in a simple black suit which, fusing with the dark ground, isolates and emphasises his strong features, piercing gaze and patriarchal white hair and beard. He is the embodiment of the statesman and fighter for Federation, while the judge and the cardinal represent the temporal and spiritual institutions which support the State. The conventions of academic portraiture remove the three figures from a particular time or place, and suggest their universality: the same conventions would be used for their counterparts in Britain, and the portraits could be hung next to them without any sense of difference.

Roberts felt himself part of the imperial civilising mission, and his art makes sense within it. He painted figures in the landscape in ways that revealed how they were making it their own; he depicted the "strong masculine labour" that shaped a nature and contributed to the wealth of Empire; he adventured hundreds of miles from Sydney to paint works that would represent the heroic life of the bush for middle-class city audiences; he portrayed the influential men whom he saw as the creators of the 'new Britannia' – and the pretty city women whose role was to civilise the new society through elegance, refinement and fostering of the arts. He intended that such paintings would record the processes that had brought the nation into being. Roberts conceived of Australia as an organic society, tied to the soil and socially harmonious. Thus his paintings never confront the class antagonisms or profound racial injustices of his time. Instead, he seems to have thought of his art as a means of contributing to social

Sir Henry Parkes, 1892, Sydney, oil on canvas, 66.0 x 56.0 cm; Art Gallery of South Australia, Adelaide, Elder Bequest Fund 1899

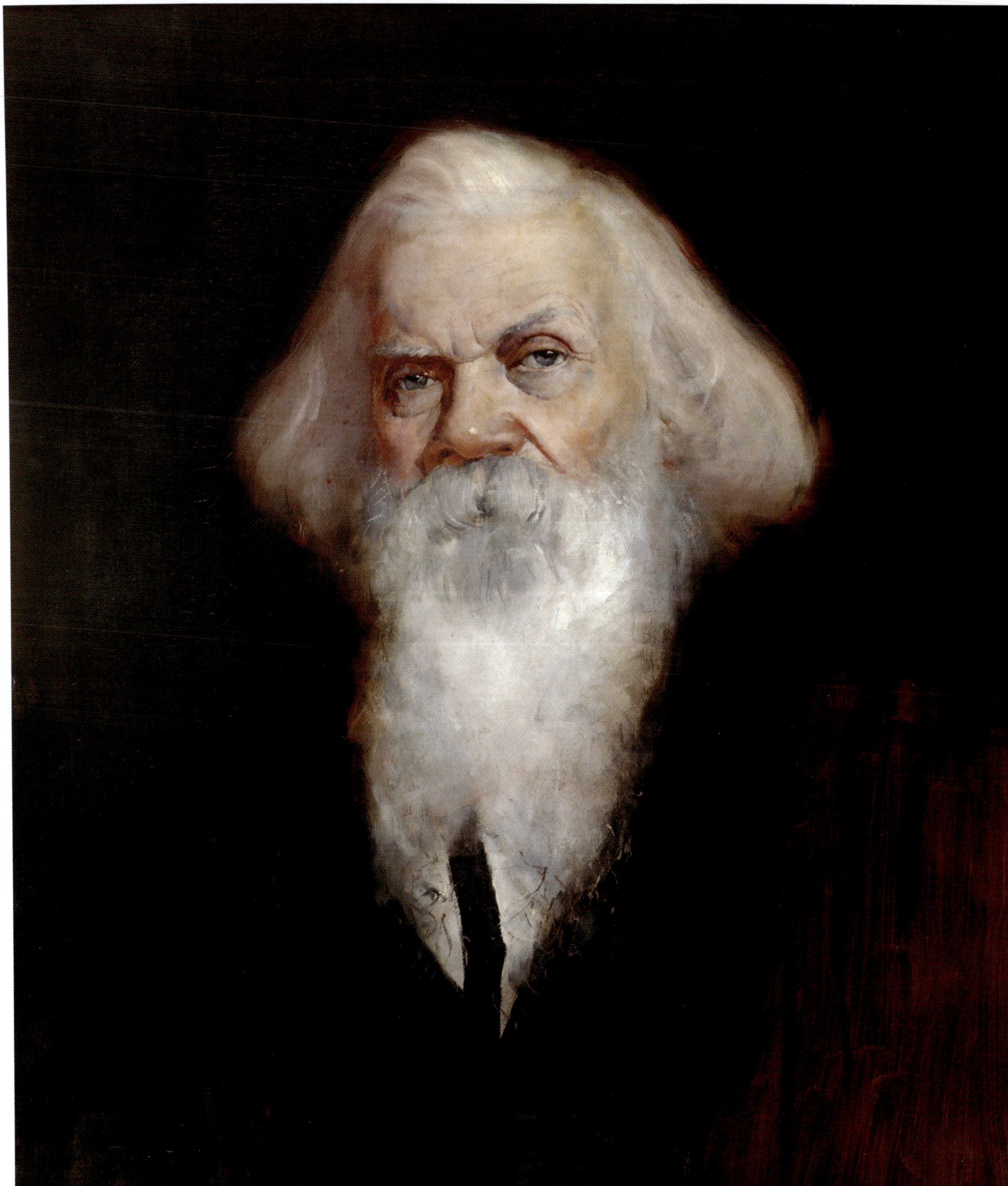

unity and to progress. By using a Realist mode of expression he also suggests that these characteristics were real – and provided a reassuring message to the progressive, educated, urban middle-classes who saw his work in exhibitions, visited his studio and bought his works.

I will suggest in this essay that, as international styles claiming scientific truth and responsiveness both to nature and to modernity, Realism and its derivatives, Naturalism and Impressionism, were integral to late-nineteenth-century European imperialism.[5] In the case of settler colonies like Australia, their insistence on the expression of the present moment was crucial to a process which had to excise the past in order to make Terra Australis 'terra nullius'.

* * *

Roberts showed *Aboriginal head (Charlie Turner)* in the same exhibition as *Church, State and the Law*. This was an unusual depiction of an Aboriginal in that it suggested that Charlie Turner was a person with his own inner life, not a debased being arrested at an earlier phase of human evolution. Roberts represented the head as a vignette, cut off from the man's body – and from his tribal group and, indeed, from any social context. Roberts used this form of composition in other portraits – particularly those of elegant young women such as *Frances Ross*. Her elaborate hat speaks of a particular moment in the modern, the moment of *that* fashion, while her vivacious expression suggests that she is in communication with someone, and thus that she is a social being. Roberts's Realism was the style which evolved in modernising, atomised societies, but he struggled to reconcile the disparate parts of Australian society in his painting. This reconciliation did not include Aboriginals.

Turner's eyes are turned upward. Traditionally this was a means of suggesting inner spiritual vision, but here the eyes seem to be almost fearful, as if Turner was looking up at some threatening authority. This troubling painting must be understood in the context of the belief that the Aborigines were a dying race. Roberts, like many European Realists, sought to record ways of life which were disappearing, making his attitudes clear in inscriptions such as "Gubbie Wellington – one of the last blacks of Corowa" (and, on the reverse, "Last of the Murray River Tribes"). Similarly, when the Art Gallery of New South Wales purchased *Aboriginal head* in 1892 (first exhibited without Charlie Turner's name), a critic wrote "that its value will grow year by year with the gradual disappearance from our midst of the *original possessor of the soil*", and in 1926 Roberts told a journalist that he had thought that his Aboriginal portraits "would have been an interesting record of a dying race".[6] The *Aboriginal head* is a poignant embodiment of the ideology of terra nullius. The floating head exists out of time, in no place. It is the image of the Outsider which unsettles Roberts's claim about the universality of an art that was "the perfect expression of one time and one place ...". In this continent, "one time and one place" meant modern time, the time of progress; one place meant British soil. Progress, modernity, the evolutionist doctrine of the survival of the fittest, justified the 'no place' of Charlie Turner. I am not suggesting that Roberts consciously held such ideas. More profoundly, his Realist style states that this is what he *saw*.

Aboriginal head (Charlie Turner), 1892?, Sydney, oil on canvas on paperboard, 39.4 x 29.8 cm; The Art Gallery of New South Wales, Sydney, Purchased 1892

* * *

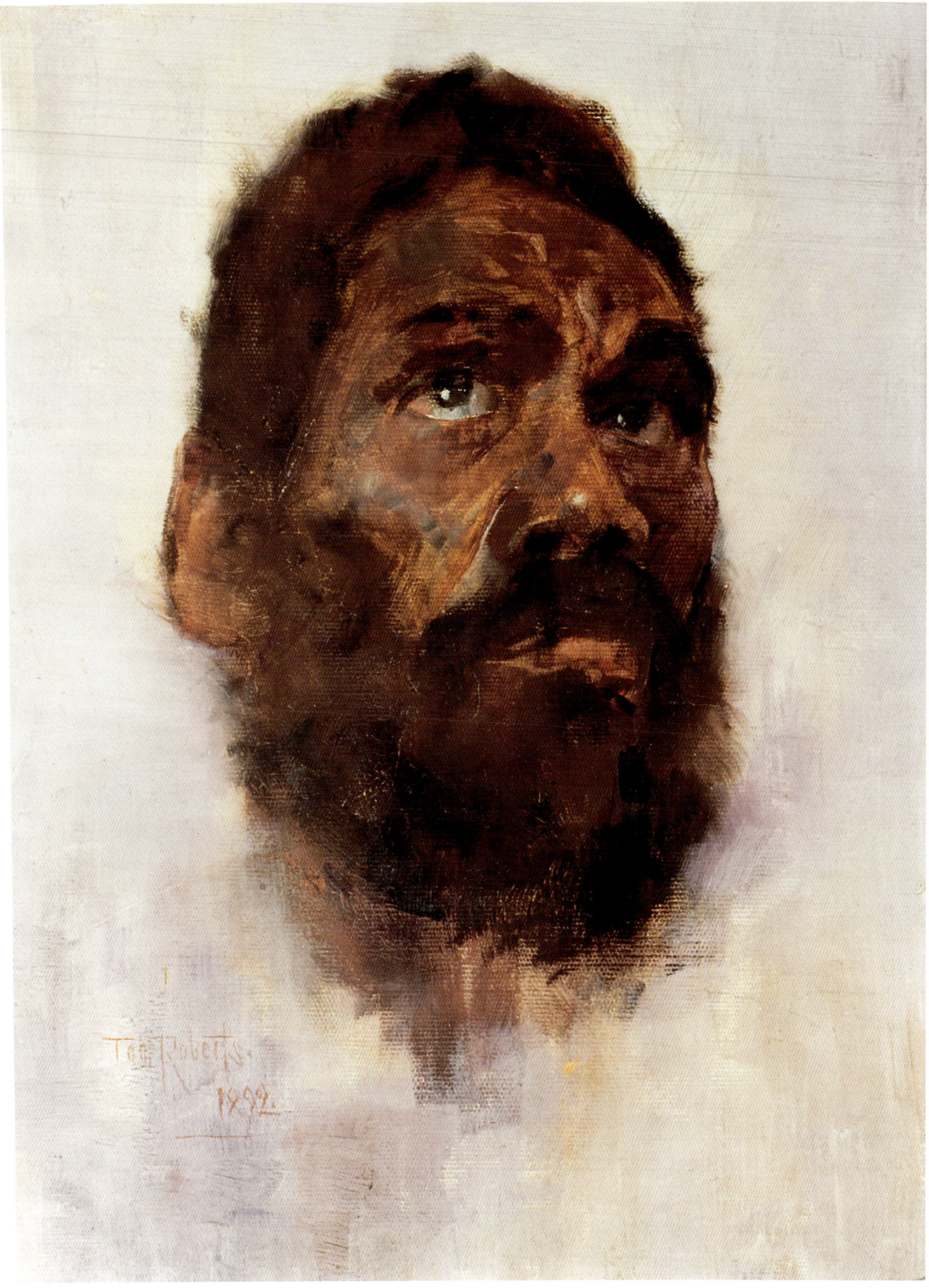

Tom Roberts

Roberts came to Australia with his widowed mother, brother and sister in 1869 when he was thirteen years old, shortly after the death of his father, a respected citizen of Dorchester where he was editor of the Dorset County Chronicle. Significantly they sailed in the True Briton. Mrs Roberts had decided to join her relatives in Melbourne, but in their early years the family lived in some poverty in the mean streets of Collingwood and the dreams of greatness offered by the Empire must have seemed very distant.

Roberts believed he had realised such a dream when he was commissioned to paint the huge *Opening of The First Parliament of the Commonwealth of Australia by H.R.H The Duke of Cornwall and York, May 9, 1901*. When he completed it in England he wrote: "Well, all this began at 2 bob a night at Collingwood [School of Design] ...".[7] He progressed from Collingwood to the National Gallery School, then located in the Melbourne Public Library, a smaller version of the British Museum's panopticon library, a fitting model for the imperial dissemination of knowledge and culture.

Roberts later said that, for a few years, "the memory of English landscape" prevented him from appreciating the Australian scenes. His new appreciation probably owed something to the plein-airists, recent arrivals from England and elsewhere, who insisted on the necessity of painting in nature.[8] Nevertheless to continue his education he decided to study at the centre of Empire, in the Royal Academy Schools in London. Several of Roberts's English works reinforce the notion of the return to the centre: two tiny Whistlerian paintings depict the Houses of Parliament and Trafalgar Square, respectively the mother of Parliaments and the triumphal centre of Empire. Roberts also painted a scene in his home county, Dorset, using the soft-misty muted tones of plein-air painting.

Thames scene, c1884, London, oil on wood panel, 12.7 x 22.9 cm; Private collection, Melbourne

Roberts returned to Australia in 1885 with the ability to work in a variety of styles: academic figure-painting; plein-airist tonal painting; painterly Realism; a descriptive Naturalism, strongly influenced by photography; Whistlerian composition and abstraction of colour; and probably some direct knowledge of French Impressionism.[9] This eclecticism is characteristic of the work of many artists who go from the periphery to the centre in that they can encounter all contemporary styles simultaneously. It was to serve Australian art well since it enabled Roberts to adapt his style to a variety of pictorial functions, ranging from fresh and immediate studies of the bush to academic portraits, and to Naturalist or painterly Realist figure-paintings on 'national subjects'. The precise sources of his styles are less important than the fact that their shared commitment to individual perceptual experience, truth to nature and to the modern suited them to the European appropriation of the world. As Bernard Smith and William Eisler have shown, European expansion in earlier centuries required realist modes of art for recording human types, as well as flora and fauna, and for depicting topographical sites.[10] However, apart from the styles used for simple description, the Neo-Classicist and Picturesque styles which inflected such forms of realism created temporal structures which, in their different ways, suggested continuity – including historical continuity between European exploration and settlement and pre-existing cultures (except for the styles used for simple description). Later-nineteenth-century Realist styles emphasised

Trafalgar Square, c1884? London, oil on cardboard, 14.0 x 28.0 cm; Art Gallery of South Australia, Adelaide, South Australian Government Grant 1988

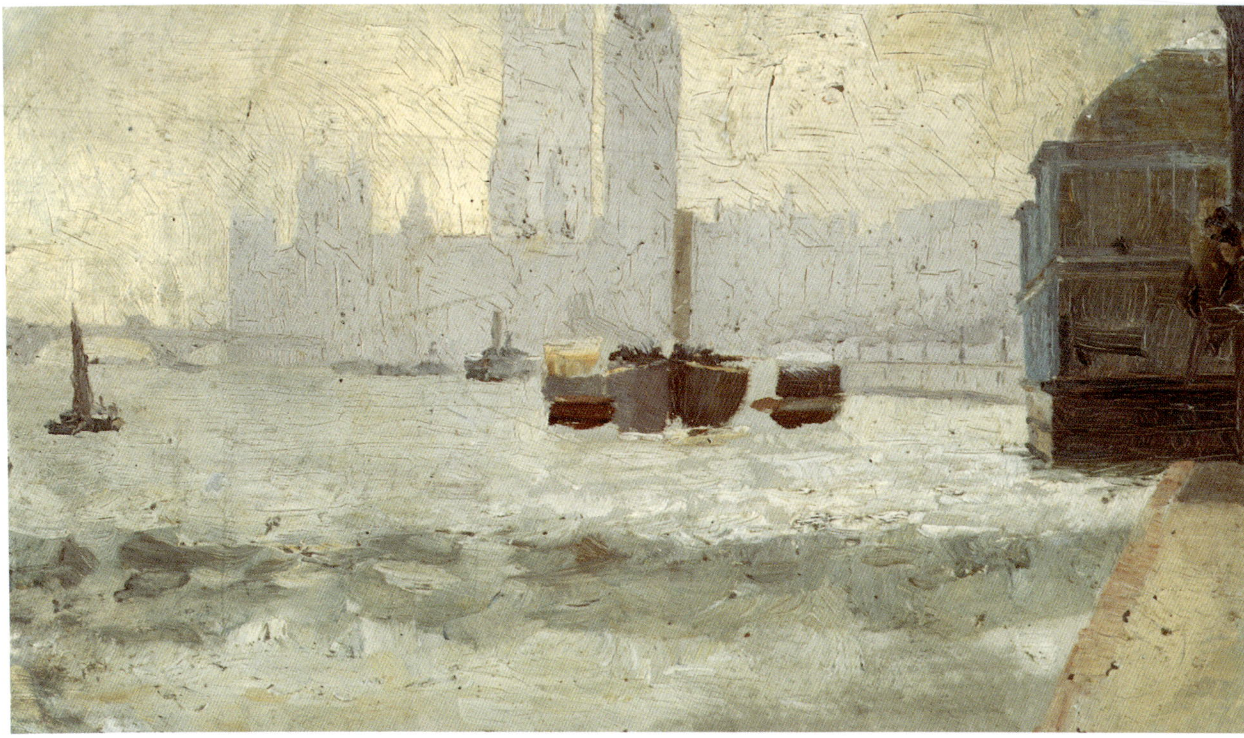

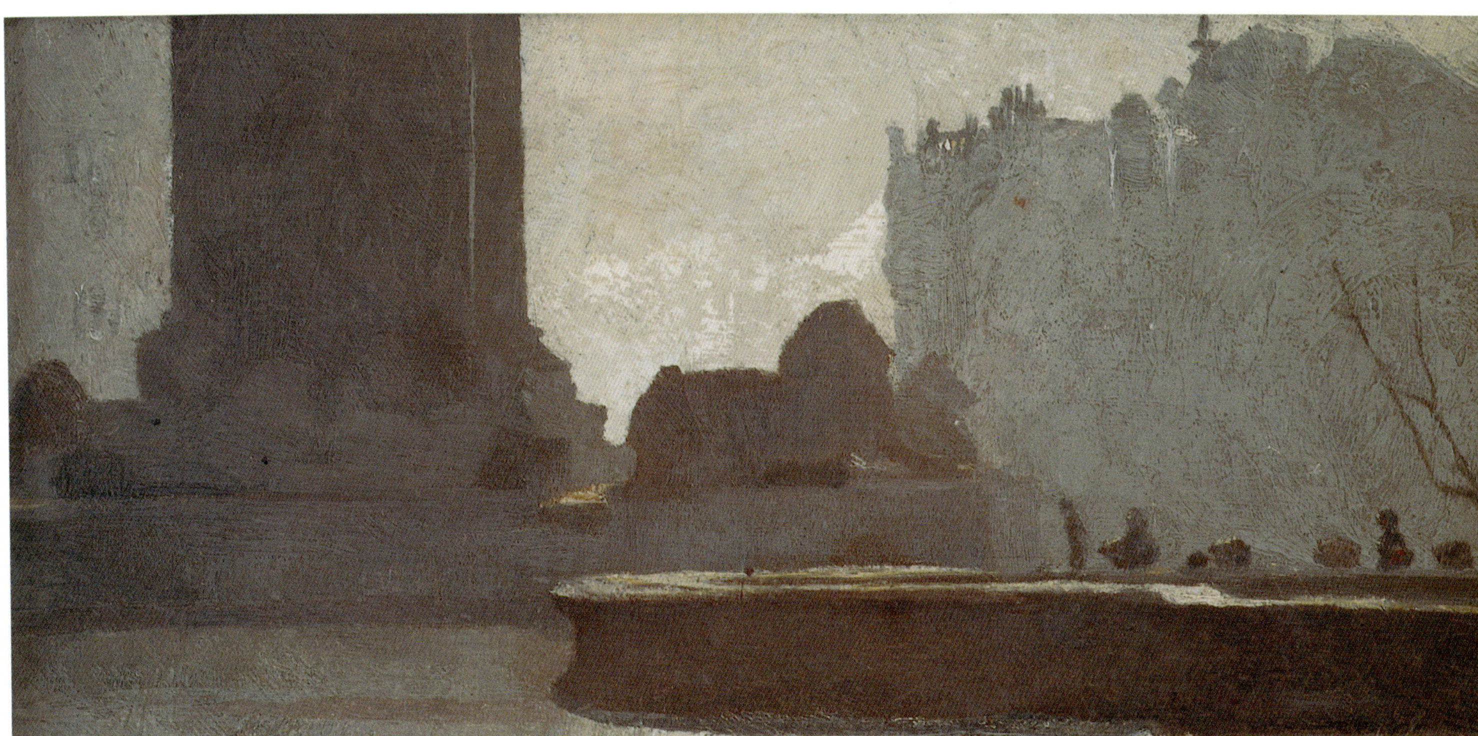

the moment of perception and thus broke the nexus between past and present. Their emphasis on individual perception rather than inherited modes of expression could result in startlingly new, even raw responses to the physical environment and to contemporary experience.

The first time I realised this was when I myself returned to Melbourne from England (in contrast to Roberts's slow sea-voyage, I was hurtled from hemisphere to hemisphere). The clear blue sky is of course a cliché – though not the less true – but what I had not expected was a sudden, overwhelming sense that the pink tonalities of *Allegro con brio, Bourke Street west* were absolutely 'true'. Melbourne's nineteenth-century architecture is not, of course, pink, so presumably what I was feeling was the visual sensation of warmth, of 'hot' light. Significantly, Roberts painted Bourke Street a few months after returning to Melbourne – and never painted in this way again, almost as if that early clarity of perception was superseded by other 'moments' of seeing, and other styles. It could be suggested that he had a kind of displaced seeing which resulted in the striking discontinuities of his pictorial exploration of the Australian scene. Roberts never again painted such a striking picture of the modernising city. The Empire rejoiced in the British cities springing up around the globe, imitating the forms of the mother-city, but generally the pictorial expression of Empire focused more on the soil than on buildings.

Roberts's painting of his return to Australia, *Coming South* – a more tightly painted, descriptive work, detailing the kinds of people who made the long trip to a Britain on the other side of the world – was sent to the Colonial and Indian Exhibition which opened in London in May 1886. This was an exhibition displaying all the products of the vast Empire and, like all the great 'universal exhibitions' of the nineteenth century, was conceived as a grandiose didactic exercise, informing its visitors about every facet of the imperial adventure. The presence of Roberts's little painting in the exhibition is indicative of the vast, controlling imperial gaze which nothing could escape.[11]

To assert the Britishness of Roberts's project is not to deny its Australianness. To the immigrant painters from England and Scotland these were one and the same thing, and they contributed as much, if not more, to the development of an Australian style and iconography than did the native-born. In 1883 a native-born Australian criticised painters who "saw Australian scenery with English eyes", as if through an "atmospheric veil". This, he said, "may please an Englishman, but I was born in the sunny south". Generally, however, paintings of Australian people, landscapes and light were seen as variations on British art-forms, rather than radical alternatives to them.[12] Moreover it was an Englishman who painted *The Sunny South*. Today we might rejoice in this painting as 'characteristically Australian' (a favourite late-nineteenth-century phrase) because of its hedonism, its brilliant blue water and warm light. But the title makes sense only in relation to the 'unsunny north' – and the painting's hot colours and its evocation of men's bodily pleasures in nature relate implicitly to the fresh greens and infinite shades of grey and more constrained bodies of Roberts's mother country.

Turning the soil (Sketch for *Charcoal burners*), c1886, Melbourne, oil on panel, 34.8 x 13.4 cm; Art Gallery of South Australia, Adelaide, South Australian Government Grant 1982

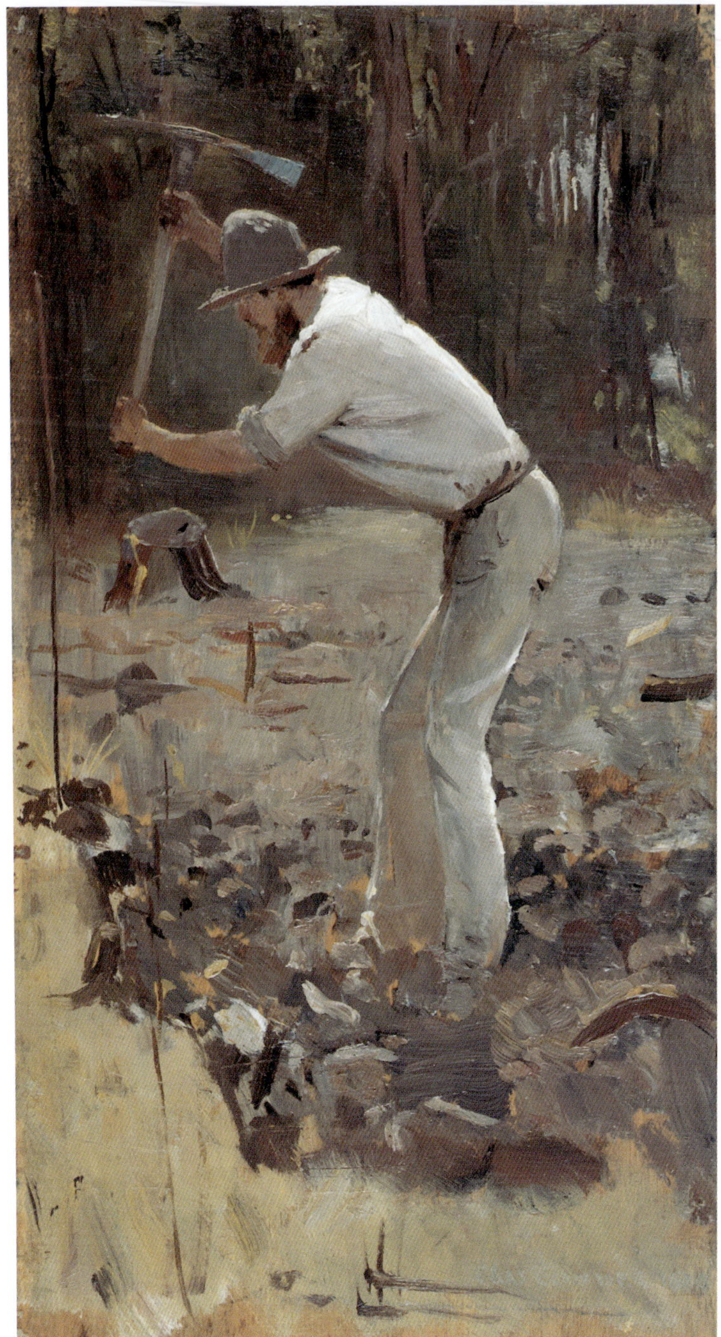

Tom Roberts

To understand the relationship between British culture and its new environment, Roberts's paintings of figures in landscapes should be read against the grain of our affection for them and of our acquired sense that they are quintessentially Australian. It is significant that in the 1880s the works of Roberts and his friends were often *seen* as 'French', despite the fact that plein-airism was as much an English as a French phenomenon. Nevertheless the critic James Smith said that works in an exhibition in 1886 showed "the general leaning of young artists and art-students towards French methods of landscape paintings" in "their avoidance of too much definition of form and their disposition to secure striking effects by colour laid on in broad masses".[13] This sense of the foreignness of the new styles may be due to the fact that their expression of individual perceptual experiences made new demands on spectators and, indeed, disturbed their existing modes of seeing the landscape.

Slumbering sea, Mentone is painted in an international style and yet suggests the absolutely local. It is an Impressionist painting of middle-class leisure, and invites delighted recognition of the particular aspects of brilliant Australian light reflected off both smooth and ruffled water. For all the happiness of the theme of messing about in boats or sitting in the sun enjoying the scene, there is a strangeness in the painting. Bourgeois ladies were relatively recent apparitions on the beaches of Australia, as they were on those of England and France – where, as Monet's paintings of the 1860s show, it was only recently that the railways and new hotels had irrevocably transformed the traditional fishing villages. Because Sydney and Melbourne are situated on the sea they did not yet need the dense infrastructure of the tourist resorts on the English Channel, so *Slumbering sea, Mentone* suggests a closer relationship between the figures and nature than did Monet's paintings of this subject. Roberts's elegant seated lady was, however, representative not just of a developing bourgeois culture, but of the complete displacement of another culture, one which cannot exist in the same frame as the theme of bourgeois leisure (as do the fishermen in Monet's *Beach at Sainte-Adresse* of 1867). On Port Phillip Bay the shores were ringed by centuries-old shell middens – which I am tempted to see in the powdering of strokes along the beach under the bank. Impressionism allows us to see whatever is there simply as coloured accents but once one thinks of the possible presence of a midden the painting cannot be the same. It perhaps makes one more aware of the dark bulk of the red cliff and its sombre reflections which seem almost to have strayed in from another painting, and suggest that the scene is not so tame, so civilised as it seems at first sight. But, fragile though she may seem in her white dress and delicate parasol, the woman stands for the implacable forces of the imperial civilising mission.

This is even more clear when – as in *A summer morning tiff* – the bush becomes the impassive setting for a sentimental incident which was the popular stuff of English anecdotal painting. There is no relationship – emotional or physical – between woman and landscape. She is simply there. The landscape provides a beautifully studied series of recognitions – the scratchy grasses, the rusty red path, the round gum-leaves, the delicate young gums with their smooth trunks or peeling bark – which invite the

"Evening, when the quiet east flushes faintly at the sun's last look", c1887, Melbourne, oil on canvas, 50.8 x 76.2 cm; National Gallery of Victoria, Melbourne, W.H. Short Bequest Fund 1944

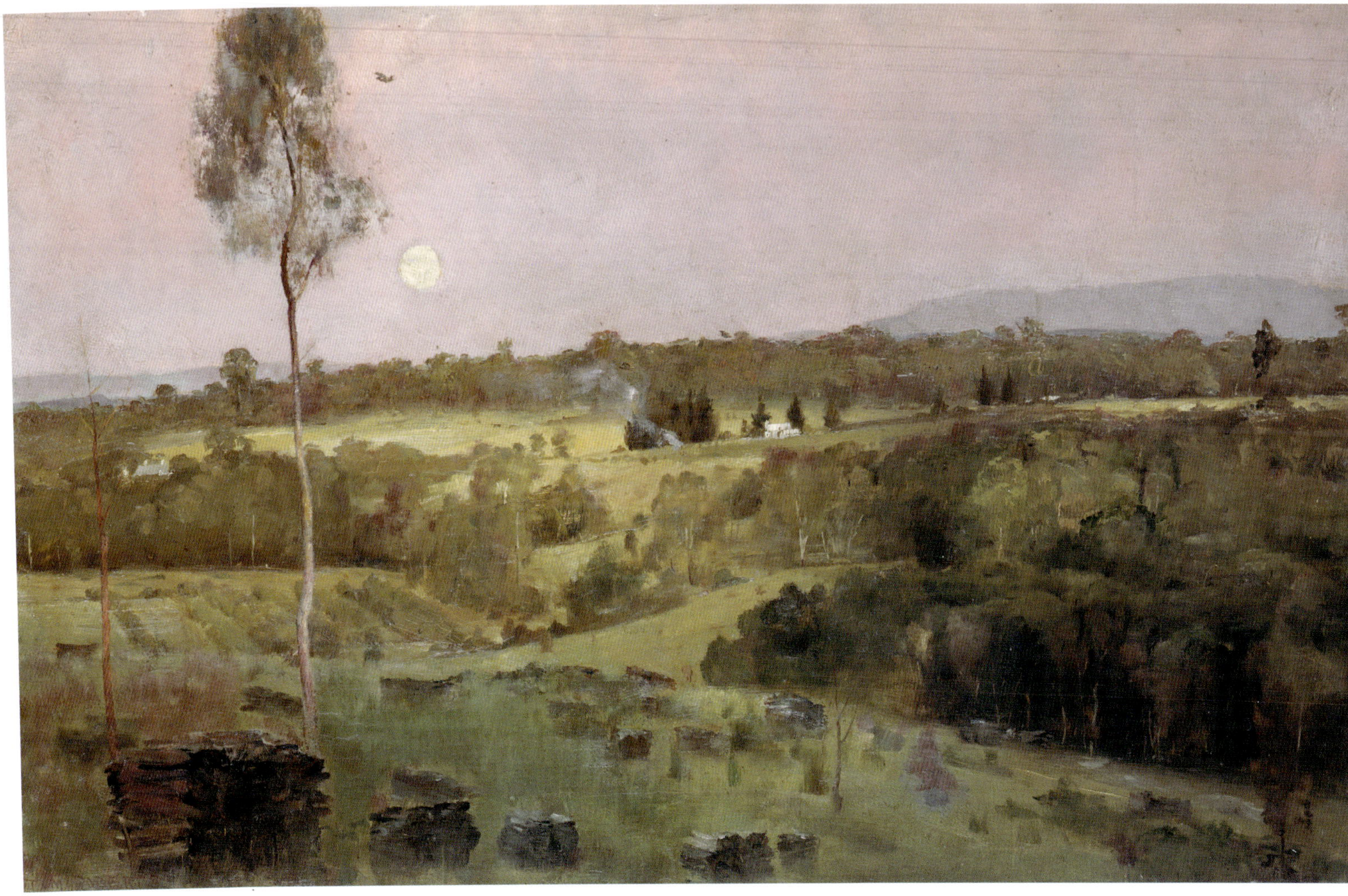

spectator's eye to enter the landscape. But the woman is not clearly located in the bush: she is dwarfed by the young gum-tree, as if she were some distance behind it, but the grasses indicate that she is quite close to it; the detail of her dress suggests she is close, the blurring of her face the opposite; while her sharp silhouette seems almost to be stuck on to the surface – as is emphasised by the little shadow beneath her skirt.[14]

When *A summer morning tiff* was shown with *The artists' camp* in the Australian Artists' Association exhibition of 1886, Smith claimed that it "shows the influence of the Impressionists" – indicating that he, at least, found high-keyed painting foreign. There is, in fact, no one form of 'Australian light', and the belief that brilliant golden light was 'characteristically Australian' was as much symbolic as real.

The witty little *The artists' camp* is a more conventional plein-airist work, but is also a fascinating example of a painter painting himself into a relationship with nature. The camp was at Houston's Paddock at Box Hill, "above the bark hut of the owners" (a reminder that pioneering bush architecture survived even close to Melbourne).[15] Roberts uses the young gums to articulate the screen of grey green foliage, and his closely related tones and smudgy colours evoke the clammy chill of a Melbourne wintry morning. The humdrum camping breakfast transforms the bush into somewhere familiar, and the painting as a whole suggests that the male comradeship in painting the bush creates a different relationship between figures and nature than that found in *A summer morning tiff*.

Roberts's "*Evening, when the quiet east flushes faintly at the sun's last look*" depicts an almost imperceptible roseate light that melds the ochres and olive greens of a summer twilight. Here the characteristic slender young gum-tree articulates the soft rolling hills, the mauve tinted sky and distant mountains. The brushstroke invites one to imagine that one is there – at the moment when the painter found the right colour for the tiny change of tone which one can discover to be smoke, a roof, a patch of cleared ground between trees. The style itself is witness to the artist's presence in the landscape and to the processes by which he came to see it. Roberts and his friends felt that this 'afterlight' was particularly characteristic of Australia, and compared it with more brilliant colours of sunset in the western sky.[16] Yet, as was characteristic of Roberts's fluctuating pictorial allegiances, the wistful associations of twilight are responsive not only to Australia but also to the nostalgic, dreamy emotions of English Aestheticism, in particular to Whistler's formal harmonies. Even here, there is a rawness in the landscape – seen most notably in the lumpy piles of sawn wood – which disrupts harmony and re-asserts the specificity of place.

While he was painting such works, Roberts was also painting the more active processes of Empire: the paintings of "strong masculine labour". They are preceded by the *Charcoal burners*, representing a small-scale pre-capitalist industry which was quite often depicted in nineteenth-century European art. There it is depicted in terms of centuries-old forest activities, frequently with a sense of nostalgia for the disappearance of forest-workers, who were seen as embodying the primeval relationship between man and forest that

The artists' camp, 1886, Melbourne, oil on canvas, 45.7 x 60.8 cm; National Gallery of Victoria, Melbourne, Felton Bequest Fund 1943

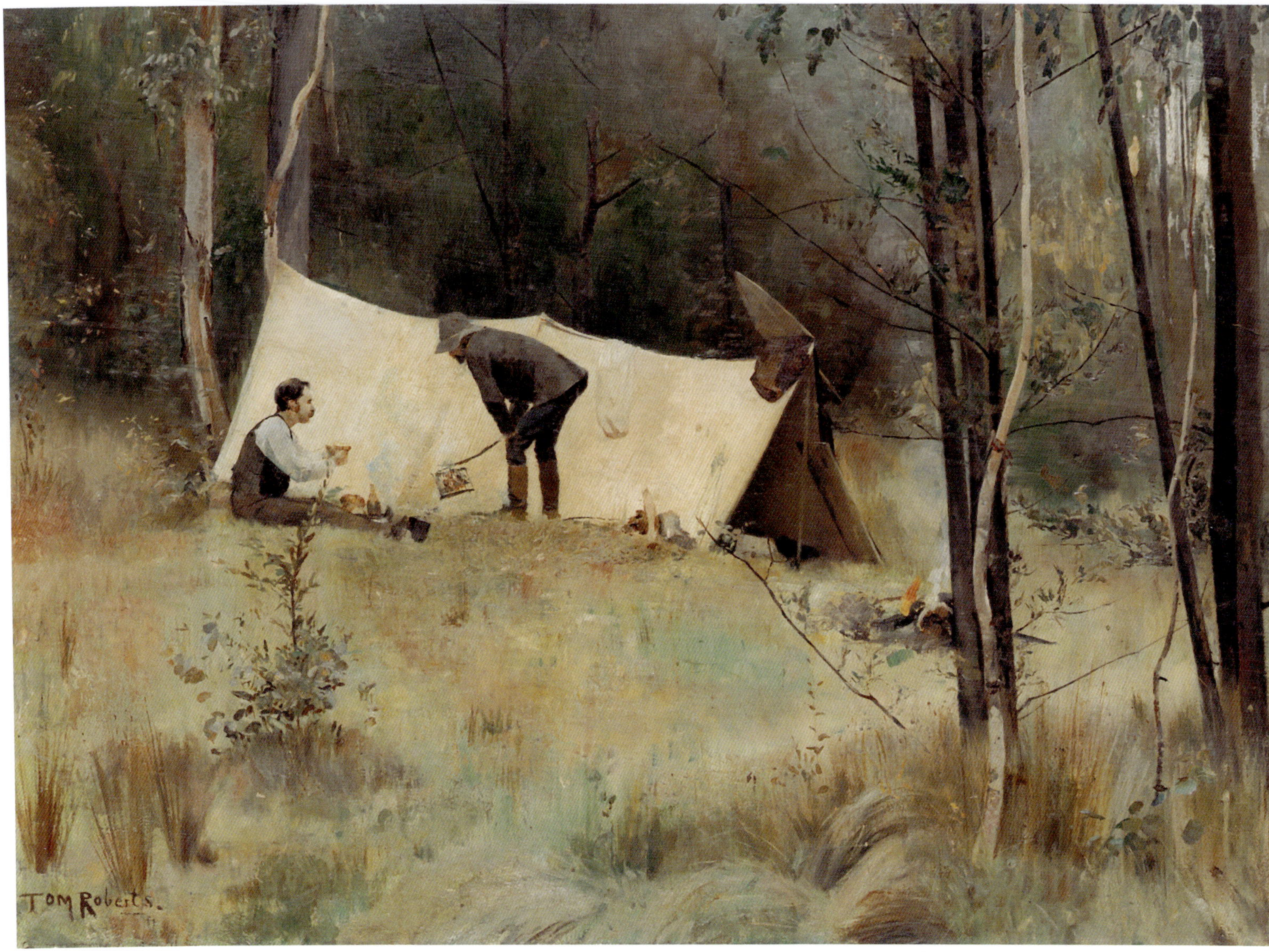
TOM Roberts.

was threatened by modernity. Rather different emotions arise in the bush scene where the casually cut tree-stumps and the methodically piled logs suggest matter-of-fact utilisation of woodland, untouched by the almost superstitious awe and sense of violence expressed in European plein-airist depictions of the cutting of trees. Nevertheless the unemphatic repetition of the theme of the cutting of wood and actual or implied clearing of land in works by Roberts and his friends (see *Evening*, some of the 9 by 5s, Streeton's *The selector's hut* and Conder's *Under a Southern Sun*) suggest that the subject had local significance. In a drawing after the lost *End to a career – an old scrub-cutter*, the stiffened body of the old man has the pathos of English representations of the rural worker as victim but it also shows the results of an active clearing of the bush. The man's body seems about to collapse, but the absence of any signs of culture suggests that it will stay where it falls, absorbed into the land that it had cleared.

Roberts's paintings of the pastoral industry embody a more active, powerful relationship between man and nature. He began *Shearing the rams* in the summer of 1888-89. The celebration of the colony's centenary quickened Australians' sense of their distinctiveness, but it also emphasised what the imperial mission had accomplished in the hundred years since the first inglorious settlement at Sydney Cove. The occasion may have inspired Roberts to paint *An autumn morning, Milson's Point, Sydney* when he visited that city in early 1888. Roberts chose to depict the birthplace of the British colony, looking across the Harbour, past the ferries at Milson's Point, the heights of Observatory Hill and Miller's Point into Circular Quay with the Customs House in the distance. For once, Roberts did not paint golden light and blue skies but an unpleasant pinky-brown atmosphere, which a Melbourne reviewer of the Victorian Artists' Society exhibition attributed to pollution: "the somewhat murky background, reminding the spectator that this is a city consuming fossil coal and not charcoal".[17] Behind the ferry's dirty plume of smoke one can see, berthed around Circular Quay where the First Fleet had moored, the ships which linked the colony to the outer world, powered by both steam and sail. The smoke from steam-driven transport was one of the favoured signs of modernity – as Roberts would have seen in the great paintings by Turner in the National Gallery, London, and may have seen in French Impressionism. However, the Realist or the Impressionist moment denies the past, so Roberts could not, even at this site, have conveyed a grandiose historical vision in the ways that Turner did. Thus despite the transformation of the forested bay into one of the chain of modern cities engendered by the great industrial Empire, Roberts conveys not the historical process, but the newness, rawness and incompletion of the city, enacting these qualities in the paint-structure itself.

An autumn morning, Milson's Point, *Evening* and *End to a career – an old scrub-cutter* were shown together in Roberts's studio. His 'Studio Wednesdays' in Melbourne were modelled on 'Studio Sundays' which in London preceded the Royal Academy exhibitions, allowing connoisseurs to view paintings in artists' studios before they were exhibited in public. In addition to such efforts to foster audiences for art, Roberts consistently sought to professionalise local art practice; he played a prominent role in

An autumn morning, Milson's Point, Sydney, 1888, Sydney, oil on canvas, 45.7 x 76.2 cm; The Art Gallery of New South Wales, Sydney, Purchased 1983

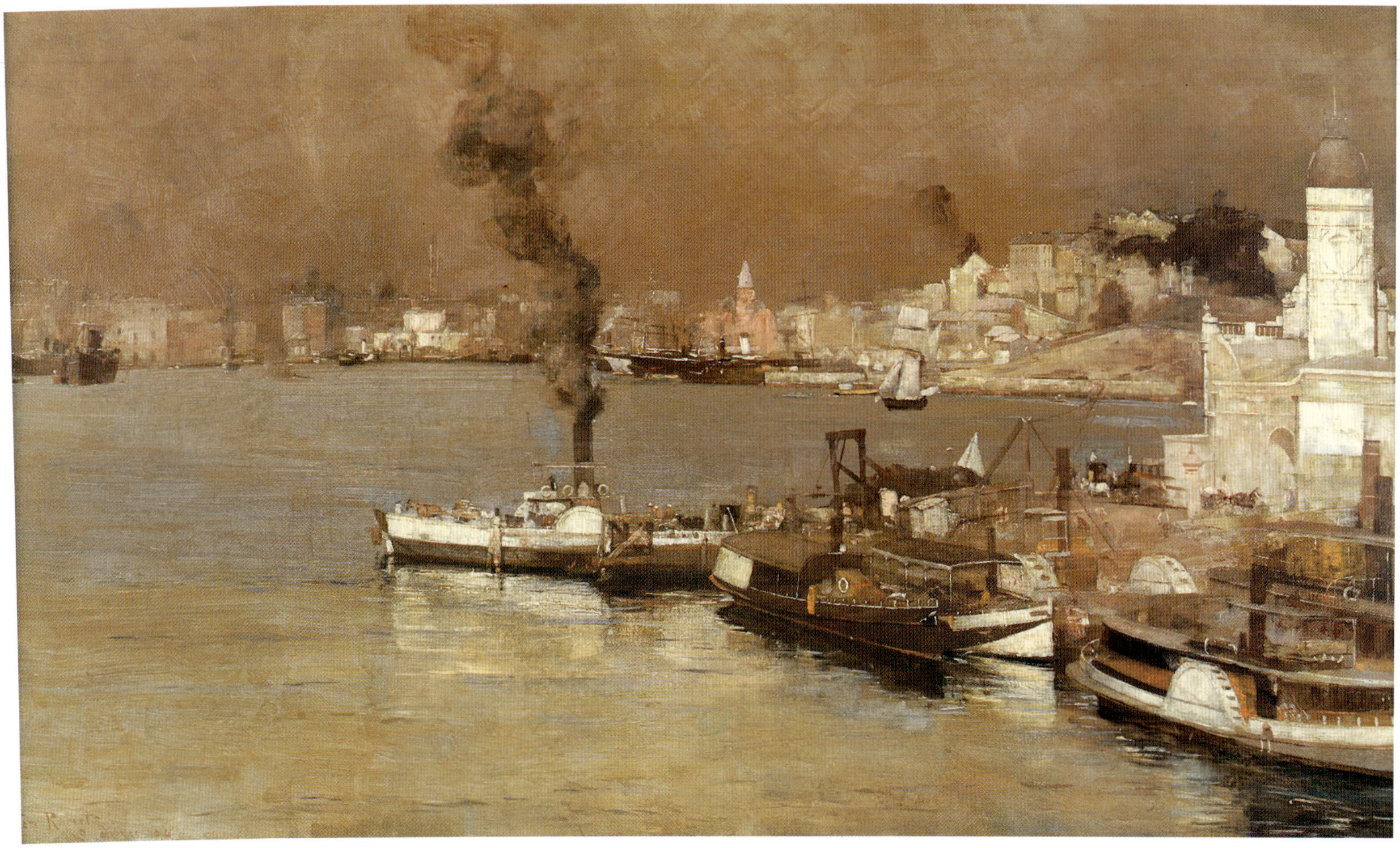

the organisation of the local art societies; intervened in debates on art in the press, repeatedly asserting the artistic value of the Australian scene and berating the public galleries for their neglect of contemporary Australian art.[18] Such activity suggests that Roberts took the British civilising mission very seriously. Melbourne was to be a microcosm of Empire, containing in miniature the cultural institutions of the centre – with the promise of a grand future.

It is therefore fitting that a number of Roberts's Melbourne portraits represent influential members of Melbourne's society, whose complex lives embodied the history and the future of the colony: besides artists and musicians, they include the commissioned life-size portrait of Alderman Samuel Amess who was not only ex-Mayor of Melbourne but also builder of some of its most important buildings, most notably the Treasury; the Professor of Moral Philosophy at Melbourne University, Henry Laurie; Henry Walker, Mayor of Collingwood, manufacturer, a founding director of the Victorian Tramway Company, and instrumental in the building of the Victoria Street Bridge; the Hon. L.L. Smith, a controversial doctor specialising in venereal diseases, who came to Australia in 1852 after medical studies in London and Paris, went gold-digging, wrote medical almanacs and became a politician. The point of these portraits was not that they looked distinctive, but that they looked like every other influential, black-suited man in the Empire. Roberts also painted the wives and daughters of prominent men, as in *Blue Eyes and Brown* which probably depicted a member of Professor Laurie's family. It is a striking example of Roberts's eclecticism: the girl's long hair and flowing dress – in the reformed clothing style promoted by the Aesthetic movement – create an elegant silhouette against the Japanese screen. But these Aestheticist qualities co-exist uneasily with the girl's serious face and thin, childish arms – and with the soulful eyes of her dog which introduce a touch of Victorian sentiment.

This painting was awarded a Second Order of Merit at the Centennial International Exhibition held in Melbourne in 1888, as was the portrait of C.S. Paterson and Paterson's loan of *Reconciliation*. In an exhibition celebrating a hundred years of British colonisation in this distinctive land, it is significant that no landscapes by Roberts were shown. His only works depicting figures in Australian nature were *End to a career – an old scrub-cutter* and *A summer morning tiff*: the pathos of the former and the sentimental anecdote of the latter would have been at home in a Royal Academy exhibition, and could have suggested that, while the environment might change, moral perspectives and emotional situations could be translated directly from the Old World to the New.

Yet 1888 seems also to have given British Australians the confidence to believe that they had something distinctive to say to the centre of Empire. In mid 1889 a group of artists, including Roberts, "tired of the slow progress of Australian art", decided to send works "with a decided leaning towards nationality" to Britain – and to the Paris Salon. The work which most closely fits the bill is Roberts's *Shearing the rams.* [19]

Shearing the rams and *A break away!* are subjects for which there are few (if any) European or British precedents. English and French painters tended to represent individual peasant labour, not the pastoral industry: flocks are guarded by a single shepherd or shepherdess;

Mending the sail, 1886-87, Melbourne, oil on canvas, 35.4 x 46.0 cm; National Gallery of Australia, Canberra, Gift of W. Booth 1947

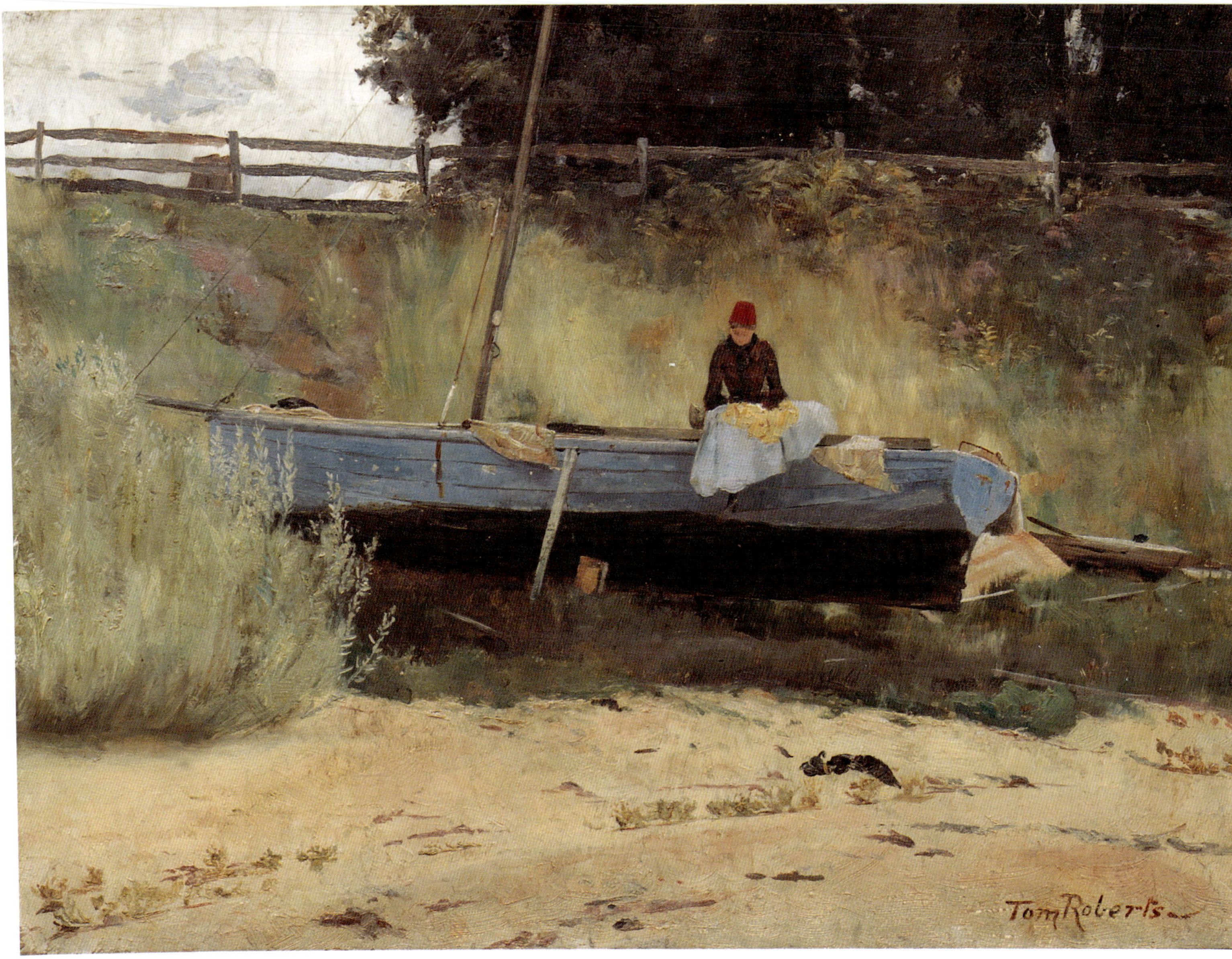
Tom Roberts

a woman shears a solitary sheep. Roberts said that in *Shearing the rams* he wanted to express "strong masculine labour", and this marks it off from most French and British Realist paintings which generally represented only women's labour on the land (Clausen's paintings of haymaking are an exception). McCubbin's and Jane Sutherland's depictions of women working on the small farms near Melbourne are closer in gender to their British and European counterparts. Roberts never even hinted at women's role in rural labour.

Shearing the rams has acquired iconic status in Australia, but has different meanings if considered in the imperial context. The image of Australia which Roberts hoped to display in Britain was of strong, healthy, harmonious labour. Since he did not depict an overseer, he represents men powerfully in control of their own work. There is not a hint of the precarious living, the exhausting work and the bitter antagonism between owners and men which, at this very time, culminated in the great shearers' strike of 1890.[20] Rather than a painting of the realities of pastoral life, this is an allegory of the masculine control over nature, in which an 'unproductive' land is turned into a productive one. The precise detail of the wooden shed shows columns of felled trees and even the glimpse of a golden landscape at the end of the shed suggests cleared land and 'the sunny south'.

The pastoral industry was frequently depicted in contemporary illustrated journals and compendia like the Picturesque Atlas of Australasia which had wide imperial diffusion.[21] But paintings in oil gave such activity a different status, that of high art, one which could ennoble that which an editorialist implied was "altogether unworthy of depiction".[22] By creating a rhythmic composition in deep space through his use of echoing and contrasting poses, Roberts gave the scene a completeness that elevated it beyond the trivial moment. He followed updated academic modes of pictorial construction, studying his subject on the spot for 'truth', composing and painting it in his Melbourne studio so that he could universalise it and make it fit for viewing at the centre of the world. Thus the "strong masculine labour" was not a matter of local conditions – of a country in economic depression, with antagonism between capital and organised labour – but of the effort that had built and was building the Empire. The primary produce of Australia enriched Britain as much as the colony, and provided Britain with markets for its goods.

Work in the bush for *Shearing the rams* was probably halted by winter. The city called for a while, with 'The 9 by 5 Impression Exhibition'. Roberts's Melbourne studio was in Grosvenor Chambers at the top of Collins Street, an imposing address containing studios especially built for artists. The artists who could afford them had to be relatively well-off – and in the colony with its limited opportunities for exhibition and sale, that meant private means, teaching or portrait-painting. Profitable portrait-painting required an artist with bourgeois manners, clothes and an elegant studio. In this context, it is fair to say that the 9 by 5 exhibition, held in Buxton's Rooms in nearby Swanston Street, was a fashionable social event rather than a revolutionary artistic one: the rooms were decorated with draperies and Japanese fans; tea was served and "Miss Fanny Bristow sang ...".[23]

Country road makers, 1923, Kallista, Victoria, oil on canvas, 72.5 x 50.3 cm; Private collection, Sydney

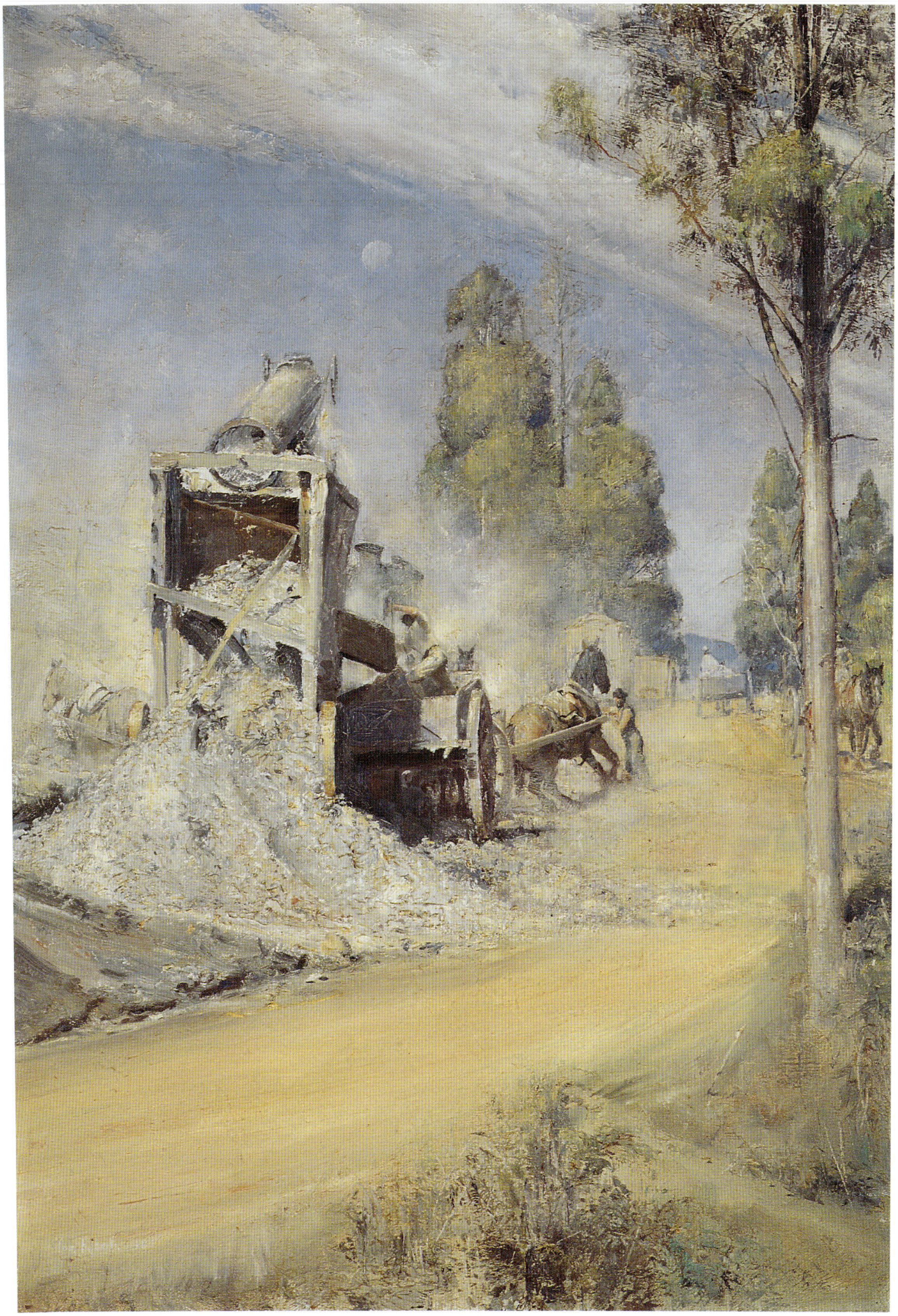

These social, feminised urban activities were the counterpart of Roberts's increasingly long stays in the bush in order to paint the epic masculine struggle against nature: he continued work on *Shearing the rams* at Corowa in the summer of 1888-89, returning there in 1891 to do studies for *A break away!*. Roberts said in 1899 that this was the work in which he had "most nearly realized his idea".[24] This "idea" has to do with the heroism of masculine labour as it struggles to control the instinctual forces of nature. This can be seen not only in the horseman's attempt to stem the great rush of the sheep but also in the ways the scene has been shaped by the new occupiers of the land: these are imported animals in a cleared landscape – as is shown by the emphatic tree-stumps and the logs used to fence in the stock route.

A journalist wrote in 1891: "This is no portrayal of any place or event. It is a 'composition' and this is its keynote: 'Time was and indeed is not yet very remote ...'".[25] This, then, is a painting of history. Yet Roberts's expression of a moment in time defined by the intersection of the dynamic movement of the horse-and-rider and of the sheep suggests that the painter was present at the scene to capture that moment. It is as if he were saying: "I was there" or, rather, "I am here". In fact, his presence was a fiction, for he would have had to be suspended far above the scene. In short, the conflict between the demands of Realism and the demands of imperial history-making is embodied in the painting itself, and is the source of much of its ambiguous fascination.

Something similar can be seen in Roberts's most straightforward painting of history: *Bailed up*. Roberts painted its landscape setting on site, after composing the essentials of the scene in a small oil-sketch. He continued painting in the great corrugated-iron hall at Inverell. Roberts thus used the processes of academic figure-painting, as well as plein-airist insistence on painting on the spot, to realise a large, highly formalised composition. The work is, however, strangely ambiguous: it depicts a bushranging incident that had occurred in 1860s, but, for all the abstraction of the composition, the painting reminds me of the coloured illustrations in the 'boys' own' books of masculine imperial adventure across the Empire. The formal structures of academic figure-painting derived from traditional history-painting in which time-before and time-after is indicated in the climactic frozen moment of the composition, thus indicating the human consequences of what was depicted. Roberts's Realist convictions meant, however, that he had to paint even a dramatic event without shaping it into dramatic form. The incident is thus deprived of any other meaning than the fact that it had once happened.

Yet this form of time has its own meaning. The transformative force of Empire had to be recorded as if it were a series of stills, each of which says "this is how it was". Realist painting and the mass imagery of illustrated journals depicted historic events in the form of time suggested by photography in which each moment is detached from the continuity of time. Such imagery was appropriate for the British and European Empires which had simultaneously to display their history and to indicate that their conquest of the world was *natural*.

* * *

Alexander Augustus Anderson (snr), 1889, Brocklesby Station, Corowa, NSW, oil on canvas, 24.1 x 19.0 cm; Castlemaine Art Gallery and Historical Museum, Purchased with the assistance of the Caltex Victoria Art Fund and Public Appeal 1979

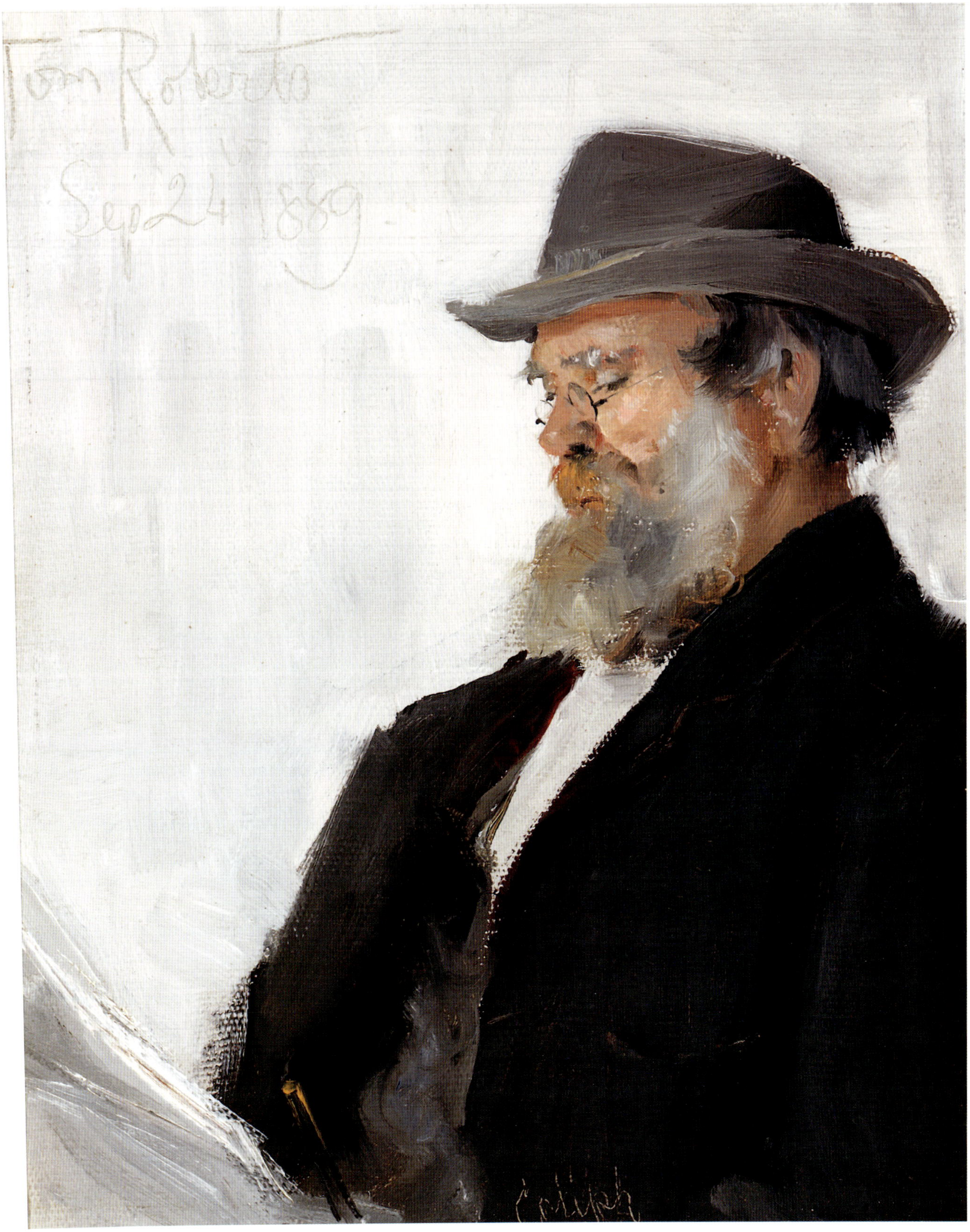
Tom Roberts
Sep 24 1889

Bailed up is the most obvious example of the fact that, after Roberts moved to Sydney in late 1891, his work became markedly more historical, not simply in the sense of looking backward, but of looking forward, envisaging his art as part of a historical process leading towards Federation, the foundation of Australia as a nation. The Depression of the early 1890s revealed class antagonisms that could not be ignored and may be another reason why Roberts tended to turn away from the representation of contemporary urban life. This tendency was, however, also one aspect of British and European Fin-de-siècle. Roberts painted relatively few landscapes – and few continued to express the delighted sense of discovery seen in those of the 1880s (except for the seductive *Mosman's Bay*, expressing the hedonistic delights of a Sydney summer day). For economic reasons, portraiture was his dominant genre, while his paintings of bush life became either more straightforwardly historical or more grandly generalised, as in *The Golden Fleece.*

For all the accuracy of detail in *The Golden Fleece* – from the actual construction of the wooden shearing-shed down to the makeshift moccasins which the men made from the hessian wool-bales – the figures suggest an almost dreamy self-absorption that suggests something more than literal truth. This 'something more' can, I believe, be found in the almost ritual moment when the dirty wool is parted to reveal its creamy golden whiteness. The whiteness is emphasised by the warm shadows within the shed. I have recently been told that no shearers would work with the hessian blinds up,[26] but the shadowy filtered light of the interior suggests that Roberts studied the shearing with the blinds down. He clearly also wanted to juxtapose the work of the interior with images of the golden landscape clouded by the silvery dust raised by the sheep. Roberts here depicts the owner, Duncan Anderson, overlooking the solemn rites of shearing. Was this a tribute to his friend, or a re-assertion of pastoral authority four years after the end of the great shearers' strike? Whatever the case, the painting has shifted from the power of the team of individual men to the creation of the Golden Fleece itself.

Even Roberts's portraiture reveals his growing belief in the historical mission of his art. *Church, State and the Law* is one example of portraiture which was both Realist and historical. So too were his small informal portraits of "familiar faces and figures" painted sketchily on wooden panels. These included actors, musicians, journalists, politicians, military men. He exhibited twenty-three of them in 1900, and expressed the hope that they might be purchased as a group because of their historic interest ("if one considers how interesting such a group would be to us now, of similar types of, say, fifty years ago ...").[27]

Paradoxically Roberts's growing historicism could have been influenced by the increasingly long periods he spent in the bush or on the coast, as if he were doing a personal exploration of eastern Australia following the first British explorers or settlers. In 1892 he went on a three months' voyage up the Queensland Coast to the Torres Straits Islands, where no-one can forget the epic trip of Cook through the Barrier Reef and into the Torres Straits to Possession Island. Roberts commented in an article on the trip that the differences between the Islanders and the mainland Aboriginals could

A Queen of gums, 1926, near Ben Lomond, Tasmania, oil on canvas, 45.0 x 35.5 cm; Private collection, Melbourne

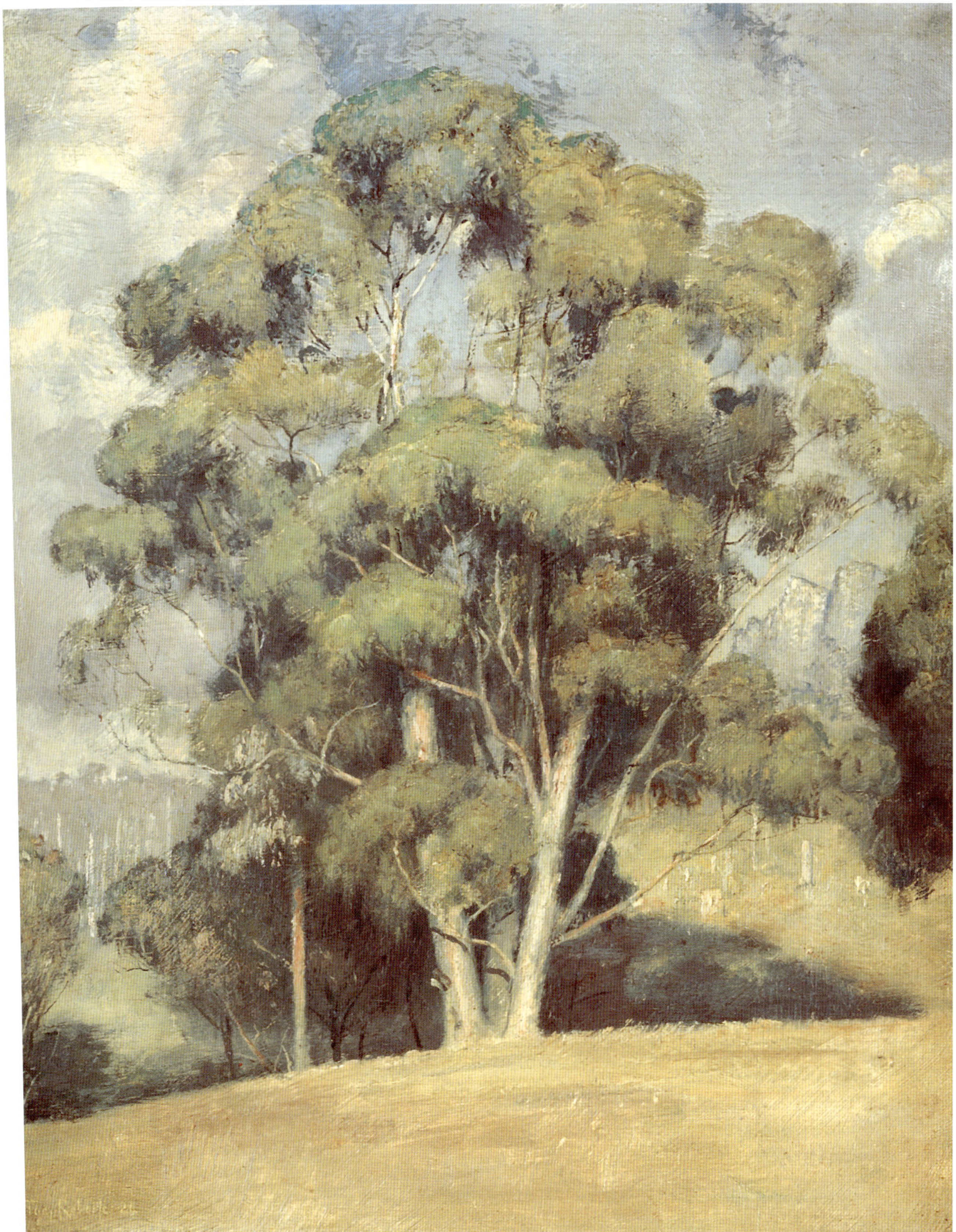

help "ethnologists try to solve the problem of the peopling of the continent".[28] In 1894-95, Roberts spent about eight months in northern New South Wales, including his visit to the Clarence River "to paint Aborigines", and these too were probably meant to find their meaning in the imperial story.[29] One of these was the portrait of Maria Yulgilbar. Another was inscribed "Billie Millera was a grown man in 46 when Ed. Ogilvie of Yulgilbar was the first white to see him". The portrait of Edward Ogilvie with its intense red background is perhaps Roberts's most vivid depiction of a man. Given Roberts's interest in forceful men who both made their own histories and contributed to the history of Australia, he was probably excited by the eighty-one-year-old pioneer who had arrived in Sydney from Scotland in 1825.[30] In the 1840s Ogilvie had been the first white man to explore the Clarence River where his property Yulgilbar was located. He learnt elements of the local language – by kidnapping an Aboriginal boy – and made a treaty with the Aborigines giving them full hunting rights over land which he wanted only for grazing. Comparatively enlightened though he may have been, the comparison between his portrait with his commanding pose and piercing gaze, and the evasive gaze and naked shoulders of the Aboriginal woman clearly reveals where the power lay. From Yulgilbar, Roberts rode 270 kilometres to stay with his friend Duncan Anderson at Newstead, before going to stay at another local property to paint *Bailed up*, his most overtly historical painting.

* * *

Despite the inevitability of Federation, Roberts had, by 1899, decided to leave Australia. He was disillusioned by lack of recognition and probably wanted the challenge of London again. His return was delayed by the commission to paint the opening, by the Duke of York on 9 May 1901, of the first Federal Parliament. The painting was the summation of Roberts's desire to create a modern history-painting, but 'The Big Picture', as Roberts called it, has generally been interpreted as a failure. Roberts ultimately found it burdensome to paint – but he was also exhilarated by the challenge, and his notes on his sitters express his excitement in discovering the varied histories which had brought them to this one moment. Certainly the task was difficult, for not only did Roberts have to represent a solemn moment, the foundation moment of the new nation, but his commission also required "correct representations" of the Duke and Duchess of York, of the first Governor-General, the governors of the States, members of the new House of Representatives and the Senate, representatives of foreign powers and other distinguished guests, "to the number of not less than 250". To paint so many detailed Realistic portraits in one composition was a challenge – and the "universal black" of the parliamentarians' suits certainly did not help. Roberts tried to animate them by massing them against the white dresses of some of the ladies and of the huge choir, and by irradiating the space with great shafts of light that pour across the Exhibition Building to the isolated figure of the Duke reading the Royal proclamation. A straight line runs from the flight of steps, across the Duchess, the Governor-General and the crowd of foreign representatives to the Imperial crown. In the shadows on the wall is a gigantic portrait of Sir Henry Parkes, the 'Father of Federation', who had died in 1896, not

Edward Ogilvie, 1895, Yulgilbar, NSW, oil on canvas, 73.5 x 58.5 cm; Mitchell Library, State Library of New South Wales, Sydney, Presented by Mrs G. Carson to the Mitchell Library 1972

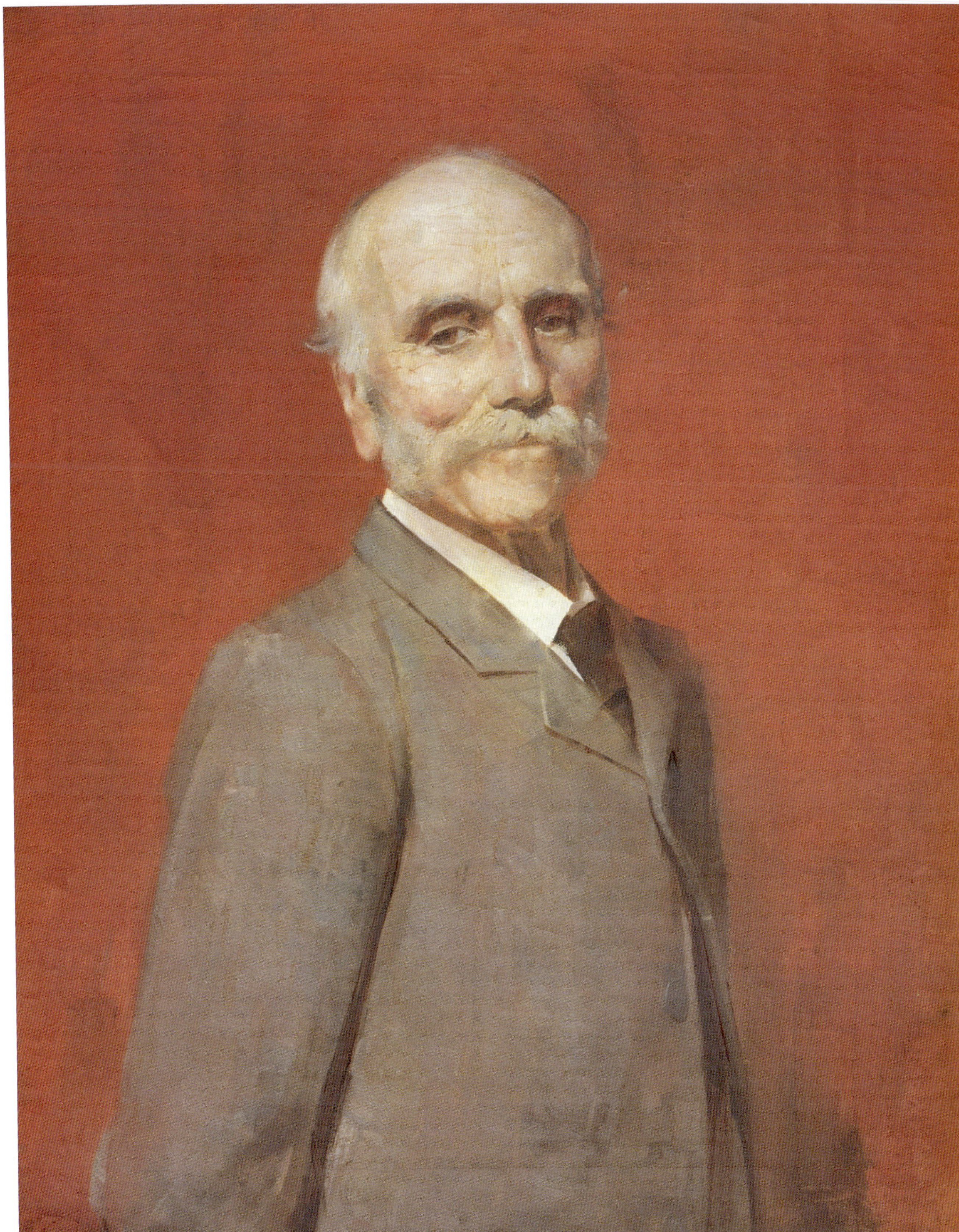

living to see the new dawn. His portrait creates a triangle which disrupts the direct linkage between the Crown and the Duke, and unsettles the massive effect of continuity. Victoria, the royal matriarch who had reigned through most of Australia's history, had died in January 1901, so the Duke was speaking in the name of his father the new King Edward. Unsurprisingly, the painting is overwhelmingly male: the women on the dais and in the small group in front of the choir are there as wives, dominated by the sullen phalanxes of black suits. The sea of white dresses beyond the places of power are there not as makers of the nation, but as decorative adjuncts to it. Roberts said that when he painted his study of the scene he saw it as a landscape and one could speculate that, in the finished work, Roberts was painting his familiar dualism: the "strong masculine labour" of the nation-creators and the undifferentiated 'feminine' Nature which they had shaped and would continue to shape.

It is in truth a painting of Empire. After it was exhibited at the Royal Academy in 1904 the Commonwealth presented it to Edward VII. In 1958, his great-grand-daughter Queen Elizabeth returned it to Australia on permanent loan.

One could argue that it was anachronistic for the new nation to be commemorated in oil-paint – and in ways which emphasised the frozen pomposities of the British-Australian establishment. But this would be to miss the point: oil paint was *the* inherited means of signifying power. Similarly, the inherited hierarchies and modes of self-presentation, and the symbolic return of the event to the centre of Empire, through exhibition in London and presentation to the King, all indicated that, although the colonial child had reached national adulthood, it remained in tutelage.

* * *

Roberts had to complete 'The Big Picture' in London since many of his sitters lived there. He, his wife and young son left Australia in 1903, not to return till after the First World War.

It has been customary to blame both 'The Big Picture' and Roberts's return to England for the 'failure' of his art of the second part of his painting life.[31] Certainly when he returned he went through a 'black period' that lasted for a several years, before he felt he could again find his way as an artist. He had been a leader in Melbourne and Sydney and, with his colleagues, he had created new styles and a new iconography for the new society. In England he was a nobody: "England does not really *want* anybody, she has everybody and everything ...".[32] One should, however, be wary about dismissing Roberts's later work, if only because the kind of art to which Roberts aspired in England in the first two decades of the twentieth century is now profoundly unfashionable. It was conservative in style, and we tend to measure it against his earlier works into which we project our own delighted recognition of landscapes we love. In England Roberts was not exploring a new landscape or a new way of seeing, but was seeking to express individual moments of personal vision within a century-old tradition. The silvery grey light in *The towpath, Putney* is more tentatively painted than his robust Thames scene

Sketch for the Opening of the First Parliament, 1901, Melbourne, oil on wood panel, 30.5 x 45.8 cm; National Library of Australia, Canberra, Purchased 1920

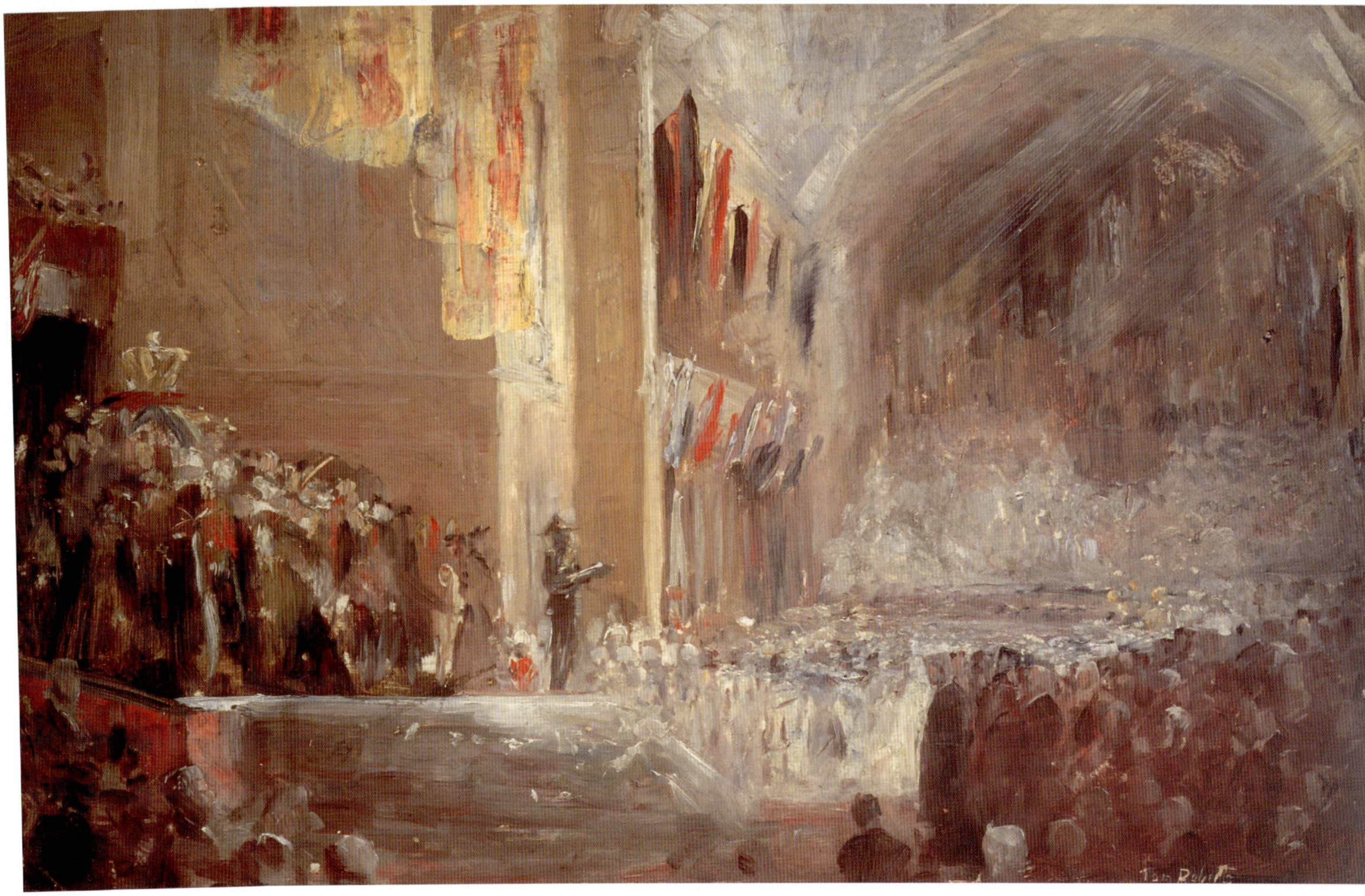

painted twenty years before, but it is sensitively observed, as is the beautiful cloud study, *Storm at sea*. His English portraits too have little appeal. The harmony of silvery greys and delicate illusionism of *Grey Lady (Mrs Ince)* give the figure the stylised elegance of fashionable Edwardian portraiture – but this is a portraiture which today seems dated.

It seems that in Australia, confronted with a new landscape and at a distance from the centre of art, Roberts had been able to use the abstraction of paint more adventurously than he could in England. This is not, however, how he saw it. In 1913 he visited the exhibition of Post-Impressionist paintings which were, he wrote "up against well worn outlooks" and "make you think":

> the painted grass of fields & painted trees & painted folds of drapery (done in the highest style of art) won't do – they look silly. Nothing but the broadest outlook & simplicity will stand against them & its right ... I suppose it's inevitable to feel one ought to have known in early years what one gets hold of now.[33]

In his "early years" in Australia he had in fact painted with "the broadest outlook & simplicity", but this was no longer the case. Nevertheless, despite its illusionism, *Grey Lady* is painted with a rather dry, pastey paint that encroaches on the illusion of "painted folds of drapery". This kind of paint was to form the basis of his style in his final Australian years.

The towpath, Putney, 1904, London, oil on board, 24.2 x 39.5 cm; ICI Collection of Australian Art, Melbourne

At the outbreak of war in 1914 Roberts accepted the obligations of Empire and of his double heritage and, at the age of 57, volunteered for the Royal Australian Military Corps, serving at the Third London Military Hospital.

Roberts visited Australia as soon as he could after the war. He wrote to his son that his return "had the sensation that as a child you thought it would be going to heaven", and he decided to return to Australia for good. *Springtime in Sussex*, painted in 1921 when he was winding up his life in England, represents the essence of his English style: its delicate, quivering moisture-filled light is embodied in thick dry paint. Roberts depicts the changeability of spring light – with the suggestion of new foliage thickening the still wintry trees and the vibration of light on the cottage and the meadows – in a manner that also suggests that this tranquil, fertile countryside is eternal. There is not a hint of the twentieth century and even the little children suggest the endless childhood of a dreamed, traditional England rather than future. The painting suggests perhaps the image of a timeless, changeless England that Roberts wanted to carry back to Australia.

* * *

Since the late 1930s the landscapes that Roberts painted after his final return to Australia have consistently been denigrated. In his own time however they were much admired, even if they were overshadowed by Streeton's grander nationalistic images. The admiration of Arthur Boyd and Fred Williams for Roberts's late landscapes should make one cautious about too easily dismissing them. The paintings are quiet and unshowy, and they suggest that, at the end of his life, Roberts's painting was a form of

Storm at sea, 1907, Mundesley-on-Sea, Norfolk, oil on canvas on plywood, 35.3 x 44.5 cm; The Art Gallery of New South Wales, Sydney, Purchased 1946

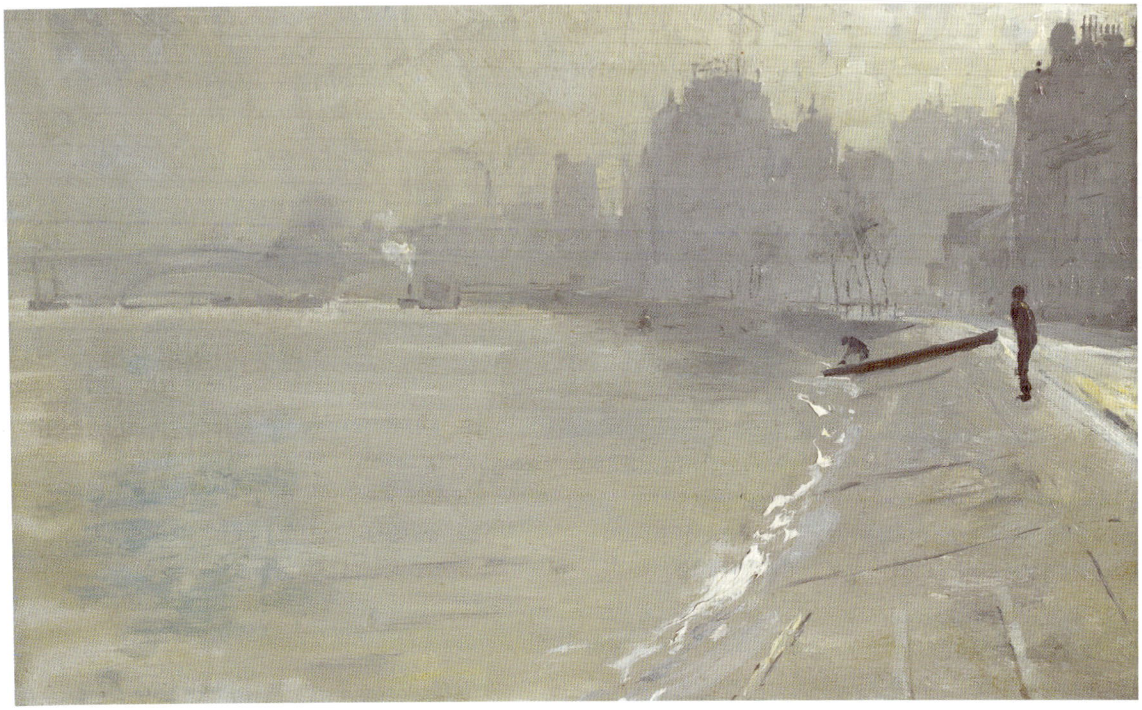

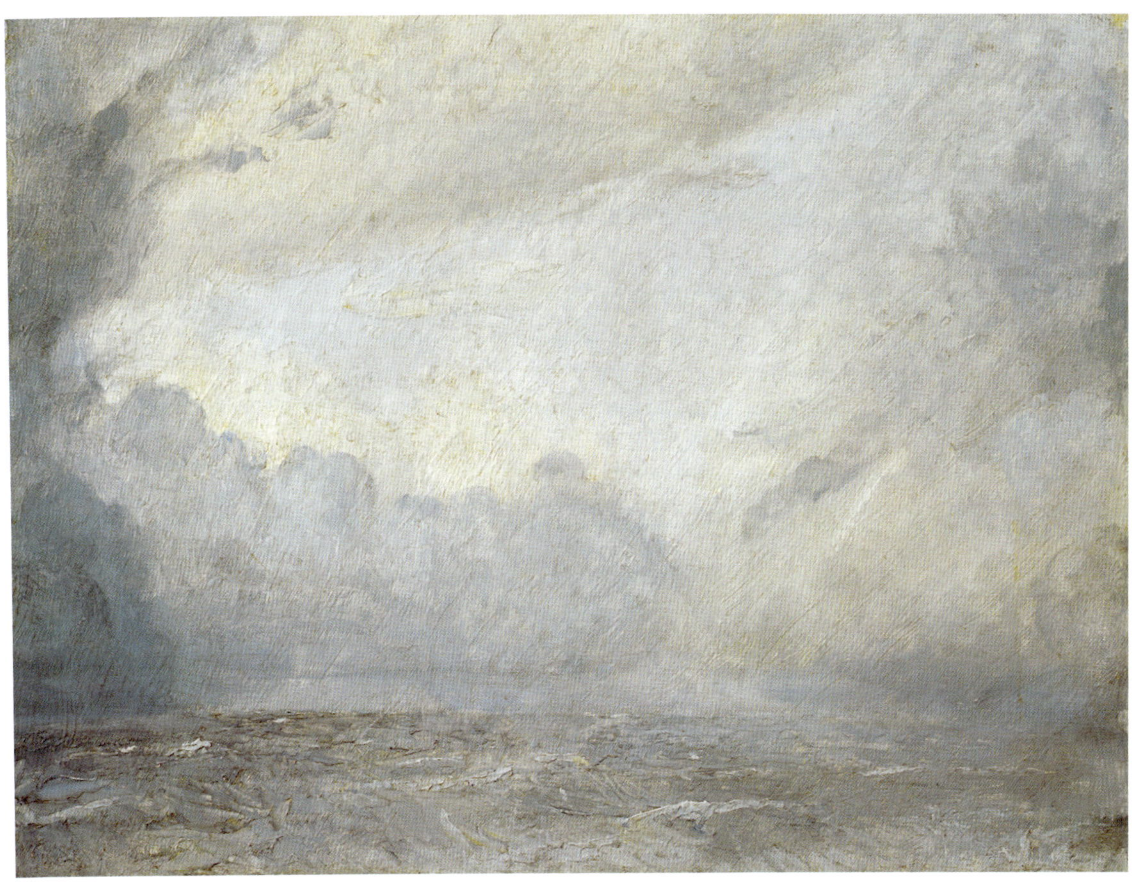

coming home, a home in which he could comfortably integrate a style which had learnt the infinitely subtle inflections of English light, but which somehow 'remembered' and absorbed his Australian past.

Unlike his earlier Australian landscapes, his late ones suggest continuity of time and completeness of the landscape. Even the *Country road makers* suggests continuity with the past rather than the raw newness of human intervention in the landscape seen in *A break away!*, while the horse and dray dwarfed by the majestic trees in *Sherbrooke Forest* do not disrupt a sense that this is a vast, centuries-old forest, unscarred by human industry, awe-inspiring but also familiar. And the familiarity, I suggest, is created as much by Roberts's paint as by our experience of such forests.

A Queen of gums rears up against the distant luminous hills, a single iconic form, filling the whole canvas.[34] The painting suggests that Roberts's fifteen years of painting English trees now led him to paint eucalypts that had denser foliage than the "slender young gums" he had painted on his first return to Australia. Yet the delicate silhouettes of branches recalls those gums – and reminds me of the twigs of eucalypts he always kept in his box of souvenirs. Here the tree suggests a heroic being, standing up against the painter, but separated from him by the expanse of bleached grass. The tree is strongly itself, a comforting presence, but also distant, indifferent, resistant to the human identity implied by the title. Similar reassuring but distancing characteristics are found in *Hillside*. Here too the trees have dense foliage; the hills are a characteristic Australian formation, but are more rounded and enclosing than those in the early paintings. The paint is also dense and rather dry and, in its abstractness, is able to register more complex effects than the rather thin, scratchy brushstroke that Roberts used in his sunbleached landscapes of the 1890s. The little house nestled among the round trees in the valley suggests continuity in that landscape, and suggests that, although farming might be hard in the stony hills, it was also secure.

* * *

As someone who, like Roberts, has spent a life moving between England and Australia, I wonder how his role in the legacy of the British Empire will survive the inevitable separation from its last constitutional links. I think of the hot light in the untidy straggle of *Allegro con brio, Bourke Street west* with its wide road rising to the top of the hill and, seemingly, dropping over it – into nothingness; I think of the lady in white so uncertainly located in space in *A summer morning tiff*; I think of the curiously unstated but constant reminders of the cutting of wood and the clearing of land – and of the men in *Charcoal burners* who seem to go through the movements of work as if in a dream; I think of the almost dreamlike character of the bushrangers in *Bailed up*; or the shearers in *The Golden Fleece*. In a sense, the paintings seem to suggest the tentativeness of "strong masculine labour" and, often, of the uncertainty of the relationship between figure and bush.

I am not saying that Roberts's paintings express alienation from the Australian landscape, or that they simply express a visitor's experience of the bush. Indeed, I feel that many works express a deep empathy with it. How can this be seen? All I can say is, "Look

Grey Lady (Mrs Ince), c1910-12, London, oil on canvas on paperboard, 76.1 x 63.3 cm; The Art Gallery of New South Wales, Sydney, Purchased 1946

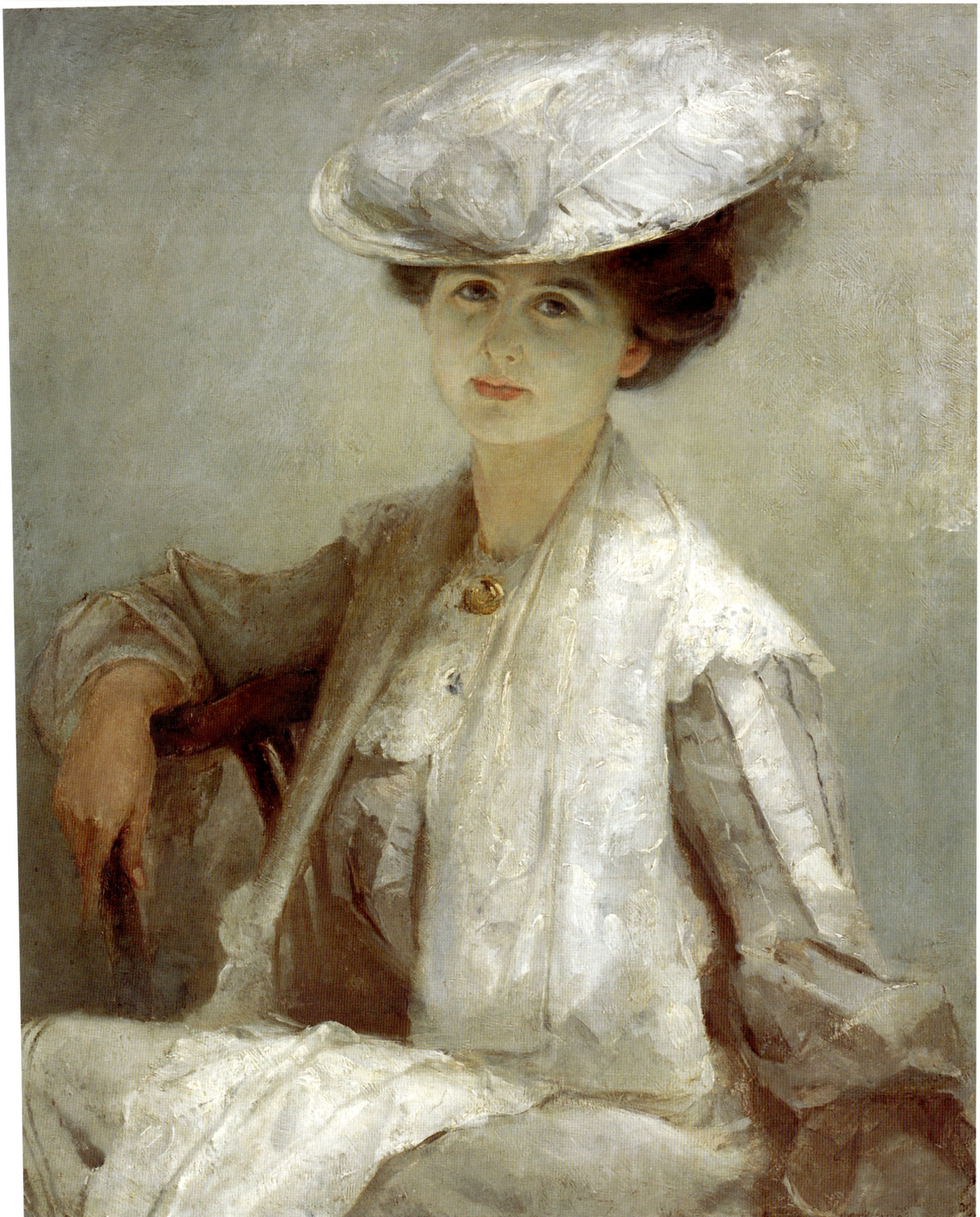

closely": look at the warm colours on the trunks of the banksias in *The Sunny South*; look at the violet tinged distant hills in *Evening*; look at the colours that suggest the heat on walls shadowed by corrugated iron in *Mosman's Bay*; look at the blue shadows on bleached grass on the hillside in *Bailed up*, look closely ...

But how can this looking be reconciled with styles that I have claimed are identifiable with the conquering eye of imperialism? Is it that I, as a beneficiary of the British creation of Australia, share the imperial vision? But now, at the end of another century? And what is my relationship to Roberts's creation of a landscape in terms of the "strong masculine labour" of the artist-creator who shapes nature, "the one mistress"? What is the relationship of those who have come more recently to this country to such paintings? What will be the life of such paintings in the century of 'globalisation' and 'virtual reality', when we are more and more divorced from a bodily relationship to our immediate environment?

Above all what is the relevance of such painting to those who first lived in the landscapes that Roberts painted? In the 1990s I do not think we can participate in Roberts's representations of figures in the bush without thinking of the invisible presences in his paintings, without recalling the fact that he recorded 'terra nullius', not an empty land, but a land emptied of those who lived by identifying with it. Perhaps the very truth of Roberts's vision – one that suggests separation from what it loves or seeks to love – will allow us, a hundred years later, to confront the pain that is inherent in our love for this conquered land which – as Roberts's painting shows – always eludes definition and slips away from us, even when it is most sensuously intense, most loved.

Hillside, 1927, Trawool, Victoria, oil on canvas, 45.7 x 53.0 cm; Art Gallery of South Australia, Adelaide, Elder Bequest Fund 1943

p. 94-95: *Opening of the First Parliament of the Commonwealth of Australia by H.R.H. The Duke of Cornwall and York (later H.M. King George V), May 9, 1901,* 1903, London, oil on canvas, 304.5 x 509.2 cm (unframed); Royal Collection on permanent loan to Parliament House, Canberra. Photography: Bruce Moore

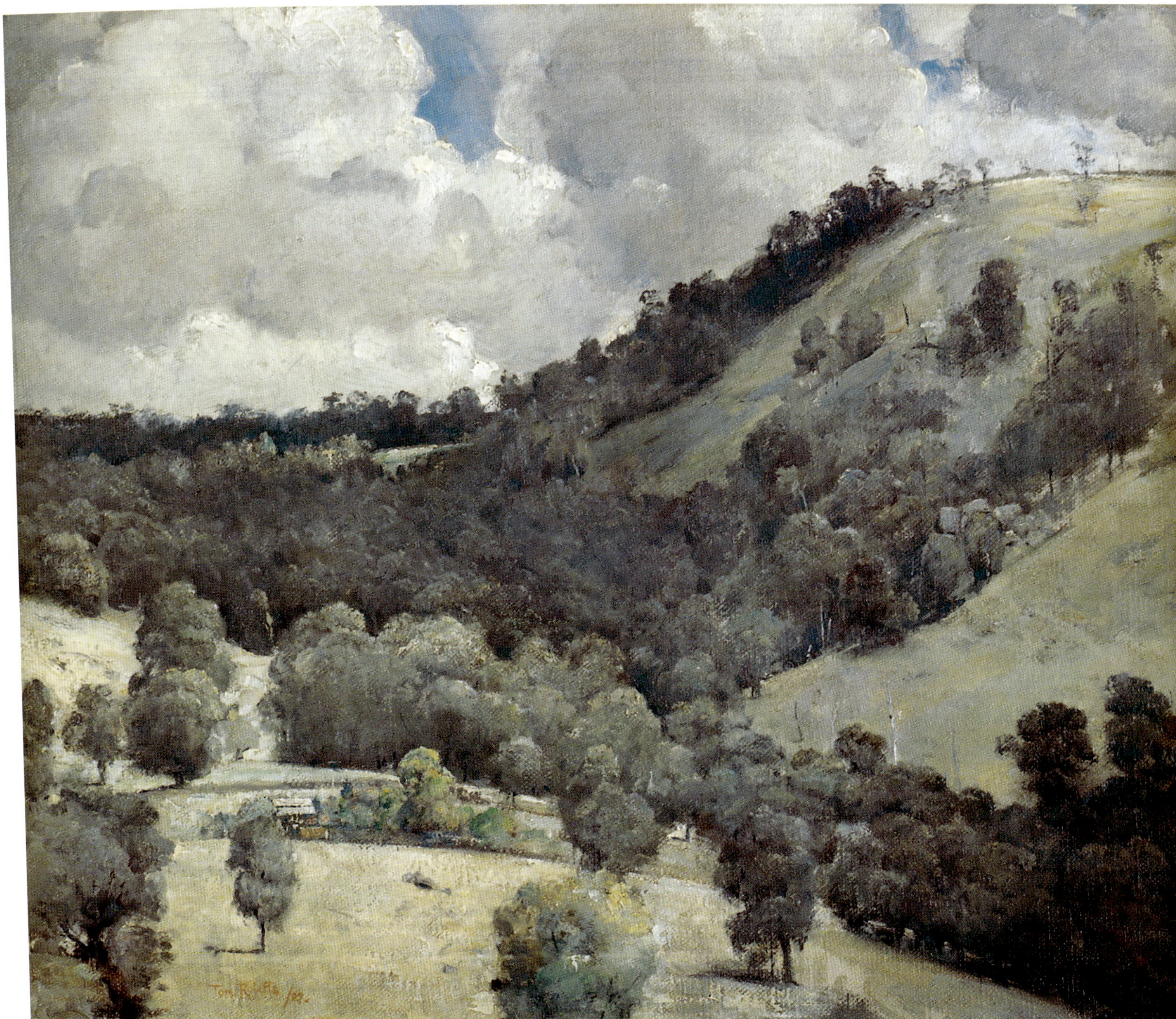

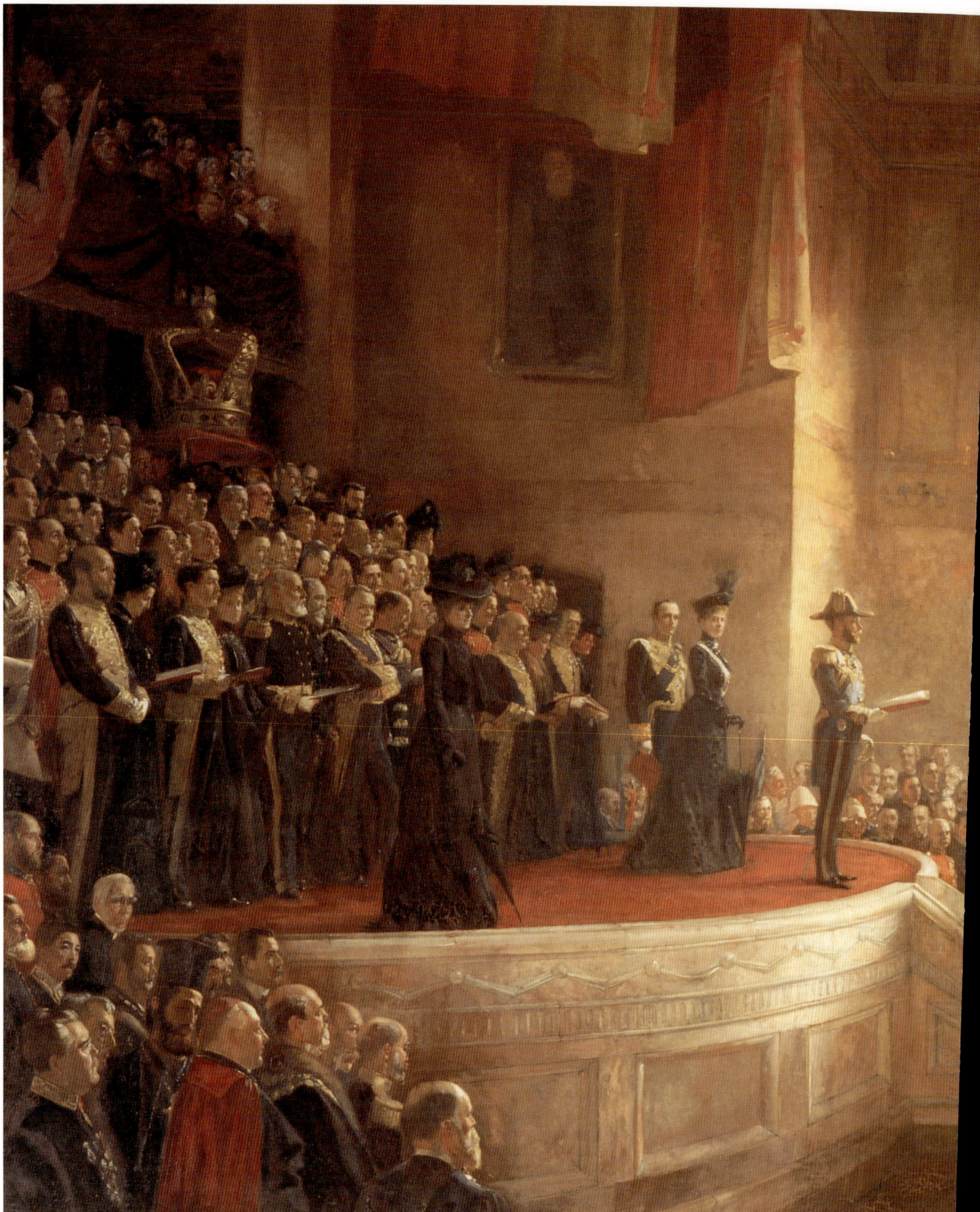

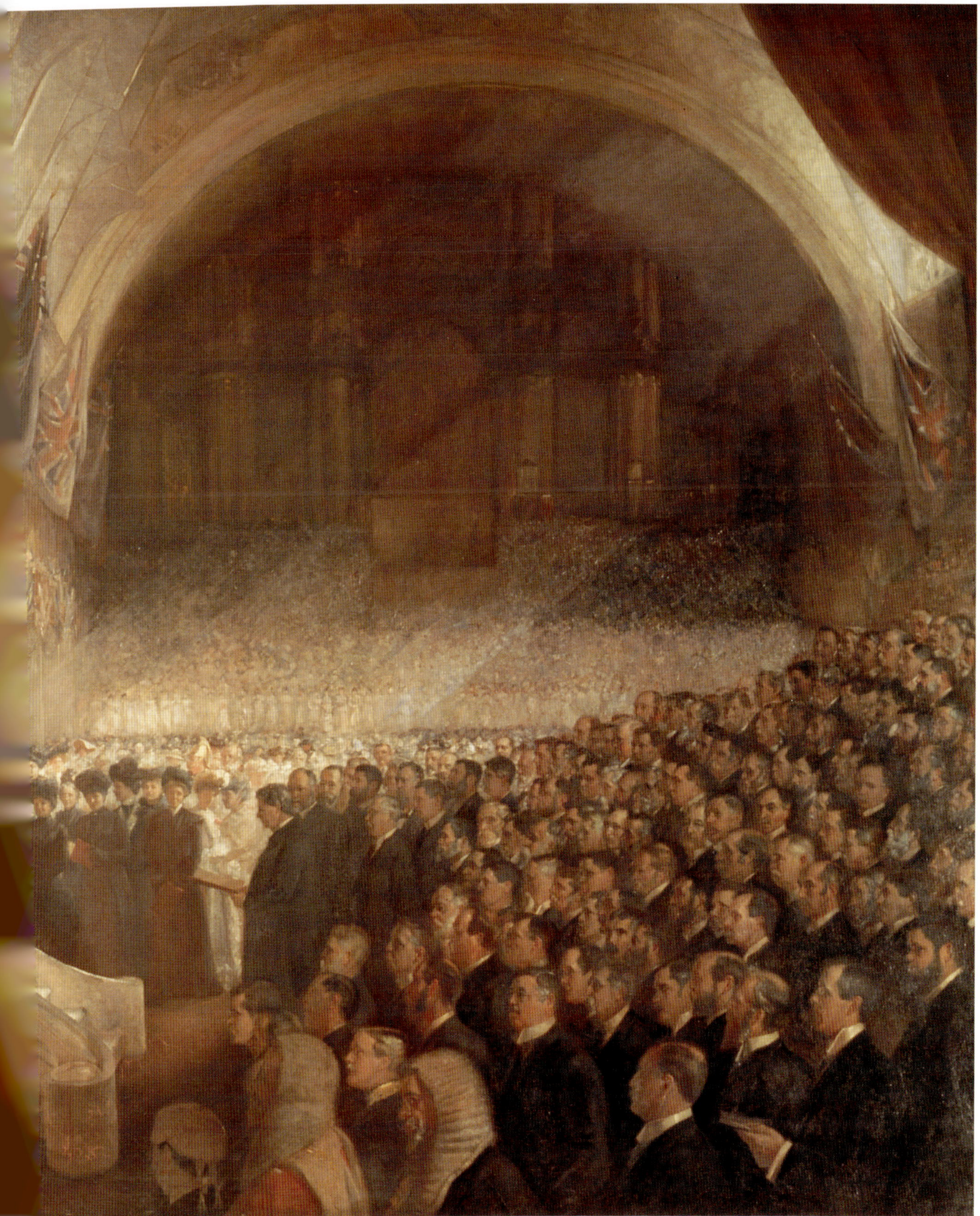

Tom Roberts

Shearing the rams, 1888-90. The Golden Fleece, 1894.

Daniel Thomas

The defence and salvation of the body by daily bread is still a study, a religion, and a desire.

Thomas Hardy, Far from the Madding Crowd, 1874.

These are public works of art. They were made so that Australians might know themselves and that foreigners might know Australians. They are a fulfilment of fellow painter John Russell's exhortation at the end of Roberts's student spell in Europe: "Go and forget style and tackle our stuff for love".[1]

First, therefore, consider what might be seen by a man or woman off the street, encountering them in an art museum or a public exhibition, in the 1890s or any time later.[2]

Human bodies fill the viewer's gaze, adult men's bodies; strong, athletic and confident in their skill at a somewhat obscure task. A few children share the men's world of work. In the earlier of the two paintings one of the animals which are the objects of the men's attention is clearly presented, and can be identified as a merino ram.

Rude timber buildings, with a decided look of age, contain the men and the sheep. The men's clothing is very interesting; it has a distinct bush style, indeed stylishness. The ritualistic, repetitive work takes place in comfortable shade but outside these rough temple-like structures the glare of sunlight is intense.

The paintings are big enough to be important but not so big as to be domineering. The first is four feet high or 120 centimetres, the second is one metre high. Foreground figures at the sides are placed for empathy with viewers standing a short distance away, so the painted bodies seem to be life size, or at least to be in the same foreshortening continuum as the viewer's body. We can readily enter this world of men in decorous, purposeful but sensuous embrace with animals. Shearers today can quietly admit that they love shearing; a former woolgrower, helping analyse one of these paintings, mentioned softly that "sheep's ears are very beautiful".[3] Although the men are not sweating and they perform the work with ease ("no sweat" says he who is confident), a spectator senses the bodily warmth of exercise and fitness. Some viewers especially note the eroticism of stripping – undressing – the animals of their normal earth-toned clothing to display white nudity, and that in the earlier painting animal heads are thrust into the male human crutch.[4]

Next consider the titles. The first, *Shearing the rams*, immediately tells the world of working woolgrowers much that has to be carefully explained to a non-initiate. The second, *The Golden Fleece*, implies, to a differently educated audience, a world of archaic myth.

Shearing the rams, 1888-90, Brocklesby Station, Corowa, NSW, and Melbourne, oil on canvas mounted on board, 121.9 x 182.6 cm; National Gallery of Victoria, Melbourne, Felton Bequest Fund 1932

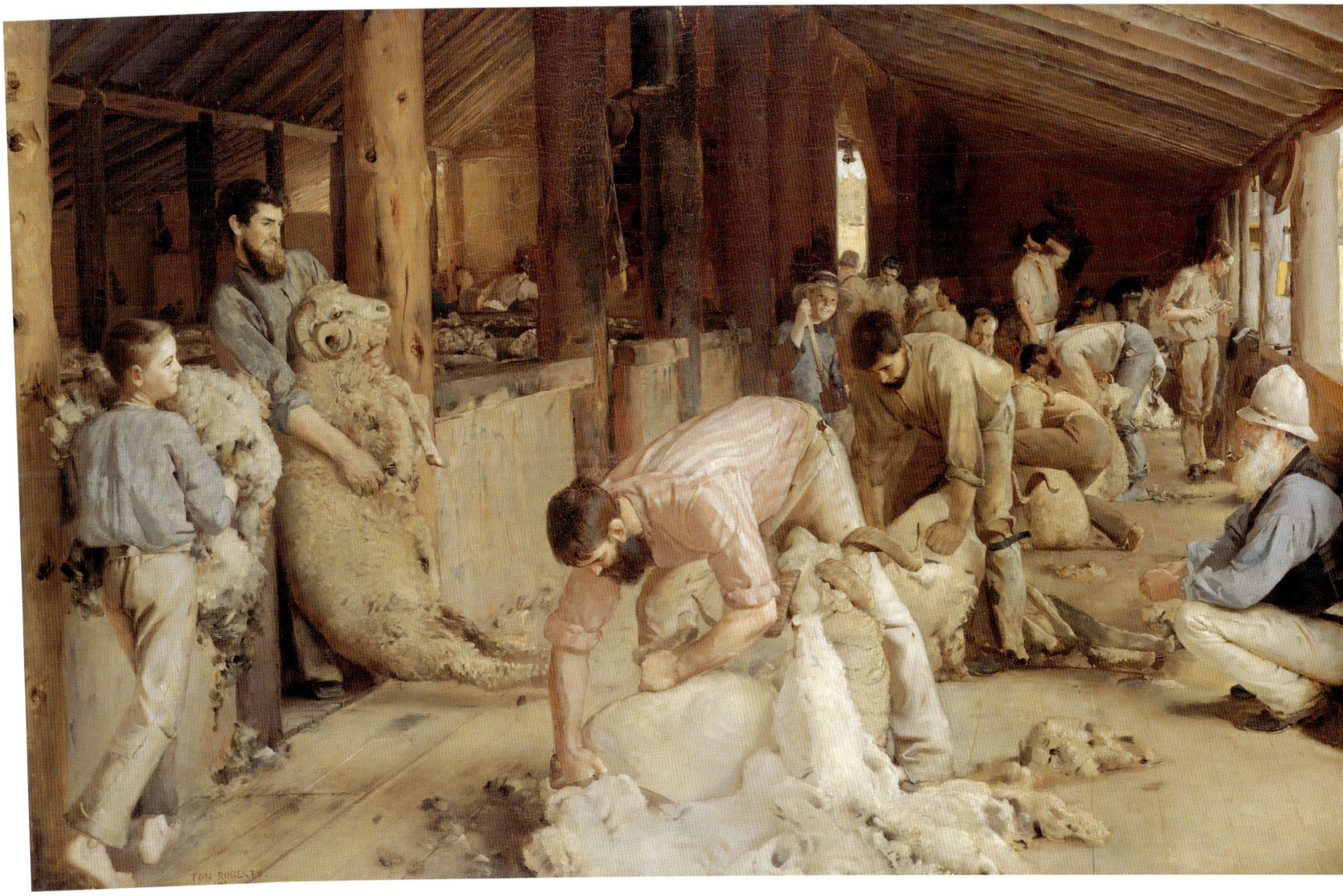
TOM ROBERTS

A flock of sheep is composed half of (female) ewes, half of (castrated, neutered) wethers. The male rams are a minute minority, their purpose not to produce bulk wool but to impregnate the breeding ewes each season with the best genes for the most wool from the largest possible drop of next year's lambs. Their fertility is reduced by the stress of shearing, so with the rams the shearers must perform unusually skilfully, both to protect their own manhood from the dangerous spiral rams' horns and to be restrained and gentle. With the production-line work on ewes and wethers there is more toleration of nicks and cuts and bleeding.[5]

Further, the shearing of the rams is left till the end. It is thereby a ritual, the climactic event in the annual cycle of work on a sheep station. The rams on this small station – only seven or eight shearers visible – would be done in less than one day. The shed and the men might already be spruced up for its transformation that night from a workplace to a place of pleasure; the shearers and their lowlier rouseabout colleagues, and friends and neighbours, will display different competitive skills as musicians, comedians and dancers. The old man squatting on the right does not look like a 'squatter', as substantial landholders were then called, nor an overseer; more likely intended as a neighbour, perhaps a parent or grandparent of one of the young shearers, he is just hanging around in a sociable atmosphere, maybe waiting for the party.[6]

Let the artist tell us – eloquently – what he intended in this painting. But first the reason for his written credo. The big canvas had returned to Melbourne from an actual woolshed in the bush. No Australian painting had hitherto been received with such excitement; it was highly unusual in its complex marshalling of many large-scaled figures and it was the first work to ennoble the central role of wool in Australia's wealth-creation. (Australia had become in the 1870s the world's largest wool producer and wool earned more than half of Australia's export income.) Table Talk on 30 May 1890 said: "A distinctly Australian picture ... not only a fine example of Australian art, but it is strikingly representative of the life of the country". The Age the same day: "The most important work of a distinctively Australian character" ever. It was hoped that *Shearing the rams* would be bought by the National Gallery of Victoria but it was not, and a Gallery trustee and critic wrote disparagingly in an editorial in The Argus:[7] Roberts hit back in a letter to the editor, 4 July 1890:

> ... It seems to me that one of the best words spoken to an artist is, "Paint what you love, and love what you paint", and on that I have worked; and so it came that being in the bush and feeling the delight and fascination of the great pastoral life and work I have tried to express it. If I had been a poet instead of a worker with the brush, I should have described the scattered flocks on sunlit plains and gum-covered ranges, the coming of spring, the gradual massing of the sheep towards that one centre, the woolshed, through which the accumulated growth and wealth of the year is carried; the shouts of the men, the galloping of horses and the barking of dogs as the thousands are driven, half seen, through the hot dust cloud, to the yards; then the final act, and the dispersion of the denuded sheep; but being circumscribed by my art it was only possible to take one view,

Shearing the rams, (detail), 1888-90, Brocklesby Station, Corowa, NSW, and Melbourne, oil on canvas mounted on board, 121.9 x 182.6 cm; National Gallery of Victoria, Melbourne, Felton Bequest Fund 1932

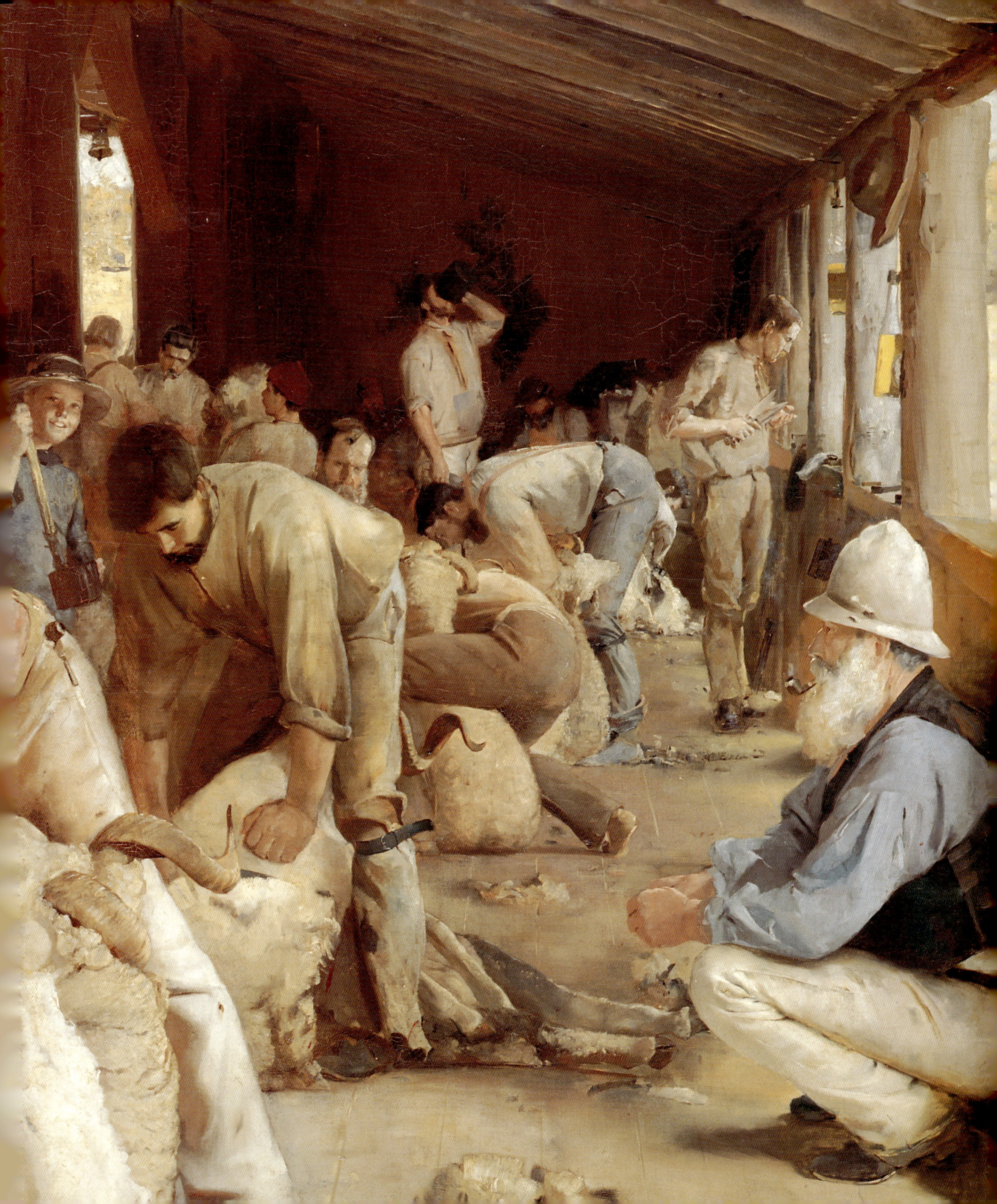

> to give expression to one portion of all this. So, lying on piled up wool-bales, and hearing and seeing the troops come pattering into their pens, the quick running of the wool-carriers, the screwing of the presses, the subdued hum of hard fast working, and the rhythmic click of the shears, the whole lit warm with the reflection of Australian sunlight, it seemed that I had there the best expression of my subject, a subject noble enough and worthy enough if I could express the meaning and spirit – of strong, masculine labour, the patience of the animals whose year's growth is being stripped from them for man's use, and the great human interest of the whole scene.

A respect for quietness was one of Roberts's attractive qualities, and perhaps "the subdued hum of hard fast working" is the key phrase in this letter to the Australian public. The "rhythmic click of the shears" applies only to the hand shears seen in these paintings. Shearing with machinery, and with today's generators for electricity in remote sheds, is unpleasantly noisy; a century later pampered prize rams are still given the special treatment of lower-stress hand shearing.[8]

Mechanical shearing had been successfully introduced only during the two years in which Roberts was working on *Shearing the rams*. It had started on the high tech mega-sheds for fifty or more shearers on the vast stations much further out than these owned by Roberts's friends: Brocklesby of *Shearing the rams* was on the River Murray at Corowa in the New South Wales southern Riverina, Newstead of *The Golden Fleece* is near Inverell in the New England tablelands of northern New South Wales. Smaller sheds did not hurry into machinery and even Newstead, a larger shed than Brocklesby's, did not switch until 1900. The assumption of technological progress was, however, so strong in popular culture that already in August 1890 the press spoke of *Shearing the rams* as "representative of a style of shearing which in pastoral history will soon be a thing of the past".[9] By 1894, when *The Golden Fleece* appeared, The Bulletin observed that it was "undoubtedly the picture of the year ... a work bearing evidence throughout of most careful study. This is emphatically a picture typifying a phase of Australian life that is rapidly passing away, and the trustees have done wisely in securing it for the National [Art] Gallery [of New South Wales] ...".[10]

The rude timber architecture of these sheds would have reinforced, for the media, an assumption that this was a disappearing Australia. Newstead's had been built in 1868, Brocklesby's probably about the same time, from logs and slabs of native cypress pine; newer sheds frequently illustrated in the press were built of sawn timbers and steel, had glass windows, and displayed great expanses of corrugated-iron roofing. An 1890 painting of a modern shed, by Godfrey Rivers, was given to the Queensland Art Gallery in 1895, perhaps in intercolonial rivalry with the old-fashioned one bought for New South Wales.[11] If the absent technology was highly visible to the first viewers of these paintings, a late-twentieth-century observer has seen, subtly, an image of possible dehumanisation by machinery but also of the profound satisfaction to be found in collaborative, skilled work. Virginia Spate says of the receding line of men shearing rams: "... look at how the bodies of the stooped men are locked together by linkage of arms and legs, and repetition

Shearing shed, Newstead, c1894, Newstead North, Elsmore, NSW, oil on wood panel, 23.5 x 35.6 cm; Private collection, Sydney

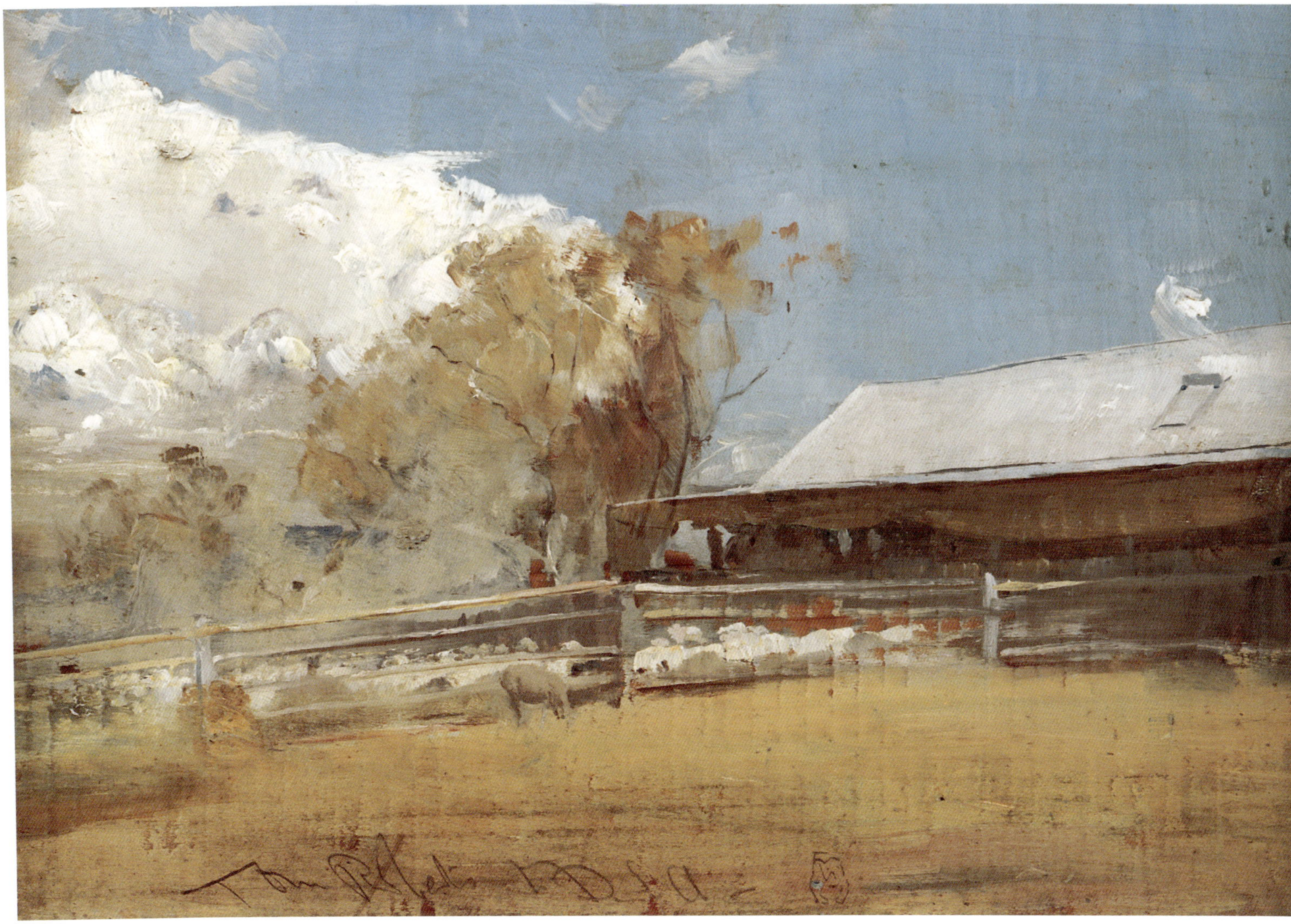

of arching backs. Thus, despite their seemingly individual features – which we struggle to see – they are not individual men working, but a single labouring machine ".[12]

The workmen own these paintings. The bosses are marginalised. In November 1889 the Corowa Free Press visited the Brocklesby woolshed and saw bosses that have disappeared from our gaze.[13] Shearing might have begun shortly after Roberts arrived and painted, on 24 September, a sketch portrait of his host Alexander Anderson. The artist could only observe and sketch while shearing was in progress, as he had already done the previous season, claiming to have made seventy or eighty studies at Brocklesby in 1888, though almost none has survived. But shearing was over by November and the shed, ten miles inland from the homestead and its Murray River lagoon, had become a studio for weekday work by the artist, living in an adjacent hut for transients, with a permanently resident stockman and family as neighbours in a second hut.

The local newspaper saw a "veritable 'Landseer' or 'Raphael' ... squatting down ... at Andersons' woolshed, at Redlands, dressed in blue shirt and moleskins ... with brush in hand, giving the last finishing touches to a picture in oils about 5ft x 4ft ...". The reporter recognised local models Frank Barnes squatting smoking a pipe, "on the shearing board Jim Coffey, busy stripping a sheep of its covering", "young Detlefsen, who is hurrying with the fleece to throw on the table before the wool-roller ..." and "in the background pressing wool, Mr A. Anderson (snr) facing his brother Charles ...".

Susie Bourne, constantly in the shed, was not mentioned by the reporter. During shearing, provided she secured her hair in a hat, she was given charge of the tar-pot, to touch the sheep's cut bodies with healing dabs. She became the only figure looking out at the viewer. It is as if she is sharing a secret with the photo-realist picture-taker; she was there and knew how much was made up. Maybe her ninth birthday, 22 February 1890, inspired her inclusion; her presence is in any case a note of thanks to the stockman's family that had kept the artist fed during his time at the woolshed hut. She was his spirit of the place.

The "finishing touches" seen being made in November sound like an artist posing for a reporter. The picture was not ready in time for the Victorian Artists' Society exhibition in March 1890 and, after a pause, was finished in Melbourne in May. A grey monochrome "First sketch for Shearing ..." shows the rhythmic line of shearers, the framing figures of a shearer fetching/displaying a ram and another standing sharpening shears, all of which survived in the final version.[14]

But the hands-on Anderson proprietors, probably identifiable with the good-sized figures at the wool table in the background of the "First sketch", eventually shrank into insignificance. A back view of Alick Anderson's head rhymes wittily from the bottom of the bright slit of outdoor light with the time bell at the top; younger brother Charles is the dark-haired man facing him across a now unseen wool table, to which a boy delivers a fleece.

The Golden Fleece, 1894, Newstead North, Elsmore, NSW, and Sydney, oil on canvas, 104.0 x 158.7 cm; The Art Gallery of New South Wales, Sydney, Purchased 1894

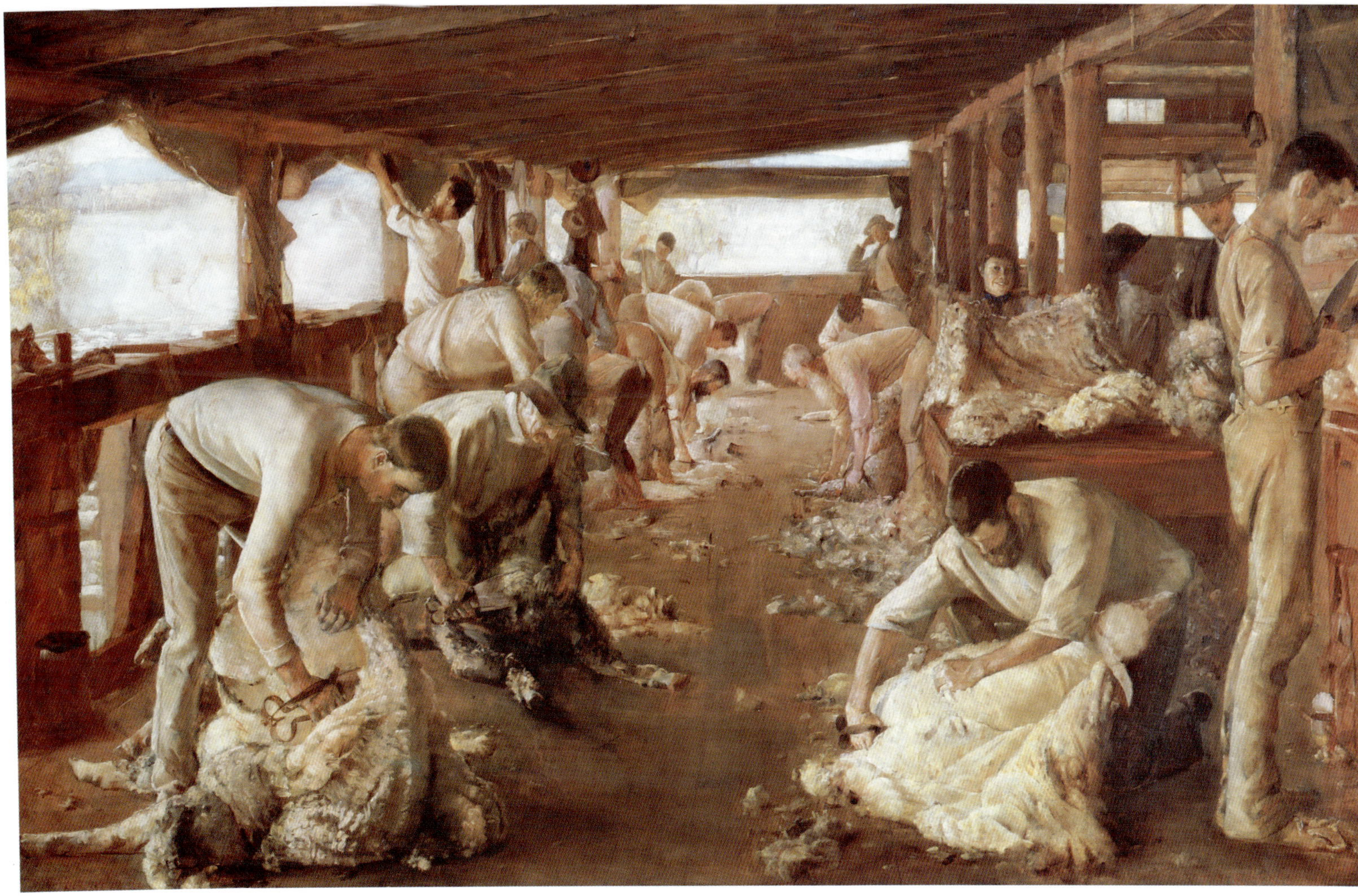

Similarly in *The Golden Fleece* the owner of Newstead North, Duncan Anderson (no relation to the Brocklesby Andersons) is far from dominant. Wearing a smart hat very different from the workers' battered bush hats, the boss peers out, a little uncertainly perhaps, from behind the shoulders of the tough shears-sharpener, foreground right. A hand from nowhere, growing out of the sharpener's back, holding a fleece, is that of the owner. His presence is so awkward, and so unresolved artistically, that one can only assume it is an afterthought. Perhaps he had declined to be included while Roberts was working at Newstead; perhaps his artist mate – they were very good friends – sneaked him in after the canvas had returned to Sydney. Perhaps on the other hand Anderson or his family at Newstead, realising that he was absent, put in a late request. The space he occupies seems to have been stolen from a now ghostly second boy rouseabout, hatted and standing in profile against a post; probably he was throwing a fleece onto another wool table, a companion action to the display by the boy who claims our attention.

It might seem strange that Roberts painted two such similar paintings. Maybe the disappearance of *Shearing the rams* into the privileged seclusion of a Collins Street boardroom-cum-office, of the stock & station agent Edward Trenchard & Co., was deemed unsatisfactory for a work that sought such a broad public audience. Maybe a second try might succeed in entering a public collection, as indeed it did, with great promptness.

The differences are real enough however. *Shearing the rams* is more beautified, less realist, though both paintings would have been recognised by an art audience as belonging to a new movement of determined naturalism, based on diligent study of the subject, and hoping to achieve a styleless style of near-photographic, truthful observation. There was then an international fashion for honouring regional ways of life and work, an anti-metropolitan attitude that sought out the typical but often obsolescent work of, say Provencal grape harvesters, Cornish fishermen – or Australian sheep-shearers.

An art audience would also have suspected that perhaps the shearers at Brocklesby were not all modelled from different men. The receding displays of "the long blow" along the animal's side or the removal of neck, belly and shoulder wool seem to be performed by men of strong family resemblance. Perhaps they were all modelled by Jim Coffey. Table Talk reported that Roberts paid £12 to "the most characteristic and picturesque of the shearers: to pose as required for a good many days".[15]

The rhythmic, sequential poses might have been perceived as referencing the recently available photographs, by Eardweard Muybridge, of animal and human locomotion, which Roberts certainly knew. The too-graceful pose of the barefoot fourteen-year-old Jack Detlefsen would have been recognised as a standard art-school ploy, a reversal of the Esau figure in Ghiberti's Florentine quattrocento *Porta del Paradiso*.[16] (And a bush viewer might wonder whether the boy's entry from the viewer's space really proved that this rather small shed was bigger than it seemed.)

The Golden Fleece, (detail), 1894, Newstead North, Elsmore, NSW, and Sydney, oil on canvas, 104.0 x 158.7 cm; The Art Gallery of New South Wales, Sydney, Purchased 1894

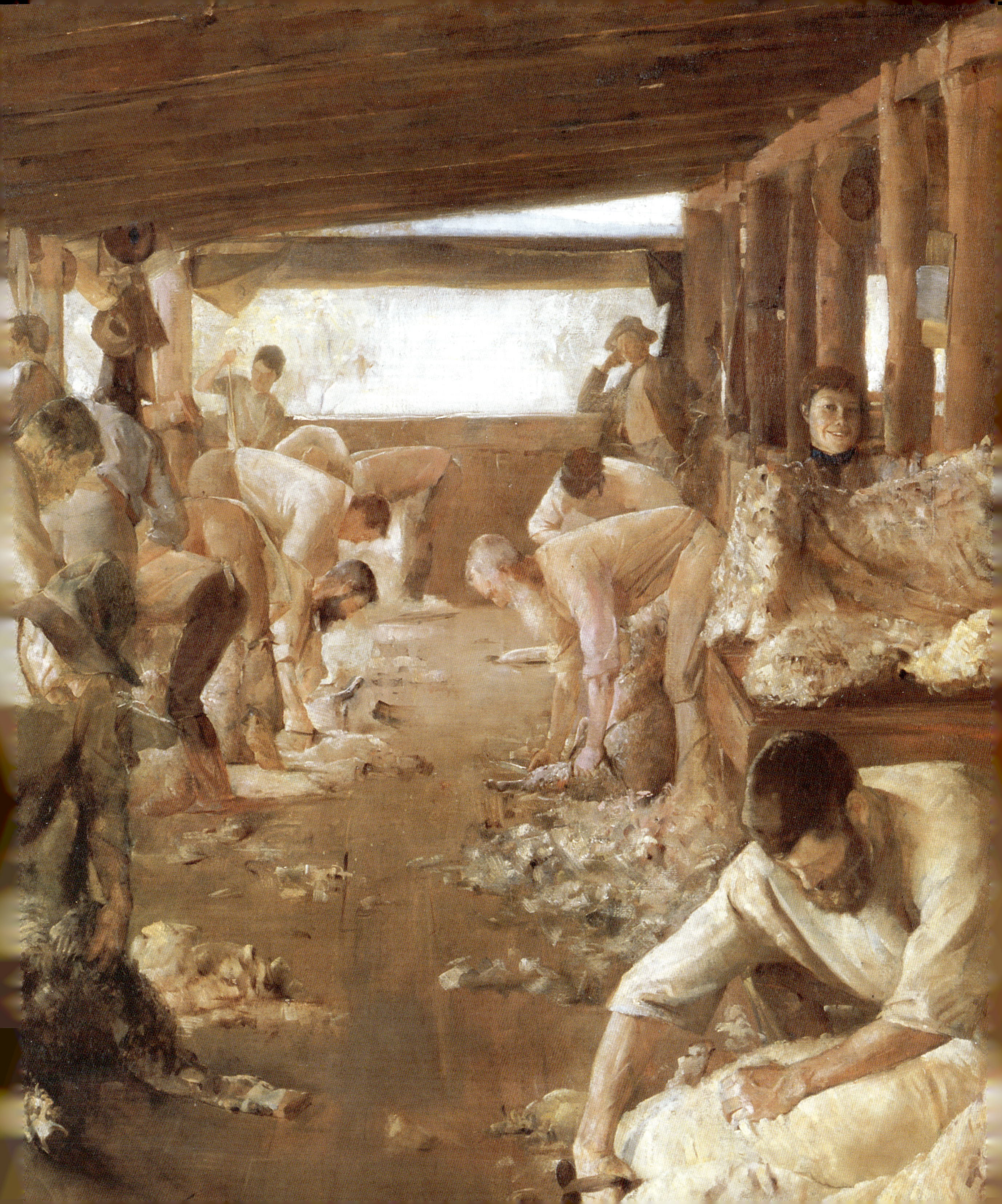

The Golden Fleece might not have been based on detailed study of shearing at Newstead. There is no evidence that Roberts had been there before his arrival for Christmas and New Year 1893, and he had finished it before the next shearing season. His oil-sketch of the shed shows freshly shorn white sheep outside so perhaps in December he caught the end of a late shearing season. He had studied the process enough at Brocklesby. The second picture looks, pleasingly, less like art.

It is a reversal of *Shearing the rams* in a few respects. The subject honours the product, the 'golden fleece', more than the process of shearing. The knowing child who displays (as well as the golden fleece) an awareness of the artist/viewer outside the painting is this time not a girl but a boy. At Brocklesby the business end of the shed – entrance, bell, wool table and wool press – was in the distant background; at Newstead the viewer stands at the entrance. Although in both sheds we are looking east,[17] in the Riverina lowlands spring can be very hot and the shearing board is on the shady southern side, also a more suitable workplace for painting conventionally even-toned naturalism. In the New England tableland spring can be too cold, so the shearing board catches the warmth of the northern sun – and the glare and the contrasts which symbolise Australia better than shadow. We also are shown the yard outside, with sheep and dust and a stockman shouting and waving. We get shearers of course – a very real diversity of unbeautified young and old, smooth and wrinkled, white-bearded and black-hatted (perhaps to hide baldness) – but we get much more.

In *The Golden Fleece* we see not privileged rams but merino wethers, workaday wool producers. At Newstead they produced fine wool, better able to claim the description golden fleece than the medium wools of the Riverina. And the Newstead boss as a child had been taken from Australia to London for schooling at Harrow; his education in little but Latin and Greek would have given him a well-layered appreciation of his place in the world. He, and Roberts, knew the ancient myths, the archaic story of the Argonauts' voyage to the end of the known world to bring back the golden fleece, an allegory of the benefits offered us by the first animals to submit to domestication.

Duncan Anderson, and Roberts, would have known that the ancient Greek Arcadia was a place of rough pastoral life, that animals were important, and those who worked with them. In 1885 a visiting English journalist, George Augustus Sala, had written a series of articles on Australia and designated her 'The Land of the Golden Fleece', a new arcadia at the end of a much larger world than that of the first civilisations. The pastoralist and the artist both delighted in a life among patient animals, among rural men of great individuality. In 1898 the Sydney cartoonist D.H. Souter drew Duncan Anderson as "Ye Gentle Shepherd", seated among his sheep, crowned with a laurel wreath, and entertaining the animals with music played on his cornet. Roberts and his host both knew that the woolshed, seen from the homestead verandah on higher ground than the isolated station church, was in its way a temple, a place to honour the good and simple life of men in harmony with animals, and perhaps with the rest of the natural world.

Shearing the rams, (detail), 1888-90, Brocklesby Station, Corowa, NSW, and Melbourne, oil on canvas mounted on board, 121.9 x 182.6 cm; National Gallery of Victoria, Melbourne, Felton Bequest Fund 1932

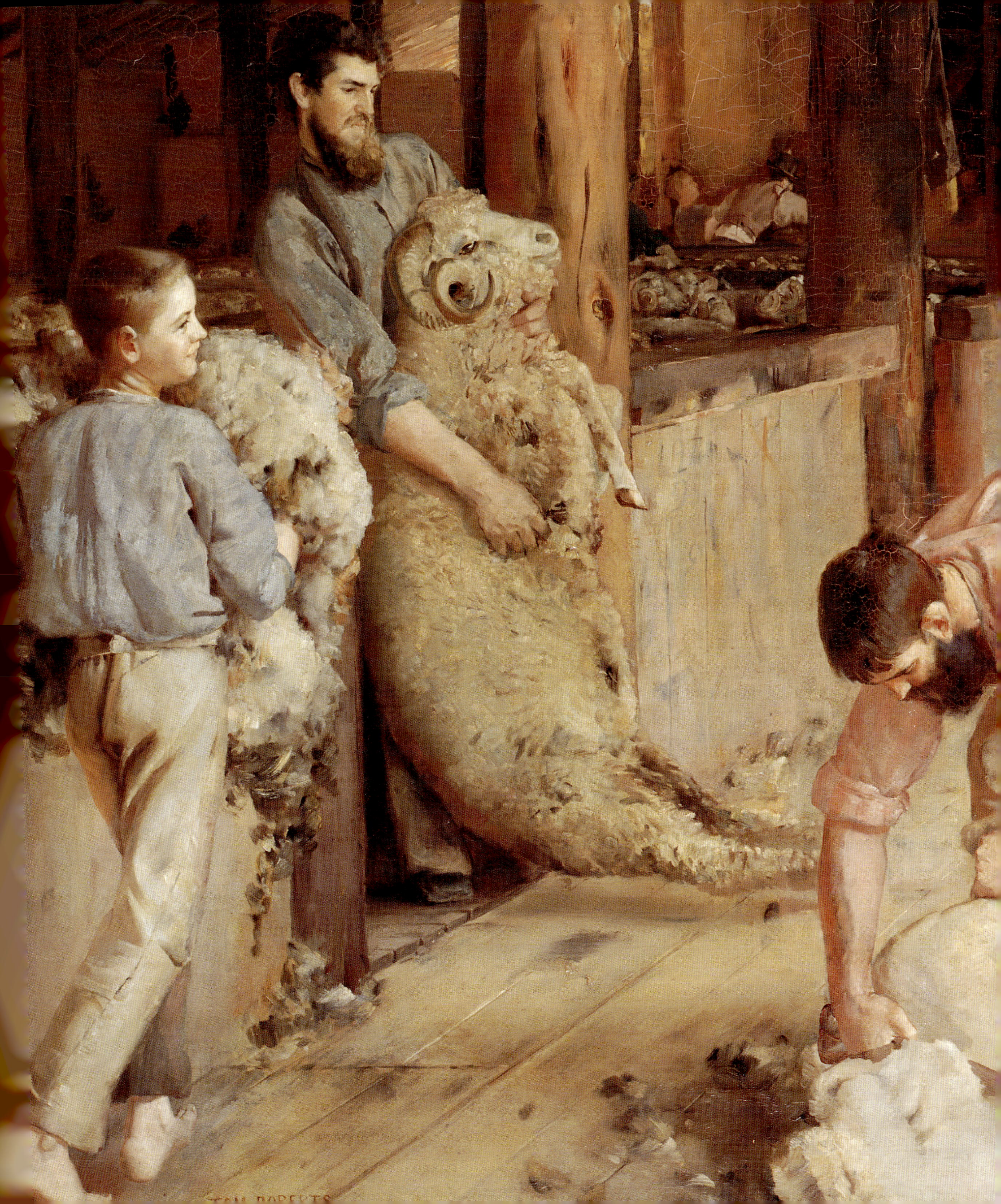

A break away!, 1891

Jane Hylton

One of the Art Gallery of South Australia's most celebrated paintings, Tom Roberts's *A break away!* has seldom been off display since 1900, the year after its acquisition.[1] Having celebrated its centenary in 1991, *A break away!* still stands as the artist intended, a symbol of Australia. As such, it remains a favourite with Gallery visitors, a key work among the national paintings by artists popularly associated with 'Impressionism'.

Viewed from a present which bears remarkable similarities to the political, economic and climatic circumstances of Australia in the 1890s, the painting's original raison d'etre seems to gain renewed strength. One hundred years ago Roberts painted his vigorous scene at a time when Australia was considering her national identity, as the colonies' Federation approached. The country was emerging from the grip of a drought which had had a devastating affect on the economy. Those late-nineteenth-century events reflect the nation's possibility now of becoming a Republic at the end of the twentieth century, after a time when Australia has again recently been in recession and drought-stricken.

The painting *A break away!* goes well beyond the spontaneity of Roberts's plein-airisme and his impressionist work of the late 1880s. In it he draws upon the 1870s work of the French artist Jules Bastien-Lepage and of the mid-nineteenth-century Barbizon School, both of great influence on the movement led by Tom Roberts. Adapting their response to humble rural labour as a legitimate subject for great art, as well as using the painterly technique evident in his own quick impressions, Roberts brings together these qualities to achieve the painting he considered his most successful. In an article published in 1899, the year the Art Gallery of South Australia purchased *A break away!*, the painting is described as "... the Riverina picture of a stockman vainly trying to stop a rushing mob of thirsty sheep who sight water" and the comment is made that Roberts "... prizes [*A break away!*] as the work in which his art has so far most nearly realized his idea".[2]

The composition of the painting is Roberts's broadest and most animated. As with much of his work, far from being a truly Impressionist or Naturalist open-air painting it was created from preliminary sketches, made in this case on Brocklesby and Collendina sheep-stations near Corowa in the Riverina district of New South Wales. The landscape motif was found quite close to Brocklesby woolshed, where in 1889-90 he had painted *Shearing the rams*; he "climbed over the boundary fence, and trespassed on the neighbouring run of Collendina", Table Talk told its readers on 13 February 1891. Roberts himself commented in 1899 on carting the large canvas cross-country for outdoor work, but it was painted mostly in the Brocklesby woolshed, and then completed in Melbourne.

A break away!, 1891, Corowa, NSW and Melbourne, oil on canvas, 137.3 x 167.8cm; Art Gallery of South Australia, Adelaide, Elder Bequest Fund 1899

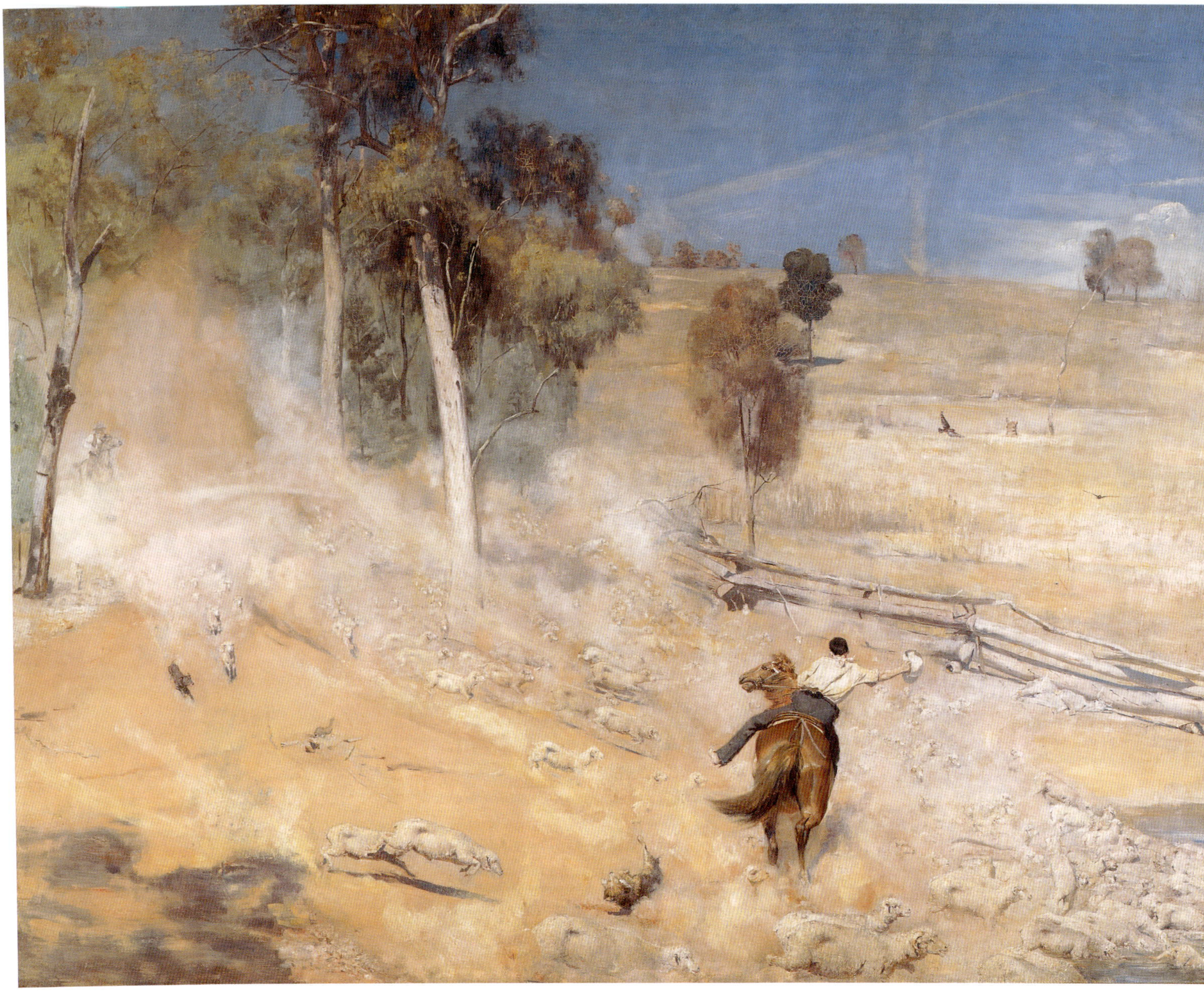

It consciously presents an heroic time of sheep-grazing pastoralism, in an image not specific to the Riverina but generalised to reflect the whole of Australia. Corowa country is by no means the outback, here it doubles for country further out. The pastoral industry, seen as the central embodiment of the Australian character, had endured a horror drought in 1888-89. The taxing period for those on the land engendered a view from the city of the Australian character as one of stoic strength, able to deal with any adverse conditions the country offered as a challenge.

In addition to this overt heroism, however, can be seen an awareness of the impact of unsustainable practices. Around 1890 wool-growing in the remote outback was suffering. Bad seasons and the rabbit plague caused the abandonment of overstocked sheep country and created general pastoral-industry unease about the dependability of Australian seasons. Australia's sheep population suddenly diminished and the figures of that time were not reached again until the 1920s. So besides the particular fear of death by trampling or by thirst, explicit in the breakaway subject, the painting expresses a general fear of degradation of the land and consequent decline of the then largely wool-dependent Australian economy.

A break away! was described in 1891 as "A bit of arid country ... positively frizzling in the heat of a January day ... An Australian incident – tragic, realistic, picturesque ...",[3] it depicts the moment all drovers in drought dread, when the flock they have driven, possibly for hundreds of miles in search of pasture, smells water and their overwhelming thirst causes the sheep to stampede. Its illustrative quality tells a story that is easily understood, about a bygone era of which most Australians are sentimentally proud. The horseman at the centre of the rush, challenged by the dry inland, does his heroic utmost to stave the rush of the sheep. Horses and dogs are incidental heroes in the painting, pitting their strenuous efforts alongside those of their human masters. The chaos of swirling dust, through which trees, sheep and another horseman are barely visible, contrasts with the extreme stillness of the hot, dry day. At the time this contrast was remarked upon; "... extremes meet, and the artist has dared to blend a fierce swirl of excitement with a perfect trance of repose".[4] Sheep are already drowning in the water, while others will surely die in the crush. Near the fence the prophetic carcass of a bullock lies desiccating in the sun.

Seeing past the slight stiffness of the central horse and horseman (the rider modelled by a rouseabout because they did the mustering),[5] and the oddly disparate composition, viewers recognise in Roberts's painting the light, the colour and areas of rapidly applied brushwork that they associate with their now beloved Australian 'Impressionist' art – and this, more than Roberts's other major paintings, has the strong outdoor light generally associated with Impressionism. Subject and style make a formidable combination. As early as 1891, however, the awkward placement and incompatibility of the finish on the dominant horseman was seen as a significant problem by the critic of Table Talk when he was commenting on the painting.[6]

A break away!, (detail), 1891, Corowa, NSW and Melbourne, oil on canvas, 137.3 x 167.8cm; Art Gallery of South Australia, Adelaide, Elder Bequest Fund 1899

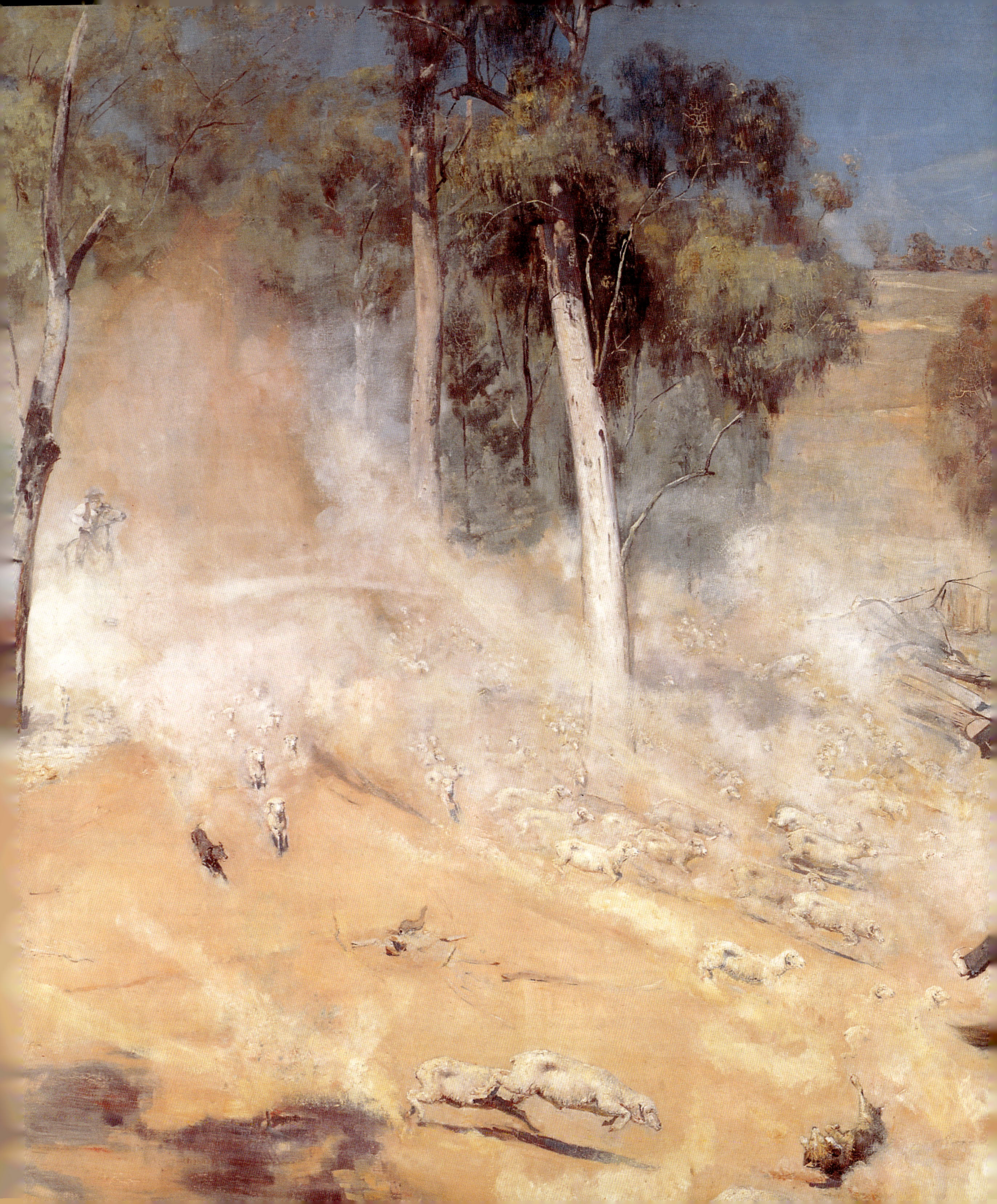

Roberts took six months to complete *A break away!* using as reference a number of vigorous on-the-spot sketches he had made in his sketchbook. A compositional sketch[7] indicates that the final work varies little from his initial roughed-out, action-filled concept. He also probably made oil sketches for the work judging by the comments of a reporter who in 1891 had come to write about "A 'BUSH' STUDIO; And The Picture In It": "Roving eyes next rest on a rough sketch ... The subject is a chock-and-log fence, with effects ... to suggest fierce overhead sunlight – a dazzling glare".[8]

The successful depiction of extreme, high-speed action in *A break away!* suggests that Roberts studied closely the movement of dogs, sheep and men on horseback. The reporter at the Bush Studio noted: "A 'still holding pool' in Riverina has been selected by the artist, and in Riverina, as a rule, only sheep are now depastured. Hence the artist has also chosen to depict sheep rather than cattle – for consistency's sake" He spent several months on Brocklesby and Collendina stations, observing for the painting[9]. He also wrote to Charles Conder discussing the difficulty of painting animals in motion, to which Conder replied suggesting the use of photographs.[10]

At the time *A break away!* was painted the Riverina border country was a place with a distinct identity. The woolshed studio and the artist's adjacent hut were ten miles out but Brocklesby homestead, to which the artist returned at weekends, was on the outskirts of the small town of Corowa, the region's centre on the New South Wales bank of the Murray River. Here on the border between two colonies issues such as Federation were enthusiastically debated by the local press, The Riverina Grazier and the Corowa Free Press; there were customs duties payable at the border crossing en route to Melbourne, which was much nearer than Sydney, the New South Wales capital. In 1891, the year *A break away!* was painted, a convention of the Australian colonies was held in Melbourne from which developed a Commonwealth Bill. At a time when the nation's political consciousness was beginning to be concerned with mutually supportive nation-building, Australians turned to the bush for inspiration and notions of cultural identity.

During the 1890s, as nationalism was becoming a significant issue, Roberts painted five works, each intended to reflect the heroic quality of characteristically Australian bush life. They were seen as being most appropriately destined for a public role in the colonial 'National' Galleries. *Shearing the rams*, 1888-90, *A break away!*, 1891, *The Golden Fleece*, 1894, *Bailed up*, 1895, and *A mountain muster*, 1897, are all paintings focusing on rural industries where the male dominated the work and are characterised therefore by masculine symbolism. In sharp contrast to the unhurried pace of *The Golden Fleece* and *Shearing the rams*, both evocative of a flourishing rural industry, *A break away!* is an expression of extreme physical energy and reflects potential calamity.

A break away! was initially priced at 300 guineas when first exhibited in Melbourne and remained with Roberts for nearly a decade. In 1898 Roberts wrote to H.P. Gill, Honorary Curator of the National Gallery of South Australia, interested to find out more about the 'Federal Australasian Art Exhibitions' of contemporary works organised for the first time that year by Gill. These exhibitions brought together in Adelaide work from

The old barracks at Collendina, c1891, Collendina Station, Corowa, NSW, oil on canvas, 40.0 x 51.5 cm (sight); Private collection, Adelaide

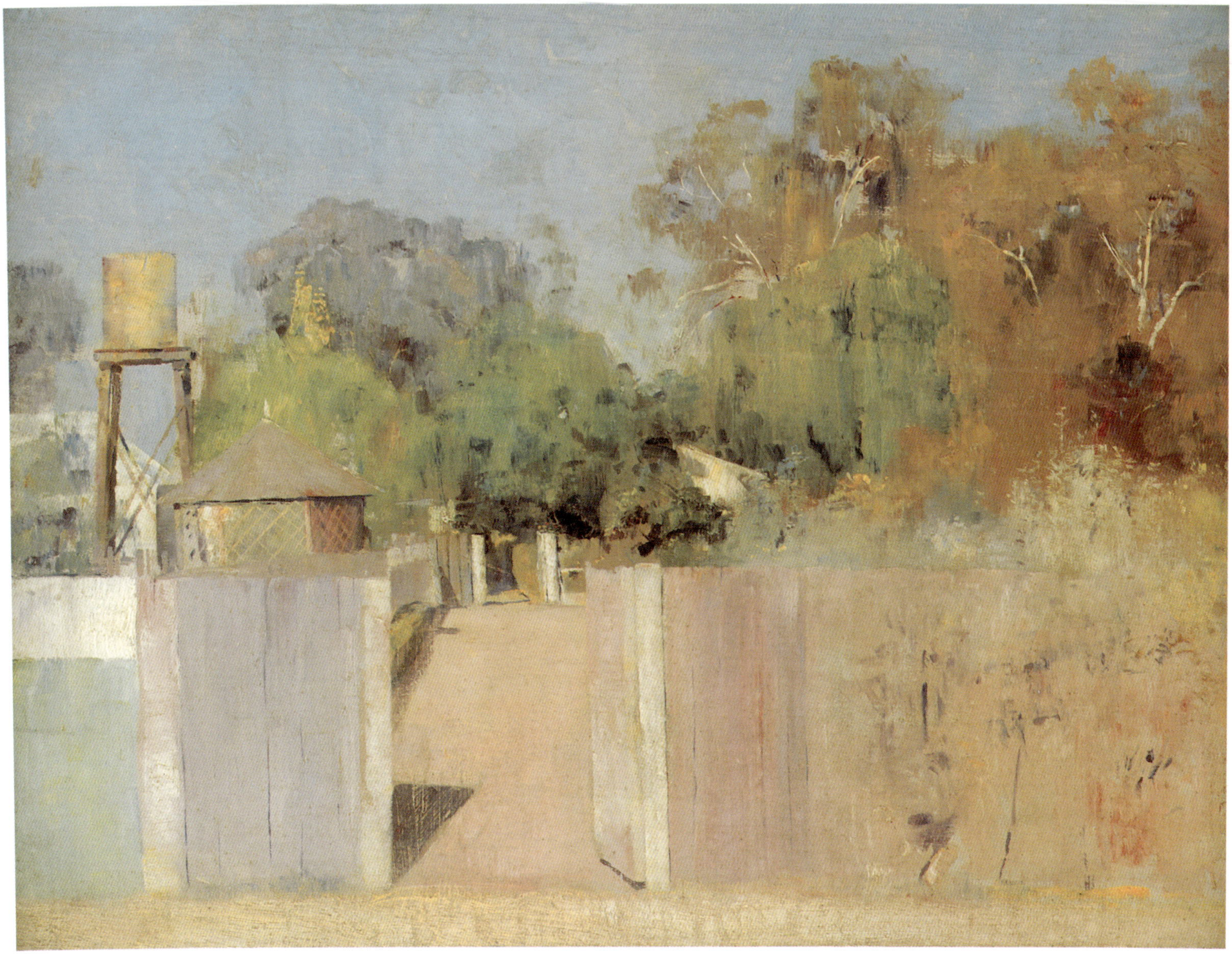

all over Australia and New Zealand, and Gill's purchases from them formed the basis of the Gallery's Australian collections. For the first exhibition Roberts sent only one painting, a portrait entitled *Christina* priced at thirty-one guineas. In November 1899 for the second exhibition Roberts again sent only one painting. This was his *A break away!*, at the significantly reduced price of 200 guineas, even though it had been much admired the previous year in the Grafton Galleries 'Exhibition of Australian Art in London' (for which the cattlepiece *A mountain muster* had been painted as a companion for this mob of sheep on the hot plains). After negotiations between the Board of the Public Library, Museum & Art Gallery, H.P. Gill and Roberts's agent Rodney Cherry of the opportunistically named Grafton Galleries, Sydney, the purchase price was eventually reduced to £150, still a remarkably expensive picture at that time.

Correspondence between Gill and Roberts while the sale was being negotiated indicates that by being away from Sydney when Gill wrote with the Board's offer the artist almost lost the opportunity. Much relieved at the finally satisfactory outcome of their negotiations, Roberts wrote to Gill, thanking him and stating of the work, "I think it is the best outside thing I have managed". He went on to say that his "... recollection of those months is always happy. From the first morning when I began carrying it on my back to my spot – the carting of it from one place to another, until it was rolled up to go down to my [Melbourne] studio". But he followed with the comment: "Then came the chill indifference of the Trustees of Melbourne and from then until now [Adelaide] not an offer or inquiry about it".[11]

The painting has inspired a number of contemporary socio-critical Australian works. In 1985 Anne Zahalka produced a manipulated photograph of *A break away!*, challenging the myth of the male role in pioneering Australia. In her *Untitled* from the series *The Landscape Re-presented* she changed the gender of the rider to female by altering the figure's short hair to a long, feminine plait. In his *Untitled from 'Breakaway' series*, Bill Young disrupts the tranquil interior of Jan Vermeer's *The love letter*, c1670, with a superimposed image of the dusty chaos of *A break away!*. Also created in Adelaide, Peter Baka's *The Breakaway after Tom Roberts*, 1987, reproduces the painting as an assemblage, whose corrugated-iron materials emphasise the unassailable Australianness.

A break away! lives on as a dramatic and compelling work fulfilling all the artist's nationalistic intentions. It is of no account that he almost certainly never saw a breakaway stampede of sheep.

A mountain muster, 1897, Newbold, NSW, and Sydney, 1910s?, England, oil on canvas, 129.5 x 147.3 cm; National Gallery of Victoria, Melbourne, Purchased with the assistance of Central Equity Limited and Westfield Holdings, and through The Art Foundation of Victoria with the assistance of The Joe White Bequest, Governor, 1995

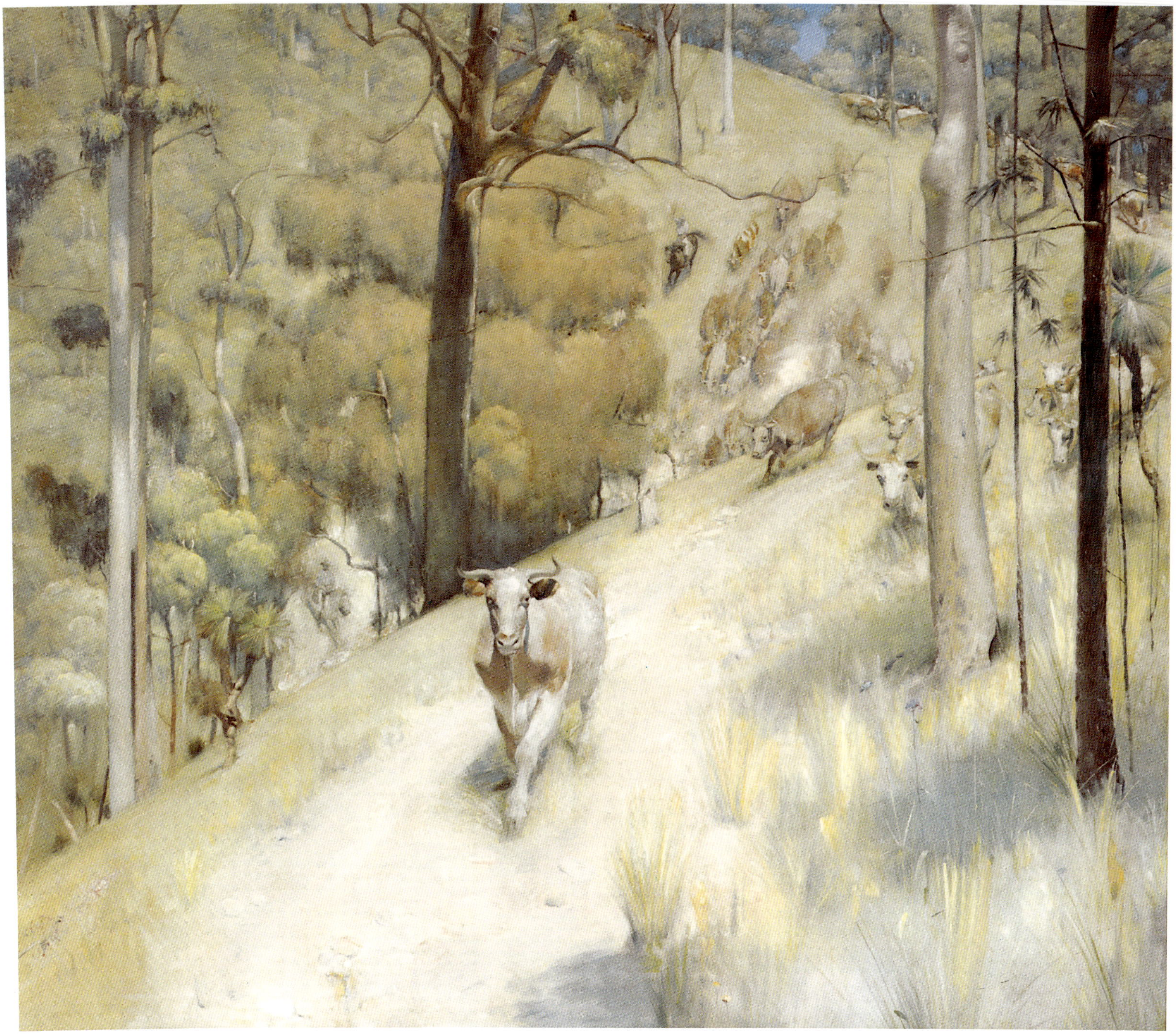

Bailed up, 1895/1927

Barry Pearce

Following a century of colonial settlement, European Australians in the 1890s began to construct an historical mythology for themselves. Much of it was to do with how they had come to terms with their landscape; how they had survived in it, how they used it, and how they felt about it. Tom Roberts was the artist best equipped to project this ethos, the evolution of which had been only tenuously heroic, indeed often exploitative. And he was able to celebrate it with the brilliant light which had largely escaped the perceptions of his predecessors.

Roberts was fascinated by pastoral life and found his greatest fulfilment in a series of bush-life paintings begun with *Shearing the rams* and continued after his shift in 1891 from Melbourne to Sydney. Whilst staying at Duncan Anderson's Newstead sheep station, near Inverell in the New England tableland of northern New South Wales, Roberts conceived the idea of a bushranging picture. In it he would present an imaginary incident from the disorderly past, within an artistically modern portrayal of the Australian landscape in its highest key. Such was the beginning of *Bailed up*.

At Newstead at the end of 1893 Roberts was already planning his second sheep-shearing painting, *The Golden Fleece*. Walking along the road between Newstead and Paradise, a neighbouring station owned by Russell Hughes, he found a setting for his bushranging picture. It was an isolated spot among grass trees and a forest of tall gums, a level bend on a long steep ascent, the last bad hill for travellers following the Macintyre River on their way to Inverell. This back road was not in fact a coaching route, but here was a good setting for Roberts's "sham stick-up": a coach would have been well and truly trapped by the great log placed across the narrow climbing road; mounted bushrangers could have waited well camouflaged in the steep forest above, and a spare horse left lurking in the shadows. It was highland country, not far from where the region's last bushranger, 'Captain Thunderbolt', had died a quarter of a century earlier.

At this ideal spot for a robbery under arms, the artist, helped by the Anderson family, built a platform of timber, bark and wire in a stringy-bark tree growing below the road, so that he could set up his canvas on this 'Perch' at the level of the road. A Cobb & Co. coach then in operation between Inverell and Glen Innes was painted in town at Inverell, together with its driver Bob Bates. 'Silent Bob Bates' had a story of being robbed by Thunderbolt some three decades earlier, and it was his laconic, hard-wrung description of the quiet nature of the incident which determined the mood of Roberts's composition – though there is apparently no attempt to distance it in time by dressing the "lady passenger" in obviously 1860s costume. Other characters were modelled by other townspeople in Inverell, and by station hands at Newstead, where the painting was completed.[1] Roberts made tiny drawings and an oil sketch of how he wanted the scene

Bailed up, 1895, Newstead and Inverell, NSW, and Sydney, 1927, Kallista, Victoria, oil on canvas, 134.5 x 182.8 cm; The Art Gallery of New South Wales, Sydney, Purchased 1933

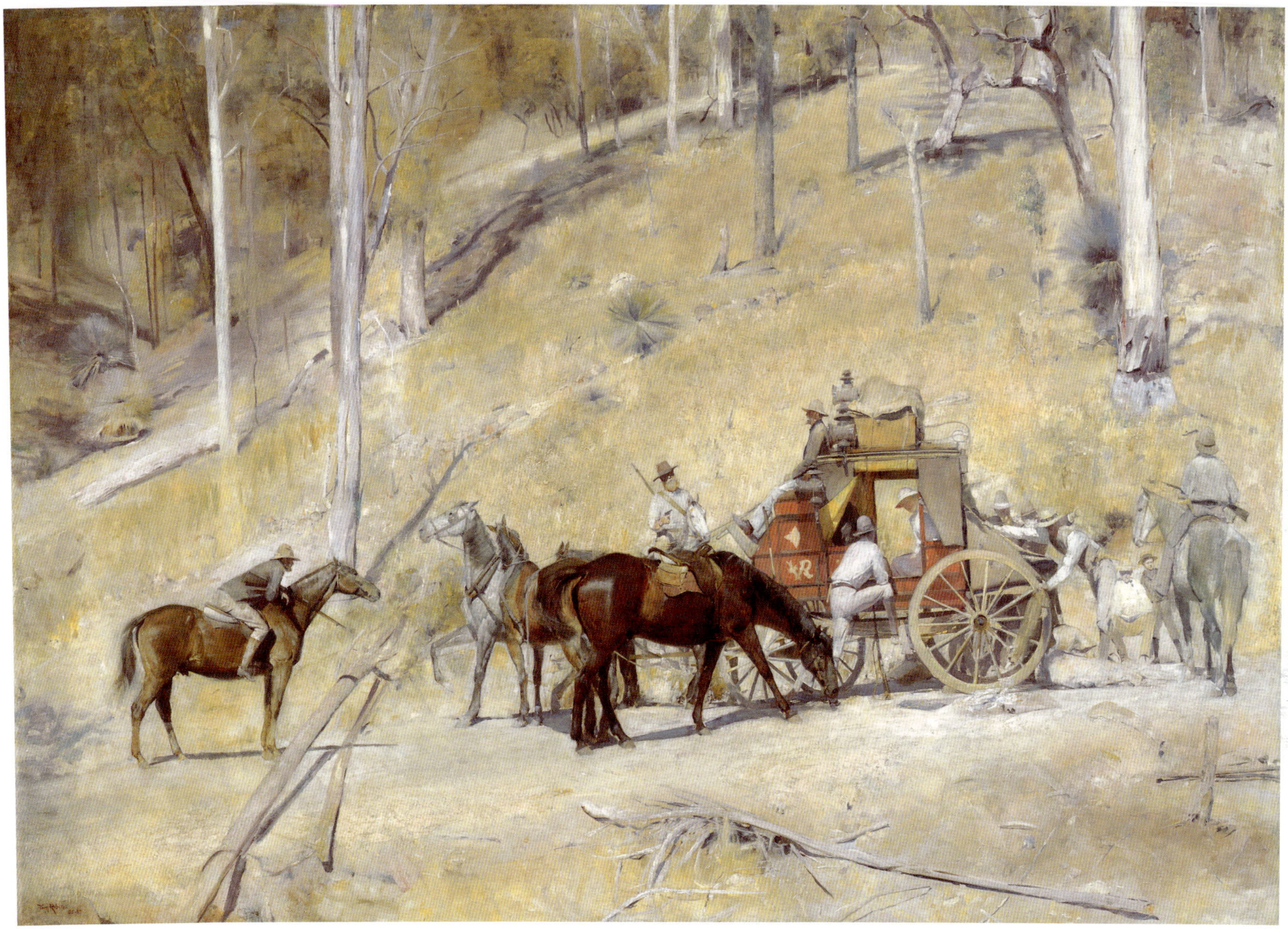

to look before he started his big canvas, in which he set out to create the most complex painting of his career to date; complex because it was not only about the seizing of a moment in the landscape but was also intended to convey a recollection of the historical past.[2] This particular watchful, shadowy place had engendered the artist's idea of a sudden, apparitional haunting by bushrangers.

Of the group of bush masterpieces that Roberts embarked upon between 1888 and 1898, *Bailed up* turned out to be the most contentious, and remains so. For in spite of the nationalistic fervour which might have guaranteed an enthusiastic reception for the painting when it was exhibited in Sydney and Melbourne in the 1890s, it neither succeeded in eliciting unanimous praise, nor found a willing buyer. Roberts dropped the price from £275 in 1895 to 70 guineas in 1900. After all the enthusiasm and trouble he took to paint *Bailed up*, Roberts could not dispatch it into the world.

Because Roberts reworked the painting in 1927 it is now difficult to assess the validity of its reception in 1895. Nagging criticisms made by the press concerned the men's legs or the horses' skin ("... the length and slimness normal in the gum tree are abnormal in the bushrangers' legs").[3] Perhaps unsatisfactory pictorial resolution was sensed, turning potential collectors away. Eventually in 1928, after Roberts had substantially repainted the background landscape, *Bailed up*, price 500 guineas, was sold from an exhibition of his work at the Macquarie Galleries in Sydney. It was bought by J.W. Maund, a solicitor, amateur painter and trustee of the Art Gallery of New South Wales. Maund promptly lent it to the Gallery, which purchased it five years later.

Since then critical opinion has fluctuated. Lionel Lindsay wrote warmly of *Bailed up* in the Macquarie Galleries exhibition catalogue, praising its rich rendering of light and comparing its subject to the prose of Henry Lawson. But as recently as 1985, when it was included in *Golden Summers: Heidelberg and beyond*, an exhibition of Australian painting from Roberts's time, *Bailed up* was hung in the National Gallery of Victoria's last room with works mainly of the Edwardian era, removed from its period of genesis. More recently still, in his biography of Roberts, Humphrey McQueen ventured the opinion that *Bailed up* was ineffectual as a bushranging story and that, because of its flat, skyless landscape and lateral disposition of figures across the composition, it was an insipid echo of the then-fashionable, decorative, Symbolist mural style of Puvis de Chavannes.

Continuing ambiguity about the efficacy of *Bailed up* as an icon of Australian art is puzzling. Why is admiration of it so tempered with caution? Is it because, notwithstanding the monumental failure of his vast *Opening of the First Parliament of the Commonwealth of Australia*, his *Bailed up* represents the most protracted struggle in Roberts's career to realise his vision on a large scale?

Perhaps answers to these questions could be found by comparing *Bailed up* with its family of bush-life paintings in one room, even though the temptation to display it with Roberts's late work may be overwhelming. Others of the family might have a

Bailed up, (detail), 1895, Newstead and Inverell, NSW, and Sydney, 1927, Kallista, Victoria, oil on canvas, 134.5 x 182.8 cm; The Art Gallery of New South Wales, Sydney, Purchased 1933

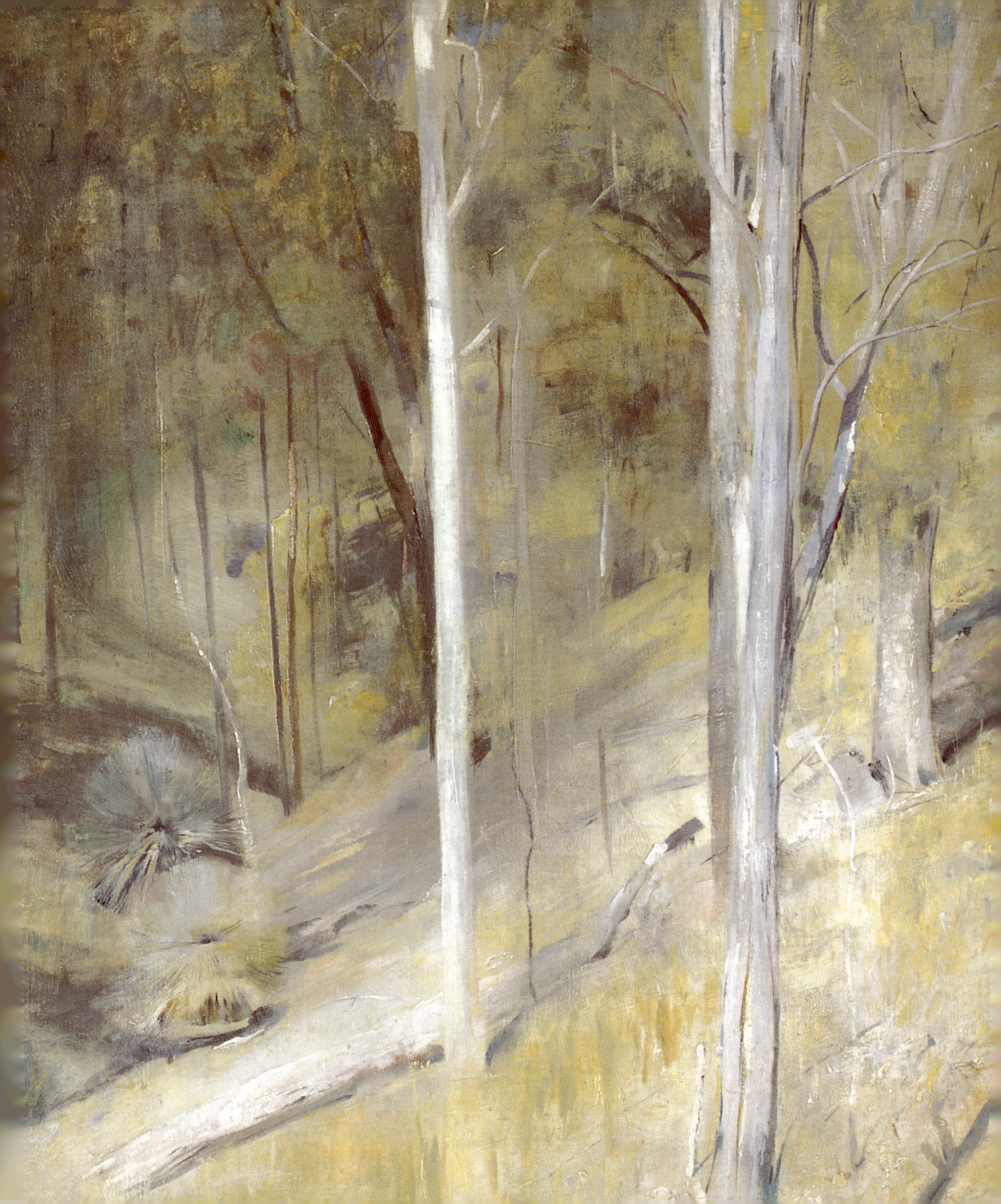

more instant appeal. The motif of *A break away!*, for example, has the impact of an action shot filmed by a swooping helicopter. It is not necessary to examine it at close quarters to feel the adrenalin rush of a moment's panic, as a rider tries desperately to stop a mob of sheep stampeding down to a water-hole. Suspended in heat and dust, like a video image halted by the pause button, the powerful dynamics of this composition can be read from far away. It evokes, especially if we can imagine substituting cattle for sheep, some of the reckless events associated with the wild American West. It is no wonder that when *Bailed up* was first exhibited in 1895 the press preferred Frank Mahony's bustling Australian paintings of Americanised 'cowboys' and 'outlaws', such as the cattlepiece *Rounding up a straggler*, 1889, and the mounted pursuit of bushrangers *As in the Days of Old*, 1892, both of which Roberts would have seen hanging in the collection of the Art Gallery of New South Wales. Time has shown Mahony's work for the trivial, overblown illustration that it always was. Against such action-packed pictures, however, the static solemnity of *Bailed up* seems to have worked against its general appeal.

This may be said even when it is compared with Roberts's two major sheep-shearing paintings, *Shearing the rams* and *The Golden Fleece*. Those two works, filled with large-scaled figures, exude a sweaty nobility and mysterious concentration of interiorised energy which make *Bailed up* appear uneventful, an effortless, artificial tableau of little figures dwarfed by nature's setting and held in bright light before the curtain closes. Yet by considering its deceptive ease, which belies the difficulty Roberts had in realising his intention, we may appreciate *Bailed up* as one of his greatest achievements.

Bailed up reveals its qualities best with a patient examination of detail. The composition has been cunningly constructed with diagonal and vertical tree-trunks and shadows leading the eye up to, around and beyond the dramatis personæ. The landscape rises to the very top of the picture – no sky, and no space for escape – and the gaze soon descends once more to the lower half, forced to contain itself within the flat parameters of the picture. Scanning the surface further brings forth the real richness of the work since, as much as *Bailed up* may be about armed robbery, or landscape, or historical mythology, it is equally about the transforming process of painting.

Roberts's struggle enabled him to arrive instinctively at a majestic synthesis. Light became paint, and paint became light and we cannot tell the difference between the two, whether it is in the radiance of the shirts and hats of the figures, or the straw-coloured grass and silvery tree-trunks of the midsummer landscape – and if the cast shadows of the trunks are painted from observation it is late afternoon on this south-west facing hillside, though it seems for the bushranging incident itself that the intention is high noon. Day after day Roberts walked three kilometres uphill on the road from Paradise, where he stayed because it was closer than Newstead, climbed up a ladder to 'The Perch' and stared at the hot stillness he was setting down on his canvas which had been wired to a railing. This was the coda that he transferred to the coach scene itself; stillness and light, investing the figures with an almost mystical calm. Indeed he created the feeling that time had stopped in the small, transient affairs of humankind. As with the unlikely

Bailed up, (detail), 1895, Newstead and Inverell, NSW, and Sydney, 1927, Kallista, Victoria, oil on canvas, 134.5 x 182.8 cm; The Art Gallery of New South Wales, Sydney, Purchased 1933

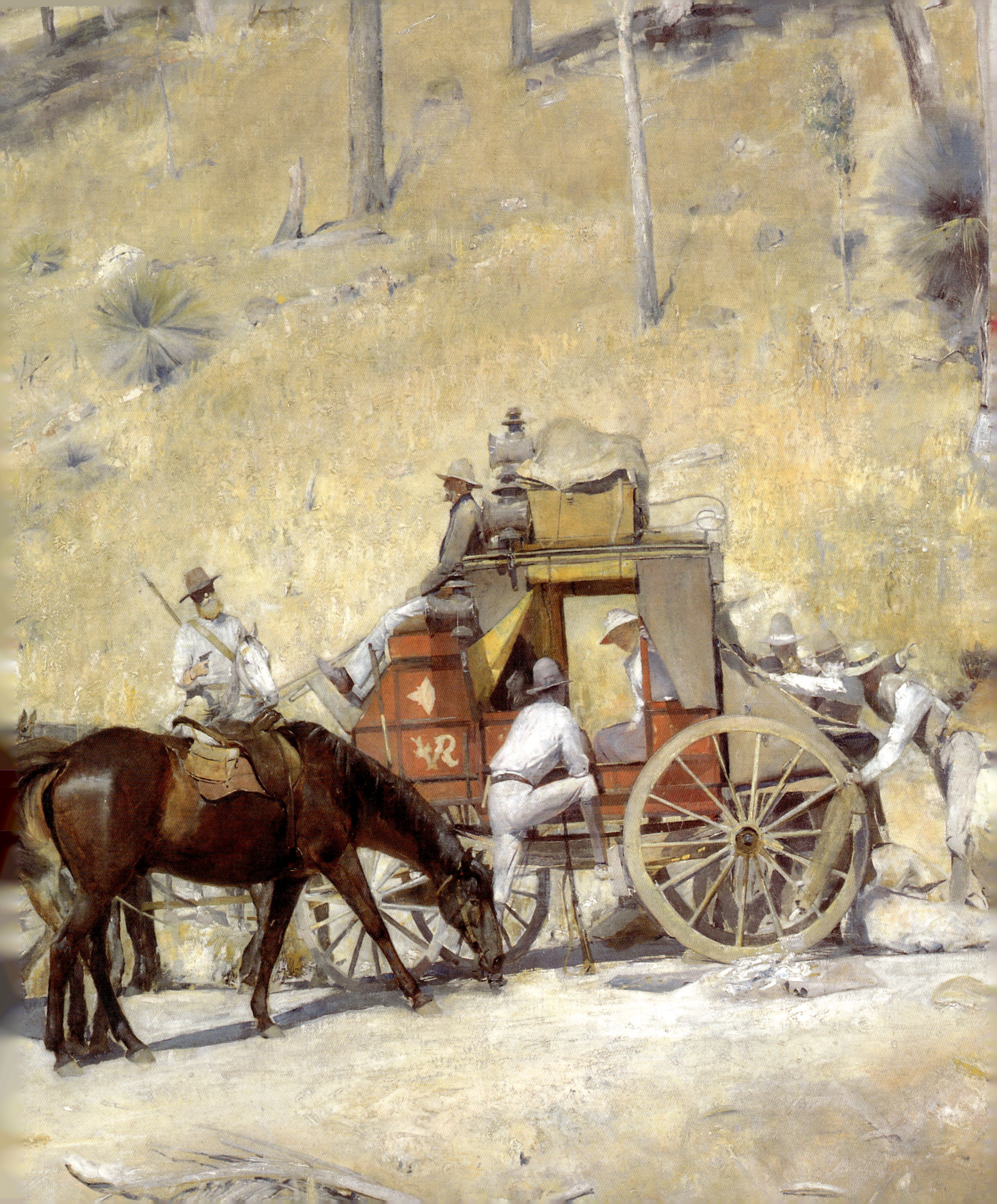

and inexplicable creatures grouped by Giambattista Tiepolo in his *Scherzi di Fantasia*, an all-pervading, all-redeeming, saturating light became the most important subject of the work. The sense that we are observing a kind of fairytale incident, strangely remote from yet hypnotised by it, was carried even more tellingly into Roberts's companion bushranging picture *In a corner on the Macintyre*, painted about the same time.[4] Nowhere in the entire history of Australian painting has such a sense been better rendered, particularly in *Bailed up*, where mystery, human incident and the experience of the Australian bush are embraced within a highly disciplined but spellbinding command of pictorial breadth.[5]

The remaining question which tantalises is a technical one, and concerns the extent to which Roberts repainted *Bailed up* in 1927. The surface of the painting – scraped, reworked, impasted, glazed, restated – is like a fossilised ocean bed, and traversing its bumps, dents and crevices with the naked eye does not easily expose what is old or new; only the impression of a miraculous embodiment of the painting's own history of making. What we do know is that Roberts inscribed two dates on the painting – 1895 and 1927 – and said he reworked it extensively in 1927 in his current manner.[6] This was at a period when he had become much more a meditative artist than a descriptive one, and thus of profound interest to certain later painters of Australian landscape. And that, in the end, is the telling factor which may distinguish *Bailed up* from the period of its conception. For although he was no Poussin, nor even a Puvis, he had an astute intuition for *the grid*.[7] In other words, at his best, he could orchestrate with genius all the aspects of a painting, be they naturalistic or abstract, into the values of a flat surface. In this way *Bailed up* straddles two worlds. It began as an idea for an historical narrative of the nineteenth century, but finished, through Roberts's difficulties, as a scaffolding by which he could be in grand scale a painter for the twentieth.

In a corner on the Macintyre, 1895, Inverell, New South Wales, oil on canvas, 71.7 x 86.4 cm; National Gallery of Australia, Canberra

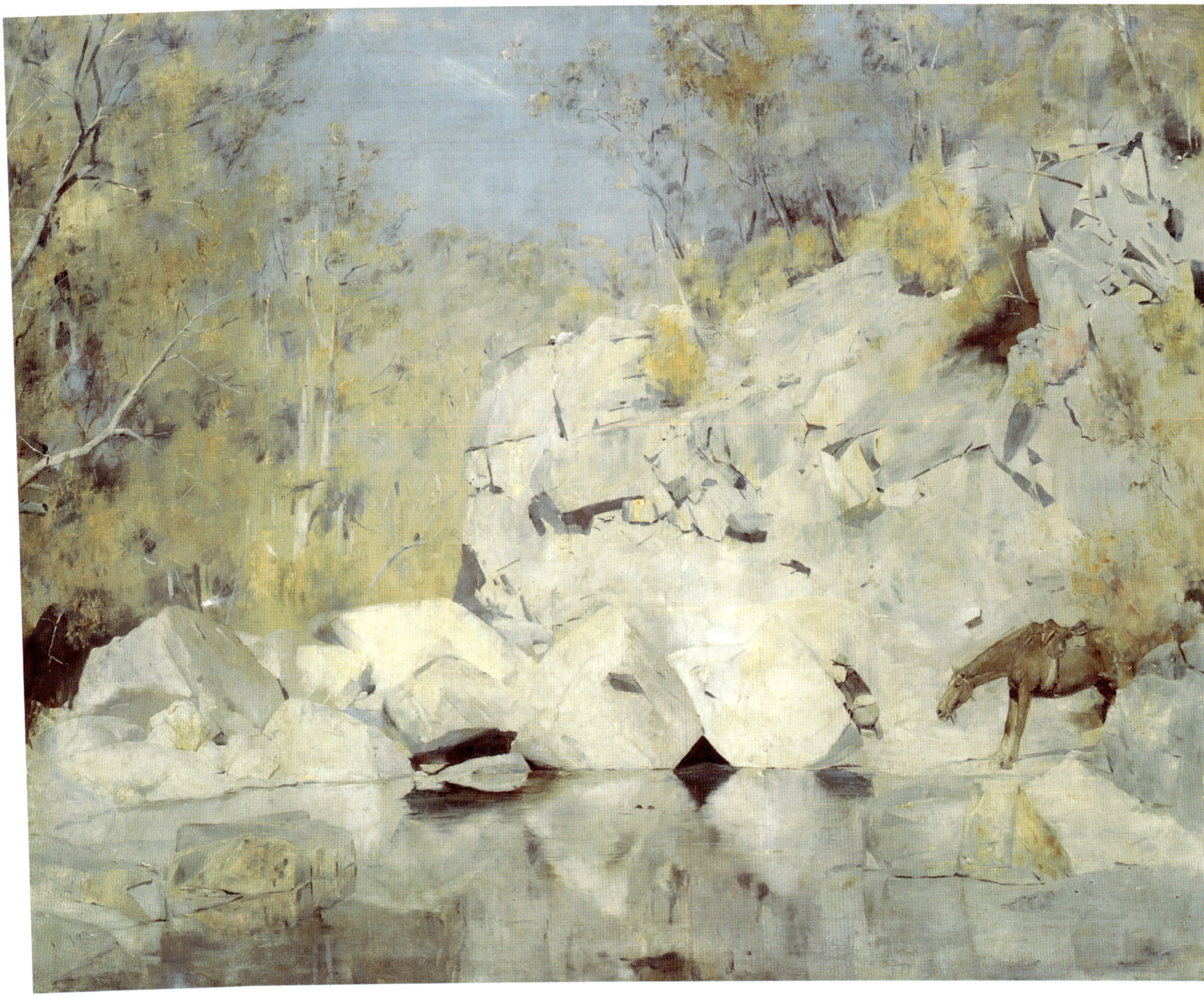

Masculinity and Modernity

Leigh Astbury

That Tom Roberts's artist friends should nickname him 'the Bulldog' suggests something of the force of his personality. Though not without a hint of criticism, D.H. Souter's description of Roberts in 1906 emphasises his formidable character:

> We saw an elderly young man, who stooped slightly, but was yet tall enough to seem above the average height of our painters ... Lean, bearded and prematurely bald, with cold grey eyes set deep beneath a domed brow. A sympathetic mouth that seldom curved in a smile; a trait all the more remarkable in a mob who thrived on laughter as we did ... We heard his voice, harsh and a trifle patronising, speaking in clear, incisive tones ... sharp crisp sentences ... but when he spoke he always had something to say, and said it in a fashion that set it beyond criticism.[1]

During the late nineteenth century when the cult of manliness still flourished, Roberts appeared to his contemporaries to be "a manly man". Years later, writing in the catalogue of Roberts's 1932 memorial exhibition, the art-museum director and critic J.S. MacDonald still saw fit to praise the artist's "masculine and robust personality", even more than his work.[2]

The masculinist bias of Roberts's art has been customarily identified in his representation of "strong, masculine labour" in the well-known pastoral figure subjects, such as *Shearing the rams* or *The Golden Fleece*. Yet at the same time that he was creating such icons of masculine labour in the 1880s and 1890s he was also establishing a reputation as a leading society portraitist, with a proclivity for sensitive portraits of women. His friend and fellow artist, John Russell, remembered his "wondrously tender manner" towards the opposite sex.[3] The obvious eclecticism of Roberts's œuvre can be partly attributed to the survival in late-nineteenth-century Australian art of distinct subject categories – such as still-life, portraiture, landscape, history painting, everyday life 'genre' painting etc. Yet to interpret his art simply in terms of an eclecticism of style and subject may be to miss the web of ideological connections which underlie and lend coherence to his work. A shrewd and committed professional artist, Roberts was subject to the dominant ideological currents of his time but he also sought to exploit some of those ideologies in his art.

Masculinism emerges as perhaps the most pervasive ideological influence on him, largely because its representation invariably intersects with that of other ideologies, such as modernity, race and imperialism. There was in this sense no singular or fixed masculine ideology directing his art, but rather a series of related masculinities which can be identified through their representation in different subjects.

Before his return to Melbourne in 1885, after an absence of four years abroad, Roberts in some of his London works had registered his response to ideas of the modernity of the city. There are small, delicate pictures, such as *Thames scene*, c1884, and *Trafalgar Square*, c1884, which followed the contemporary example of James McNeill Whistler in cloaking

Lumbering, c1893-96, New South Wales, watercolour on paper, 59.7 x 99.5 cm; National Gallery of Australia, Canberra Purchased 1978

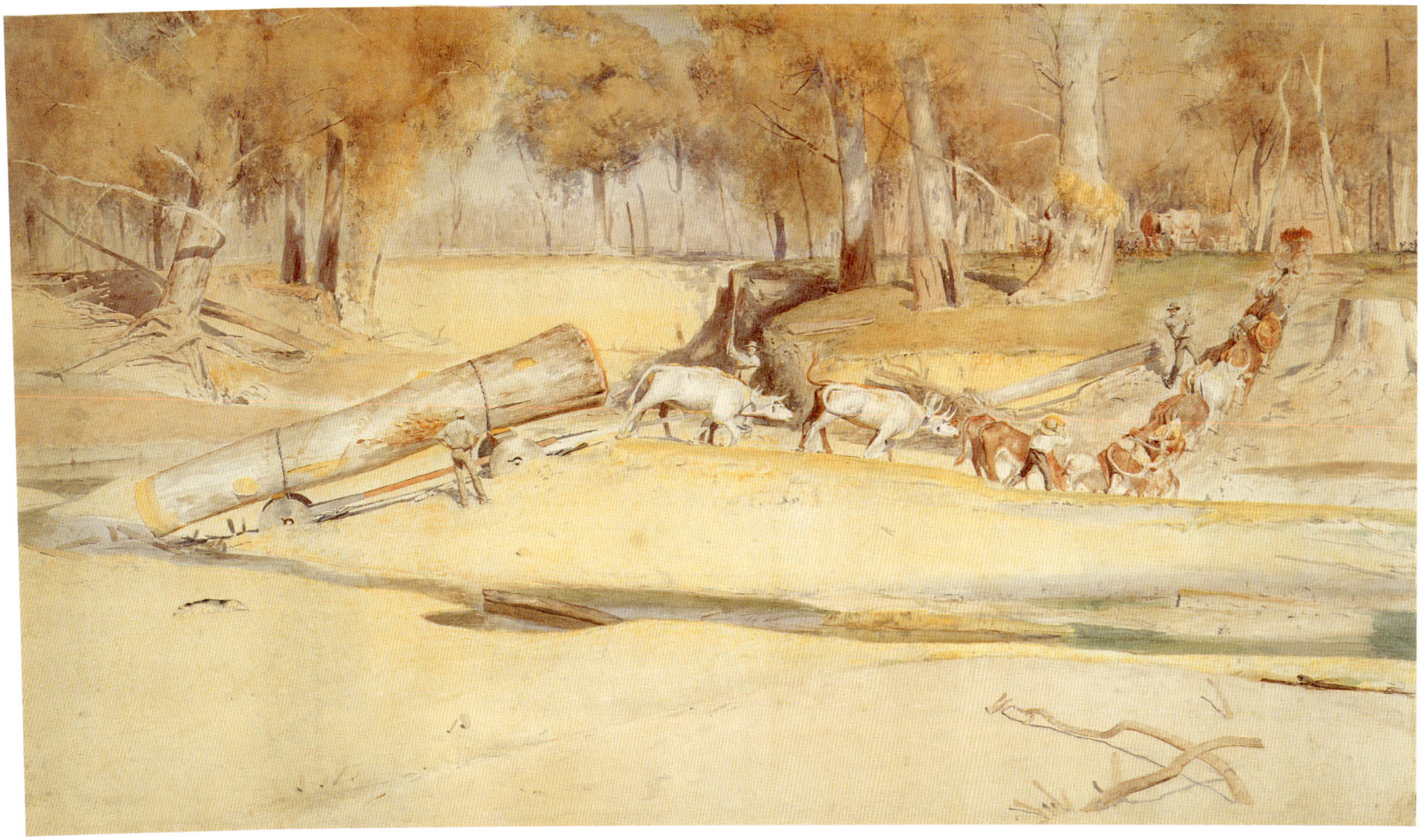

the forms of the city in a veil of atmosphere, revealing its hidden poetry while simultaneously disguising its less palatable commercial or industrial features. More descriptive in character are some monochrome wash drawings which signal Roberts's early interest in the urban crowd scene and the fashions and leisure activities of the bourgeoisie, especially the theatre.[4] The task that confronted Roberts in painting the local urban scene on his return to Melbourne was, then, comparable with that faced by immigrant artists, such as Girolamo Nerli or Ugo Catani, whose recent presence in the city's art circles added to their cosmopolitan flavour. Like the immigrant artists, he would have recognised the commonality of urban experience that characterised all great European cities. Yet in Australia the ease with which the experience of Old World cities could be translated into artistic conventions established by a painter such as Whistler could be weighed against what was perceived to be distinctive and dynamic, if not perhaps occasionally vulgar, in the corresponding experience of New World cities.

The call for a painter capable of expressing "the heroism of modern life [that] surrounds and presses upon us" had been voiced with consummate eloquence by the French poet Charles Baudelaire. His seminal ideas regarding the nature of modernity and the necessity for contemporaneity in art were gradually disseminated in the discourse of English-speaking art criticism. In 1887 the English critic Frederick Wedmore wrote for the Magazine of Art an article "Modern Life in Modern Art" in which he declared that "the real historical painting of our time is the record of the characteristics of our life – its labour, its pleasure, its principal personages". The "real world" must be the motive of pictorial art, Wedmore argues:

> It must paint the atmosphere that rolls over our great cities. In its character-painting does it not show already that it is not hard to be interested in the modern physician, in the man of business, in the woman of society? In its draughtsmanship of the figure it may learn, I think, more and more to take heed of and to chronicle those types of force and flexibility and serviceable beauty which, in our ideals of to-day, take precedence of those old types of ascetic reticence and timid restraint.

It is as though Wedmore is predicting the direction to be followed in the late 1880s and 1890s by Roberts's portraiture and figure subjects. He identifies the emphasis on the present as being part of the literary discourse of the era: "Literary art comes to us, as in Browning, as in Walt Whitman, in new forms, refreshed with the later experiences, renewing its youth, and being ... an alert guide for us today".[5]

The issue of modernity had indeed become a crucial one for Australian artists and critics by the close of the 1880s. In 1890 the visiting American art critic Sidney Dickinson gave to the Victorian Artists' Society a lecture titled "What Should Australian Artists Paint?" He stipulated in Baudelairean terms that "It should be the ambition of our artists to present on canvas the earnestness, rigour, pathos, and heroism of the life that is about them. These qualities exist if we will but open our eyes to them". Singling out Tom Roberts and Frederick McCubbin as painters who had already made "some efforts in this direction", Dickinson argued that "the mixed life of the city and characteristic

Ulverstone, 1890s, Tasmania, oil on canvas, 40.6 x 68.7 cm; Private collection, Melbourne

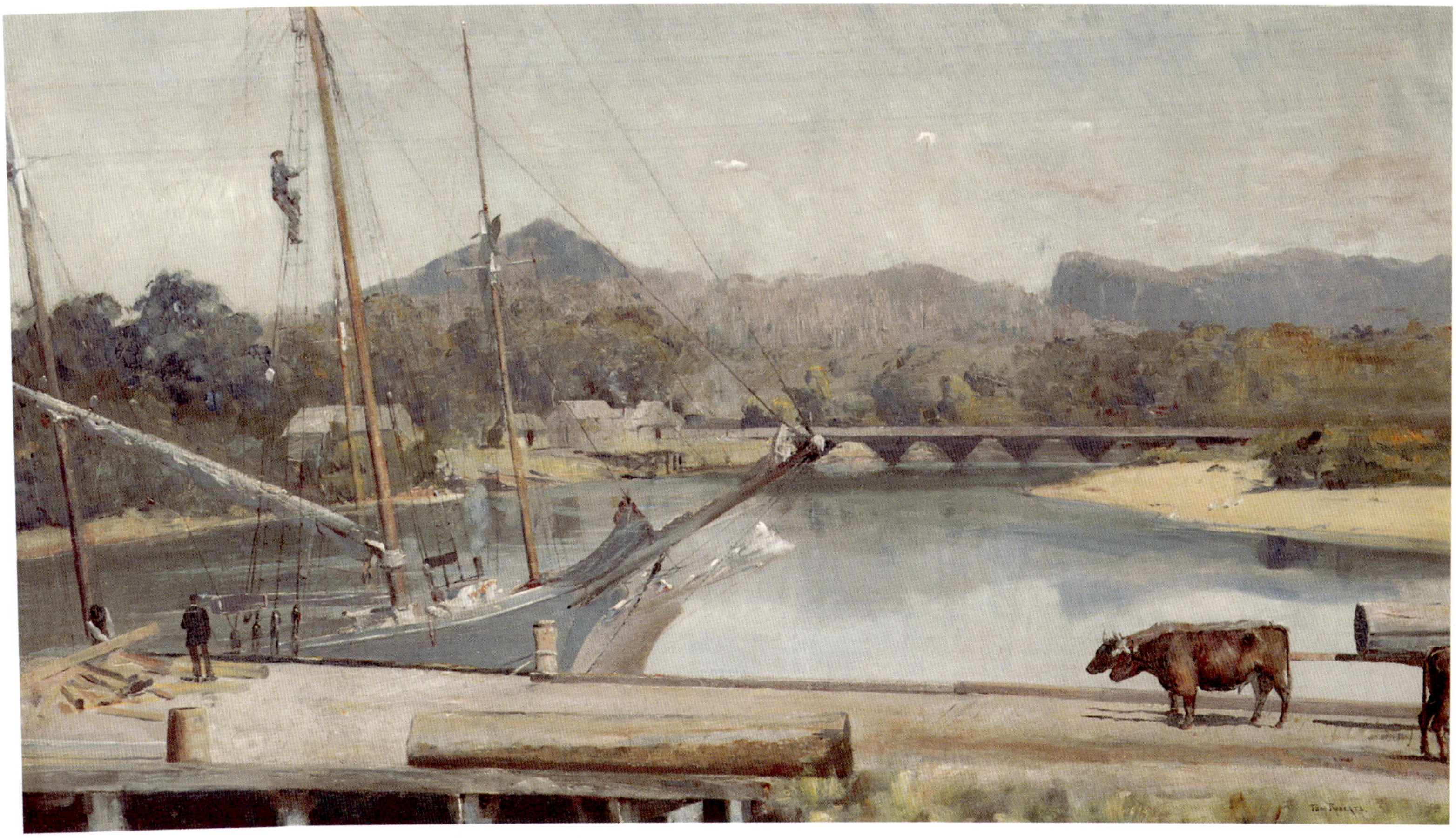

life of the station and bush furnish countless subjects, whose successful description would attract universal attention in the galleries and saloons [*sic*] of Old World exhibitions, but are here ignored because of their familiarity".[6] The heroism of modern life, to be located in *both* city and bush subjects in the New World, was thus counterpoised with the potential attraction of such subjects for art audiences in the Old World.

Frederick Wedmore had similarly associated the "new forms" of Walt Whitman's poetry with the spirit of modernity. In Whitman's robust, masculine verse contemporaries found confirmaton of how the "muscle and pluck" of free, individual men on the American frontier were instrumental in creating the nation and building its cities. As if by a process of imaginative transference, the Old World was to be somehow re-invigorated and made youthful by new societies at its margins.[7] This was also representative of the critical response to Whitman in Australia. In 1890 Charles Conder variously described him as "rough & to the point" and as "a rugged genius".[8] After his death in 1892 Whitman was increasingly lauded as a poet capable of expressing "the spirit of modern democracy". The anonymous writer of an obituary article titled "Walt Whitman, By One Who Knew Him" that appeared in the Illustrated Australian News of 2 May 1892 found that "comradeship is the central note of that democracy which he was ever celebrating". The democratic tenor of his ideas and beliefs was said to derive from his sympathetic understanding of the particular qualities of modern life. Thus the poet and critic William Gay found him in "complete rapport with modern life, he is the poet of the great movements in which that life is expressing itself".[9] In 1894 Roberts's friend John Le Gay Brereton, later Professor of English Literature at the University of Sydney, wrote that Whitman "expresses the modern man, because his poems are intensely subjective". He went on to elucidate how "the pain, satisfaction, and greatness of love are to be experienced in comradeship – 'adhesiveness', as Whitman calls it – 'the dear love of man for his comrade, the attraction of friend to friend'. This 'manly attachment' is pure, passionate love".[10] The critical reception and influence of Whitman in Australia suggests some of the ways in which the project of modernity could be easily elided with masculine ideologies in contemporary discourse.

The city of Melbourne in the 1880s boom years experienced rapid change, expansion and disruption, conditions symptomatic of the dynamic force of modernity. The fabric of the city and its buildings was changing so incessantly that it appeared to take on a provisional nature, as observed by Richard Twopeny in his *Town Life in Australia*, published in 1883:

> In spite of the abundance of large and fine-looking buildings, there is a rather higgledy-piggledy look about the town ... There are no building laws, and every man has built as seemed best in his own eyes. The town is constantly outgrowing the majority of its buildings ... there are still gaps in the line of the streets towards the outskirts.[11]

The unfinished and arbitrary character of the city mirrored other aspects of social dislocation as older, established patterns of conducting colonial commerce and industry

Christmas flowers and Christmas belles, c1899, Sydney, oil on canvas, 52.1 x 36.2 cm; Manly Art Gallery & Museum, NSW, Gift of Colonel A. Spain 1940

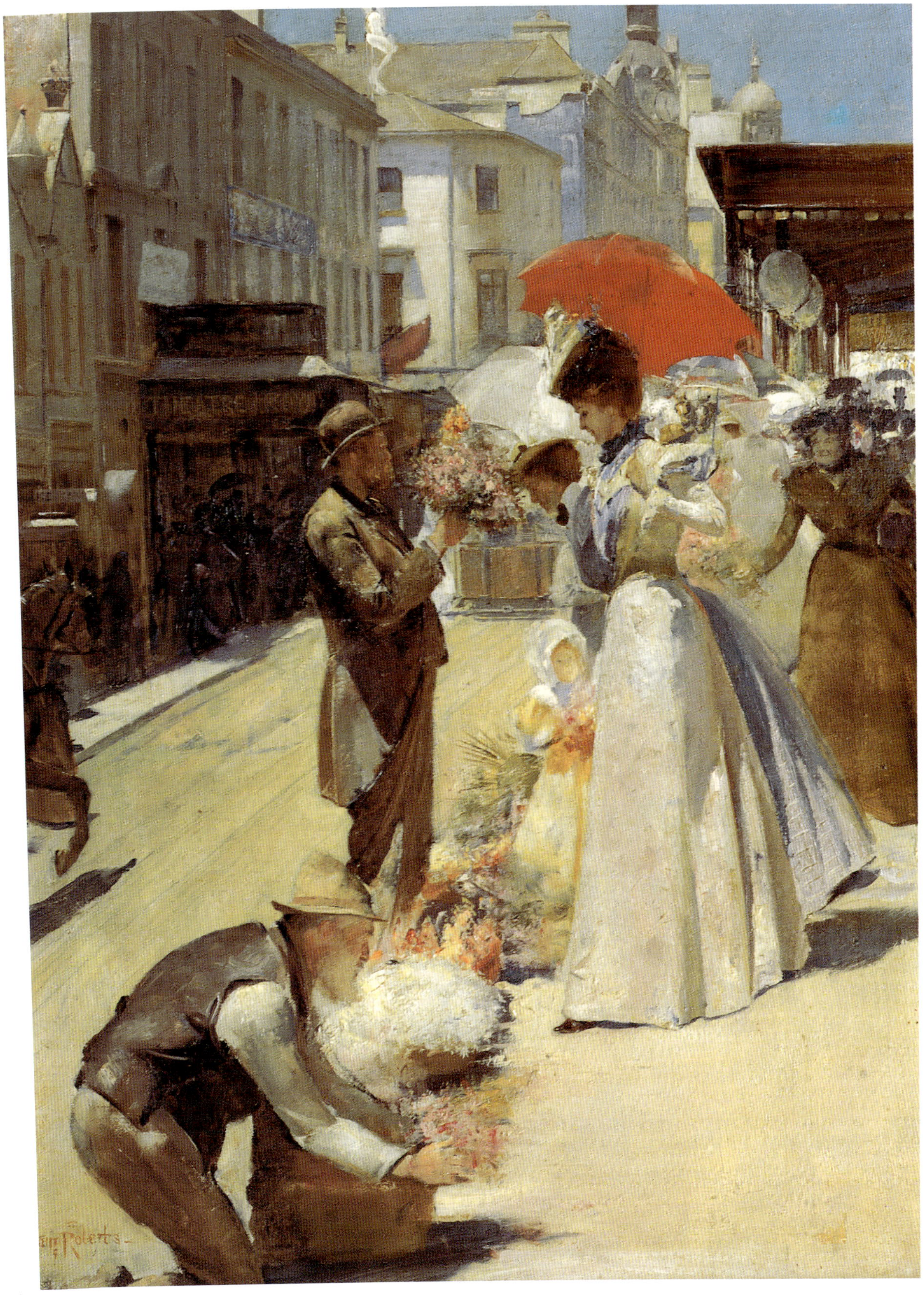

were at first threatened and then transformed.[12] Yet it was impossible to ignore the outward signs of pride in the headlong progress of 'Marvellous Melbourne' – as it had been designated in 1885 by George Augustus Sala, a celebrity journalist, visiting from London. The Australian Building, at the corner of Elizabeth Street and Flinders Lane, completed in the 1888 Centennial Year, was a mixture of English and American architectural styles; for a short time it could claim to be one of the tallest buildings in the world. With the benefit of hindsight occasioned by the economic depression of the early 1890s, Roberts became critical of the rebuilding of the city during the boom: "the architect has unworthily helped the client to rear edifices which reflect perfectly the period of their making, and whose note is expensive vulgarity ... and so the styles are like the money that made them – borrowed".[13]

Against the sense of uncertainty and contingency which is one side of the experience of modernity, Roberts appears to have responded positively to the energy, excitement and cosmopolitanism that characterised Melbourne in the 1880s. In a more muted form than Paris of the 1860s and 1870s, Melbourne took on elements of self-fabrication and display that are linked to the idea of the society of the spectacle. Twopeny observed that there was "undoubtedly that general love of display, which is almost as characteristic of Melbourne as it is of Paris". That Melbourne had "decidedly the best set of shops" in Australia was indicative of the city's "metropolitan and fashionable character". Shop windows were "dressed anew every week, and with a taste which reminds one of Paris". Melbourne "nearly always has its dress-clothes on", with women's fashions being closely attuned to very recent developments in Paris.[14] The repeated references to Paris as the source of what was current in the realm of fashion and display in Melbourne emphasise a social dimension of modernity to which Roberts responded.

In his famous essay on "The Painter of Modern Life" Baudelaire had nominated fashion as a defining feature of modernity:

> Fashion should thus be considered as a symptom of the taste for the ideal which floats on the surface of the crude, terrestrial and loathsome bric-à-brac that the natural life accumulates in the human brain ... [Fashions] should be thought of as vitalised and animated by the beautiful women who wore them.[15]

For Baudelaire it was the flâneur, the disengaged male spectator who wanders anonymously in the crowd, who is capable of discerning the social and psychological dimensions of fashion and dress. In a complementary strategy, Roberts adopted the role of dandy or Aesthete as his artistic persona during these Melbourne years. Just as the dandy was traditionally renowned for his impeccable sense of dress and manners, Roberts was noted to have worn the first opera hat seen in Melbourne. The continental, and especially Parisian, character of local bohemia in late-nineteenth-century Australia was also often remarked upon. With his command of French, Roberts responded to such paradigms by opening his "picturesquely arranged" studio to the public on one afternoon each week and staging polite gatherings where the latest French journals were discussed. In 1886 two works from his relatively rare ventures into the field of commercial illustration took as their subjects the sophisticated ambience of Melbourne's

Mosman's Bay, 1894, Sydney, oil on canvas , 63.5 x 106.2cm; New England Regional Art Museum, Armidale, NSW, Gift of Howard Hinton 1933. The Howard Hinton Collection.

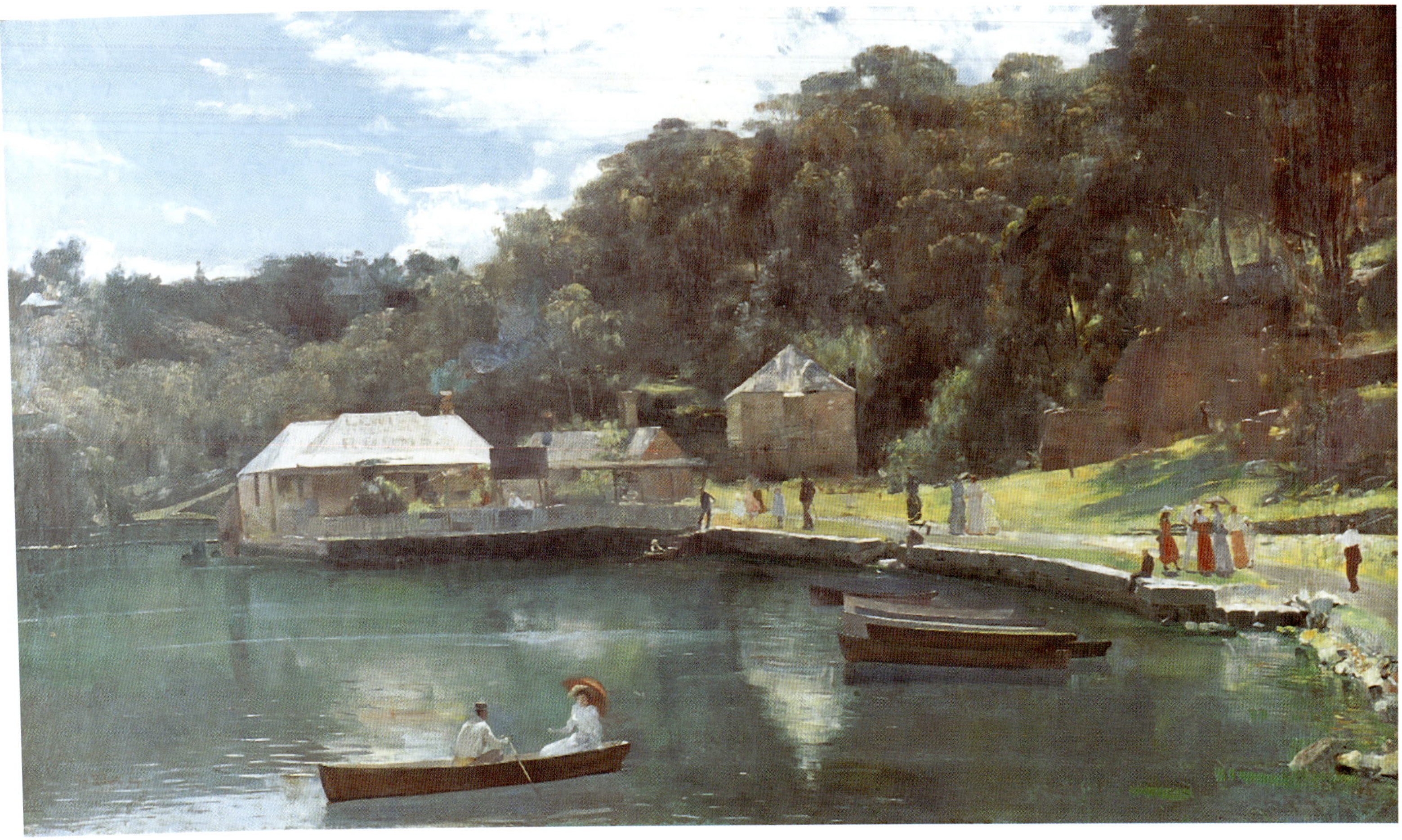

social life. A pen & ink drawing, *At the Melbourne Cup*, evidently intended for publication in The Bulletin, treats the prime event in the city's social calendar and portrays a crowd scene with splendidly attired men and women; an illustration, *Promenade, Queenscliff*, published in the Illustrated Australian News, similarly focuses on fashionably dressed men and women promenading at what was then one of Melbourne's popular seaside resorts.[16] Both images depict the bourgeoisie at leisure, a theme popularised in the art of the French Impressionists and their followers, and both deal specifically with the meaning of fashion and display in modern society.

Almost of necessity, the experience of modernity in New World societies was a hybrid one. Both the inhabitants of New World cities and overseas visitors invariably gauged their achievements and distinctiveness in relation to those of the Old World. This became a convenient formula, for example, within the genre of late-nineteenth-century travel writing. Some of these tensions between Old World and New World conceptions of modernity are subsequently played out in Roberts's different approaches to urban subjects. *Going home* and *Evening train to Hawthorn*, which were exhibited in 1889 in 'The 9 by 5 Impression Exhibition', follow the spirit of his earlier Whistlerian London scenes in showing the city rendered anonymous and then transformed by nightfall, mist or fog. A famous passage from Whistler's 'Ten o'Clock Lecture', first delivered in February 1885, evokes the poetic mood of the urban scene:

> And when the evening mist clothes the riverside with poetry, as with a veil, and the poor buildings lose themselves in the dim sky, and the warehouses are palaces in the night, and the whole city hangs in the heavens, and fairyland is before us – then the wayfarer hastens home ... [17]

Going home, c1889, Melbourne, oil on cedar cigar-box lid, 23.2 x 13.5 cm; National Gallery of Australia, Canberra, Purchased 1976

The expression of modernity in *Evening train to Hawthorn* seems similarly ambivalent, being conveyed as much through the portrayal of phenomena – steam, smoke and the atmospheric sky – as by the concrete symbols of progress in the train and the telegraph pole seen teetering on the left. Whether consciously or not, the image juxtaposes the old and new in the city's development: the spires of the Scots and Independent Churches, silhouetted against the city skyline, are emblematic of an earlier period, the 1860s and 1870s. It was the rapid expansion of Melbourne's suburban railway networks in the 1880s, aided by the punctuality gained from the railway telegraph, that was vital in enhancing the leisure opportunities of the bourgeoisie, while paradoxically ordering and regulating them.[18] As in European cities, the introduction since the 1850s of gas street-lighting had created new public spaces for evening leisure; the play of light, glitter and shadow on reflective street surfaces imbued the city with an aura of romance and magic. Promenading the streets at night, as seen in *Going home*, became a fusion of private and public experience: bourgeois couples and lovers could feel the pleasure of being alone at the same time as they presented themselves to the public gaze.[19]

Compared with the sophistication and cosmopolitanism of the urban images that Roberts – and his younger colleagues Charles Conder and Arthur Streeton – showed at the 9 by 5 exhibition, the immediate impression conveyed by his *Allegro con brio, Bourke Street west* is that of the energy and bustle of a frontier town. The city rendered anonymous

Evening train to Hawthorn, c1889, Melbourne, oil on cedar panel, 14.0 x 22. 6 cm; The Art Gallery of New South Wales, Sydney, Stinson Bequest Fund 1991

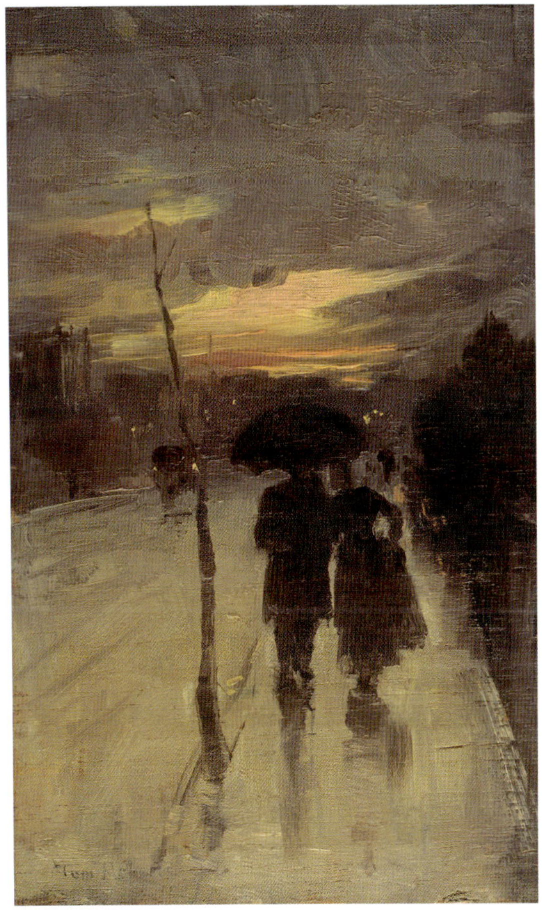

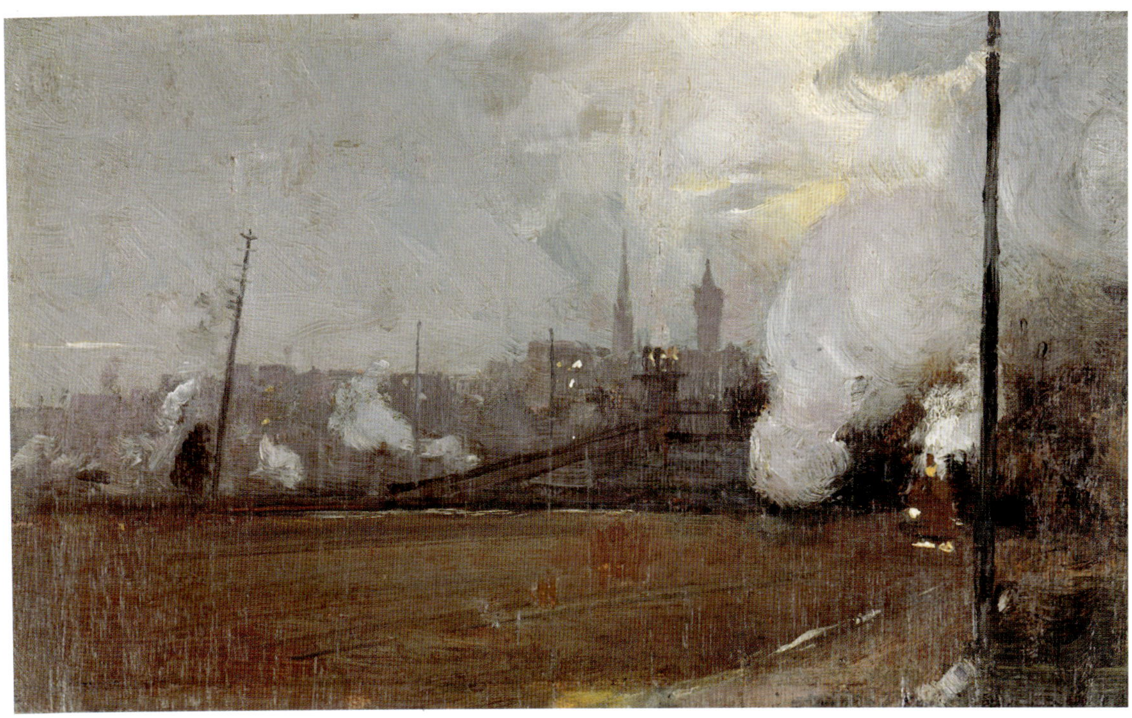

by nightfall is here replaced by a readable portrayal of a well-known local street, captured in the full sunlight of an Australian summer. Table Talk on 28 November 1890 explained how the view of Roberts's "animated subject ... is taken from the north-side of Bourke Street, looking towards Queen Street, thus enabling the artist to focus on all the hustle and bustle and life that congregates near the Post Office". The painting was probably completed in the summer of 1885-86 (that is, before the first cable tram travelled down Bourke Street on 2 October 1886) but Roberts returned to it in his Melbourne studio in late 1890, and added the trio of young women, lower left. The frontier associations of *Allegro con brio, Bourke Street west* are, then, best understood in the context of developments occurring in Australian art closer to its date of completion. Scarcely a week after the opening of the 9 by 5 exhibition in August 1889, Table Talk carried a report that a group of artists, including Roberts and Streeton, had become "tired of the slow progress of Australian art" and were making a bid for European recognition by sending paintings "with a decided leaning towards nationality" to the Royal Academy and the Paris Salon.[20] *Shearing the rams*, which Roberts completed in his Melbourne studio in May 1890, may have been one of these paintings intended for exhibition overseas. At the March 1890 exhibition of the Victorian Artists' Society Streeton had shown his picture *The selector's hut: Whelan on the log*, an Australian national subject inspired in part by Whitman's line, "Muscle and pluck forever". Roberts thus finished his Bourke Street picture during a period when he and other local artists were painting subjects "with a decided leaning towards nationality", conscious of the potential appeal of such subjects to overseas audiences.

Visitors to Melbourne in the 1870s and 1880s frequently remarked on the fact that it was an 'American-style' city, compared with, for example, the more old-fashioned picturesqueness of Sydney. Melbourne bore the signs of the robust vigour of a New World city: its material prosperity and pulsating commercial life; the energy and 'get up and go' attitudes of its citizens; the newness of its architecture and its constantly changing appearance; and its wide streets laid out according to a grid structure. Roberts's Bourke Street cityscape derives much of its meaning and effect from his skilful interweaving of New World and Old World interpretations of modernity. The wide, hot and dusty street, with its distinctive verandahs offering refuge from the sun, conveys something of a frontier rawness. The Picturesque Atlas of Australasia described the western section of Bourke Street in terms which evoked this rough vitality:

> Here congregate the saddlers, harness makers and farriers, and here, too, are the numerous horse bazaars, resonant with the clatter of iron-shod hoofs, the cracking of whips, the hum of bidders discussing the 'points' of the horses put up for sale, and the stentorian voice of the auctioneer ringing through the vaulted mews.[21]

Contemporary descriptions of this section of Bourke Street imply that an insider's knowledge of horses and the horse-trade was part of the experience of a frontier city, and this may help to explain why Roberts chose to omit reference in his picture to the coming of the cable trams. For long-time residents of the colony his subject also held memories and associations of 'the early days' when crowds thronged the Melbourne

Lady with a parasol, early 1890s, Sydney, oil on canvas mounted on board, 45.7 x 28.2 cm; Private collection, Sydney

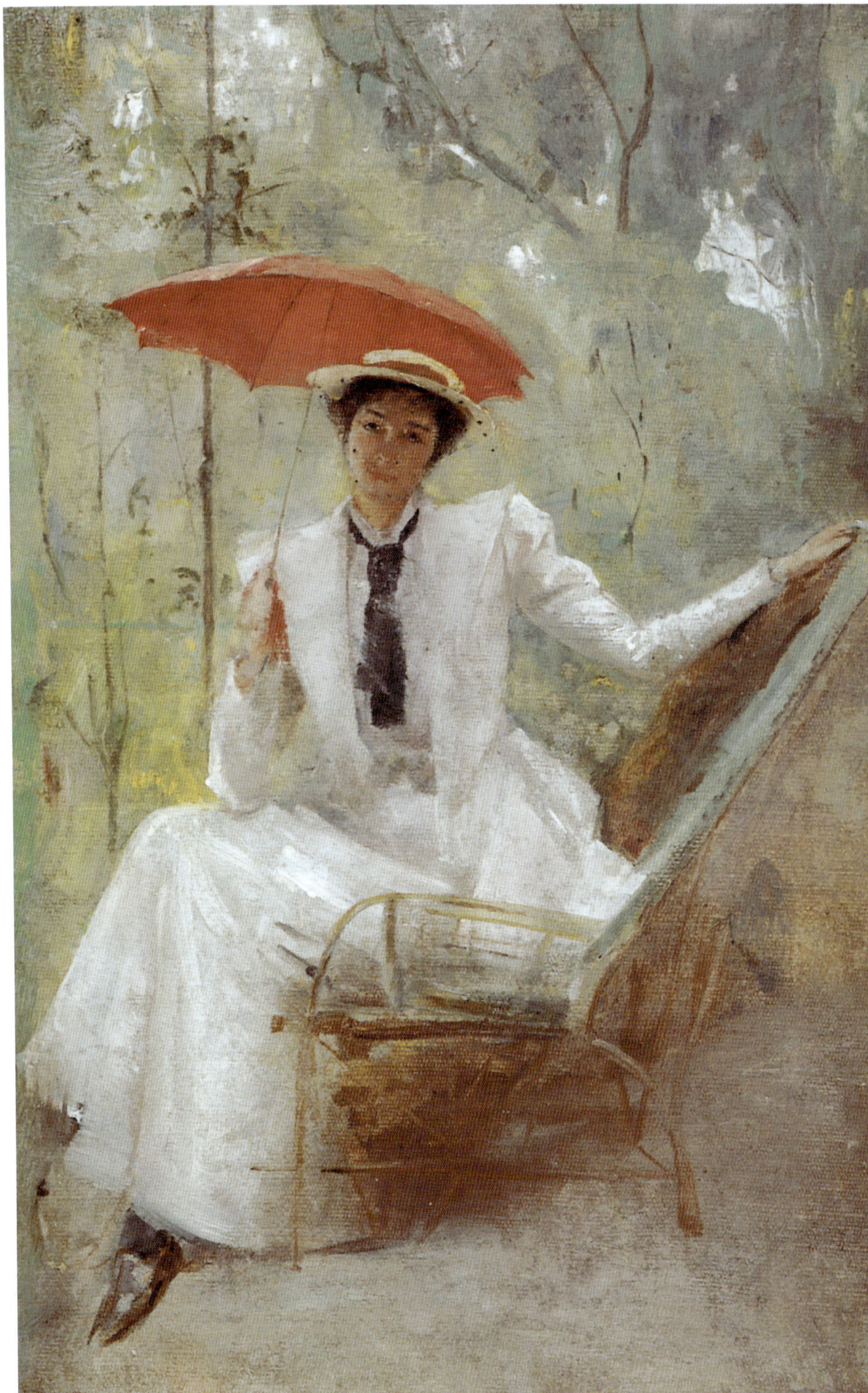

Post Office on the arrival of the monthly mail.[22] Since then, communications had been revolutionised by the advent of the telegraph and the streets of Melbourne were colonised by towering telegraph poles, the conspicuous presence of which in Roberts's picture would have been interpreted by contemporaries as a sign of progress.

The *Allegro con brio* of Roberts's title – "lively with spirit" – celebrates the energy and vitality to be found in this less salubrious area of Marvellous Melbourne. At the same time it pays homage to Whistler, with his fondness for employing musical titles. The formal influence of Whistler can be detected perhaps in the way in which the bright pastel shades of the picture are orchestrated into an overall colour harmony; or perhaps in the manner in which the dark forms of the horse carriages and the men's suits are organised to create zig-zag patterns and calligraphic accents up the rise of the hill. As important, however, as any stylistic influence, the Whistlerian allusion also signals Roberts's attempt to represent modernity in Bourke Street as a somewhat incongruent amalgam of the sophisticated manners of an Old World metropolis with the rough-edged dynamism of a big colonial city. His incisive rendering of costume and fashion suggests ambivalent aspects of a society in transition. Many of the women are shown carrying black umbrellas, or more fashionable dome-shaped parasols, to shield prized, pale complexions from the effects of the harsh sun. Twopeny had noted in 1883 an increased sophistication and restraint in ladies' fashions; his comment that "bright colours are still in vogue, but they are not necessarily loud or unpleasant beneath the austral sun" could be used to describe Roberts's last-minute portrayal of the figures of Miss Elizabeth Anna Fraser, her sister and a young friend as an up-to-date accent imposed on the left foreground of *Allegro con brio*. In the 1880s most Melbourne businessmen still wore black frockcoats, trousers and top hats, seen in Roberts's picture. They had adopted this conventional attire in the previous two decades as a sign of their metropolitan status and newfound commercial respectability. The unsuitability of such British urban fashions for Australia's hot weather led Twopeny to ask caustically: "Can you imagine yourself wearing a black coat and high hat with the thermometer jogging about from 70° to 110° in the shade?".[23]

For Roberts fashion and dress could be read as social signs: they were equally implicated in the role of the artist as dandy or flâneur, the detached observer of modern life. Baudelaire had long ago espoused the poetic beauty and universal equality of the dress-coat and the frockcoat as "the necessary garb of our suffering age".[24] The wide streets or boulevards of the planned city, with their regular straight lines, seem to have encouraged the complementary processes of urban display and voyeurism that came to characterise one experience of modernity. The high viewpoint employed by Roberts in *Allegro con brio, Bourke Street west* allows the spectator to view the ebb and flow of the crowd with moral detachment; there is a sense of energy and flux as the figures move in alternate, almost random, directions. Within this field of perpetual mobility, time becomes fleeting and contingent; the blurred movement of a figure on the left is registered only by an ambiguous blue smudge. Our eyes may finally come to rest, at the right, on a dark-suited figure in a top hat, standing alone next to a pole, his upper torso silhouetted

Frances Ross, c1898, Sydney, oil on wood, 62.3 x 47.0 cm; The Art Gallery of New South Wales, Sydney, Purchased 1954

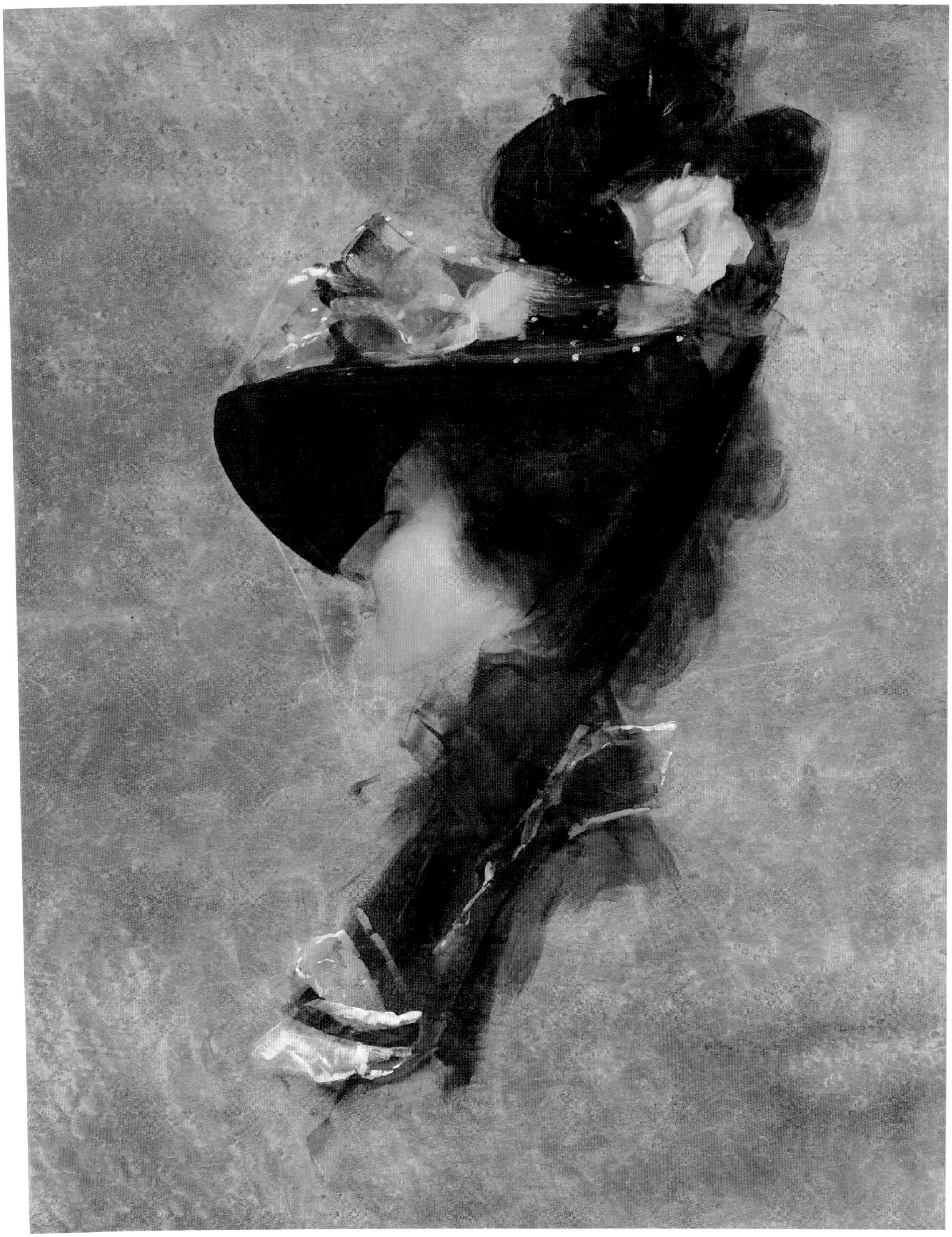

against a patch of sunlight. Perhaps this figure is Roberts's equivalent to the Baudelairean flâneur, an urban voyeur who surveys the scene with the customary cool detachment affected by the artist dandy. The disengaged male spectator representing the detachment of vision occurs elsewhere in Roberts's art: he may be found, for example, in the bowler-hatted gentleman of the bourgeoisie who leans languidly against the ship's decking to the left in *Coming South*; or even, perhaps, in the figure of the bushman who casually rests his head on his hand while he observes the busy shearing activity from the back of the shed in *The Golden Fleece*.

Roberts rarely treated the theme of vice and poverty in the modern city, a subject which attracted the attention of contemporary illustrators and slummer journalists. His etching *A Chinese cook shop*, 1887, is an exception. It shows a young caucasian woman, standing in what might be interpreted as a provocative pose, in the company of some Chinese men in the murky atmosphere of the cook shop. Slummer journalists characteristically represented the slums and opium dens of Little Bourke Street as a dark and menacing other world, the underside of the confident public spaces of Melbourne's predictable grid street pattern.[25] Women were especially vulnerable and prey to the evils of opium peddled by the Chinese in this morally depraved environment. In 1887, for example, Cassell's Picturesque Australasia devoted a separate chapter to Little Bourke Street: here were to be found "women of all sorts", most of them addicted to opium; neither education nor class could protect them from the evils of addiction, the writer noted, as the "graceful outline of a well-dressed girl brushed me in passing". The chapter included an illustration, *At Work: A Chinese kitchen*; such Chinese kitchens and workshops were often supposed to be disguises for their real purpose as opium dens. Roberts's etching no doubt carried similar associations and meanings for his contemporary audiences. In this etching the artist's treatment of race and gender conveys an ambivalent attitude towards modernity and evolving sexual roles. If the flâneur was free to wander anonymously amongst the city crowds, the spaces of modernity were nevertheless gendered; fashionably dressed women might promenade casually on the streets, but there remained certain 'foreign' areas of the city where the solitary, respectable woman did not venture without risk to her reputation.[26]

In two key images where he paid tribute to the dynamism of the modern city – *Allegro con brio, Bourke Street west*, 1885-86/1890, and *An autumn morning, Milson's Point, Sydney*, 1888 – Roberts chose to portray nodal points in the city's structure, centres of transport and communications. With the construction in 1886 of a cable tramway from Milson's Point to the heights of the North Shore at Ridge Street, the Milson's Point ferry terminal, seen in Roberts's picture, had recently become a busy site of transport interchange for ferries, vehicular punts, horse-drawn vehicles, trams and trains. The steam, smoke and pollution which cast a coppery light over the atmosphere serve to 'naturalise' the forces of industry and commerce which drive the energy of the city. The imagery of both these well-known pictures is, then, inseparable from the representation of the thriving energy of the work-day world. Roberts's portrayal of bourgeois leisure in the suburban bush or on suburban beaches is defined by its opposition to the vibrant movement of

Smike Streeton age 24, 1891, Sydney, oil on canvas, 45.7 x 35.7 cm; The Art Gallery of New South Wales, Sydney, Purchased 1945

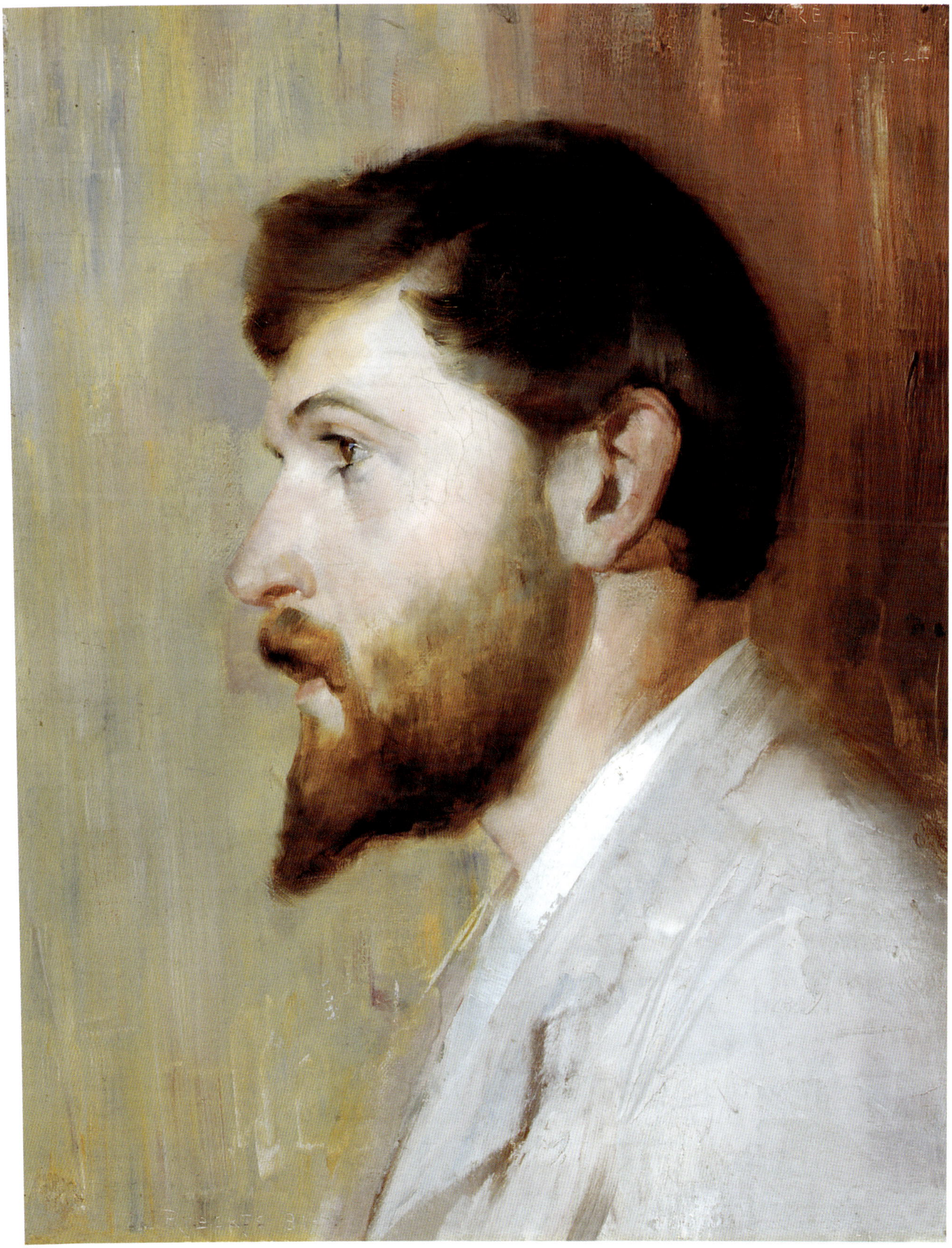

city crowds: these leisure pictures focus on an alternative urban ideal – the escape from the pressures of work and city living. In *The artists' camp* and *A Sunday afternoon picnic at Box Hill* the bush is presented as a site for respectable bourgeois recreation but the apparent solitude of these secluded scenes has been achieved through the artist carefully avoiding any hint of the suburban sprawl from the nearby township of Box Hill, its encroachment aided by the recent extension of the railway to the area. Emphasis falls on the perceived exclusivity of the bourgeois experience of nature and leisure; it is the cultivation of the individual sensibilities of the participants that matters in these scenes.

Yet the proximity of sites of work in the city to those of suburban leisure was acknowledged by most commentators as a positive advantage. Twopeny remarked that all Melbourne's more expensive suburbs "are connected with town by railway. A quarter of an hour will bring you ten miles to Brighton, and twelve minutes will take you to St. Kilda, the most fashionable watering-place".[27] In his 1887 seaside-suburb painting *Slumbering sea, Mentone*, Roberts did not dissolve distinctions between nature and culture as did Charles Conder in his image of the same place, *A holiday at Mentone*, painted a year later. Conder presented the Mentone shore as a spectacle to be consumed by the leisure-seeking bourgeoisie in their elegant costumes; Roberts, on the other hand, conveys the commodification of urban leisure by emphasising the contrast between the sophisticated dress and manner of the women and the natural wildness of the coastline. With the pristine whiteness of their fashionable dresses, these middle-class women are portrayed by Roberts as visitors within the landscape, presumably willing to pay for the privilege of hiring a boat and boatman for the occasion. There is little happening here to disturb the tranquil stillness of the balmy, sunlit day. Leisure, it seems, is represented as the antithesis of work. Yet the peaceful leisure activities of these genteel women could also be read as a reflection of the wealth generated by the commercial and industrial drive of the city.

Mosman's Bay provided a convenient Sydney Harbour location in the 1880s and 1890s for members of leisure-seeking urban society who wished to enjoy the natural beauties of their city in an atmosphere of ease and comfort. In his *Mosman's Bay*, 1894, Roberts succeeds in capturing the sense of display, stylishness and urban sophistication that characterised the lower-middle-class pursuit of leisure and recreation in this pretty, sheltered spot. It was painted during the period he was living a bachelor's existence as a resident of Curlew Camp at the adjacent Little Sirius Cove. Part of Mosman at this time was also set aside as a military reserve. It was no doubt the carrying out of manœuvres that provided inspiration for his painting, *"A" Battery Field Artillery, New South Wales*, 1896, in which the dashing uniforms of the soldiers, their mannered poses, and the nonchalant ease with which they perform their actions, all contribute to its aura of theatre and spectacle. The two pictures suggest parallels between military display and the decorous display of conventional leisure in well-ordered society.

The *"A" Battery Field Artillery*, in particular, suggests the elision of the values and ideologies of modernity, masculinism and imperialism. Such ideas were hardly new in the history

"A" Battery Field Artillery, New South Wales, 1896, Sydney, oil on canvas, 30.7 x 50.9 cm; Australian War Memorial, Canberra, Acquired 1951

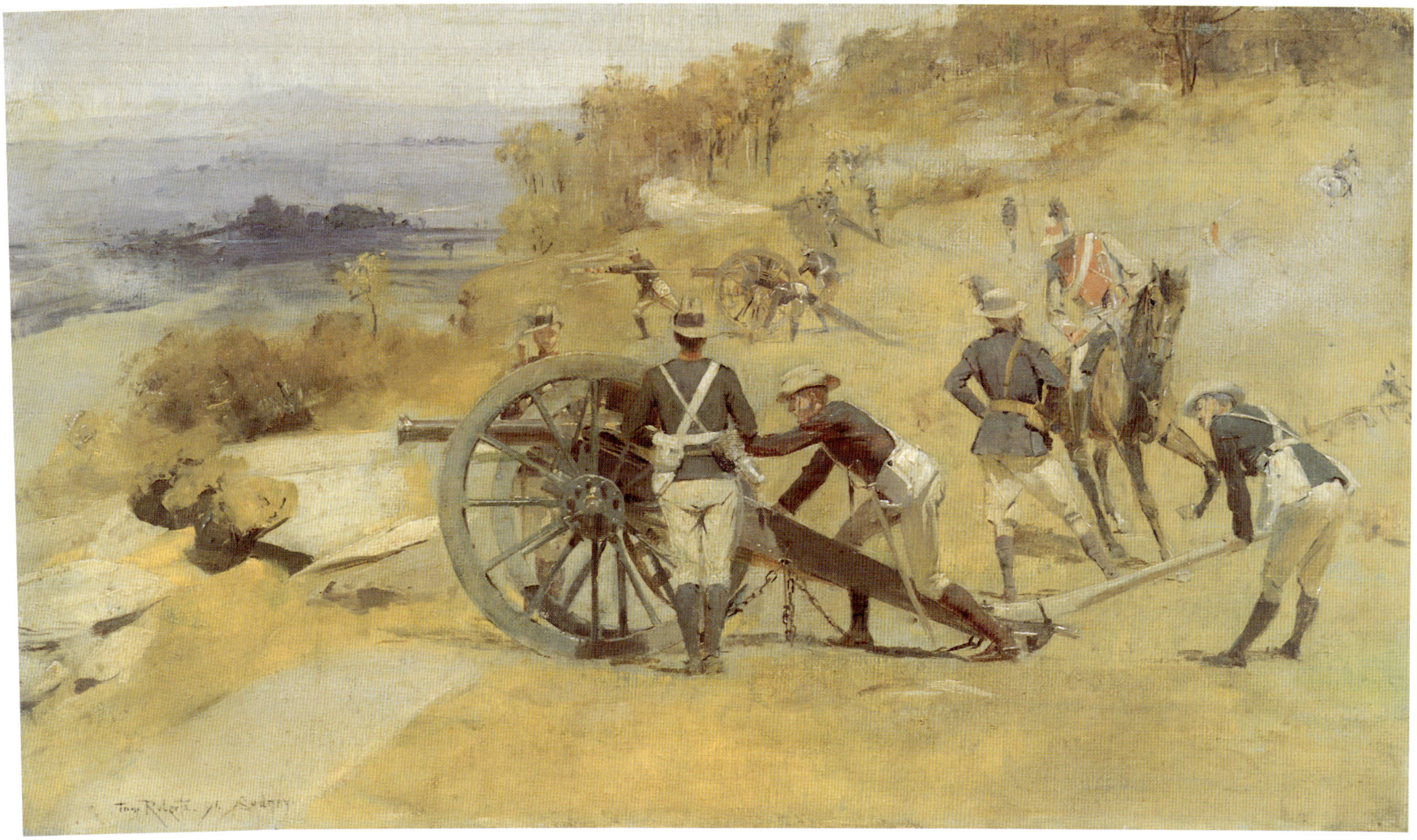

and literature of modernity. Baudelaire, for example, had praised "the pageantry of military life, of fashion and of love" and he declared that "the military man has his beauty, just as the dandy ... a kind of martial nonchalance, a curious mixture of calmness and bravado".[28] Roberts's 1896 portrait of Sergeant R.D. Fraser of the New South Wales Mounted Rifles seems in sympathy with Baudelaire's views in representing Fraser in a stylish, self-confident pose, lending his figure a dandyish elegance. Yet Roberts need not have read Baudelaire in order to absorb the link between military display and modernity. In the late nineteenth century the Australian public turned up in great crowds to watch military manœuvres and reviews; the spectacle of these occasions was enthusiastically recorded in paintings and in numerous illustrations in newspapers and magazines. Some of these images acknowledged the presence of the crowds, but Roberts chose not to indicate their presence in his *"A" Battery Field Artillery*, perhaps for similar reasons to those that led him to excise the presence of women from the rural communities represented in his paintings of "strong masculine labour".

The values of the New Imperialism in the 1890s endorsed the representation of sexual separation and homosocial activities seen in *"A" Battery Field Artillery*. The processes of colonisation allowed for the reassertion of masculine prerogatives in a new country, symbolised by the figure of the 'Coming Man'; if women went to these new countries, they usually went in their traditional roles as wives and servants. Roberts does not confront the idea of the actuality of battle in his picture, but his imaginative identification with the masculinism of Empire is nevertheless present in this and other of his military subjects. As early as 1883 he had drawn an illustration of *The Deserter*, depicting the guilty culprit being brought back to custody by a uniformed soldier. In an article on the collection of the National Art Gallery of New South Wales, written by Roberts in 1891, he saw fit to praise Alphonse de Neuville's contemporary historical picture, *The Defence of Rorke's Drift*, 1880, which portrayed an 1879 Zulu War battle where some eighty British soldiers successfully defended their fort from an attack by 4000 Zulu warriors. These military subjects, focusing on the themes of 'desertion' or 'near defeat', can be interpreted in retrospect as attempts to interrogate the masculinising norms of war, such as patriotic duty and personal valour. The death of General Gordon at Khartoum in 1885 had the symbolic effect of fuelling latent British anxieties about the efficacy of expansionist imperialist policies, as well as raising inner doubts as to the innate superiority of the British race. Rudyard Kipling's emphatic reassertion of an imperial ideal in the face of such doubts and anxieties does much to explain the popularity of his writing with both Roberts and Streeton in the 1890s.[29] Streeton praised Kipling's novel, *The Light that Failed*, 1890, to Roberts as being "wonderfully fine and true". Significantly, the hero of the novel, the war artist Dick Heldar, after being 'emasculated' by city life and the New Woman, as represented by his relationship with Maisie, returns to the all-male world of the war zone in the East to have his masculinity finally vindicated in an heroic death.[30] Even more directly than Kipling, the poetry of Walt Whitman tends to reduce the primary meaning of war to that of male comradeship, strongly permeated in Whitman's case by feelings of homo-eroticism.

Sergeant R.D. Fraser, Mounted Rifles, 1896 Sydney, oil on oak panel, 62.2 x 28.3 cm; Australian War Memorial, Canberra, Acquired 1974

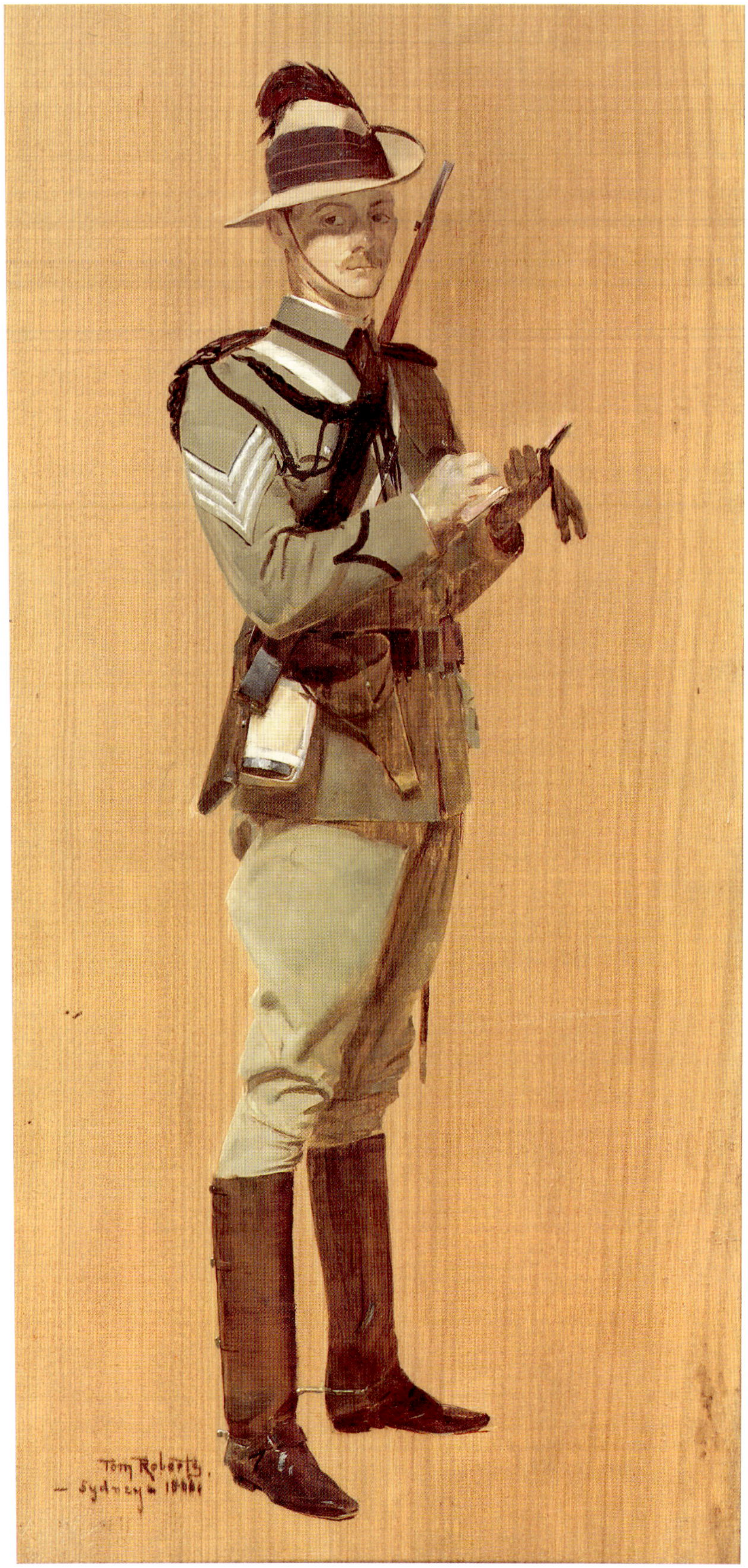
Tom Roberts.
Sydney

Tom Roberts

After he moved in 1891 to live in Sydney, Roberts's practice as a portraitist continued to flourish. The need to survive financially was no doubt behind his considerable output as a portraitist in the 1890s, but it is too easy to dismiss his efforts in this area as mere 'face making'. Aside from economic considerations, he also sought, in Wedmore's words, "to chronicle those types of force and flexibility and serviceable beauty" which represent "our ideals of to-day". With such aims in mind, by the mid 1890s Roberts had begun a series of "character portraits" with the intention of portraying "all who were famous in Art, Literature, Science and Drama".[31] Many portraits from this period are of men and women he knew quite intimately from his immediate social milieu and for whom he felt a strong degree of professional sympathy. His famous profile portrait of *Smike Streeton age 24*, 1891, emphasises the youthful sensitivity of Streeton's personality: in this sense it embraces the Whitman ideal of the "manly attachment" of a slightly older male to a younger man or youth at a time when intense male friendships were still encouraged.[32] Other portraits indicate his ambition to create a network of professional contacts and influence in the society in which he moved, an understandable strategy for a male artist who took his professional status as seriously as Roberts did.

It is in the realm of the arts – especially art, music and theatre – that Roberts's portraiture of the 1890s most clearly acknowledges the incursion of women into the contemporary workplace. As actresses or musicians, some of his female subjects can be seen to participate in the new entertainment and leisure industries associated with the advent of modernity in the late nineteenth century.[33] In undertaking portraits such as those of the artists' model *Ada Furlong*, c1895, or the actress *Frances Ross*, c1898, who went on the stage following the break-up of her marriage, Roberts would have been aware of the changing role of women epitomised by the figure of the 'New Woman'. Some of his most sensitive portraits, including those of the artists *Eileen* [Tooker], 1892, and *Florence Greaves,* c1898, treat their subjects with detachment: the women are portrayed in introspective mood, eyes slightly downcast, their wistful expressions further softened by a veil. As with the portrait titled *The Paris hat*, 1892, Roberts pays close attention to details of the latest fashions in which Eileen and Florence are dressed.[34] Beyond this recording of fashion, he seems to have realised how costume of the day was designed subtly to eroticise women's faces and bodies. As the Australian performance artist Linda Sproul has observed, his concentration on textures such as hair, fabrics, fur, veils and lace tends to lend Roberts's portraits of women a slightly fetishistic quality.[35] In *Elizabeth and Carmen Pinschof*, 1900, for example, there is a suggestion of erotic interest in the long, wavy tresses and dark gaze of these adolescent daughters of the artist's patrons, Carl and Elise Pinschof.

Like most male artists of his generation, the process by which women were objectified in Roberts's art began very early in his career, almost as a matter of course. In order to raise money for his fare to Europe in 1881 he had painted a copy of Edwin Long's popular picture, *A Question of Propriety*, 1870, which had been purchased in 1871 by the National Gallery of Victoria. Long's picture shows a tribunal of Spanish clerics who sit in judgement on the morals of a dance performed by a gipsy; the male viewer was

Elizabeth and Carmen Pinschof, 1900, Melbourne, pastel on paper, 62. 0 x 63. 0 cm; National Gallery of Victoria, Melbourne, Bequest of Caleb Roberts 1984

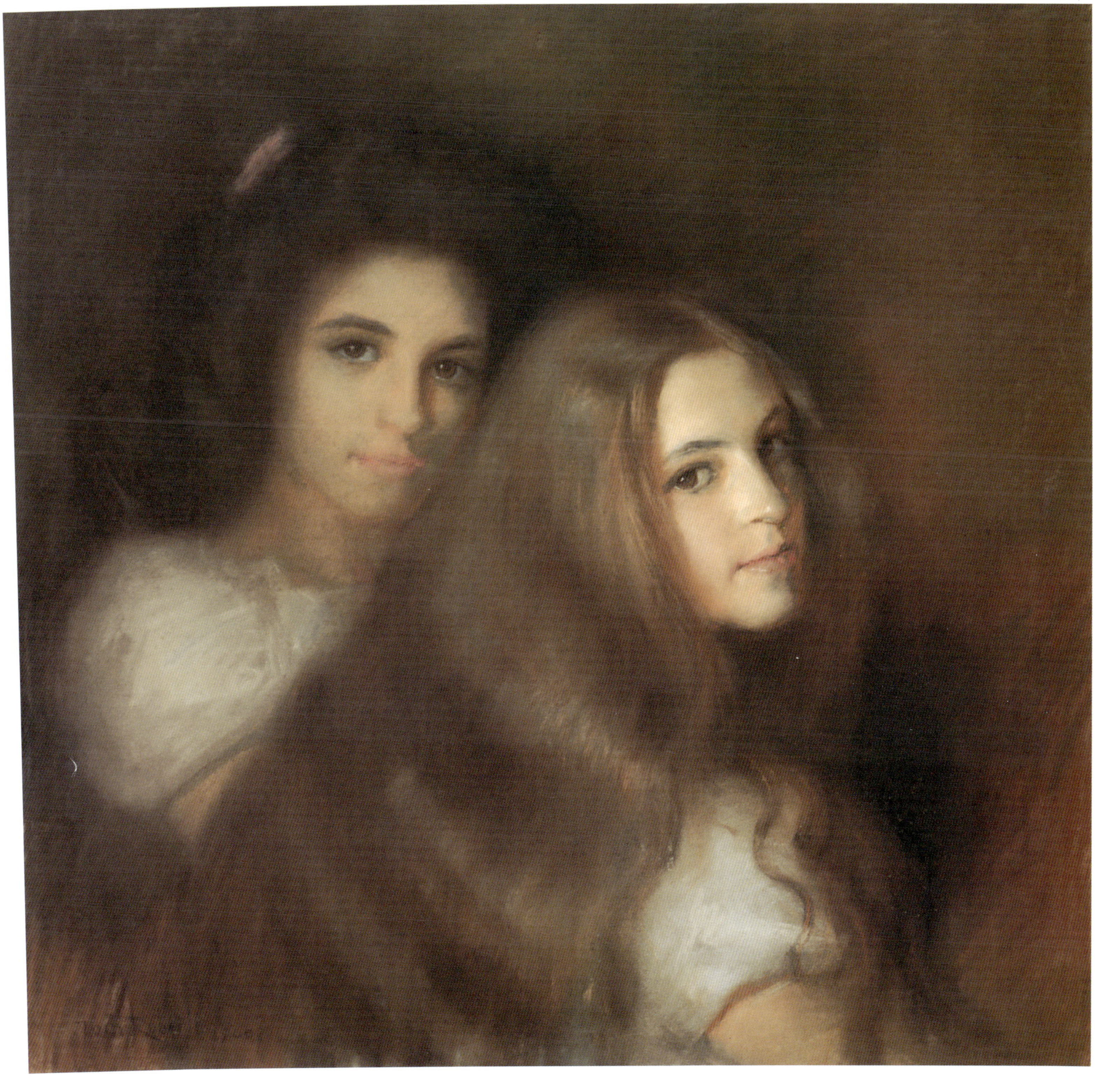

inevitably expected to identify with the objectification of the female and her submission to the authority of the male gaze.[36] As the cultural theorist Edward Said reminds us, the phenomenon of Orientalism in nineteenth-century culture describes an attitude of mind imposed by Western culture on the otherness of 'the Orient' or 'the East', rather than referring to a specific geographical location. Some of this fascination with the 'mystery' of another, foreign culture informs Roberts's portrait of *A Spanish Beauty*, c1883-4, which shows the woman clad in a dark mantilla.[37] Figures of female sexuality were frequently represented as both exotic and veiled in late-nineteenth-century art and culture. The veil becomes a metaphor for the mystery and otherness of female beings, "a kind of permeable border" which both conceals and reveals their sexuality.[38]

The role of the veil as a metaphor for female sexuality suggests links between the apparent detachment of Roberts's treatment in his conventional portraits of women and his more direct objectification of them in imaginative subjects, such as the *femme fatale* figure. Both approaches could be interpreted as signifying a masculinist response to anxieties raised by women's sexuality and their increasing emancipation in society. In *An Eastern Princess*, 1893, the dark and sultry enchantress addresses the viewer with a bold and seductive stare; the form of her body is glimpsed voyeuristically beneath the diaphanous veil of her muslin dress. The everyday has here been transformed to represent the exotic. The model for this Eastern fantasy was Lena Brasch, the attractive young sister of the Brasch brothers who were Roberts's fellow residents at Curlew Camp. As Mary Eagle has noted, the Princess's mode of dress, including the narrow gold headband across her brow, was a conventional costume fantasy in theatre performances of the day. With its imaginative translation of fact into fiction, *An Eastern Princess* presents the intersection of ideologies of race, gender and imperialism.[39] A later femme fatale subject by Roberts, *A Circe*, 1899, evidently conveyed the temptress's sensuality but was less convincing in creating an illusion of her mystery and exoticism: the critic 'De Libra' (James Green), commented on "the voluptuous figure with her diaphanous drapery that ill conceals the ravishing contours of a distinctly Australian figure and the rich warm glow of flesh and blood".[40]

Roberts cannot be described as an artist of active ideological persuasion. Yet his art was shaped and given meaning by some of the major ideologies of his time. What is customarily seen as evidence of his eclecticism and his pragmatic social attitudes and actions could be better interpreted as the outcome of a dominant masculinist outlook. This gave him the freedom and confidence to move fluently from one subject to another, yielding a web of ideological connections in the process. His treatment of modernity, for example, was not simply a matter of stylistic influence but rather a reflection of his ability to locate signs of modernity in the fabric of the society wherein he lived and worked. Roberts responded readily to the various ideological threads which helped define the nature of Australian society in the late nineteenth century. Ironically, his sense of the opportunity afforded by the Empire may have created false expectations of his chances of artistic success when in 1903 he left Australia for England.

The camp, Sirius Cove, c1899, Sirius Cove, Sydney, oil on canvas on paperboard, 25.4 x 34.6 cm; The Art Gallery of New South Wales, Sydney, Purchased 1940

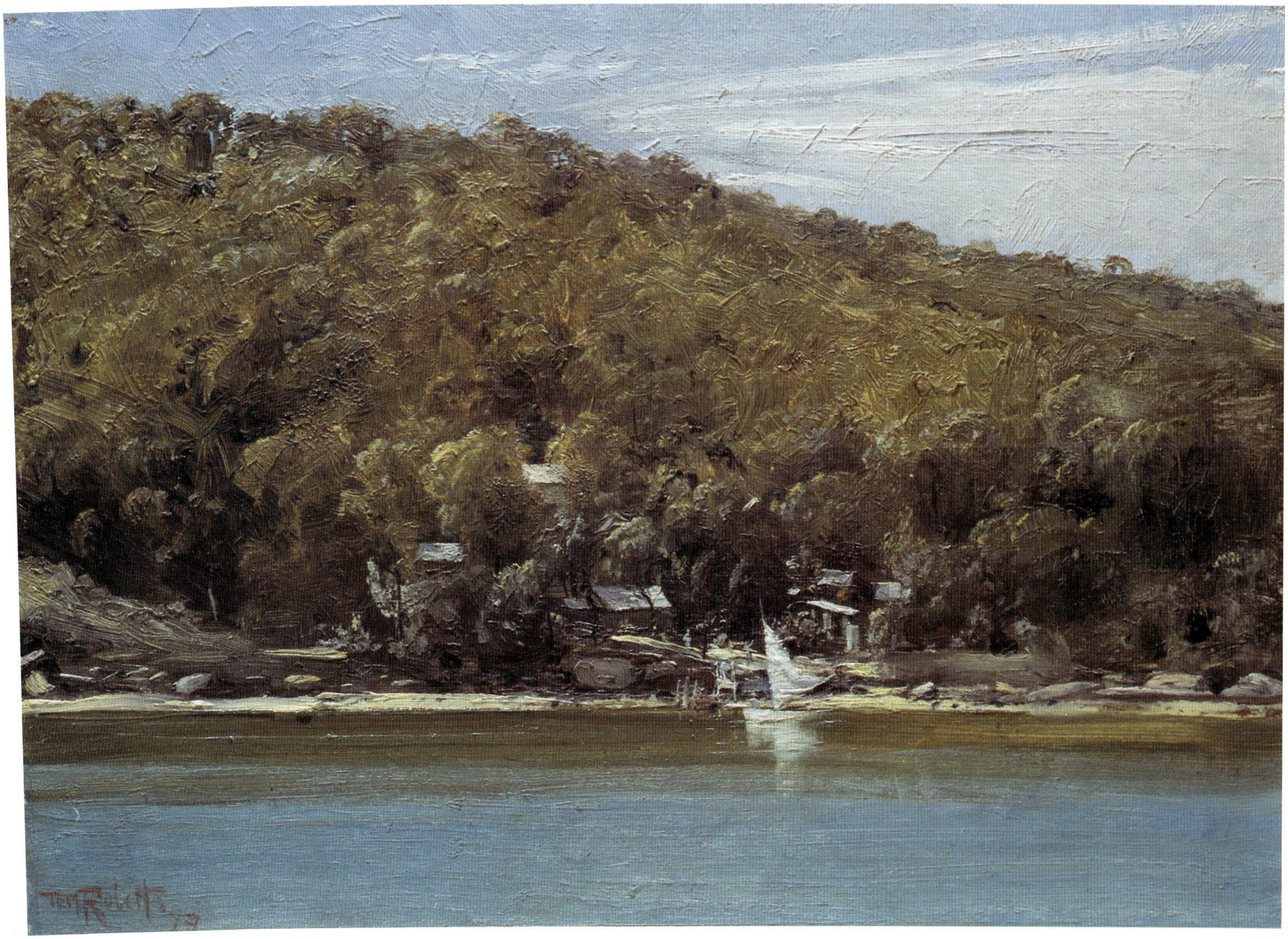

Tom Roberts

Portraiture and Nationalism

Helen Topliss

All history takes on the appearance of inevitableness after the event. Looking backward the future will be tempted to say that Australian Union was Australia's destiny from the first and that nothing could have prevented its consummation. But if this be true, it is certainly not true of its present accomplishment, whatever might have resulted in later times, hereafter, with other men and other means.

Alfred Deakin, c1900[1]

Deakin, one of the key forces behind Federation, Prime Minister of Australia three times, described himself as an Independent Australian Briton and wrote a personal account of the Federation movement from which the above epigraph is derived. Deakin's sense of history in the making was shared by his friend the artist Tom Roberts.

Roberts's major claim to fame has not been his portraiture, yet his concern to record Australian history and the personalities behind the deeds distinguishes him as much as his more famous subject pictures. Tom Roberts in the 1890s painted a series of small, informal panel portraits of Australian celebrities which he described as being of "familiar faces and figures". The twenty-three panels were exhibited in Sydney in November 1900, on the eve of Federation of the former colonies. In the catalogue for this exhibition Roberts expressed his wish that the series be kept together as a representative gallery of types:

> ... the painter feeling that the interest of such a collection if broken up, would be to a great extent lost, especially when one considers how interesting such a group would be to us now, of similar types of, say fifty years ago ...[2]

This miniature gallery of Australian characters has been given little attention, mainly because it was dispersed; as the small wood panels were readily collectable most soon found their way into private ownership. They are deserving of attention because, as much as Roberts's well-known paintings of 'heroic masculine labour', they indicate his thoughts on the subject of nationalism. The panel portraits are part of a programmatic design to record Australian character, both urban and rural. Roberts's singular achievement within the context of Australian painting was his ability to work, successfully and simultaneously, on almost all artistic categories. He could extend an equal degree of seriousness to very different subjects, from the heroic themes of rural life in *Shearing the rams* and *Bailed up*, to informal, intimate portraits of lively metropolitan celebrities.

Roberts's return to Australia in the mid 1880s was fortunately timed. It was a period of intense artistic activity and Roberts, fresh from studies in London, could detect the beginnings of a new art movement which gained momentum from the move towards

Miss Minna Simpson, 1886, Melbourne, oil on canvas, 59.5 x 49.5 cm; Private collection, Canberra

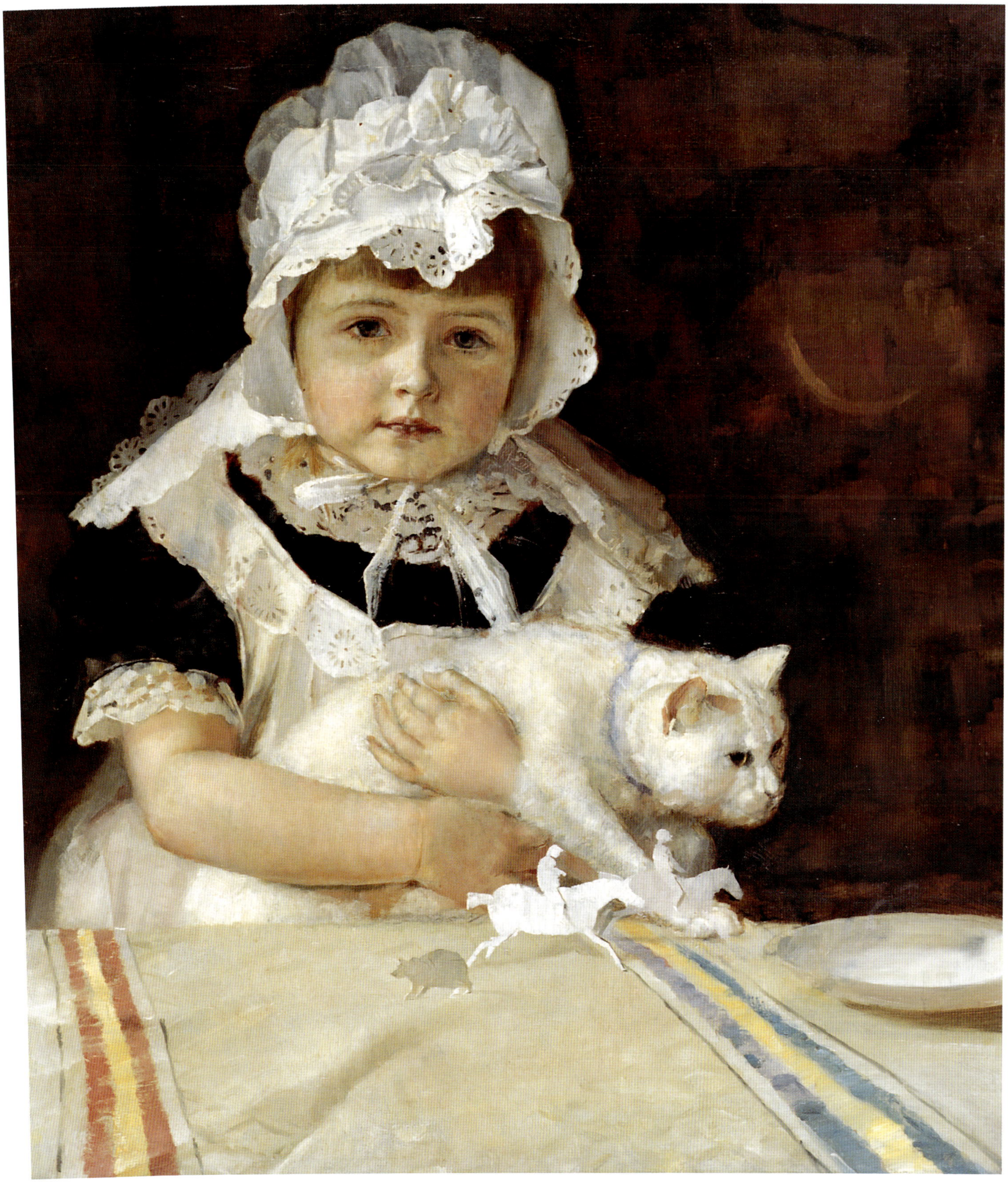

Federation. The artist responded to the political and cultural aspirations of the period. He interpreted an evolving national identity in plein-air subjects painted in the latter part of the 1880s, in his portraiture and in his subject pictures. During these years of incipient nationalism in the arts the predominant mood was a Romantic one and national identity for Roberts was linked to romantic reflections on the outer-suburban landscapes at Box Hill, Eaglemont and various seaside locations on Port Phillip Bay.[3] Nationalism emerged in Europe in the late eighteenth century with the Romantic movement; Romantic poetry such as Wordsworth's and Shelley's expressed national sentiments in relation to the landscape, echoing religious and national ambitions. Roberts and his younger colleague Arthur Streeton, both of whom were fond of quoting the British Romantic poets, painted several landscapes with specific stanzas in mind.[4]

In the succeeding decade of the 1890s Roberts directed his work further afield, to the northernmost point of the continent and to the pastoral districts of New South Wales. His vision was expansive, but he found that his ambition to record Australian history subjects was limited by an economic recession. Perhaps for this reason he rechannelled his art into more realisable and marketable formats, such as his portrait heads of Aboriginal people in New South Wales and further afield.[5] His documentary nationalist enterprise is present in the Aboriginal portraits as well as in those of artists, actors, musicians and politicians.

Roberts's romantic 1880s evocation of the landscape around Melbourne gave way in the 1890s to a naturalist interpretation of typically Australian themes, as seen in *Shearing the rams* and *Bailed up*. Roberts's ambitious, naturalist subject matter however was delimited not only by the economic climate but also by the prejudice of an art establishment whose values had been shaped by Victorian aesthetics. In order to earn a living as a painter he had to content himself with the pragmatic requirements of portraiture, although he did distinguish between the official commissions of mayors, aldermen and politicians and the informal portraits that he frequently painted, with evident pleasure, of friends and associates. Roberts's twenty-three panel portraits are of the latter category; they reveal his desire to paint a series representative of Australian characters and Australian talent. As a group it also reflects an attempt to integrate the art of portraiture into something more significant than mere likenesses. Higher purpose is born out by Roberts's later correspondence with Alfred Deakin on the importance of establishing an Australian portrait gallery of Australians distinguished in public affairs.

At this point some observations should be made about Roberts as a history painter. For him, history painting was the highest artistic expression. It was his constant regret that he could not afford to paint more large, heroic works like *Shearing the rams* and *Bailed up*, which subsequently became icons of Australian nationalism. The production cost of *Shearing the rams,* for instance, was greater than the price that Roberts asked, and received, when he sold it to Edward Trenchard, a prominent Melbourne pastoral-industry agent. When it was first exhibited a reviewer calculated that a chief shearer or a shearers' cook employed for one season earned more than the artist who had dedicated two shearing seasons to paint the picture.[6]

Madame Pfund, c1887, Melbourne, oil on canvas, 142.2 x 98.1 cm; National Gallery of Victoria, Melbourne, Purchased 1948

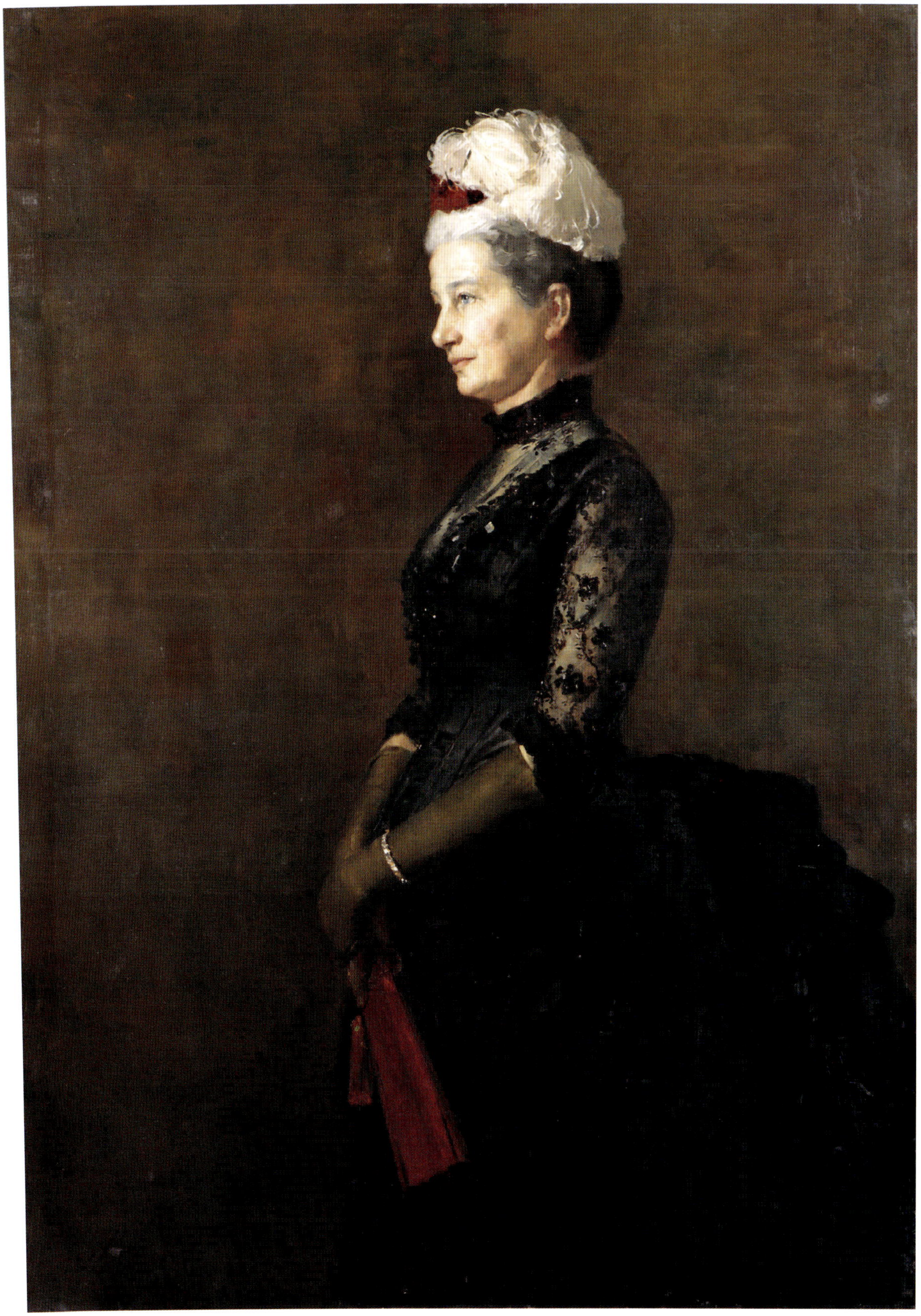

Such paintings were not favoured by the trustees of the National Gallery in Melbourne. James Smith, a trustee of the Gallery and a prominent art critic, panned the work for not being sufficiently universal. His review expressed the tacit classicist and imperialist bias held by an establishment which maintained that classical or Biblical subject matter were the major themes for artists. Roberts's defence of his painting as being "the perfect expression of one time and one place", thus making it representative of "all times and all places", was a naturalist's rejoinder to classical aesthetics.[7] Notwithstanding the poor response of the establishment and the slowness of patronage, the 1890s Depression was a period in which an unprecedented output of literature and art helped foster a sense of Australian identity and thereby gave impetus to the political movement which culminated in January 1901 in the declaration of Federation. Roberts played a major role in this cultural movement and he also took a significant part in the history of Federation by accepting a commission to paint the members of the first Federal Parliament at its opening ceremony. This event altered the course of Roberts's career; ironically, it took him away from the newly designated nation and from further opportunities to paint heroic subjects from characteristically Australian life.

Unlike most of his Australian contemporaries Roberts received his artistic training in London at the Royal Academy. He adhered to the standards and ideals of the Royal Academy and his attachment to that institution continued after he returned in 1885 to Melbourne. Roberts corresponded with his British friends on his return to Australia, remaining very keen to receive news of their achievements. Many of his peers at the Royal Academy Schools such as George Frampton, Robert Anning Bell, Harry Bates and Maurice Greiffenhagen achieved official prominence as artists in Edwardian England. All the above painted and sculpted classicising or mythological subjects, thus qualifying as history painters or sculptors. When Roberts returned to London a second time, some twenty years later, in 1903, he found that although he had been commissioned to paint what he considered an historic and major picture for the new Australian nation he thereby gained no credibility as a major artist within the context of establishment British art. Roberts's first year in London saw him attempting to obtain likenesses of the Royal couple who had taken part in the Australian Federation ceremony in Melbourne, and he felt very shabbily treated when the future George V did not grant him more than one sitting. In accepting the commission to paint this memorable event Roberts had also committted himself to paint 250 likenesses of the participants. His *Opening of the First Parliament of the Commonwealth of Australia by H.R.H. The Duke of Cornwall and York, May 9, 1901* is the kind of official work that should have been painted by an artist with a large studio and with pupils to assist him. Roberts was too financially restricted but nevertheless he felt duty-bound to record good likenesses of all the sitters. Rather than being an heroic work like Jacques-Louis David's *Coronation of Napoleon*, Roberts's *Opening of the First Parliament* is a series of individual likenesses placed together on a huge canvas, more than three by five metres. It serves as an historic monument and document of the occasion, but as a history picture it is lacking in focus and incident. It proved to be the Waterloo of Roberts's aspirations.

Blue Eyes and Brown, 1887, Melbourne, oil on canvas, 126.8 x 76.0 cm; National Gallery of Victoria, Melbourne, Purchased 1960

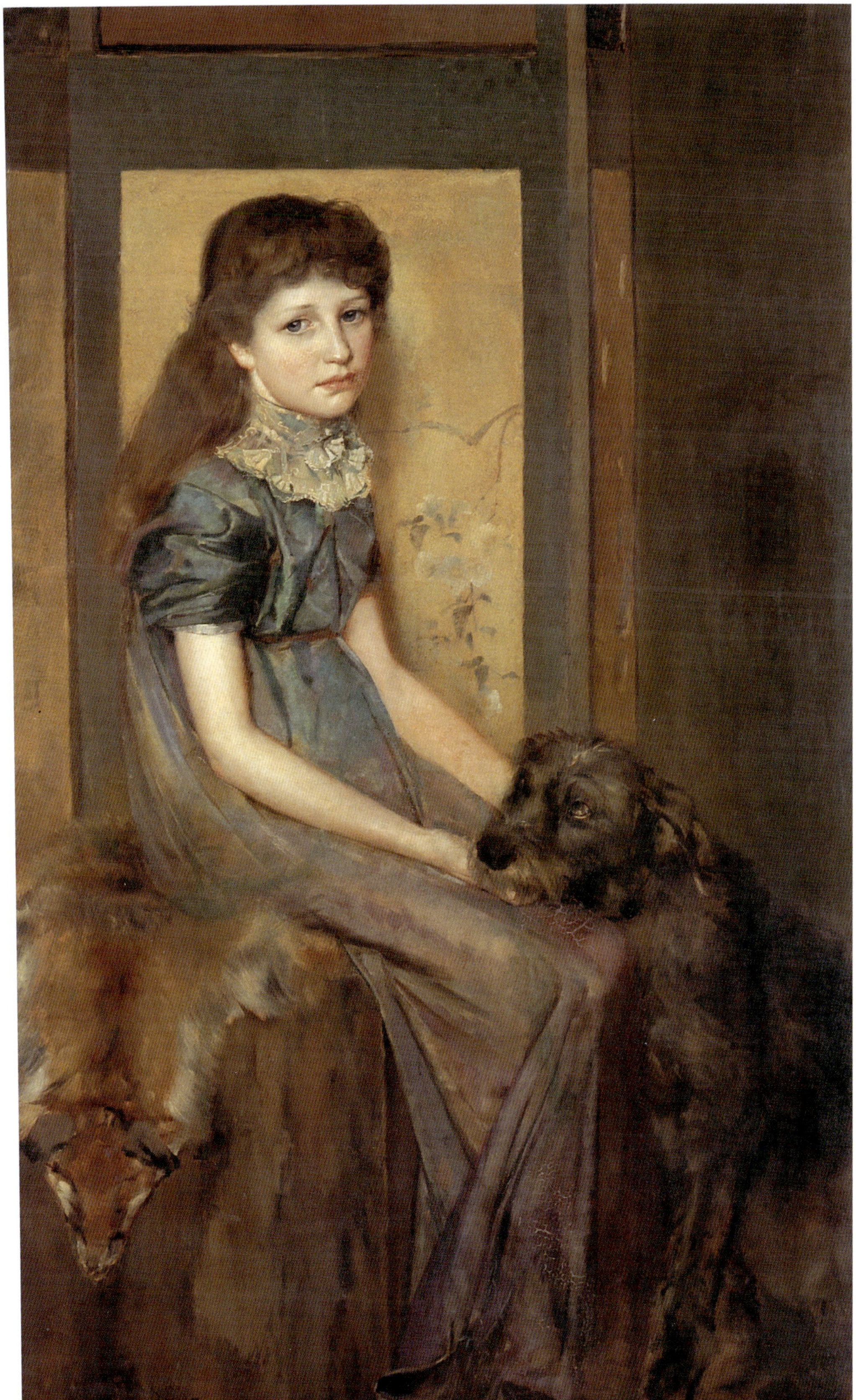

Tom Roberts

Prior to his departure from Sydney, Roberts had complained frequently that he was forced to earn his living by painting politicians' portraits. When he accepted the commission to paint 'The Big Picture' he felt that his career was finally on the right track and that this work would ensure his future success. Sadly, it was his high esteem for history painting and his nationalist convictions that led him to accept this onerous task which also took him away from his natural talents and ambitions as a painter. His patriotism was often expressed, and in a letter to Alfred Deakin on finally completing 'The Big Picture' he wrote: "... of course you know how proud I am to have put my little bit to the Australian history; whether it will impress people as the scene and the 2 years work impressed me, remains ...".[8] Roberts left for London in March 1903 and by November of that year he had completed his work on 'The Big Picture'. The patronage that Roberts had expected in the wake of this commission was not forthcoming and over the next few years his paintings were often rejected at the Royal Academy – in his nineteen years in London only eight works were accepted by the Royal Academy and most of those were portraits. In an interview with The British Australian in 1906 Roberts remarked that England didn't really need anybody in the arts: "The supply is in excess of the demand. The only thing is to try to make her want you, and that is difficult, for she really only wants the exceptional in any line".[9]

As can be seen from the catalogue raisonné of his work, Roberts painted many portraits of different kinds throughout his career. The total is roughly 250 portraits, which represents a third of his artistic output. The official portraits were not always uninteresting commissions, especially when Roberts knew the individual concerned. That was the case with Sir Henry Parkes, whose portrait he painted twice – thrice if we include his symbolic portrait at the rear of the Big Picture, where Roberts included him as a presiding spirit over the ceremony.

Roberts also painted many portraits of women, revealing his love of female personalities and his response to decorative aspects of their dress. Some of these portraits, such as *Eileen,* and the two of *Florence Greaves*, are beautiful studies hardly equalled by any other Australian artist of the day. His first works to enter a public collection were portrait heads: the pretty *Eileen* and the *Aboriginal head (Charlie Turner)*, both bought in September 1892 by the National Art Gallery of New South Wales.

The small panel portraits are standing figures and thereby form a distinct group within his artistic output. What makes these Australian national portraits so appealing is that they were informal representations painted in a spontaneous manner by an artist who had personal insight into the characters. Indirect models for these panel portraits are the bohemian sketches made by nineteenth-century painters of their fellow artists, or of well-known literary figures. The direct lineage was from full-length portraits by Whistler, such as *Arrangement in Black: Portrait of Señor Pablo de Sarasate*, painted in 1884. Sarasate was a violinist and the picture demonstrates Whistler's musical theories: the major colour, like a dominant key or chord in music, establishes the mood of the picture. Roberts, who had also been influenced by Whistler's small cityscape paintings

Mrs L. Abrahams, 1888, Melbourne, oil on canvas, 40.6 x 35.6 cm; National Gallery of Victoria, Melbourne, Purchased 1946

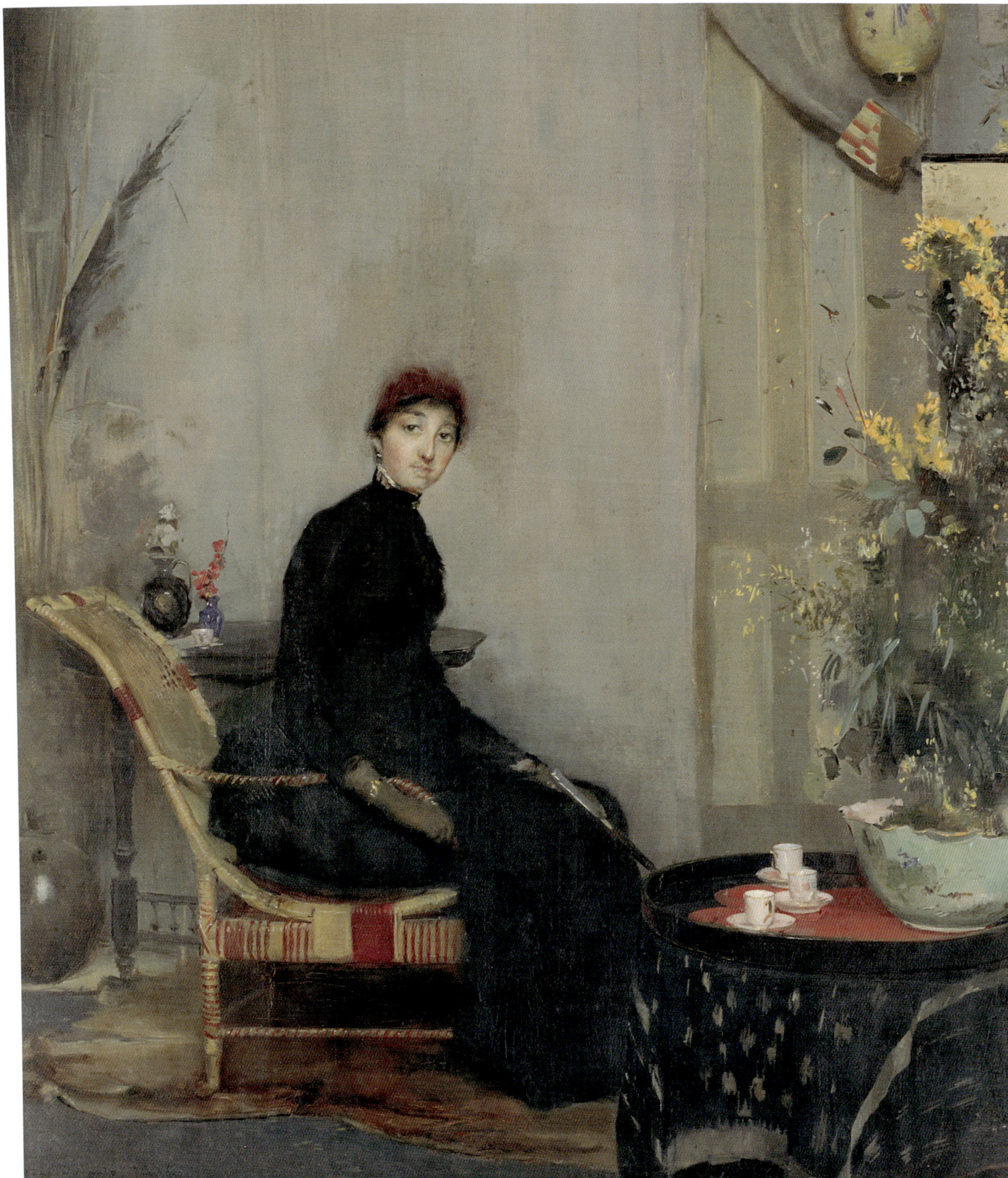

exhibited in London that same year, employed dominant tones in his own little 9-by-5 inch pictures of the river Thames, painted in 1884 in London. The influence was continued in a series of small paintings painted on cigar-box lids after Roberts's return the following year to Melbourne. Like Whistler's small paintings these were called 'impressions' but unlike most of the works by the French Impressionists the time of day represented is sunset, or twilight, which became an important signature tune for Roberts's landscapes, also in keeping with Roberts's Romantic influences.

Whistler's formula for his informal portraits was to set the figure against a dark ground. Roberts followed this example for his small works of the 1890s in selecting a wood support which he left unprimed and unpainted and covered with a thin, dark oil applied in subtle brown or black pigment. The important exception is the portrait of the musician G.W.L. Marshall-Hall, a brilliant coda to the series; he is represented against a bright oak background, wearing a light tan suit. Roberts's theatre personalities included George Coppin, J.C.W. Nicholson, Robert Brough and Dion Boucicault, there were musicians such as Alfred Hill, Henri Kowalski and Johann Kruse, newspaper figures such as Livingston Hopkins, Arthur Adams and Andrew Garran. There were military men, businessmen, politicians and one pastoralist, the lively, cornet-playing Duncan Anderson.

When Roberts exhibited these panel portraits in 1900 he hoped to sell them as a gallery of Australian celebrities and types.[10] An article in Review of Reviews, in 1896, mentioned that the portraits were hanging as a group on Roberts's studio walls in Sydney, demonstrating the artist's pride in the collection as well as his effort to publicise them.[11] With the exception of some of his portrait heads of women (which also included theatre and art personalities) this series of small full-length panel paintings of creative men – and a couple of women – are amongst his most accomplished and evocative works. It is quite clear that Roberts distinguished between the bread-and-butter portraits of politicians and aldermen and those done out of an interest in the character or aesthetic quality of the subject. It is also clear that Roberts realised the historical and national importance of portraiture.

Roberts's working method was programmatic; he tended to work thematically and to plan a series of pictures on the same subject or mood, as can be see in the 1890s pictures dealing with heroic masculine labour and earlier in his landscapes and sketches painted in the suburban bush and coast around Melbourne. From his female portraits such as *Lena Brasch* we can see that Roberts's observation of personality could be effected even in very sketchy portraits and that he was adept at making the background reflect the sitters' personality, as in the inclusion of the soulful-looking dog in *Blue Eyes and Brown*.

Tom Roberts's fate as an artist reflects in some measure Australia's relationship to the mother country. Although Roberts was a nationalist he was still tied by his own heritage to Britain and to British institutions such as the Royal Academy, whose acceptance he

Miss Florence Greaves, 1898, Sydney, pastel on paper, 38.1 x 31.8 cm; The Art Gallery of New South Wales, Sydney, Bequest of Florence Turner Blake 1959

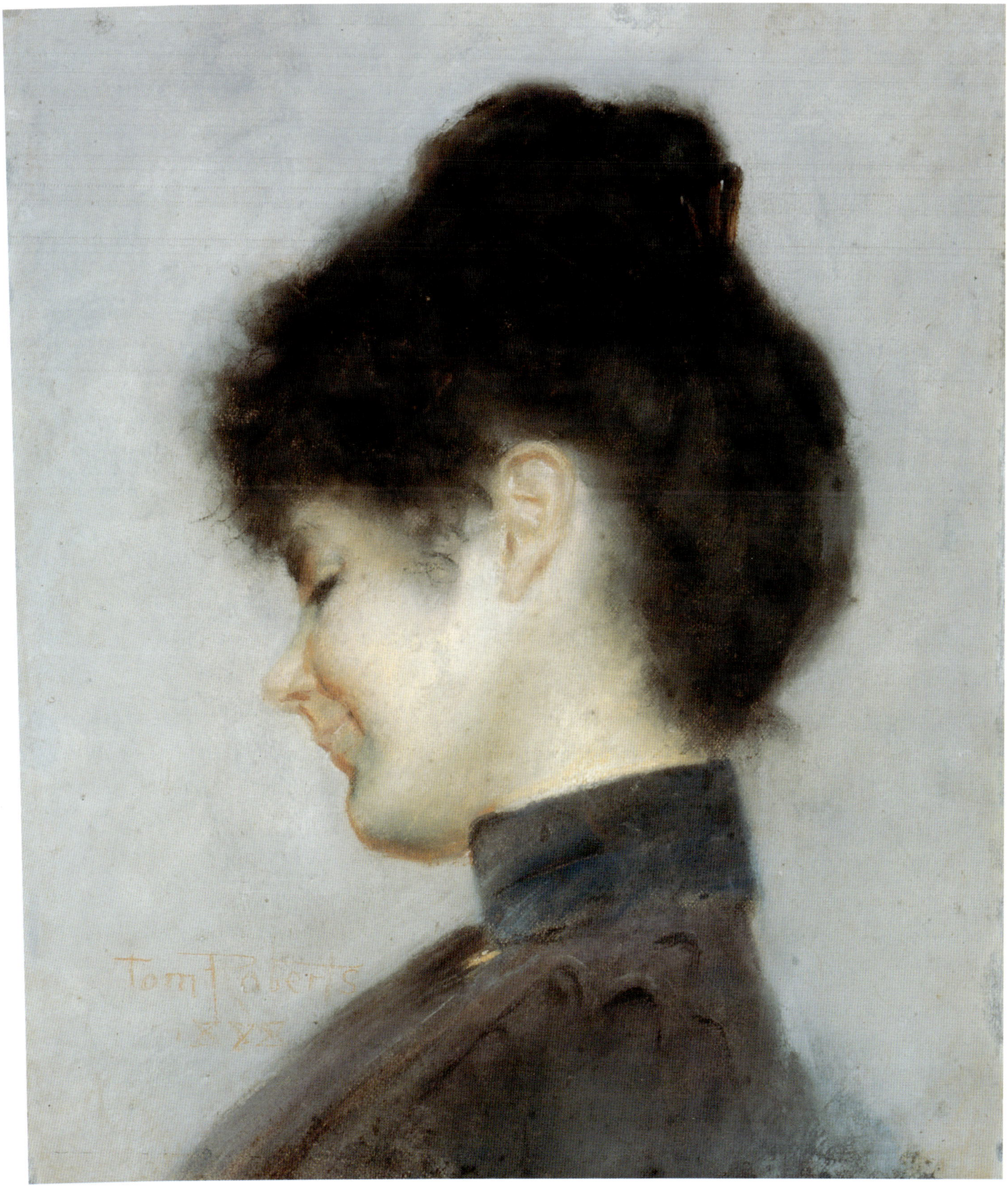
Tom Roberts
1888

needed in order to feel that he had arrived as an artist. Roberts congratulated himself that in obtaining the commission to paint 'The Big Picture' he would achieve the recognition that he had been waiting for. He also thought that it would facilitate his later career in England. However this was not to be the case. He was a colonial painter working on a painting that did not rate highly within the Academy's scale of values. Roberts had had ambitions in the more acceptable field of mythological or historical subject matter and when he completed 'The Big Picture' he attempted a mythological scene entitled *"The Sleeper Awakened"*, based on the *Arabian Nights*. Eventually exhibited at the Royal Academy in 1913, the idea went back to a sketch-club drawing Roberts had done as a young man in the early 1880s. In 1912 Roberts wrote to his colleague Frederick McCubbin about this picture, admitting to all the difficulties that he had experienced with it: "I know the whole business is old fashioned and out of date. It wants the swish of 25 – and though [I'll?] probably kick it one immediately, never mind, up it goes ...".[12] From all acounts it was an outdated subject for the time and a friend of Tom Roberts described it as being of "nude figures dancing in flimsy net", a somewhat absurd subject for a naturalist painter.[13] The abortive painting, which is known only from photographs, reveals Roberts's loss of direction in London and highlights the fact that his best work was carried out when the artist felt in accord with a national movement and when he felt that history had still to be made. This was not to be the case when he worked in isolation in England after Federation.

The intensive work on 'The Big Picture' sapped Roberts's energies and must have affected his eyesight. He complained about his eyes – photographs begin to show him wearing glasses – and immediately after completing the commission he experienced what sounds like a mental breakdown. Roberts worked his way slowly out of this crisis by painting small landscapes reminiscent in size of his earlier 9 by 5 impressions. On the advice of James Quinn, a younger Australian artist working in London, he painted in reduced tones of grey/blue and grey/green, but without the earlier confidence of handling and subtle gradations of tone. Roberts's return to London as a mature artist burdened with an impossible commission served to highlight the conflict he had felt earlier in his career. It was a conflict that was inherent in his desire on the one hand to paint major history pictures (which in the Australian context he had succeeded in doing but which had not attracted the necessary financial reward), and on the other hand his pragmatic pursuit of portraiture to earn a living. There was also the conflict arising from the values imposed by the Royal Academy which denigrated realist subjects in favour of romantic or idealist ones. It is certain that Roberts felt this conflict because after completing 'The Big Picture' he struggled for some eight years with the literary historical subject "*The Sleeper Awakened*" as if to prove that he was capable of the more highly-regarded type of subject. In the 1880s Roberts had impressed Jane Price, a fellow artist, with his ambitions of painting significant subject pictures. Price recalled:

> I remember one day sitting in his studio and looking over a portfolio which he carefully drew out from some place where it was hidden away. He explained to me that he rarely showed it to anyone ... I was very much surprised and impressed,

Lily Stirling, c1890, Melbourne, oil on canvas, 85.5 x 65.5 cm; National Gallery of Victoria, Melbourne, Purchased through the Art Foundation of Victoria with the assistance of the Chase Manhattan Overseas Corporation, Fellow, 1981

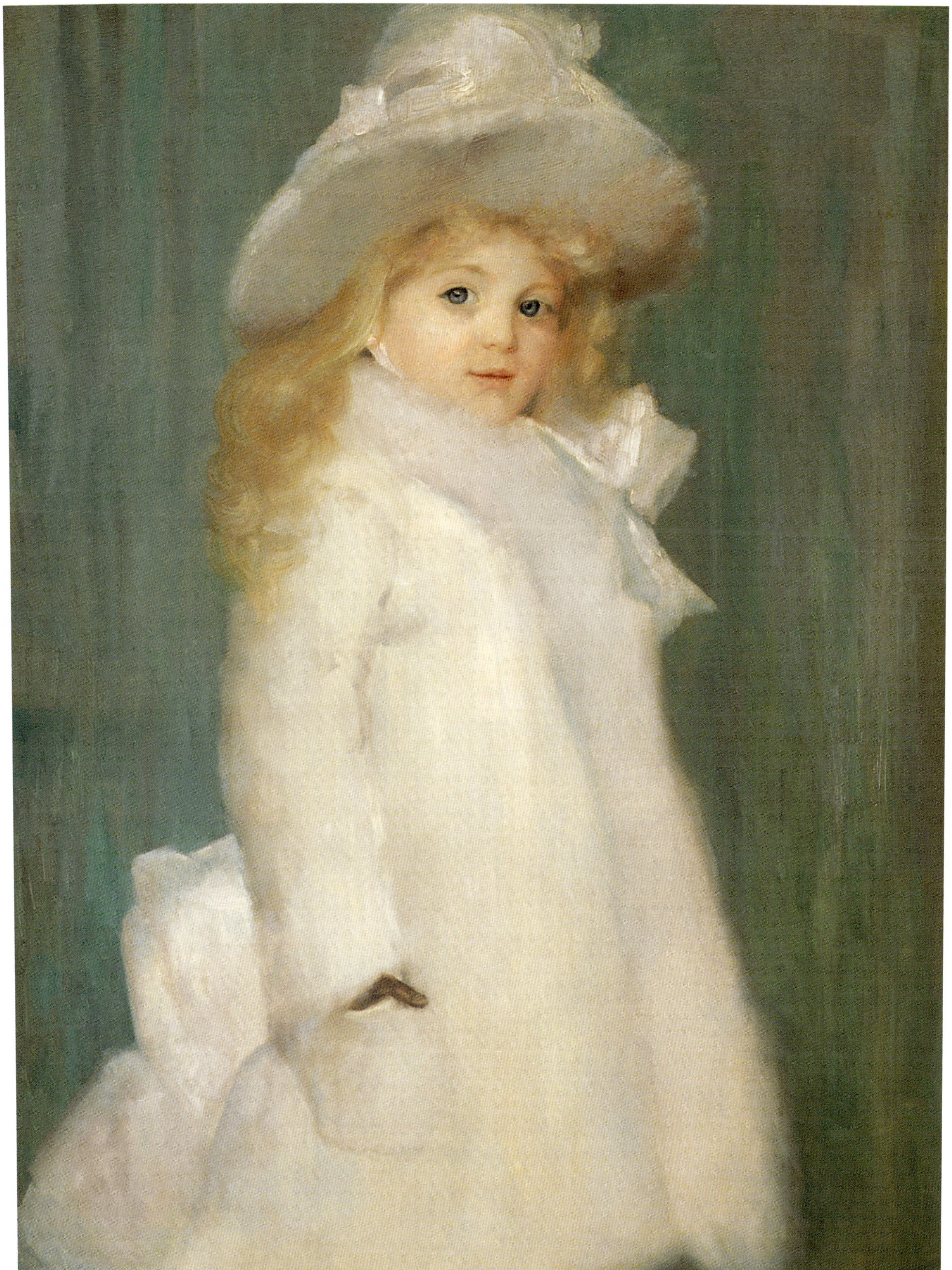

> and I saw great possibilities in his work ... It was work that seemed to me far beyond anything I thought he was capable of.[14]

A.G. Stephens, the political journalist and writer, also referred to these drawings in an 1899 article on the artist and observed that due to lack of patronage he had been forced to paint portraits.[15]

In his desire to express Australia's emerging national culture Roberts was attuned to what could be the defining themes for the new nation, themes that would distinguish Australia from the mother country. The subjects he chose for his major works were all realist themes of "masculine labour" and these representations came to be recognised as national icons. For his minor works he painted small landscapes (and a few medium-sized ones) of characteristic scenery in Victoria, New South Wales and Tasmania as well as a series of portraits of Aboriginal people, by definition quintessential Australian types – and of course, the series of small panel portraits of Australian celebrities.

Tom Roberts was characteristic of that immigrant generation of artists, writers and craftworkers who had arrived in Australia at a sufficiently early age to adapt to the needs of a new country. Robert Prenzel, a designer and cabinet-maker, revolutionised furniture design in Australia by utilising jarrah, Queensland rosewood, silky oak and pittosporum, all native woods.[16] In the crafts there were a large number of artists interpreting Australian flora and fauna, most of them in an Arts & Crafts or Art Nouveau style then popular in Europe. Prenzel came to Australia at the age of twenty, having already received an education in his chosen craft in Germany. In 1923 Prenzel commented on his change of orientation after arriving in Australia:

> I came to Australia to continue work along the classical lines upon which I had gone entirely. The Gothic, and the wide sweeps and delicate outlines of the Renaissance design. But I did not go far with that type of work. Mr Panton,[17] my friend and counsellor of those early years, advised me to carve things which would be more readily understood ... the flora and fauna of Australia. That is why you find me at work on native bears, kookaburras, gum-leaves, and the studies of Aboriginal heads.[18]

Unlike Prenzel, Tom Roberts was trained in Melbourne, being only thirteen when he arrived from Dorchester with his brother and sister and widowed mother. The art training that he received at Melbourne's National Gallery School in the late 1870s and early 1880s was incomplete and founded on outmoded classical ideals, endorsed by the Director of the gallery and school, Eugene von Guérard. These classical principles were found to be irrelevant by young artists who were eager to paint landscapes in plein air. Roberts acknowledged the poverty of Australian art education at this early stage and felt that he had to complete his artistic education in London if he were to succeed as an artist. In London he spent three years in the Antique and Life schools of the Royal Academy but left before he could complete his training in the Upper School of Painting. It is possible that Roberts did not find what he required at the Royal Academy since the orientation at the Academy schools was classical and traditional, and only those

Eileen, 1892, Sydney, oil on canvas, 49.0 x 36.0 cm; The Art Gallery of New South Wales, Sydney, Purchased 1892

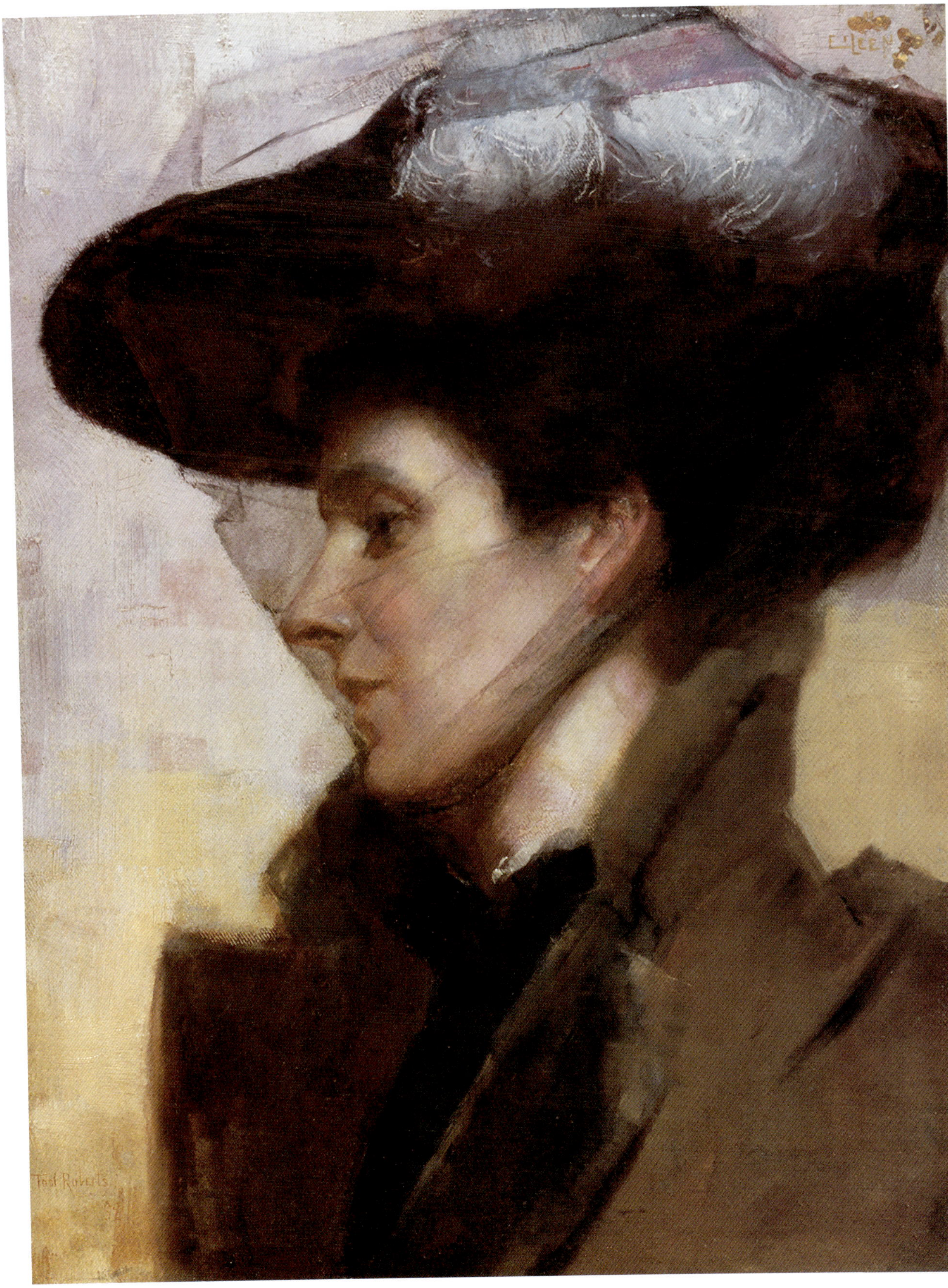
EILEEN
Tom Roberts

artists succeeded who followed its prescriptions, like Roberts's friends Anning Bell and Frampton. At this point in his career Roberts was searching for alternate models in French naturalism and in tonal impressionism. During Roberts's studies at the Royal Academy Schools not one of his masters was a landscape painter; they were all history or subject painters in a variety of historicising modes. When he first returned to Melbourne Roberts must have been anxious to make his own contribution to Australian culture and if we look at his work in the succeeding years it is clear that he was consciously trying to coin national subjects, as can be seen in his atmospheric 9 by 5 landscapes and interiors, and his major effort at a naturalist history painting, *Shearing the rams.*

As a result of his 1903 shift to London, in middle age, and once again at a crucial point in his career, it would seem that Roberts lost the sense of identity that he had achieved earlier on in Australia. Roberts's problem was that, unlike Arthur Streeton who also lived in London during the Edwardian period, he felt a conflict of identity and allegiance since he was British by birth and also by training, conditions which did not apply to Streeton. Although Streeton was also unsuccessful in London and was on the outer of British artistic circles, he could reject these as irrelevant since he was undeniably an Australian. When Streeton returned to Australia with his wealthy wife he embarked on a successful publicity campaign and emerged as the hero of Australian landscape painting. Roberts had been struggling with portraiture and poverty in England, only to return to Melbourne in 1923 as an old and almost-forgotten man unable to re-launch himself as effectively as the younger Streeton. The issues that are brought to the fore by Roberts's career are that as an artist he was particularly sensitive to the needs of the moment, and that as a young man newly returned from the seat of empire he identified and read the mood of the period leading up to Federation of the Australian colonies. There is no doubt that Roberts was a leader in the movement to characterise Australian life and nature. Moreover, he realised that not only had the landscape to be defined for a new audience that saw itself as predominantly Australian, but that Australian life itself also had to be anatomised in major paintings reflecting the pastoral industry, such as *Shearing the rams*, and in events which gave voice to Australian history, for instance *Bailed up*. In his 1895 speech to the Society of Artists in Sydney, Roberts outlined all the subjects available for the artist and the importance of representing events of the 'colonial past' that would be forgotten in twenty years' time.[19]

Roberts's series of portraits in the 1890s was painted with a similar intention of providing a nationalist gallery for the emerging nation-state. In many ways it is regrettable that in the period following Federation Roberts was one of the expatriate painters in London. Unlike his more successful Australian expatriate contemporaries, such as John Longstaff and George W. Lambert, he was unable to adjust to the demands of the British art market. Whereas Longstaff had a fashionable studio in St Johns Wood, Roberts ended up in a cottagey house at Golders Green, a new garden suburb at the end of the underground line. As late as 1910 Roberts, who conducted a regular correspondence with Alfred Deakin, was attempting to establish an Australian portrait gallery of politicians connected with Federation, to which end he was prepared to return to

Plink-a-plong, 1893, Sydney, oil on canvas, 68.5 x 50.8 cm; Art Gallery of South Australia, Adelaide, Elder Bequest Fund 1948

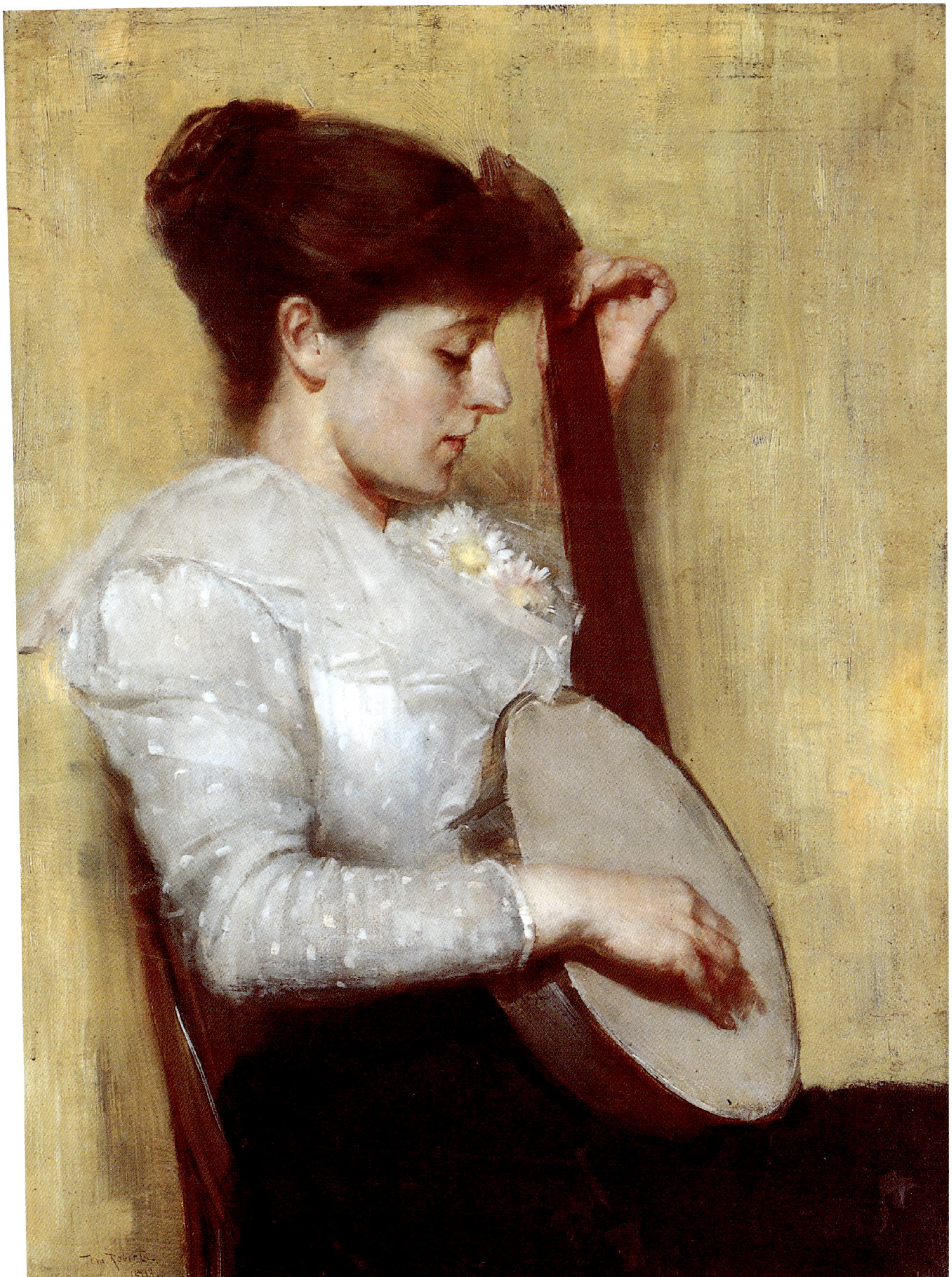

Australia for six months to undertake the work. In one letter Roberts wrote, "... it disturbs me to think that most of you are likely to go on till the inevitable comes, and leave nothing that will give the future anything that will show what you all were as men to look at ...".[20]

It is a pity that Roberts did not have the opportunity to paint some of these portraits, particularly since Deakin was entirely sympathetic to his aims. Deakin himself from 1898 to 1900 was engaged in writing a series of 'pen portraits' of Australian politicians involved in the Federation movement, though "The Inner History of the Federal Cause, 1880-1900" was intended to remain unpublished in his lifetime. Deakin was prime minister during 1903-04, 1905-08 and 1909-10 and, like Roberts, had a concern for recording historical events before they were forgotten. In the first section of his 'Inner History' he comments: "Memory affords a less and less trustworthy witness as the years roll on, and hence this sketch, undertaken while the last series of events are fresh in recollection and almost all the actors in all the stages still upon the scene ...".[21]

Deakin's pen portraits of the participants are more incisive and acerbic than Roberts's cameo portraits embedded within 'The Big Picture' or than his Federationists portrayed elsewhere, and Roberts never did get the opportunity to record the participants in this historic event. However, if we juxtapose one of Deakin's pen portraits such as that of the 'Father of Federation', Sir Henry Parkes, with Roberts's paintings, we see how an acute literary observation can complement an artist's painted likeness. Deakin wrote of

> ... Sir Henry Parkes, than whom no actor ever more carefully posed for effect. His huge figure, slow step, deliberate glance and carefully brushed-out aureole of white hair combined to represent the spectator with a picturesque whole which was not detracted from on closer observation. His voice, without being musical and in spite of a slight wooliness of tone and rather affected depth, was pleasant and capable of reaching and controlling a large audience ... He had always in his mind's eye his own portrait as that of a great man, and constantly adjusted himself to it.

Not all the participants fared well under Deakin's sharp pen. On the British aristocracy and royalty he was painfully frank. Of the Duke of York, later King George V, he noted that he was a "still more commonplace edition of his father and his wife reported to be but little more individual than the palest of pale personalities". He was vehement in his observations of the class system, and of Britain in general Deakin formed a very low opinion:

> Vast in size, wealth, appetite, profusion, energy and variety of life, London was apoplectic, stertorous, unwieldy, unhealthy, philistine and gross, greatly in need of a strong regimen and severe reform if it was to continue to be the centre of an empire and the seat of its intellectual, spiritual and political government as its power, position and resources entitled it to be.[22]

Miss Isobel McDonald, 1895, Sydney, oil on canvas, 46.3 x 41.3 cm; National Gallery of Victoria, Melbourne, Purchased 1957

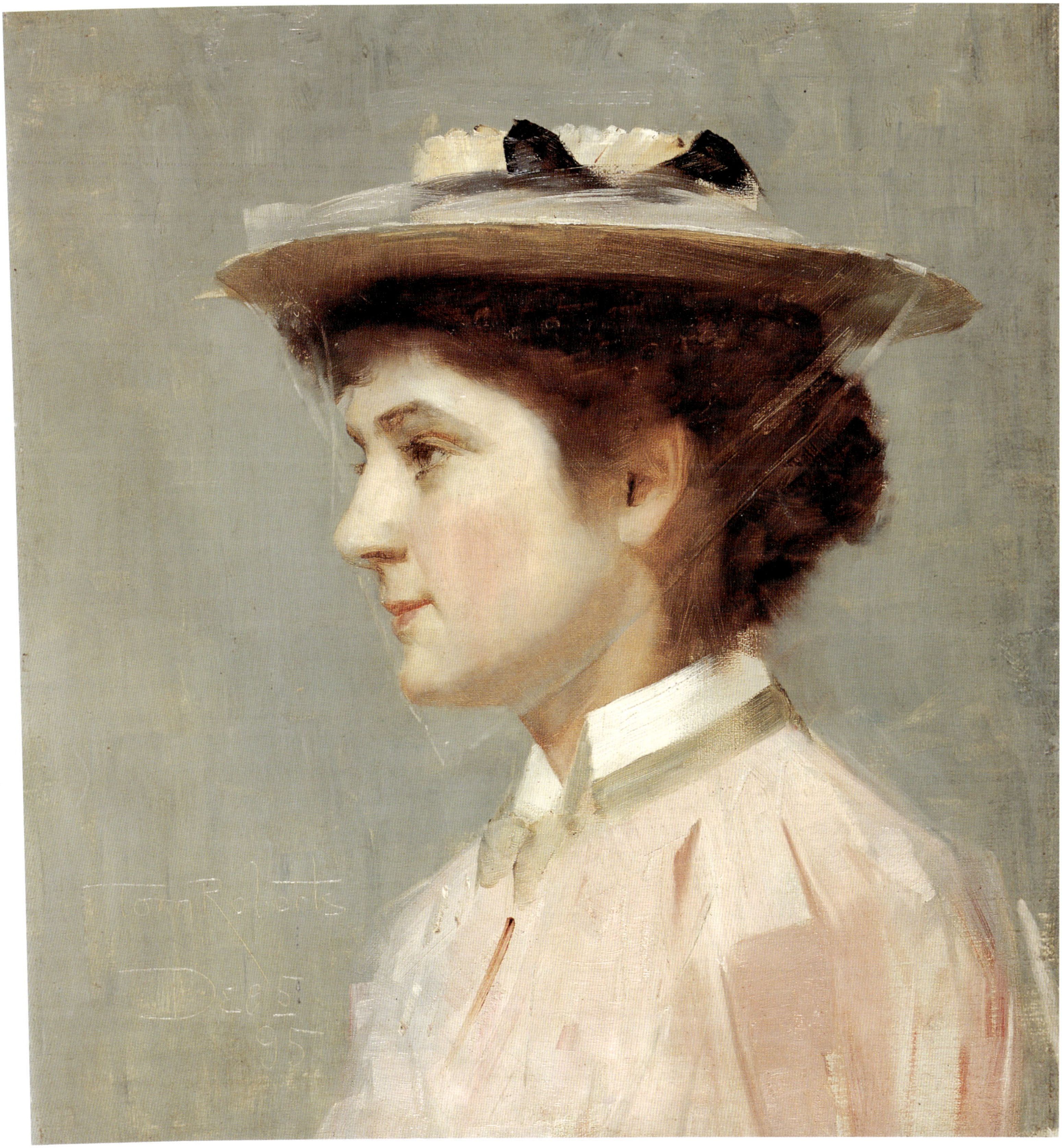
Tom Roberts
95

On that point Roberts and Deakin were not of the same mind. Deakin was after all a politician and he was extremely perceptive about people's characters. Deakin was also a native-born son of immigrant parents, which made his perspective securely Australian. Roberts, born and trained in England, had split loyalties. Roberts's British birth also counted against him in the succeeding period when history was being retold by its participants. Under the new history of a national art Roberts's place was demoted because he was not Australian-born and because in the period when Australia's art history began to be re-written he was still in England and no longer on the scene.[23]

Although Roberts's major contributions to Australian culture, his large subject pictures, are still considered to be the most important and typical works of their period his portraiture has never been reappraised, nor considered in its context. With the centenary of Federation due in 2001 it is important to take pause and to view these works anew. They were painted by an artist who had set himself the task of recording Australian life and Australian types for the benefit of posterity, just as his friend Alfred Deakin had written his inside story of Federation for Australians of the future.

Portrait of an Aboriginal woman (Maria Yulgilbar), 1895, Yulgilbar, NSW, oil on canvas, 38.0 x 34.5 cm; Dixson Galleries, State Library of New South Wales, Sydney, Presented by Sir William Dixson, March 1943

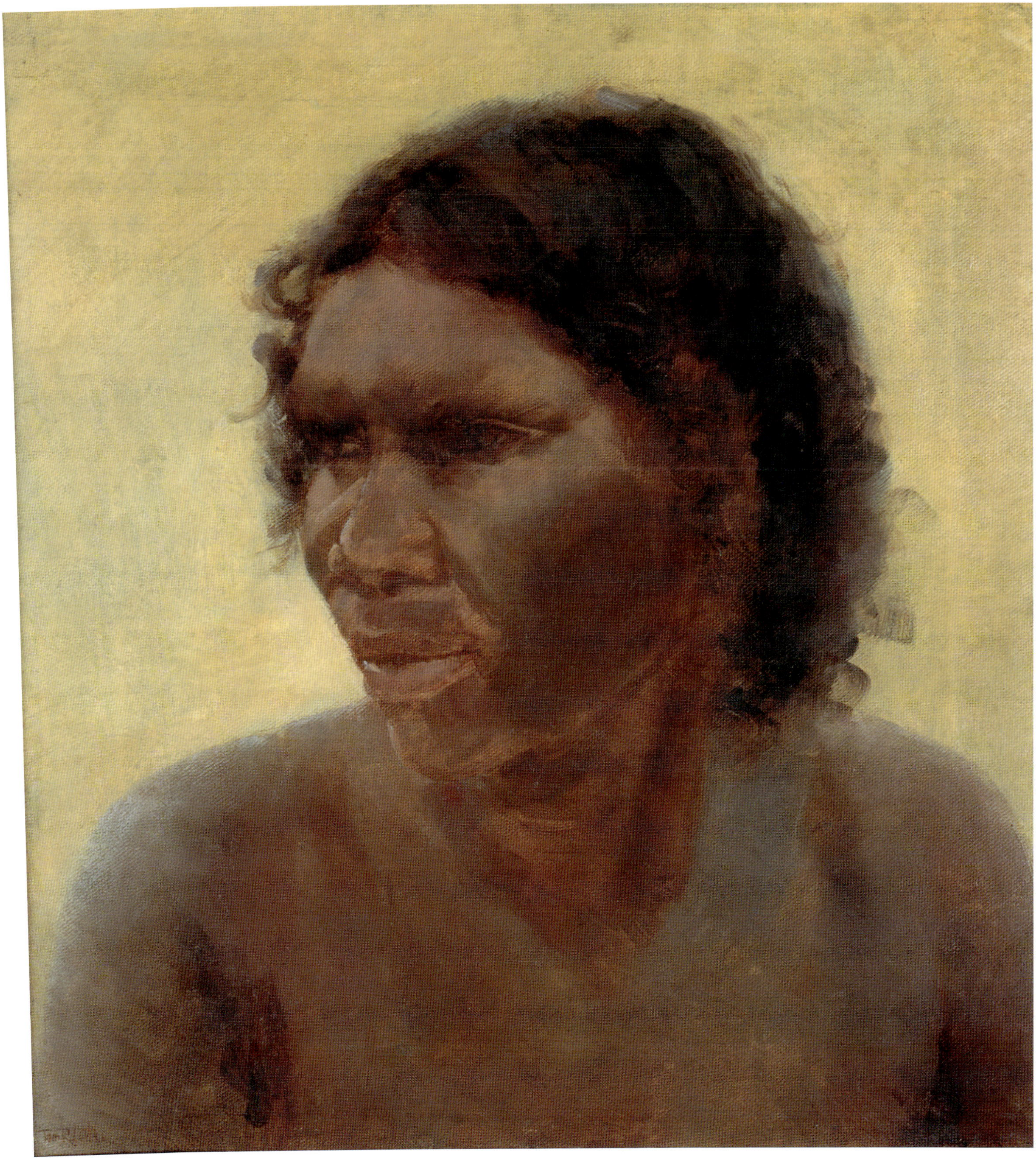

Reflections on the late work

Barry Pearce

It cannot be said that when Tom Roberts died in 1931 at the age of seventy-five his career had been flushed with success. Critically and commercially his last few years in Australia were modest. The state galleries in Adelaide and Sydney had made an effort to represent him adequately during his lifetime but in Melbourne, where his career began and ended, the National Gallery of Victoria had purchased just one painting, an indifferent portrait of the daughter of his friend W. S. Pring.[1] His close friends and associates supported him to the end, he was respectfully acknowledged throughout the art world as the key founder of an Australian school, but the general consensus of the time seemed to be that he was essentially a painter of the past. Indeed during his last ten years the vision of Roberts seemed to fade behind a curtain of humility, his paintings miniaturised in scale and detail, like the world viewed through a reversed telescope, almost underplaying their true lyrical quality compared with the more vigorous drama of his earlier work.

But if in the late works of Roberts there was a sense of retreat which was endemic to his character and circumstances, appreciation of them has perhaps been further disadvantaged by comparison with the more robust approach to picture-making which progressively infused Australian art during the 1920s. General interest in that period has tended to focus on the growth of modernism, and rightly so. Indeed by the end of the decade Margaret Preston had triumphed in Sydney with the exhibition and publication of the highly simplified paintings and woodcuts with which she exemplified her idea of the Australian modern style. In 1930 Dorrit Black had established the Modern Art Centre in Sydney, and in 1931 in Melbourne Arnold Shore and George Bell discussed the partnership with which they would the next year form a modern art school under Bell's name. Even Hans Heysen and Elioth Gruner, those two bastions inspired to preserve the popularity of Pastoral impressionism, had recently adapted their landscapes towards the new style by painting flatter or more austere compositions. This had not a little to do with George W. Lambert, who had returned from London to Australia in 1921 to become an all-conquering influence on the art scene. Lambert was no modernist, but he encouraged everyone to strengthen the formal, linear properties of their work.

All these factors contribute to a conundrum in arriving at a balanced assessment of Roberts's late works and their place in Australian art. Against such a modernising context it has been easy to regard them as echoes or pale memories, out of sorts with their time. Yet, ironically, they may now be seen in hindsight as far more potent by association with a future generation of painters than they have been given credit for; more potent indeed than the works of Streeton, Heysen, Lambert and Gruner which at the time buried Roberts's reputation.

Putney Bridge, London, c1905-c1908, London, oil on canvas on cardboard, 34.5 x 44.0 cm; Art Gallery of South Australia, Adelaide, M.J.M. Carter Collection

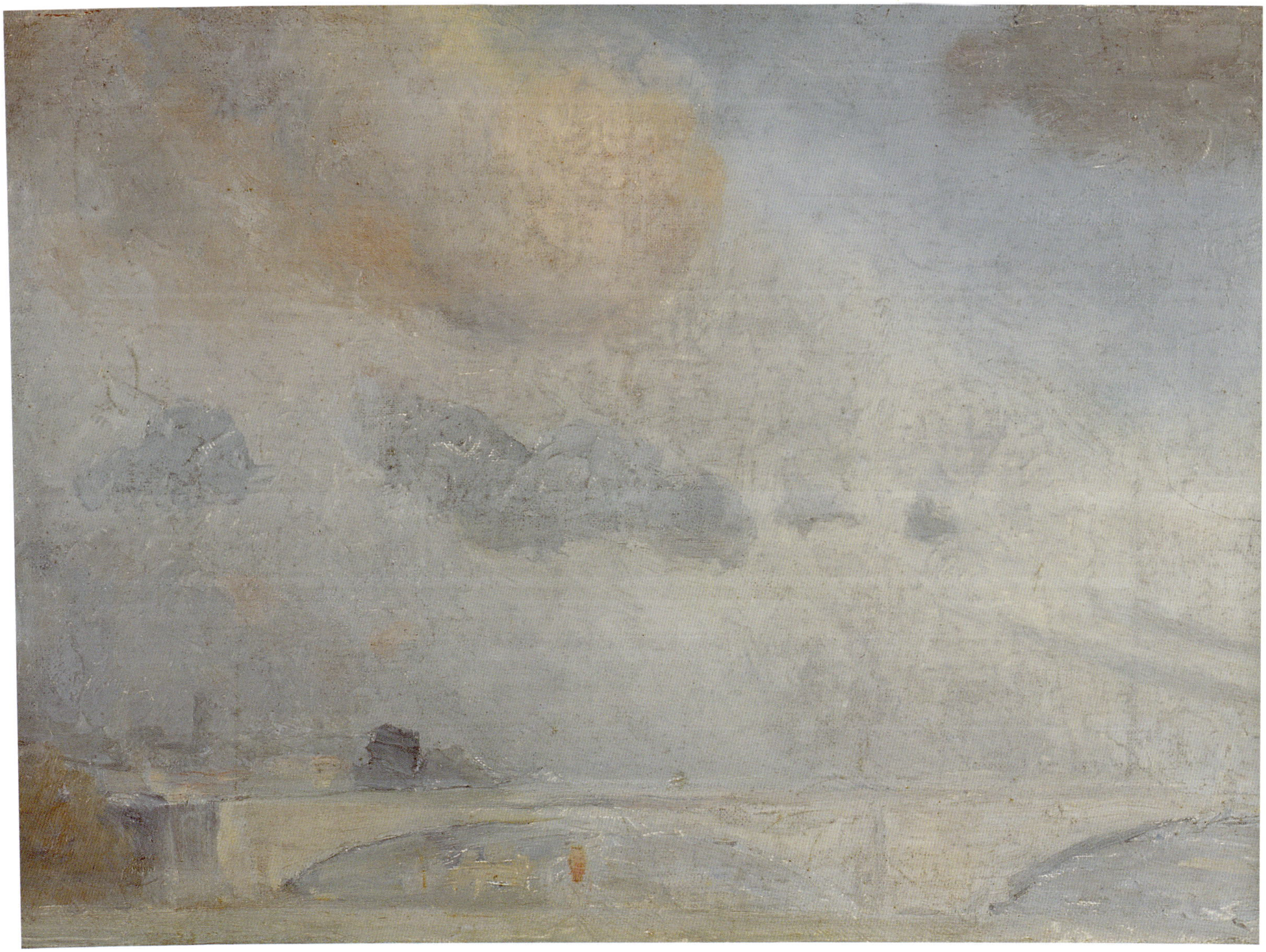

Tom Roberts

There is no shortage of opinion that from 1903, the year of completion in London of his painting *Opening of the First Parliament of the Commonwealth of Australia*, Roberts was a failure, and that that monstrously difficult commission was largely to blame. It damaged his eyesight, enervated him, and did not bring the critical acclaim he might have hoped for. If in the unlikely event some Royal Academician experienced in rendering large-scale official events with many figures had been asked to do the painting instead, the career of Roberts may have not, one suspects, progressed much differently. Roberts might have undertaken his journeys between hemispheres at different times, but his basic problem would have been the same. For just as he straddled loyalties between Australia and Empire, between vocation and career, and between the essential imagery of Australia and a precept of academic respectability in England, so at the beginning of the twentieth century his painting became stultified by an ambiguity of purpose. It would seem, from the evidence, that much of that ambiguity was imprinted in his psyche at the very outset of his life as an artist.

No such problem existed for his friends Frederick McCubbin, Arthur Streeton and Charles Conder. By 1912, the year of Roger Fry's second Post-Impressionist exhibition in London, McCubbin, after his first and only trip overseas, was blossoming back in Australia through his discovery of Old Master painting.[2] Streeton, with his bravura style and commercial success, seemed boundlessly confident.[3] Conder had been dead three years, already a self-fulfilled legend of the *fin de siècle*.[4] In 1912 Roberts wrote to McCubbin, "Well Prof where are we? Which way are we going? Damme!".[5] Since 1903 he had fallen by his own definition into a "black period". He tried cutting back on colour, painting a few modest landscapes which echoed Whistlerian subtlety, such as *The towpath, Putney* or *Putney Bridge, London* or *Storm at sea*. He produced a long-gestated but misguided subject painting entitled *"The Sleeper Awakened"* which was finally accepted by the Royal Academy in 1913, and a number of low-key but sensitive portraits including *Grey Lady (Mrs Ince)*, influenced in its monochromatic colours by discussions with James Quinn. Quinn, a younger Australian artist then in London, had advised Roberts to reduce his palette to a range of yellow ochre, light red, white and black. The resulting grey tonality seemed to suit Roberts's growing propensity for understatement.[6] However, continued rejection from the Royal Academy, and only the most subdued acknowledgement by Australian officialdom, compounded a severely damaged morale.

It was time for friends to act, and Roberts's wife Lillie, in no small way responsible for his financial stability, was supportive of an effort to revive his confidence. In 1913 he was invited by Madame Ruby Hartl, subject of an earlier portrait by him, to stay at her eighteenth-century Villa Passalacqua at Lake Como in northern Italy.[7] The sight of mountains plunging to the edge of the water, and gentle hues created by cool envelopes of air across the lake, stirred memories of his landscape painting in Australia. In the following year he exhibited his Italian pictures at Walker's Gallery in London, the rental costs having been guaranteed by Roberts's old friend Duncan Anderson, and achieved moderate commercial success.[8] But for his art it was an Indian summer. With

Winter, England, c1920, London, oil on board, 48.0 x 38.8 cm; Private collection, Melbourne

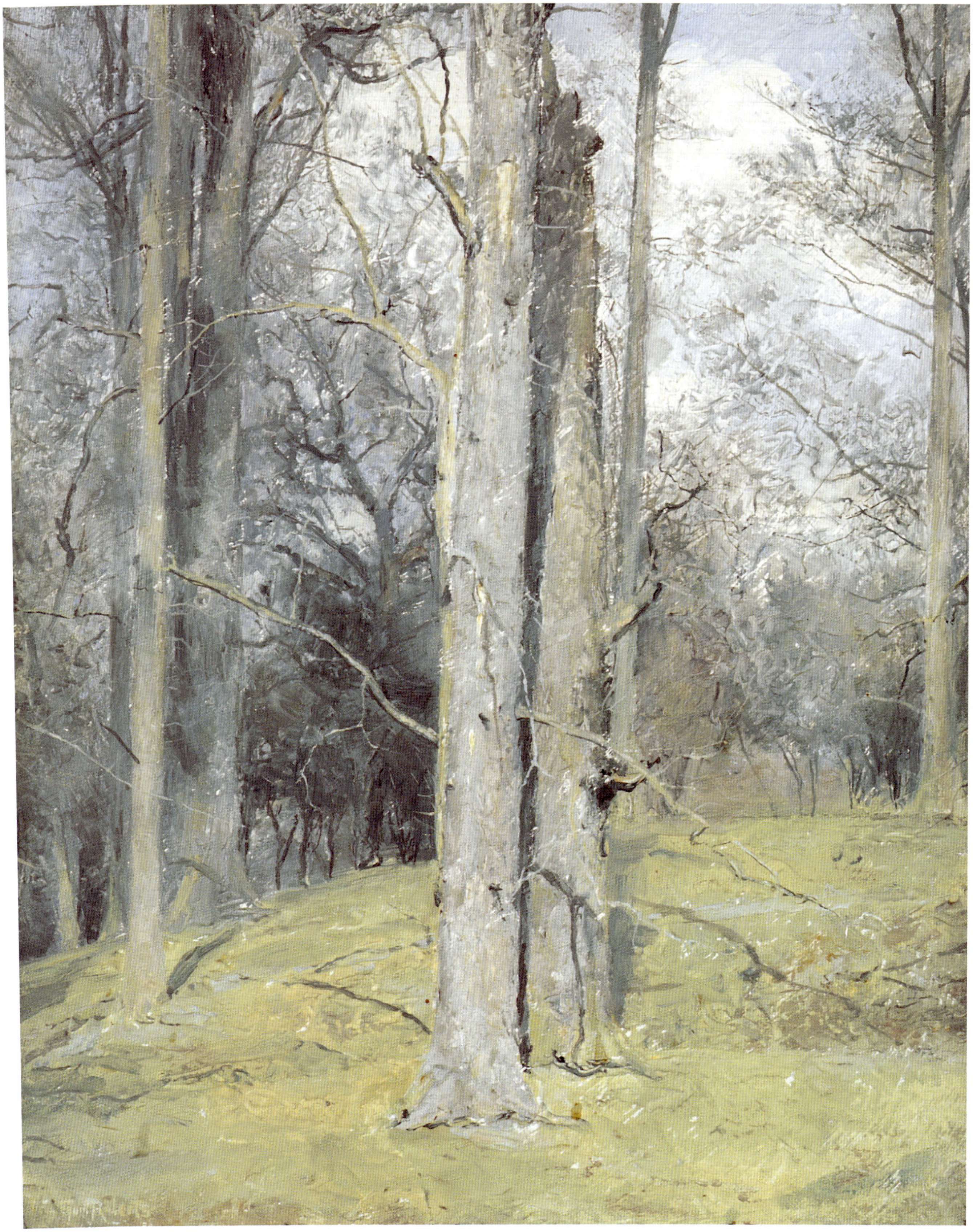

the advent of war, and Roberts's voluntary enlistment in 1915 as an orderly with the 3rd London General Hospital at Wandsworth, his painting virtually ceased for four years.

The first two decades of Roberts's twentieth-century career therefore may be seen as a hiatus by a combination of circumstance, flawed self-perception of direction and purpose, and some peculiar aspect of his nature which remains to be clarified in spite of Humphrey McQueen's recent extensive biography.[9] Why was Roberts so peripatetic, so restless in those years? Was the question of what and how to paint simply too hard to face? It ran counter to the meaning of his famous statement of 1890 "... by making art the perfect expression of one time and one place, it becomes art for all time and of all places".[10] In contrast, McCubbin stayed in his Australian garden, mining it for all the poetry it was worth and became a much better painter for it. Streeton was a traveller, but his mind was more commercially honed, and his eye and hand had the adaptive and voracious swiftness of a journalist who could go anywhere with certainty. On the other hand Roberts's frequent movement seems strangely concomitant with a descent into self doubt. Not that he was completely gloomy; he channelled more energy into bonhomie and friendships than promoting his own interests as a painter.

Judgement on Roberts's late work actually becomes more favourable by putting aside those first two decades of the new century, and focusing on his rediscovery of Australia. When he visited his country of adoption during 1919-20 there was an oxygenating effect which determined him to return for good, which he did at the beginning of 1923. Indeed he felt euphoric, declaring to his wife in a letter, "It had the sensation that as a child you thought it would be going to heaven; I don't exaggerate".[11] He would continue to feel undeserved neglect – the National Gallery of Victoria was not to acquire a major painting by him until the year after his death when in 1932 it purchased his early masterpiece *Shearing the rams* – and, as McQueen has pointed out, he was omitted by the magazine Art in Australia from its occasional monographic special issues and books. But he was at least able to regain a sense of the engagement with landscape which in the last two decades of the nineteenth century had been of such special significance to Australian art.

Between 1920 and his death in 1931 Roberts painted around two hundred works, of which about twenty were portraits and a little more than a handful were still-lives or flowerpieces.[12] The rest were landscapes, mainly small of scale, their subjects from around the area where he and his wife settled after their permanent return to Australia, and also from her family's country in Tasmania. Within a few weeks of arriving in Melbourne they bought land in the Dandenong Ranges at South Sassafras (later renamed Kallista), forty-five kilometres to the east of the city. There, in a former orchard, they began to build a house which they called Talisman.[13] The pace of Melbourne had picked up dramatically in twenty years. Its electrification, and development dictated by the imminent growth of automobile traffic, minimised the sense of provincial distance from London. In the Dandenongs Roberts and his wife recreated the London garden

Springtime in Sussex, 1921, England oil on canvas on plywood, 35.4 x 45.3 cm; The Art Gallery of New South Wales, Sydney, Purchased 1932

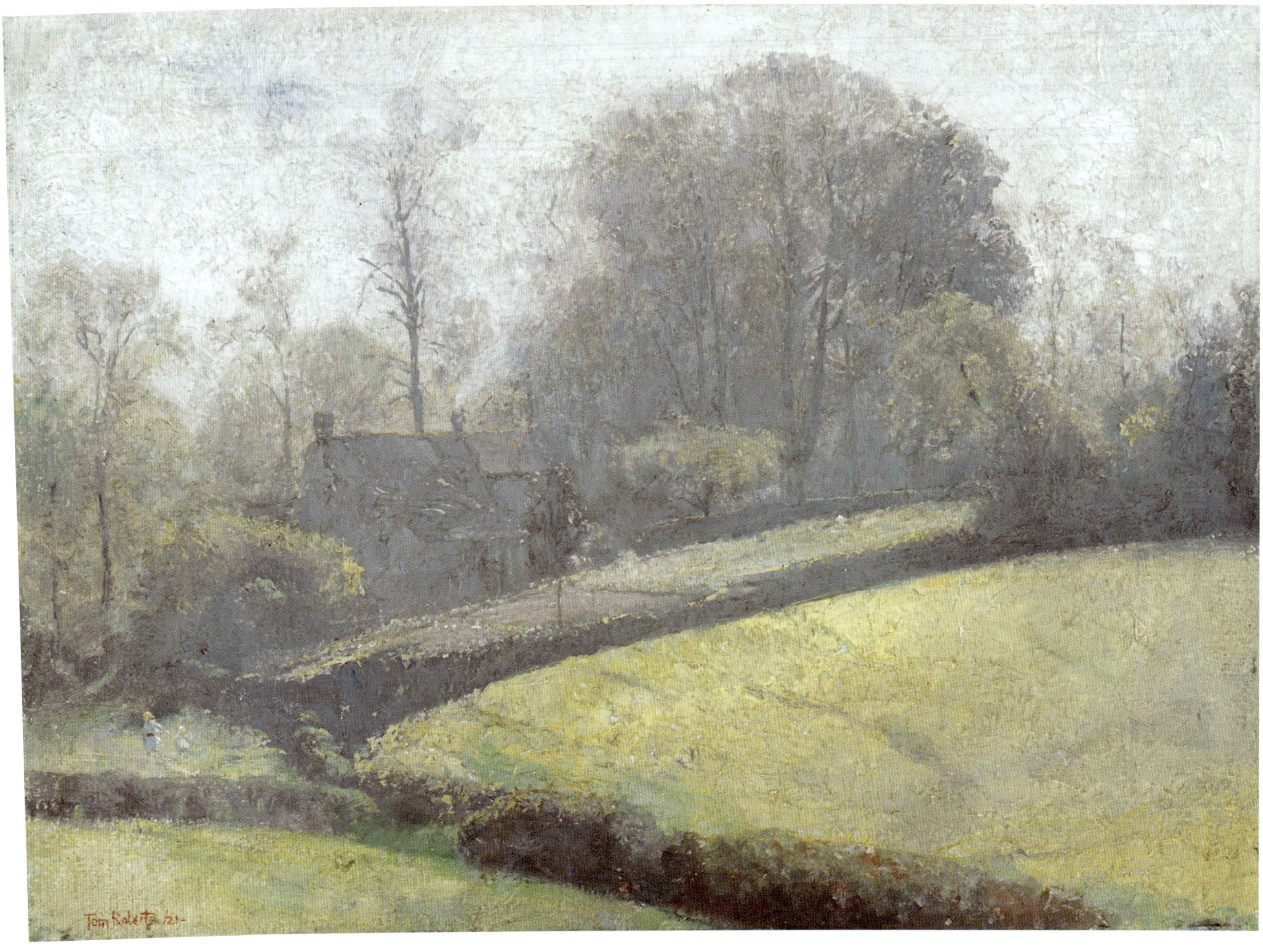

they had grown at Golders Green, and found something of the bucolic highland atmosphere which they had enjoyed being next to Hampstead Heath. The decision to return to Australia saved him as a painter in his twilight years. Moreover by living in the country Roberts may have instinctively sought to distance himself from modernist tendencies which were an inevitable part of a rapidly changing city.

Not that he could have been entirely unaware of, or even uninterested in, the presence of new ideas in the practice of his younger contemporaries. There was little evidence of it to be seen in the state galleries in Sydney and Melbourne, but Roland Wakelin and Roy de Maistre had exhibited their colour-music paintings in Sydney just before Roberts made his first return visit there and, principally through the efforts of Margaret Preston and Thea Proctor, an interest in modernism began to appear in the pages of Art in Australia and The Home magazine. Having seen the Post-Impressionist and Futurist exhibition at the National Gallery in London at the end of 1913 Roberts wrote to McCubbin with a feeling that high academic realism and finish seemed no longer relevant.[14] There is little evidence that this appreciative response had any impact on his painting, except later perhaps in his landscapes which exemplify simplicity over detail. For example as in *Hillside* where the focus travels through a sequence of dark and light masses around the edges of the picture surface, or in *Sherbrooke Forest* where the formal rigour of vertical trees is relieved by a curving foreground. Roberts's interpretation of the latter motif was to elicit considerable admiration from a later generation of artists, notably from Fred Williams, who lived and painted in the 1960s at Upwey near Sherbrooke and Kallista.

The modern era in painting, however, was not just to do with surface geometry. It was also to do with energy; and energy was light. Fundamentally, Roberts embraced the pictorial conventions of a nineteenth-century artist, but there was a certain intensity about his translation of small luminous sensations into paint, and his enduring fascination with the colour of light, which carried his vision not only into his own late period but also into the future more significantly than any of his contemporaries. The term Streetonesque conjures seductive images of Sydney Harbour, and heroic spaces of sky and sunlight, which have become part of the picture-postcard industry of Australia. The influence of Roberts has a far different association. His haiku-like intimacy of vision, the quality of which continued to be present so quietly but movingly in his late work, preserved a vital nerve-link to a quintessence of landscape painting in Australia. It reached back to Louis Buvelot, whom Roberts regarded as the father of the Australian landscape school, and perhaps even further to certain aspects of John Glover whose transparent way of depicting the bush to give it radiance Roberts surely admired, and it gathered forward momentum in the twentieth century with Elioth Gruner, Lloyd Rees, Arnold Shore, Arthur Boyd and Fred Williams. All the latter acknowledged their respect for Roberts at some part of their careers.[15]

Roberts was to these artists as Corot was to many French painters of the modern era (although in the early twentieth century writers drew a comparison more between Roberts and Manet). This relationship was something to do with the psychological need to

Washing day, Kallista, c1923-25 Kallista, Victoria, oil on canvas on composition board, 35.5 x 52.3 cm; The Art Gallery of New South Wales, Sydney, Gift of Mrs W.G. Buckle 1947

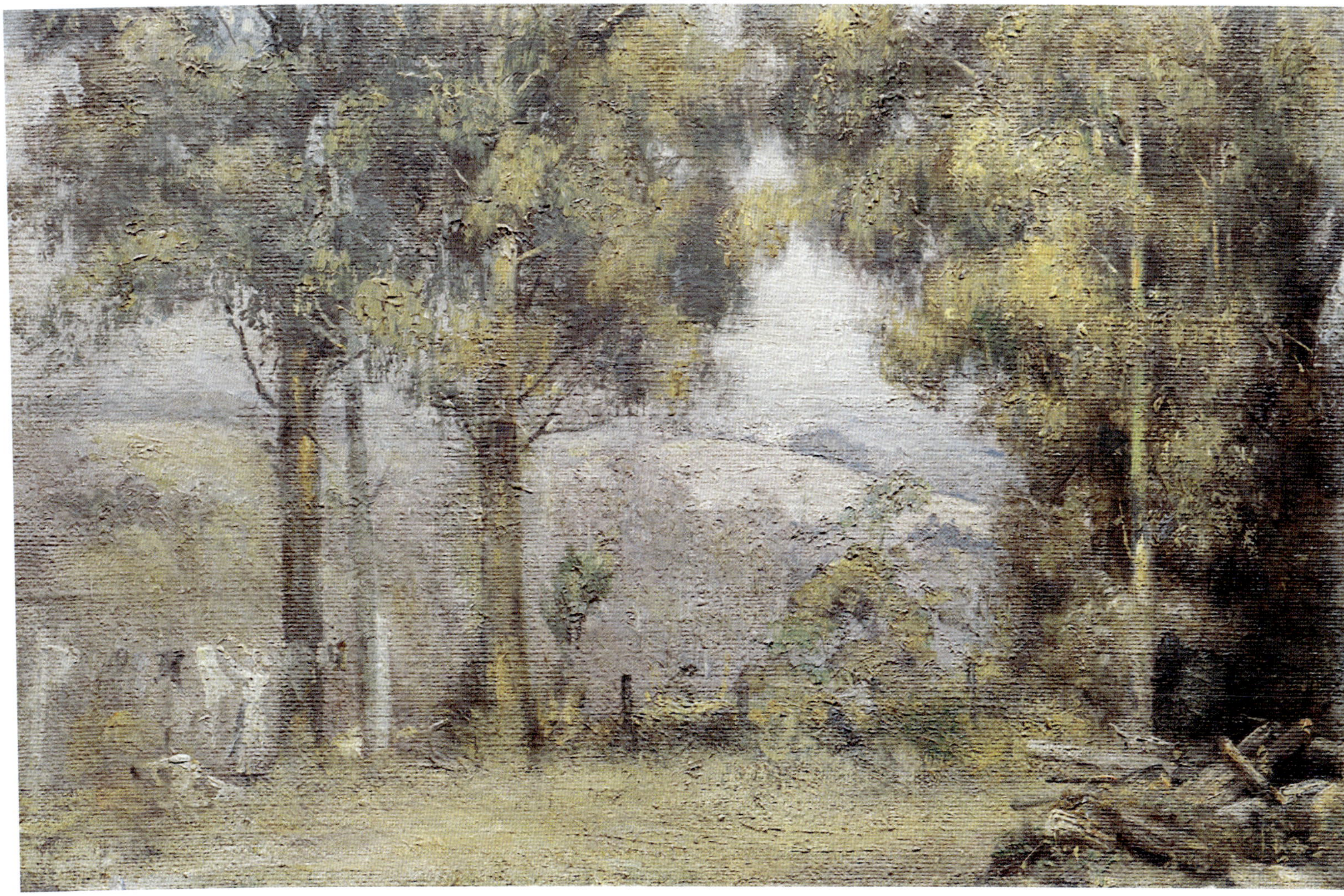

record a response to landscape in a painterly language which was soliloquous. For although each of these artists had, like Roberts, public ambition, a private response was the cornerstone, the basic module, of their painting. In his darkest moments of old age, when public success seemed so fragile, Roberts conceded that the most important thing for an artist to do was please himself.

A few years after Roberts died Arthur Boyd began to explore with his paint trolley the fields, creeks and beaches of the Mornington Peninsula in the footsteps of the earlier generation. The style, subject-matter and composition of his paintings then were closer to the late works of Roberts than anything else; little encrustations of light, impastoes bleached with Antipodean sunshine. Arnold Shore did something similar with his landscapes of the 1940s, and much later in his Shoalhaven landscapes Boyd expanded into grander conception the radiance and format of Roberts's *Bailed up* and *In a corner on the Macintyre*. It is instructive meanwhile to compare the early landscapes of both these artists with such paintings by Roberts as *Springtime in Sussex*, purchased in 1932 by the Art Gallery of New South Wales (where its intense, almost citric glow was noticed by Lloyd Rees), and *Sherbrooke Forest* and *Washing day, Kallista*, both acquired by New South Wales in the 1940s.[16] The intimacy and paint handling of these works, in particular *Washing day, Kallista*, goes beyond mere descriptiveness into visual poetry. One of the most beautiful of Roberts's late paintings, it depicts a woman at a washing line framed into the left-hand side of the composition by a copse of gum trees, an idyllic landscape glimpsed beyond. Distant focus of all elements in the picture is typical of Roberts at the time, yet this work contains the hermetic privacy of a still-life by Chardin, and was executed with the tenderness of an artist who loved his paint.

These three works were made over a five-year period, the first, *Springtime in Sussex*, in England in 1921 and the other two soon after Roberts and his wife had settled at Kallista. Taken as a group they reflect Roberts's pleasure at returning to the landscape of Australia, as expressed in a letter in 1924:

> We go on quietly – I'm doing no portraits, but am on, with great delight, to landscapes – and here is a very tempting surrounding. I had a show a few weeks back in Melbourne, and did well. People seem to like my new work. Up here are the most wonderful clouds; one goes at 'em, and is almost afraid to look next day at the result, for fear of disappointment – High piled cumuli reared up over a shadowed hill are inspiring. They seem so still but – [17]

Then in 1926 he wrote to Walter Barnett, gathering further enthusiasm:

> here we have something new yet old, no tidy self-contained elms and chestnuts that reflect every mood of these days. Think of the red gums of a Murray flat, how they stretch their arms one to another, they are a great tree, showing all their great construction. Difficult to paint with their silver grey branchwork gilded by sunlight to something warmer. [18]

Poppies, 1921, London, oil on canvas, 46.0 x 33.0 cm; Private collection, Canberra

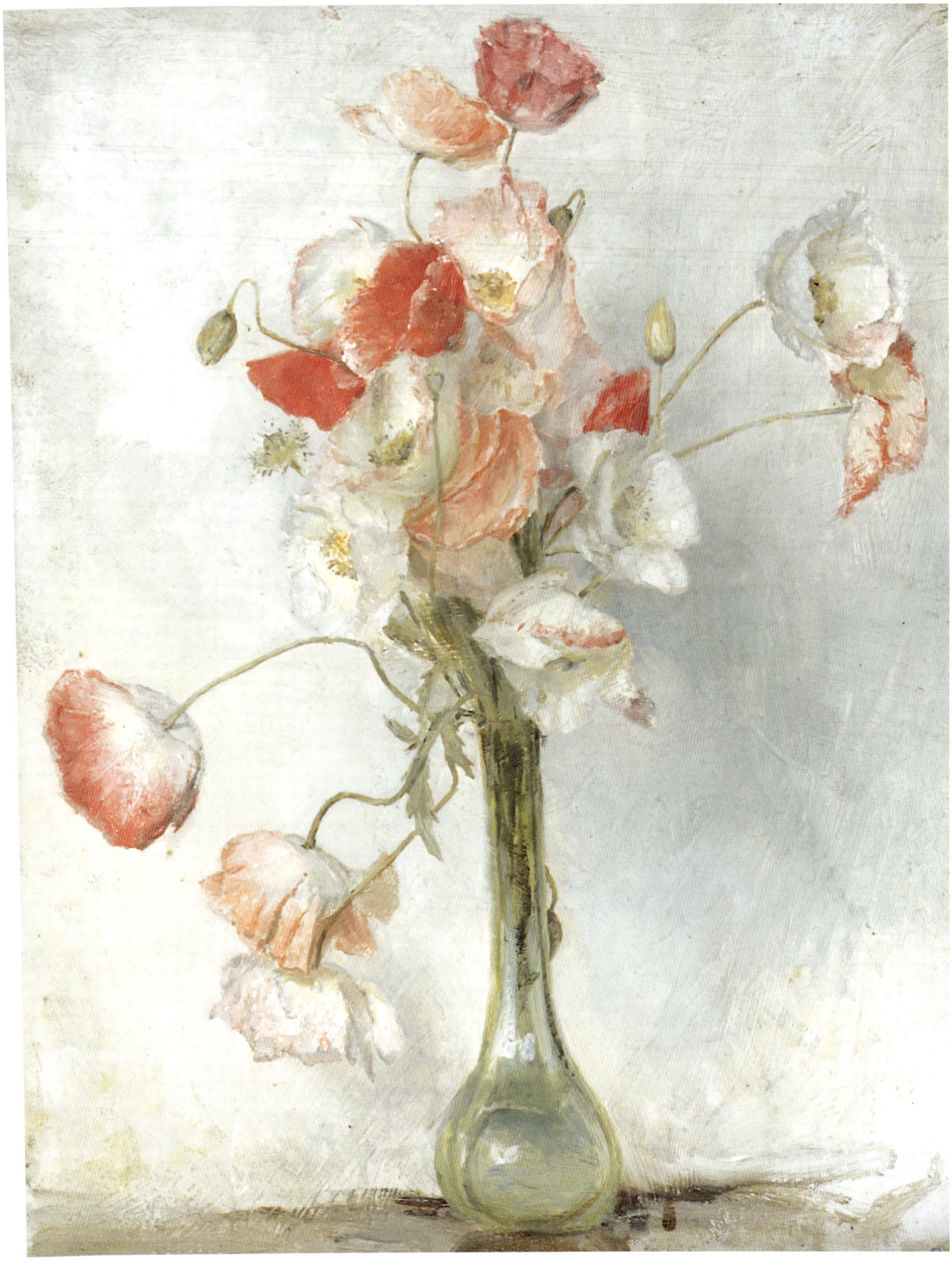

Tom Roberts

Any discussion of Roberts's late work must make reference to *Bailed up* which the artist painted in 1895, but the background of which he repainted extensively during 1927. He had experienced a good deal of anguish over it, failing to find a buyer for more than thirty years, not to mention his struggle with its technical resolution. But this was a blessing by default in many ways because in 1927 he made it a tour de force of his late style. The dilemma for a retrospective is whether to show *Bailed up* with the earlier or later period. To either it is equally relevant, for within this great painting there are two clear intentions divided by a huge gulf of time. The first was to celebrate a nationalist ethos which, in looking towards the Federated unity of Australia, gathered in a mythology of the recent pioneering past. The second intention was to transfix the mysterious stillness and glare of the Australian bush, in the process of which he created a dazzling crucible of light, paint and pentimento texture. One can imagine the background of *Bailed up* divided by a grid into many units, each one part of the whole but able to stand as a landscape painting of the late period in its own right; each a microchip of the artist's particular way of looking and translating his response into pigment.

Finally, there remains one more painting worthy of reflection concerning the late works of Roberts, and it involves a shift of focus from one of his largest paintings to one of his smallest. In 1927, the year Roberts repainted *Bailed up*, the Art Gallery of South Australia purchased *Saplings*, painted on a cigar-box lid and bearing a signature 'Charles Conder', which implied a date of c1889, the year when the artist friends made paintings on these tiny panels for 'The 9 by 5 Impression Exhibition'. This work was later reattributed correctly to Roberts. Who else but Roberts could have taken such an unremarkable slice of nature – a few gum saplings against a steep hillside without sky, illusionistic depth or narrative subject – and make out of it a talisman? This jewel of Roberts's œuvre addresses his late work, and far beyond. It projects an arc across time to Arthur Boyd, Fred Williams and even perhaps to Roberts's distant relative, William Robinson.[19] It welds the final phase of Roberts the landscape painter with his beginning. Most importantly, together with his late works, it reminds us that between this artist and his motif there was a profound, fundamental engagement that fading limelight did not diminish.

The quarry, Maria Island, 1926, Tasmania, oil on canvas , 60.3 x 50.2 cm; National Gallery of Australia, Canberra, Bequest of Henriette von Dallwitz and of Richard Paul in honour of his father Dr Oscar Paul 1965

p. 80-81: *Sherbrooke Forest*, 1924, Dandenong Ranges, Victoria, oil on canvas on paperboard, 48.0 x 68.4 cm; The Art Gallery of New South Wales, Sydney, Purchased 1946

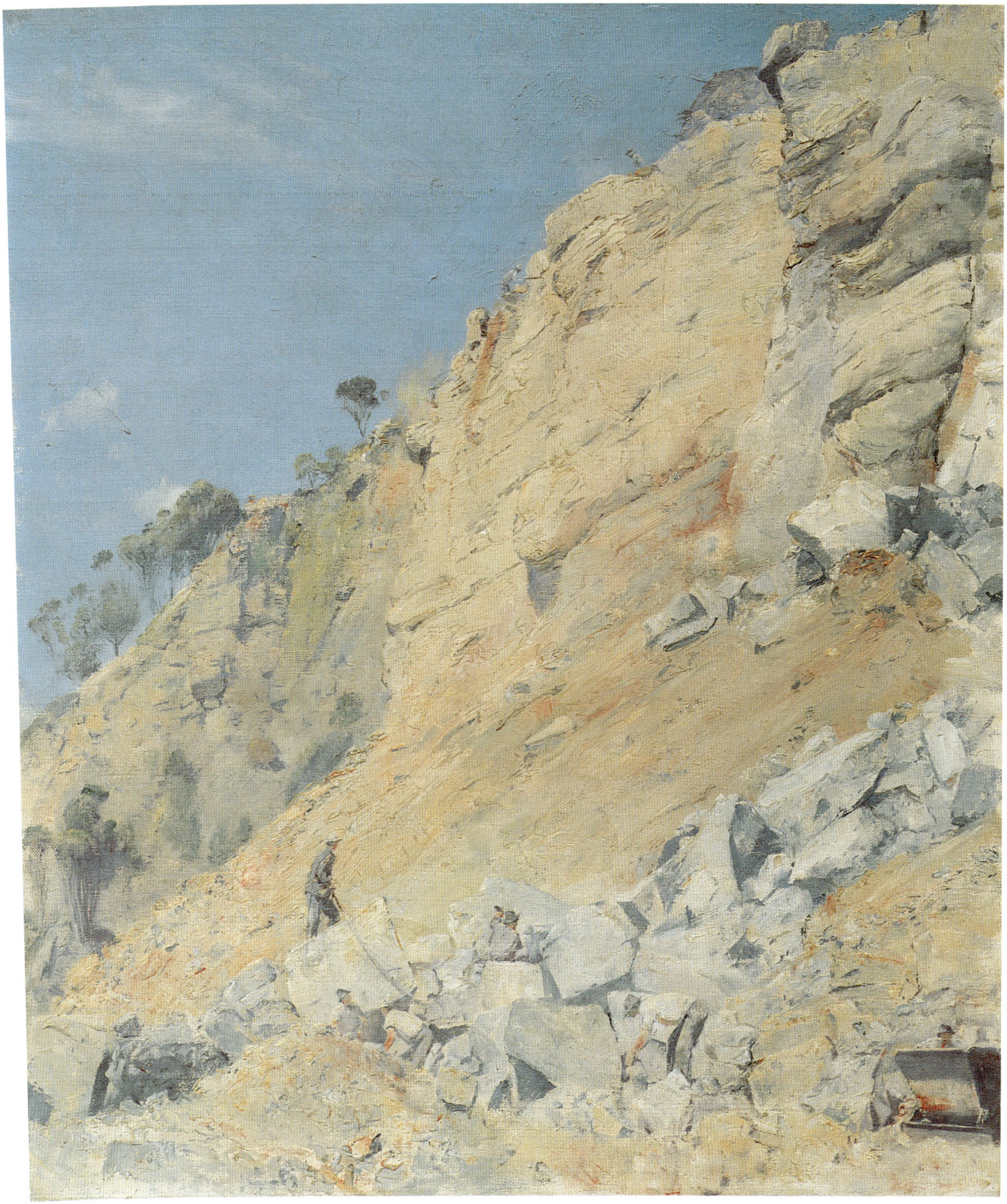

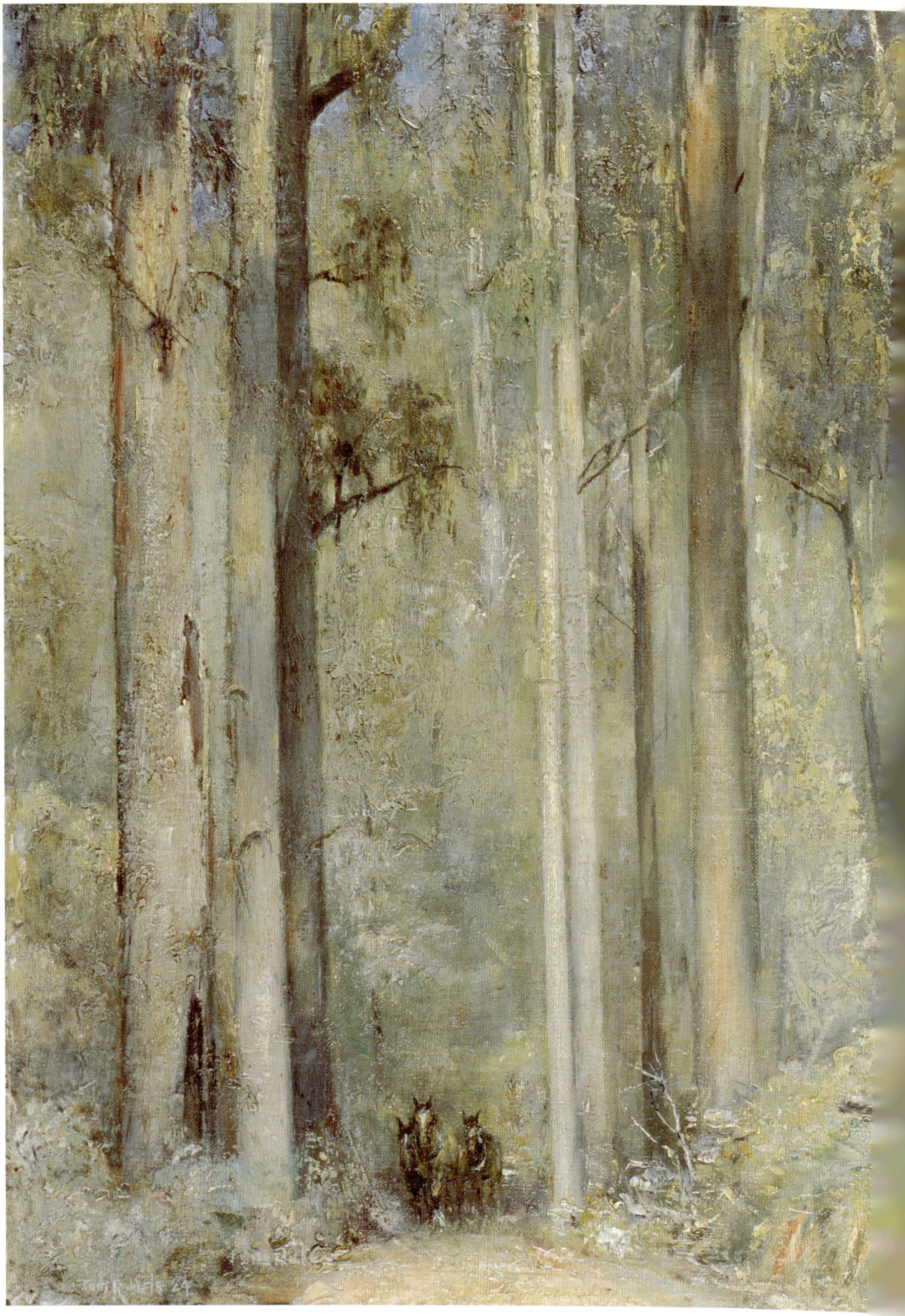

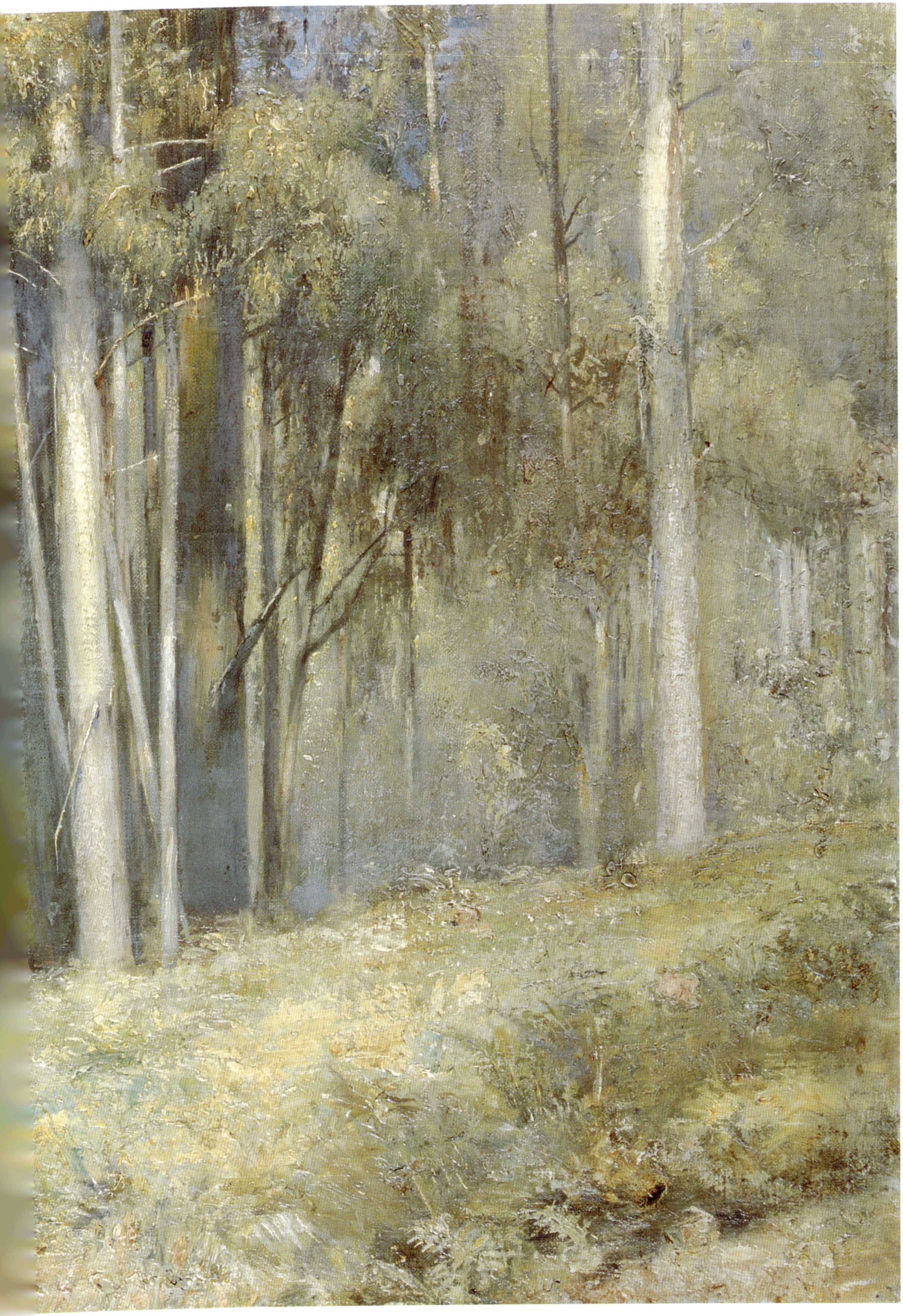

Tom Roberts, Etcher

Roger Butler

Tom Roberts first exhibited his etching *A Chinese cook shop* in 1887 but it was more than thirty years before it was seen in public again. The other six prints known to be by Roberts were never exhibited contemporaneously.[1] Despite this, Roberts's contribution to Australian print history is significant for his prints are amongst the most enduring etched images of the 1880s.

Fresh back from England, Roberts set the style in Australian artistic circles. In Melbourne in January 1886 he issued "... an artistic invitation card, etched by himself, inviting his friends to view ..." the four paintings destined for London's Colonial and Indian Exhibition.[2]

His choice of etching to produce an 'artistic' invitation was unprecedented. It no doubt stemmed from his recent English sojourn, where the Painter-Etcher movement was gaining popularity, and where such invitations were becoming fashionable.[3] In England he might also have learnt the rudiments of the technique.

A landscape etching, *At Phillip Island*, followed the January 1886 invitation card.[4] A number of fellow artists could have assisted Roberts in the production of these first Melbourne prints: Cyrus Mason, founder of the Buonarotti Club, who had technical expertise and owned a printing press;[5] Louis Abrahams, an early etcher; or John Mather whose studio in 1886 adjoined Roberts's first studio at 95 Collins Street and who, after 1893, became an accomplished etcher and teacher.

With *A Chinese cook shop* Roberts showed himself to be more ambitious – encouraged perhaps by seeing an etching, after a watercolour by Mather, that Abrahams had exhibited in 1886, or after receiving a letter from Buxton Knight, an English friend who was making money from etching.[6] For the composition and subject matter of *A Chinese cook shop* Roberts drew on his knowledge of Whistler's prints of the late 1850s, such as *A kitchen at Lutzelbourg* and *La Marchande de moutarde.*

Roberts planned to have this cook-shop plate professionally editioned in London.[7] But before doing so he exhibited an impression, priced at ten shillings and sixpence, in Melbourne in October 1887, in the Australian Artists' Association exhibition. Judging from the lack of contemporary impressions now in circulation one suspects that sales were non-existent.

The few other prints by Roberts cannot be dated with certainty – though a chronology can be attempted.

The Chinese cook shop, 1887, Melbourne, etching on paper, 20.4 x 15.2 cm; National Gallery of Australia, Canberra

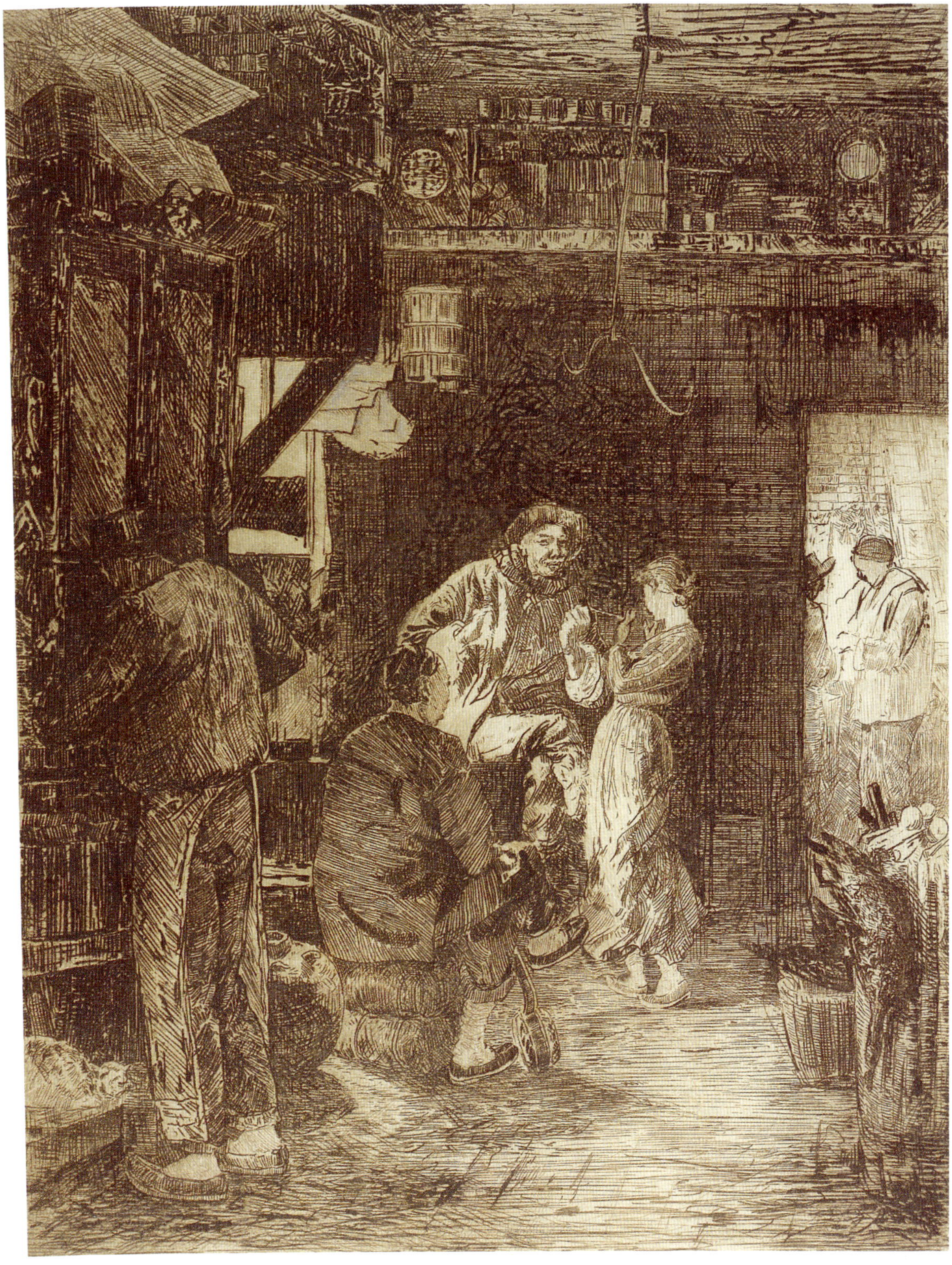

Tom Roberts

The portrait of *Louis Buvelot* – the largest print that Roberts made, based on a similar-sized pen & ink sketch of 1886 – was probably produced after Buvelot's death in May 1888 as a memento mori. An impression of Roberts's *A drover's wayside stop*,[8] is inscribed by him "June 88". *Fisherman's Bend on the Yarra* is known only by a reference in a letter dating it to 1889.[9]

In Sydney, where Roberts was based in the nineties, there was less knowledge of printmaking than in Melbourne. An article of 1892 observed that "... in Sydney, you cannot even buy an etching-plate, and as for getting it printed, you might as well go to Timbuctoo".[10]

This report seems to have encouraged Livingston Hopkins to promote etching among his artist friends, for the following year it was reported that "An Etching Club has been lately started in Sydney, which aims at high-class work rather than numerous members ... Meetings take place once a month for the discussion of matters relating to etching, plates, and proofs".[11]

Although the Etching Club existed for only two years, some of the most important prints of the 1890s were made by members. Hopkins produced his drypoint *Self-portrait*, 1894; A.H. Fullwood *The 'Black Horse', Richmond, N.S.W.*, 1894; Julian Ashton his views of Sydney, 1893; and B.E. Minns *The Harbour*, 1893.

Roberts's contribution to the Etching Club, *Ring o'Roses*, c1895, recalls the poetic etched work of Claude Lorrain, of which he had a collection.[12] The decorative composition of the print became the basis for his frieze-like painting *Australian Pastoral.*[13]

The first exhibition of the Australian Painter-Etchers Society, in Sydney in 1921, was concerned as much with giving the movement a history as with presenting the work of contemporary printmakers. Roberts's etching *A Chinese cook shop* was included, retitled as *The Opium Den.*

Plates from previous decades began to be reprinted – Julian Ashton's works of 1893, Benjamin Duterrau's of the 1840s and even the early attempts of Lionel Lindsay.[14] Roberts's copperplates that had been 'lost' also reappeared. Cyril Dillon found the plate for *A Chinese cook shop* in his own studio,[15] and Jessie Traill discovered other plates in hers.[16]

The majority of existing impressions of *A Chinese cook shop*, the portrait of *Louis Buvelot* and the landscape *At Phillip Island* are from the 1920s and later. These later impressions printed by Traill and Dillon reflect the prevailing soft, pictorialist fashion of the period. Printed in sepia with lush painterly plate tone they are far removed in feeling from the simple printings in black ink favoured in the 1880s and '90s by Roberts.

Roberts approved of these new printings, for some prints are signed. Their nostalgia was in keeping with the emotive values of his late paintings.

Abraham Louis Buvelot, c1886-87, Melbourne, etching on paper, 30.5 x 24.8 cm; Art Gallery of South Australia, Adelaide, David Murray Bequest Fund 1954

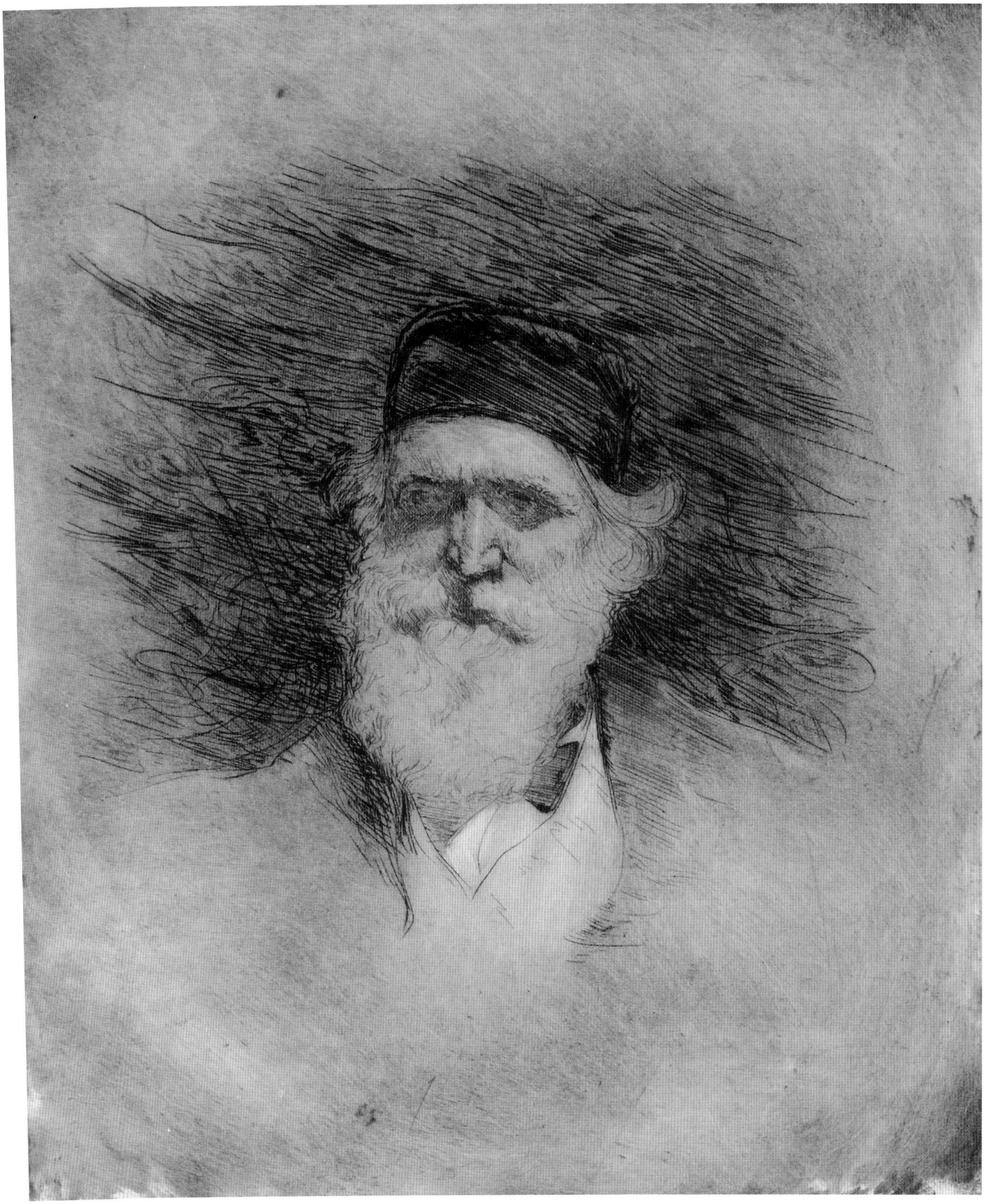

Tom Roberts

Biographical Timeline

collated by Jane Hylton from Humphrey McQueen's *Tom Roberts*

1856	8 March: Thomas William Roberts born at Durngate Street, Dorchester, Dorset, England, third child of Richard (1827-1868) and Cela Matilda Roberts (née Evans, 1828-1881).
1860s	Attended Hardye's Grammar School, in Dorchester; by 1865 was living at Wollastan Terrace. Roberts possibly met the author Thomas Hardy of Dorset during his school years. Roberts's father, who was editor of the local newspaper, died on 30 December 1868, aged forty-one.
1869	20 March: sailed from London on the True Briton, with his widowed mother, and younger siblings Alice and Dick, arriving at Geelong, Victoria, on 22 June; the family settled in Collingwood, Melbourne. Mrs Roberts's widowed mother had emigrated from England to Melbourne with six of her children twenty years earlier.
1871	Commenced formal art training (night classes), at the East Collingwood Artisans' School of Design.
1871-1874	The Roberts family resided at Dight Street, Collingwood; Tom worked at Hewitt's photographic studios, Collingwood; also assisted his mother with leatherwork for her brother Francis Evans's leathergoods business.
mid 1870s	Worked for Stewart's photographic studios, Melbourne.
1874	Resided at 113 Johnston Street, Collingwood; from 1875 his mother resided at 7 Budd Street, Collingwood. Attended the Trades Hall School of Design, Carlton (where Louis Buvelot taught); won a prize for landscapes; enrolled for evening classes at the National Gallery School (where Thomas Clark, 1814-1883, was head of the School of Design until mid 1875); met Frederick McCubbin and others at this time.
1876	Applied unsuccessfully for the position of Master in the School of Design, National Gallery School.
1877	Visited Tasmania; in Launceston met the Williamson family.
1877-79	Studied in the School of Painting at the National Gallery School (under Eugene von Guérard, 1811-1901) allowed an afternoon from employment to attend.
1878	Resided at 170 George Street, Fitzroy, with sister Alice; later resided at Nicholson Street, Fitzroy. With C.D. Richardson attended anatomy lectures at the University of Melbourne; Roberts and his fellow male students also employed a male model to pose nude for life studies.
1879	Visited Tasmania.
1880	Roberts's future wife Elizabeth Sarah (Lillie) Williamson enrolled at the National Gallery School. Roberts's oil, *Morning study*, exhibited in the Victorian fine arts court at the Melbourne International Exhibition; listed as member of Victorian Academy of Arts (VAA); two of Roberts's drawings, inspired by poet Henry Kendall's *Orara*, published as engravings by the Art Union of Victoria. The artist at this time still signed his work "T.W.Roberts"; made copies of paintings in the National Gallery of Victoria to sell to fund overseas travel and study.

1881 20 January: sailed from Melbourne on the Garonne, arriving at Gravesend, London, 11 March. 5 July: enrolled at the Royal Academy Schools, having passed the June probation examination. 6 December: commenced as a full-time student (three-year course). Resided at 10 James Street, Haymarket, working at Cologne Chambers, 8 York Building, the Strand. 5 November: *The Graphic* first published an engraving of one of Roberts's illustrations.

1882 Roberts became interested in the work of French artist Jules Bastien-Lepage (1848-1884).

1883 August: travelled through Spain with Australian friends, the radical physician William Maloney, the artist John Russell and Russell's architect brother; saw works by Velázquez and Murillo; during trip became friendly with two Spanish art students from Paris, Laureano Barrau and Ramon Casas. Casas produced out-of-doors oil sketches in Roberts's presence. Still in Spain in October. Arrived back in London in late 1883, perhaps via Venice and Paris.

1884 April: visited Venice (and/or again in October). Moved to Camden Town, London. 17 May: James McNeill Whistler's exhibition 'Notes – Harmonies – Nocturnes' opened in London.

1885 20 February: Whistler delivered his 'Ten o'clock Lecture' in London (Roberts apparently not present). Visited Paris briefly. 4 March: departed England on s.s. Lusitania, arriving in Melbourne 25 April; took up a previously accepted position with the photographic firm of Barrie & Brown, Bourke Street, Melbourne. Painted *Coming South* as a result of his ship-board experiences. Started supplying *The Bulletin* (and later other periodicals) with work for engraved illustrations. October: Buxton's artistic stationery and art supplies opened a new emporium in Swanston Street, including an art gallery. Roberts took studio space with George Ashton and John Mather at 95 Collins Street; continued correspondence with overseas colleagues, including John Russell. 14 October: accepted offer of Associate membership and began exhibiting regularly with the VAA. October: Whistler's painting, *Note in Blue and Green* shown in the Anglo-Australian Society of Artists exhibition, Fletcher's Gallery, Melbourne. Painted at Darebin Creek and Gardiner's Creek. By late 1885 Roberts was painting in four main categories: portraiture, streetscape, genre and landscape; commenced *Allegro con brio, Bourke Street west.*

1885/86 Summer: Tom Roberts, Frederick McCubbin and Louis Abrahams camped and began painting at Box Hill, just out of Melbourne.

1886 23 January: elected a member of the Buonarotti Club (proposed by Frederick McCubbin); 4 May: 'The Colonial and Indian Exhibition' opened in London; included four of Roberts's works among those provided by the VAA. 14 October: became a founding member of the Australian Artists' Association (AAA); exhibited regularly with the Association at Buxton's Gallery. December: visited Brocklesby Station at Corowa in the southern Riverina district of New South Wales, attending a cousin's wedding to the daughter of one of the station's owners, Alexander Anderson.

1886/87 Summer: Roberts, Louis Abrahams and Frederick McCubbin rented a cottage near Mentone, a small beach-side township on Port Phillip Bay, and also painted at nearby Ricketts Point, Beaumaris. Roberts met up with Arthur Streeton painting at Beaumaris. Streeton joined Roberts, McCubbin and Abrahams painting at Box Hill.

1887 2 February: elected to chair a meeting of the AAA, held at his studio. Moved studio to St James Building, 59 William Street.

1888 March: founding member of the Victorian Artists' Society (VAS), an amalgamation of the VAA and AAA; exhibited regularly with the Society. 19 March: arrived in Sydney, there met Charles Conder who had settled in Sydney in early 1887; the two painted together at Coogee. 9 April: arrived back in Melbourne. Mid April: moved into a residential studio, Grosvenor Chambers, Collins Street east. 20 April: exhibited with Frederick McCubbin, Arthur Streeton and George Walton at the official opening of Grosvenor Chambers; established a routine of full-time work. 30 May: death of Louis Buvelot. 19 June: initiated *conversaziones* at his new studio. August: eight paintings selected for the Melbourne Centennial Exhibition; these won six awards; sublet rooms in his Grosvenor Chambers suite to Jane Sutherland, Jane Price and Clara Southern while he went to Brocklesby at Corowa making sketches of shearers at work. October: Charles Conder arrived in Melbourne to stay with Roberts, moving into his own quarters around February 1889.

1889 5 March: best man for Frederick McCubbin at his marriage to Annie Moriarty. 17 August: 'The 9 by 5 Impression Exhibition' opened at Buxton's Gallery, Swanston Street; Roberts, instrumental in organising the exhibition, was one of seven artists (including Streeton and Conder), showing sixty-two of the 182 works; the value of his sales totalled fifty-five guineas.

1890 4 March: travelled to Tasmania; during his absence Charles Conder left Melbourne for Europe. 6 May: arrived back in Melbourne. Late May: after eight months he completed *Shearing the rams*, working on it mostly in the woolshed at Brocklesby Station. Late June: exhibited *Shearing the rams* (price 350 guineas) in his studio. June/July: the painting was shown at the rooms of Gemmell & Tuckett, auctioneers. July: sold *Shearing the rams* to stock and station agent Edward Trenchard, who hung it in his office in Collins Street. July: spent a few days on Alecha at Lindenow, East Gippsland. 5 December: an auction of works by Roberts, Streeton and McCubbin was held by Gemmell & Tuckett. December: exhibited *Allegro con brio, Bourke Street west*, in a loan exhibition organised by the VAS at the Exhibition Buildings, Melbourne, having added in three figures, late November.

1891 February: travelled to Corowa to sketch for a proposed droving picture, *A break away!*; while staying at Brocklesby visited the adjoining station, Collendina (property of the Hay family), where he also made sketches. 9 September: Roberts and Streeton left Melbourne for Sydney, staying in the city and then Mosman's Bay; the two shared a studio in Pitt Street; worked on commissioned portraits, sketched around Parramatta and occasionally sent articles to *The Argus* in Melbourne.

1892 May: sent *A break away!* to Melbourne to show in the VAS exhibition. 28 July: worked his way north along the coast to Cape York, crewing on the ketch Jessie. Late August: visited Thursday Island; the flower painter Ellis Rowan was on that leg of the journey. September: exhibited at Art Society of New South Wales, Sydney; the National Art Gallery of New South Wales purchased from this exhibition *Eileen* and *Aboriginal head (Charlie Turner)*, the first of Roberts's works to enter a public collection.

1893 April: portrait of *Henry Parkes* accepted for exhibition at the Royal Academy, London; also later forwarded work for exhibition at the Chicago Exposition; continued to send work to Melbourne for exhibition at the VAS. Autumn: visited Melbourne; after return to Sydney continued to paint commissioned portraits. August: exhibited work with the Queensland Art Society, Brisbane. December: visited Newstead North Station (property of Duncan Anderson, no relation to the Andersons of Brocklesby), near Inverell, northern New South Wales.

1894 January: at Newstead North commenced another shearing-subject picture; in September *The Golden Fleece* was purchased by the Art Gallery of New South Wales. May: had a new studio in Bathurst Street. October: again visited Melbourne, and returned to Sydney via Brocklesby Station. 2 November: went prospecting near Tenterfield, northern New South Wales, arriving by December at Yulgilbar, property of Edward Ogilvie, on the River Clarence; painted Ogilvie's portrait for £20.

1895 January: stayed again at Newstead. 1 February: moved from Newstead to neighbouring station, Paradise, owned by Duncan Anderson's cousin, and commenced *Bailed up*. Early April: moved into Inverell to continue the painting; painted *In a corner on the Macintyre* at this time. May: accompanied drovers for perhaps six weeks. July: travelled via Bathurst and Corowa to Melbourne. August: returned to Sydney with Arthur Streeton; exhibited *Bailed up* at the Society of Artists exhibition. 7 October: Lillie Williamson arrived in Sydney and was escorted around the city by Roberts. 31 December: left Sydney on a cruise aboard the Antidote, returning 26 January 1896; divided his time between his Bathurst Street studio and the camp at Little Sirius Cove, Mosman.

1895 President of the Society of Artists, remaining in position until 1897.

1896 30 April: married Elizabeth (Lillie) Sarah Williamson at St Hilary's Anglican Church, East Kew, Melbourne; the couple left the same afternoon for their honeymoon in Tasmania. 15 May: the Robertses returned briefly to Melbourne and on 18 May arrived in Sydney. July: sent a painting for exhibition at the Queensland Art Society. August: painted in the Blue Mountains; continued to exhibit regularly with the Society of Artists. October: exhibited *Bailed up* at the VAS, Melbourne.

1897 The Robertses moved to 7 Paul Street, Balmain.

1898 31 January: Caleb Roberts born. April – May: thirteen paintings were included in the 'Exhibition of Australian Art in London' at the Grafton Galleries, London, including *A break away!*, *A mountain muster* and *The Golden Fleece*. Mid-year: studio in Vickery Chambers in George Street. October: sent a portrait to the 'First Federal Exhibition', which opened in November in Adelaide.

1899 November: exhibited *A break away!* in the 'Second Federal Exhibition' in Adelaide; the painting was purchased by the National Gallery of South Australia.

1900 7 March: arrived in New Zealand, called on the artist Frances Hodgkins; left Dunedin on 5 May. May: Robertson & Moffat, Melbourne, published an engraving of *Shearing the rams*. September: commissioned by the Art Gallery of New South Wales, the Earl of Beauchamp. November: solo exhibition in Sydney of 113 works at the Society of Artists, to raise funds for a trip to London.

1901 February: showed Frances Hodgkins around Sydney. 5 May: the Robertses arrived in Melbourne; later resided in Heidelberg. 9 May: attended the opening of the first Federal Parliament in Melbourne by the Duke of York. 20 May: signed a contract to paint that event, the commission due for completion by March 1903; the studio provided for working on 'The Big Picture' was in the Melbourne Exhibition Buildings.

1902 Continued to paint portraits for the Parliament commission. May: travelled to Adelaide to paint the South Australian Governor, Lord Tennyson, and his wife.

1903 March: re-negotiated his contract for completion and acceptance in London by November of 'The Big Picture'. 17 March: the Robertses left Melbourne for London, arriving in April, and taking temporary lodgings in Manchester Square before residing at Kenilworth Court, Putney; Roberts took a studio in Warwick Square; commenced sittings for royal portraits for the Parliament commission. 16 November: completed this commission (in the South Africa room of the Imperial Institute) and sent the painting to Paris for engraving at Goupil & Cie. Over a period of nearly two-and-a half years he earned nearly 2000 guineas from 'The Big Picture'. In London Lillie Roberts took up wood-carving (possibly resuming a previous interest); she learnt to gild in the expectation of making frames for Roberts's works, and to sell; she later began receiving more commissions for frames than she could manage.

1904	February: two weeks holiday in Devonshire. April: *Opening of the First Parliament of the Commonwealth of Australia by H.R.H. The Duke of Cornwall and York, May 9, 1901* exhibited at the Royal Academy. June: travelled to Furtzberg, Bavaria, to paint a portrait of Marquis of Linlithgow, (first Governor General of Australia) commissioned by the National Gallery of South Australia.
1905	May: moved studio to 390 Harrington Road, South Kensington. 25 November: Lillie's father Caleb Williamson died, leaving her a small inheritance. Roberts suffered trouble with his eyesight during this period.
1906	Mid year: the Robertses holidayed in Holland.
1907	April: a bust of Caleb and the painting *"The Sleeper Awakened"* (on which he had been working for two years) both rejected by the Royal Academy. Became involved with the Chelsea Arts Club. Frederick McCubbin arrived in London from Australia, visiting the Robertses.
1908	26 March: exhibited *"The Sleeper Awakened"* and a group of portraits in his studio; his work was once again rejected by the Royal Academy. The Robertses visited Norfolk for six weeks. November: attended a Savage Club dinner for Australian expatriate artists.
1909	9 February: death of Charles Conder. September: the Robertses moved to a combined home and studio at 1 Bigwood Road, Golders Green (near Hampstead Heath), financed by Lillie's inheritance. October: work accepted for exhibition by the Royal Institute of Oil Painters.
1910	April: two works hung at the Royal Academy, one 'on the line' (eye-level). October: work included in an exhibition in Melbourne sponsored by the VAS of works by Australians living in Europe. Late in the year the Robertses visited Norfolk.
1911	Portrait by Roberts and Derwent Wood's bust of the artist exhibited at the Royal Academy; showed two oils with the Royal Institute of Oil Painters.
1912	June: exhibited *Ladies of the Summer* at the Fine Art Palace at White City. November: exhibited *A Norfolk barn* at the Paris Salon.
1913	The Royal Academy accepted *"The Sleeper Awakened"*. June-August: visited Italy, staying at Lake Como and briefly in Rome. October: visited Lake Como again. December: commissioned to paint a full-length portrait of Lord Tennyson, commenced in May 1914; paid 250 guineas.
1914	9 February: solo exhibition at Walker's Gallery, London; exhibition visited by Queen Mary. August/September: holidayed again at Lake Como and also in France.
1915-1916	July 1915: commenced duties as an orderly at 3rd London General Hospital, Wandsworth; promoted to corporal in charge of Wandsworth's Dental Department in late 1916; painted little during his four service years.
1917	December: death of Frederick McCubbin in Melbourne.
1918	November: peace declared; showed work in an exhibition 'War and Peace', at Burlington House, London.
1919	April: the Robertses holidayed in Cornwall. November: Roberts alone left London for Melbourne; met with the Trustees of the National Gallery of South Australia in Adelaide. December: spent time painting in the Dandenong Ranges, near Melbourne.
1920	30 March: solo exhibition opened at the Upper Athenæum Gallery, Collins Street, Melbourne; sold 500 guineas worth of work. The National Gallery of Victoria purchased *Penelope*, the first painting by

Roberts to enter its collection; the National Art Gallery of New South Wales again acquired work. June: travelled to Sydney via Corowa; returned to Melbourne in July. 6 August: solo exhibition (including *A mountain muster*) opened at Hordern Gallery, Sydney. September: invited (with other artists) by the National Art Gallery of New South Wales to paint a self-portrait for its collection; travelled to northern New South Wales, and then to Brisbane. October: travelled north again and then returned to Melbourne.

1921 January: returned to London. April: gave up his Sloane Street studio, to spend time away from London. June: holidayed (with his son) at Poole, Dorset. September: travelled to Normandy. December: had work hung at the Royal Society of Portrait Painters; holidayed in Italy at Lake Como.

1922 February: the Robertses visited Dorset. 30 September: Caleb Roberts married Norah Watson. October: the Robertses sold their house at Golders Green and moved temporarily into London; they returned for a fortnight to Dorset.

1923 6 January: Tom and Lillie Roberts left England for Australia on the Suevic, which berthed at Port Adelaide on 15 February before continuing on to Melbourne; visited the National Gallery of South Australia. March: the Robertses purchased land at South Sassafras (later re-named Kallista) in the Dandenong Ranges, and built a house which they named Talisman.

1924 July: sent a painting to Artists' Week in Adelaide (29 July – 16 August). 17 September: solo exhibition opened at the Fine Art Society, Melbourne.

1925 Visited Adelaide to repair portrait in National Gallery of South Australia's collection. Autumn: travelled to Tasmania, visiting Lochmaben and Longford, and painting around the Nile River. September: Caleb and Norah Roberts arrived in Melbourne.

1926 February/March: spent six weeks in Tasmania, including a visit to Maria Island. 14 June: attended the opening of his exhibition at Hordern Gallery, Sydney; late in the year re-visited Corowa.

1927 The Federal government's Historical Memorials Committee commissioned Roberts to paint a postumous portrait of the Australian poet Henry Kendall for 100 guineas. November: the Robertses took three weeks holiday at Trawool in the Goulburn River valley.

1928 3 January: death of Lillie Roberts; buried at Kew cemetery on 5 January. Roberts went to Apollo Bay to rest. March: exhibited the re-worked *Bailed up* at Macquarie Galleries, Sydney; it was purchased privately for 450 guineas and lent to the National Art Gallery of New South Wales. Travelled to Hepburn Springs and Yea, and Evandale, Tasmania, visiting the Boyes family. June/July: returned to Trawool, for five weeks. 27 August: married Jean Boyes and stayed on in Tasmania painting around the Nile; restored the artist John Glover's grave at nearby Deddington. Late September: returned with Jean to Kallista.

1929 Summer: the Robertses spent three months in Tasmania returning again later the same year. April: sailed from Launceston to Melbourne, spending a week before returning to Kallista. 24 June: an exhibition of nine artists, including Roberts, opened at the Athenaeum Gallery, Melbourne. July: the Robertses travelled to Mallacoota, Victoria.

1930/31 The Robertses returned to Lochmaben, Tasmania; Roberts painted around the town of Penguin.

1931 June: surgery for cancer; returned to Kallista for three months' rest. 14 September: Tom Roberts died at Kallista; his ashes were buried in the Boyes family plot at the Illawarra church, near Longford, Tasmania.

Catalogue

This catalogue has the benefit of much new research. It has been compiled by Helen Topliss, author of the 1985 catalogue raisonné of Roberts's work but it incorporates some changes that have been proposed since then for dates and titles. Mary Eagle's research for her forthcoming catalogue of the paintings by Roberts (and some of his contemporaries) held by the National Gallery of Australia has been especially useful as has Jane Clark's & Bridget Whitelaw's for the 1985 *Golden Summers* exhibition book. Humphrey McQueen's new biography has clarified many uncertain dates. Other revisions have been credited where possible. However, final responsibility for all revisions published here is accepted by the curator of the exhibition, Ron Radford.

Reinstatement of an artist's first publicly applied title is accepted as best curatorial practice, and is the most frequent reason for the changes.

Abbreviations used in this catalogue and in the various authors' endnotes, can be found on this page and a select bibliography on pages 223-224.

Exhibition tours

1974-1975 *Ladies in Landscapes.*
BFAG, November 1974 – January 1975; AGNSW, February 1975.

1975 *The Australian Landscape 1802-1975.*
Beijing Cultural Palace of the Nationalities, 2 – 17 September; Kiangsu Art Gallery, Nanjing, 23 September – 7 October; AGNSW, 14 – 30 November.

1985-86 *Golden Summers: Heidelberg and Beyond.*
NGV, 30 October 1985 – 27 January 1986; AGNSW, 21 February – 20 April; AGSA, 9 May – 29 June; AGWA, 30 July – 14 September 1986.

1988 *The Great Australian Art Exhibition 1788-1988*
QAG, 17 May – 17 July; AGWA, 13 August – 25 September; AGNSW, 21 October – 27 November; TMAG, 21 December 1988 – 5 February 1989; NGV, 1 March – 30 April; AGSA, 23 May – 16 July 1989.

1995 *Australian Colonial Art: 1800-1900*
AGWA, 10 May – 24 June 1995; QAG, 5 July – 20 August; Auckland City Art Gallery, New Zealand, 1 September – 23 October 1995.

Abbreviations

AAA	Australian Artists' Association, Melbourne.
A&A	Art and Australia (periodical), Sydney.
ADB	Australian Dictionary of Biography.
AGSA	Art Gallery of South Australia, Adelaide formerly National Gallery of South Australia.
AGBSA	Art Gallery Board of South Australia, Adelaide formerly National Gallery Board of South Australia.
AGNSW	The Art Gallery of New South Wales, Sydney formerly National Art Gallery of New South Wales.
AGWA	Art Gallery of Western Australia, Perth.
ASNSW	Art Society of New South Wales, Sydney (later Royal ASNSW).
BFAG	Ballarat Fine Art Gallery, Ballarat, Victoria.
CA	*Creating Australia: 200 Years of Art 1788-1988.* (Exhibition book for 'The Great Australian Art Exhibition 1788-1988', see bibliography, Thomas 1988).
GS	*Golden Summers: Heidelberg and Beyond.* (Exhibition book; see bibliography, Clark & Whitelaw)
LT	La Trobe Library, State Library of Victoria, Melbourne.
ML	Mitchell Library, State Library of New South Wales, Sydney.
NGA	National Gallery of Australia, Canberra formerly Australian National Gallery.
NGV	National Gallery of Victoria, Melbourne.
NLA	National Library of Australia, Canberra.
QAG	Queensland Art Gallery, Brisbane.
SA	Society of Artists, Sydney.
SASA	South Australian Society of Arts, Adelaide (later Royal SASA).
SLNSW	State Library of New South Wales, Sydney.
TMAG	Tasmanian Museum & Art Gallery, Hobart.
VAA	Victorian Academy of Arts, Melbourne.
VAS	Victorian Artists' Society

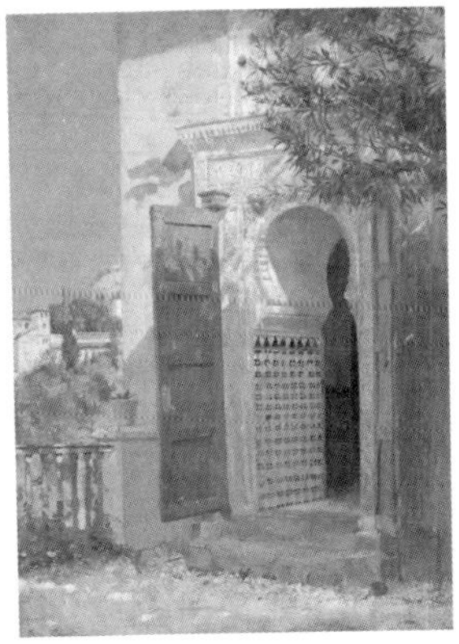

Moorish doorway
1883 Granada
oil on canvas
48.3 x 33.0 cm
Signed l.l. corner red oil, 'Tom Roberts'; dated l.r. oil, 'Granada Oct./83'.
Joseph Brown Collection
[For exhibition in Adelaide only]

Painted during Roberts's tour of Spain in the summer and autumn of 1883. Roberts selected typical picturesque motifs which had been made popular by French academic painters earlier in the nineteenth century, such as the Salon painter, Jean-Léon Gérôme. (Another Orientalist subject from Spain was *A Seated Arab*, Topliss no. 25). During this trip Roberts met a Spanish art student who had been instructed by Gérôme at the Académie Julian, Paris.

Exhibitions: 1980 *The Joseph Brown Collection*, NGV; 1985-86 *Golden Summers*; 1989, 4 May – 18 June, *Australian Paintings from the Joseph Brown Collection*, AGNSW.

Reference: Spate pp. 23-4; Thomas 1973, p. 27; Topliss no. 20; GS pp. 50-51; Barry Pearce (introd.), *Australian Paintings from the Joseph Brown Collection*, Sydney: AGNSW, 1989.

Provenance: probably Dick Roberts (Roberts's brother) – Molly Joske (his daughter) – Miss B.M. Joske (her daughter) .

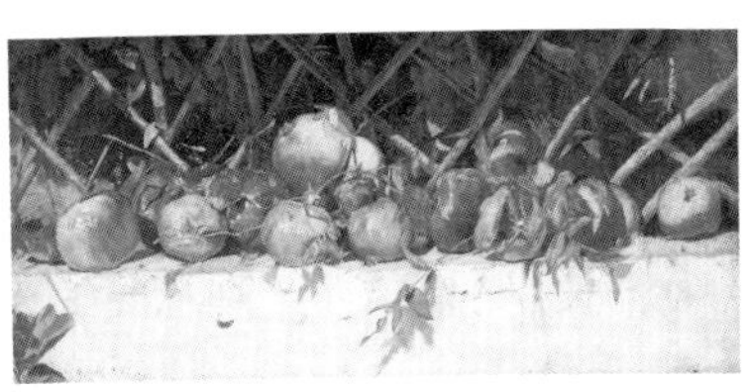

Still-life with pomegranates
c1883 Spain?
oil on canvas mounted on board, 31.1 x 64.3 cm
Not signed. Not dated.
Private collection, Melbourne

Tom Roberts's sister-in-law, Fanny Burchill (original owner of the picture) claimed that this was a school work painted by Roberts in London. It has the firm modelling and lush tones of Roberts's paintings of the mid-1880s, such as *The sculptor's studio*, 1884-85, and *Coming South* 1885-86. It is a study in the rendering of three-dimensionality and chiaroscuro as well as being a pleasing, decorative design. However the painting was possibly painted or sketched during Roberts's trip to Spain where pomegranates were more readily available than in London; the very bright sunlight and shadows would also substantiate this. It is also possible that it was painted in Venice.

Reference: Topliss no. 46.

Provenance: Dick Roberts (Roberts's brother) – Mrs Fanny Burchill (Dick Roberts's widow) – Gilbert Burchill (her son).

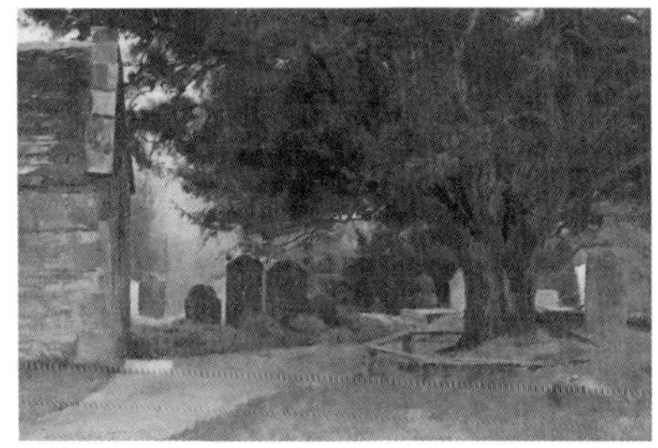

Churchyard at Shillingstone
1884 England
oil on canvas
30.5 x 45.5 cm
Signed and dated l.l., oil 'Tom Roberts-Jan. 84'.
Inscribed l.r., oil 'at Shillingstone'.
Private collection, Queensland
Inscribed reverse on mount 'Roberts Esq. Govt. Printing Office'. Label back of frame, "At Shillingstone".

Shillingstone is on the north Dorset downs. Roberts had an historical interest in his native county of Dorset, also the birthplace of the novelist Thomas Hardy. Roberts was familiar with Hardy's novels which described rural life in Dorset and he made allusions to Hardy's writing in his paintings. In later life Roberts retraced Hardy's steps in Dorset and painted a number of landscapes there (Topliss nos 416, 428, 525, 545-551). It is possible that another landscape painting similar in technique represents another view of the same churchyard (see Topliss no. 29).

Reference: Spate p. 24; Topliss no. 28; McQueen p. 126.

Provenance: Dick Roberts (Roberts's brother) – possibly Molly Joske (Dick Roberts's daughter) – Richard Roberts (her son) – Mrs M. Roberts (Richard Roberts's wife) – Spring 1980 Joseph Brown Gallery, Melbourne.

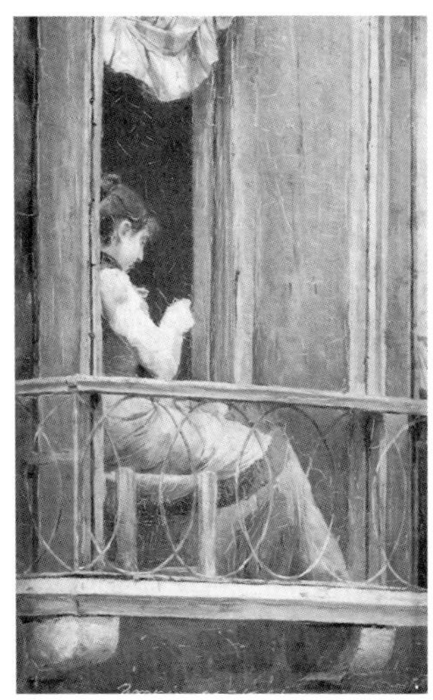

Woman on a balcony
1884 Venice
oil on academy board
21.7 x 13.1 cm
Not signed. Dated l.c., incised 'Venezia Oct. 28 '84'.
Private collection, Melbourne

Roberts possibly first visited Venice in 1883 after his sojourn in Spain; the inscribed date on this painting confirms a visit in 1884. Roberts was now developing an experimental brush technique with square brush strokes and a more fluid handling. The influence of Whistler's atmospheric panel paintings can be seen in this study as can also his more abstract technique using a simplified and freer brush technique. Another painting, *Lido, Venezia* (Topliss no. 43) is dated 'Apl. 20 '84'. However Roberts's inscribed words are difficult to read with certainty; for example an outdoor oil sketch of Brocklesby homestead (Topliss no. 150), the inscribed date of which has been read as 'Ap', could equally, and more likely, be 'Aug' or 'Oct'.

Exhibition: 1985-86 *Golden Summers*.

Reference: Spate pp. 30, 66; Topliss no. 45; GS p. 51.

Provenance: Dick Roberts (Roberts's brother) – Mrs Fanny Burchill (Dick Roberts's widow).

Tom Roberts

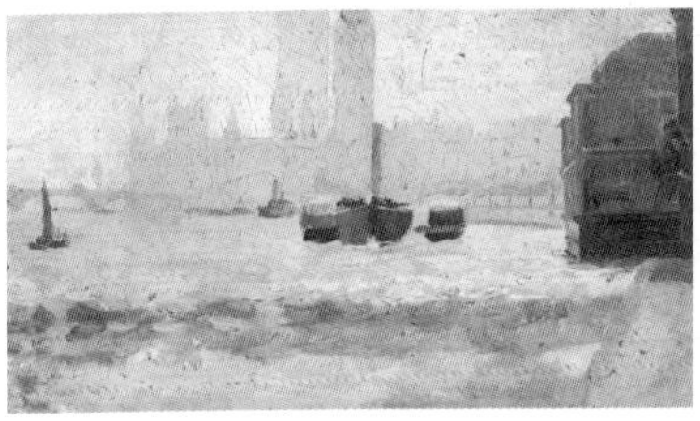

Thames scene
c1884 London
oil on wood panel
12.7 x 22.9 cm
Not signed. Not dated.
Private collection, Melbourne

Painted from the Thames Embankment looking at the Houses of Parliament covered in mist, this work has the subtle, muted tones of Roberts's early works and is painted with crisp square brush strokes not found in his late works. A letter attached to the verso written by Aubrey Gibson, November 1955, quotes information obtained from Dr Clive Stephen (sculptor), who thought the painting was exhibited in The 9 by 5 Impression Exhibition, 1889. Roberts used to go on Thames trips on two tugs called the Fox and the Eclipse.

Exhibitions: August 1889 *The 9 by 5 Impression Exhibition,* possibly no. 1, *Fog, Thames Embankment* (1 gn.); December 1973 – January 1974, BFAG, *Moonrise*; 1985-86 *Golden Summers.*

Reference: *Age*, 17 August 1889, p. 15; Spate pp. 24, 27, 30; Topliss no. 41; GS p. 118; Astbury 1989, p. 89; McQueen p. 533.

Provenance: Mrs Fanny Burchill (Roberts's sister-in-law) – Dr Clive Stephen, until 1955.

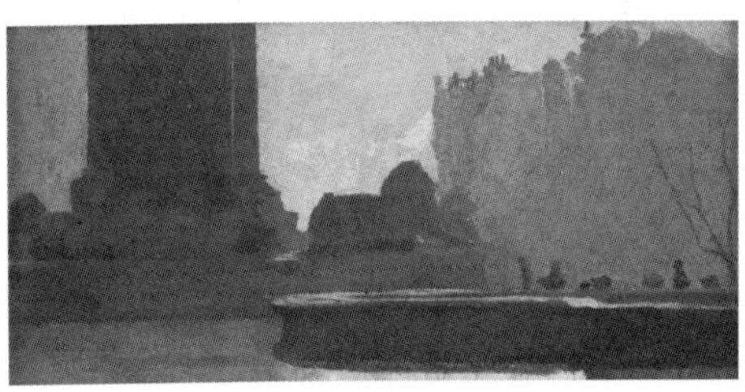

Trafalgar Square
c1884? London
oil on cardboard
14.0 x 28.0 cm
Not signed. Not dated.
Art Gallery of South Australia, Adelaide
South Australian Government Grant 1988

This panel was in Roberts's studio at his death and was purchased by his friend Mr W.G. Buckle. Roberts kept some of his early works and they became talismans for him in his later years. There remains the possibility that it was painted after he returned to London in 1903 or that he worked on it again at a later date.

Exhibitions: 1987, 25 November – 11 December, *Australian and Australia-related Art: 1830s-1970s*, Deutscher Fine Art, Melbourne; 1995 *Australian Colonial Art 1800-1900.*

Reference: Spate 1964; Topliss no. 42; Radford & Hylton pp. 147, 157.

Provenance: estate of the artist 1932 – Mr W.G. Buckle – Mrs W.G. Buckle – November 1987 Deutscher Fine Art.

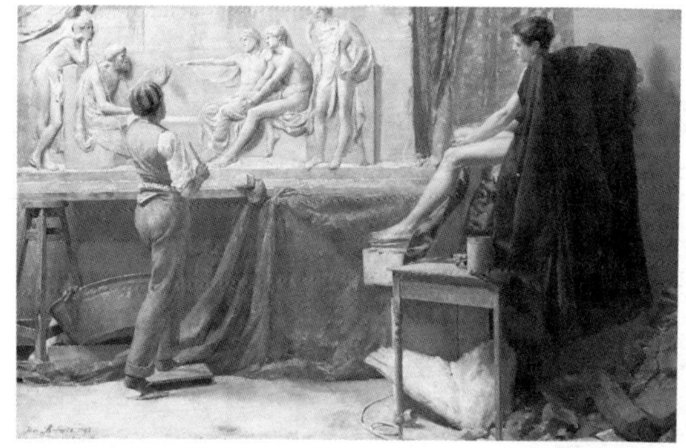

The sculptor's studio
1884-85 London
oil on canvas, 61.0 x 91.5 cm
Signed and dated l.l., red oil 'Tom Roberts 1885'.
National Gallery of Australia, Canberra
Purchased 1972

Roberts's scrap-book at the Mitchell Library contains a series of photographs of Roberts's sculptor friend George Frampton in his studio and also a number of reproductions of Frampton's work (Topliss illus. 13-18). However, it is more likely that this painting represents Roberts's other sculptor friend, Harry Bates, who had achieved a reputation for his classical reliefs and statues. This was probably Roberts's entry for the painting school at the Royal Academy. Though dated 1885 it would have been substantially worked on in 1884. It sums up three years of training and displays his ability to paint a contemporary subject which includes drawing and painting from the antique as well as from the life model. The relief being modelled here is based on the Parthenon Frieze at the British Museum, of which there were casts at the Royal Academy Antique School.

Reference: Spate p. 24; Gleeson p. 95; *Victorian and Edwardian Decorative Art: The Handley-Read Collection*, London: Royal Academy, 1972, p. 105 (for Bates's work); Topliss no. 48; McQueen p. 301.

Provenance: 24 September 1969, Christies – L. Voss Smith, London – 1972 NGA.

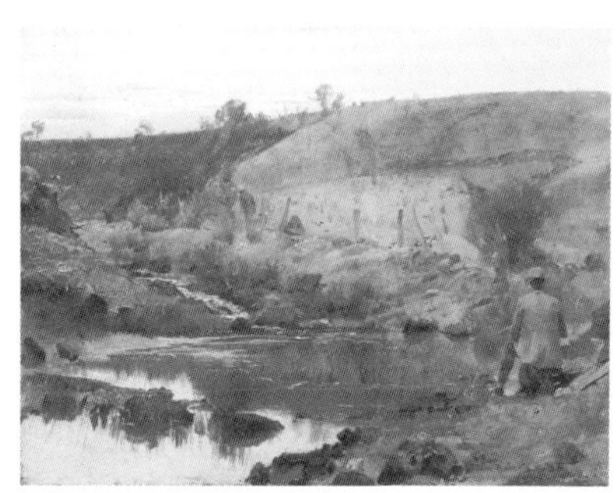

A quiet day on Darebin Creek
1885 Melbourne
oil on pine wood panel
26.6 x 35.2 cm
Signed and dated l.r., oil 'Tom Roberts – 85'.
National Gallery of Australia, Canberra
Purchased 1969

On the verso is another landscape sketch largely obliterated by a fragmented label. Label verso, 'A Quiet day on Darebin Creek [illeg] Roberts/ In – a – Melbourne/ e – [a]fter the exhibition to Mrs/ [Wh]itelaw – Woronzow Road St John's Wood/ – per order/ Tom Roberts'.

Exhibitions: May 1886 *Colonial and Indian Exhibition*, London; 1985-86 *Golden Summers.*

Reference: *Age*, 19 January 1886, p. 6; *Once a Month*, 1 March 1886, p. 265; Spate p. 38 (as *Merri Creek*); Topliss no. 49; GS p. 60.

Provenance: Mrs William Whitelaw, London – Wade, NSW – 1969 Artarmon Galleries, Sydney.

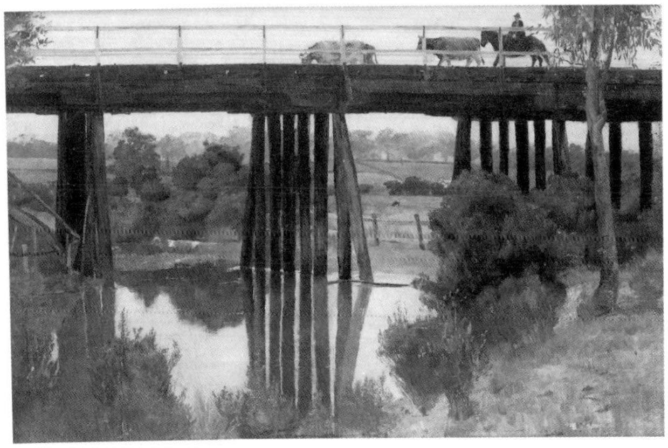

Winter morning after rain, Gardiner's Creek
1885 Melbourne
oil on canvas, 47.0 x 66.0 cm
Signed l.l., black oil 'TOM ROBERTS'. Not dated.
Art Gallery of South Australia, Adelaide
M.J.M. Carter Collection 1996

The location was Gardiner's Creek at Hawthorn. The *Age*, at a studio viewing before its departure for exhibition in London, noted that this picture showed "that Mr Roberts is quite as facile in landscape as he is in portraiture and genre".

Exhibitions: May 1886 *Colonial and Indian Exhibition*, London; April 1932, *Tom Roberts, Memorial Exhibition of Paintings*, Fine Art Society, Melbourne, no. 56 (dated 1882); 29 September – 12 December 1993 *The M.J.M. Carter Collection: A Private View of Australian Colonial Art*, AGSA; 1995 *Australian Colonial Art 1800-1900*.

Reference: *Age* 19 January 1886, p. 6; *Once a Month*, March 1886, p. 265; *Age* 21 June 1932; Spate pp. 33, 38-39; Topliss no. 53; Radford 1993 pp. 53, 58; Radford & Hylton pp. 16, 141, 142, 146, 150.

Provenance: Mrs Fanny Burchill (Roberts's sister-in-law) – Richard Roberts (Roberts's nephew) – private collection, Melbourne – 1 April 1984 Leonard Joel, lot 100 (illus. front cover).

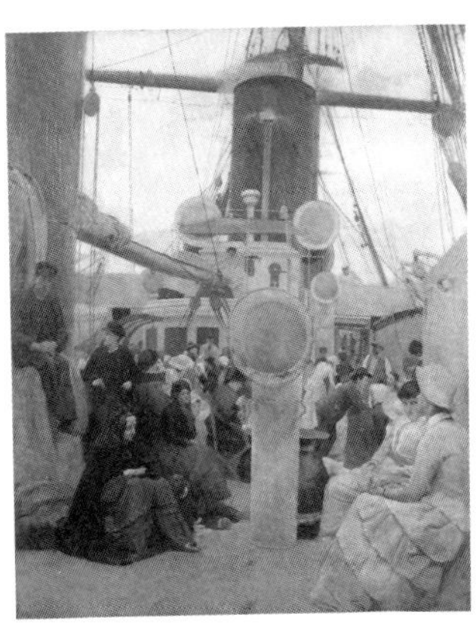

Coming South
1885-86 Melbourne
oil on canvas, 63.8 x 50.5 cm
Signed and dated l.r., grey oil 'Tom Roberts 1886'.
National Gallery of Victoria, Melbourne
Gift of Colonel Aubrey Gibson in memory of John and Anne Gibson, settlers (1887), 1967
Inscribed l.l. 's.s. Lusitania'. Verso, title inscribed on J. and T. Thallon framing label, and (Roberts's studio address) 'Tom Roberts, 95 Collins St'.

The Lusitania was the ship that brought Roberts from England to Melbourne in March – April 1885. There was a vogue for shipboard pictures in the 1880s; the fashionable French painter James Tissot painted two such scenes in London. The *Age* called this the most important picture of those destined for the Colonial and Indian Exhibition and admired the "careful and well drawn work full of character and very tender and harmonious in colour", and also noted the French influence. Although dated 1886, it must have been substantially completed in 1885 if it was shown to the press in January 1886.

Exhibitions: May 1886 *Colonial and Indian Exhibition*, London; 1947-48 *Tom Roberts Retrospective Exhibition* (as *Lusitania)* AGNSW, NGV, AGSA; November 1955 *Canberra Art Club Loan Exhibition*; 1985-86 *Golden Summers*.

Reference: *Age*, 19 January 1886, p. 6; *Table Talk*, 22 January 1886, p. 11; *Once a Month*, 1 March 1886, pp. 264-65; *Magazine of Art*, 1886, p. 400; Spate 1964, p. 262; Spate pp. 50, 73; B. Smith 1962, pp. 88, 120; McCulloch pp. 18, 154; Finemore p. 23; Splatt & Bruce, pp. 36-37; Topliss no. 62; GS p. 52; Astbury 1989, p. 180.

Provenance: Dick Roberts (the artist's brother) – 1890s Joseph Kendall – L.P. Kendall – 1967 Joshua McClelland Print Room, Melbourne – Col. Aubrey Gibson – 1967 NGV.

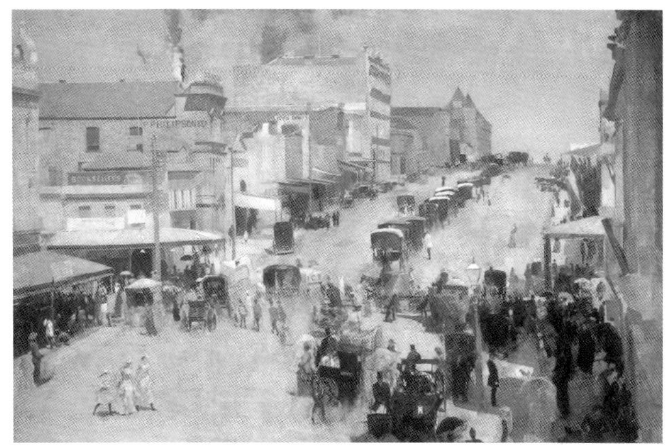

Allegro con brio, Bourke Street west
c1885-86 and 1890 Melbourne
oil on canvas
51.2 x 76.3 cm
Signed l.r., oil 'TOM ROBERTS' Not dated.
National Library of Australia, Canberra
Purchased 1920 by Parliamentary Library Committee
On loan to the National Gallery of Australia, Canberra

This picture was first exhibited in 1890 as *Allegro Con Brio, Bourke St. W.* and in 1893, at the VAS, as *Bourke Street Looking West*. It was painted in the summer of 1885-86 before the introduction of tramlines in Bourke Street in the second half of 1886.

Tom Roberts's scrap-book in the Mitchell Library contains a reproduction of the painting under which is written "Bourke Street Done from Buckley and Nunn's Balcony 1885-6". (In 1886, Buckley and Nunn's, Drapers, was no 23, Bourke Street, numbered from the Post Office Corner. See Topliss illus. 26 and 27). Mrs Anna M. Reay (née Fraser), whose family lived at Heidelberg, recalled that when Roberts made an addition to the Bourke Street painting he asked her and her sister Lottie Fraser to pose for the foreground figures: "Our figures may be seen in the picture at the lower left-hand corner crossing the street, while I am leading a small pupil by the hand" (Croll p. 31). In this painting Roberts has carefully represented and identified a series of buildings, from Dunn and Collins booksellers, to P. Philipson jewellers, to John Danks gasfitter and brassfounder, to the Menzies Hotel at the top of the hill. The painting was owned by Roberts until 1903 when he either gave or lent it to the McCubbins; Mrs McCubbin heard that

Tom Roberts

Roberts was in financial difficulties, sold it in 1920 to the Commonwealth Parliament (as an historical document relevant to Parliament's (then) location in Melbourne, looking west down Bourke Street) and gave the proceeds to Roberts.

Exhibitions: 3 December 1890, Gemmell, Tuckett & Co., Auction of works by F. McCubbin, A. Streeton, T. Roberts, Melbourne (auction held 5 December), no. 3 (Roberts exhibited 17 works); August 1893 *VAS Exhibition of Australian Art Past and Present*, NGV, no. 153; 1895 *VAS Jubilee Exhibition Australian Art*, no. 153; September 1896, SA no. 41 (dated 1886 in the catalogue); November 1900 *Exhibition and Sale of Paintings* previous to leaving Australia, Sydney, no. 51, *Bourke Street, East, Melbourne, before the trams* (35 gns); April 1918 AGNSW *Loan Exhibition of Australian Art*, no. 232 (lent by Mrs F. McCubbin); April 1932 Fine Art Society, Melbourne, no. 1 (lent by Commonwealth Government); November 1947-48 *Tom Roberts Retrospective Exhibition*, AGNSW, NGV, AGSA; 1951 *Jubilee Exhibition of Australian Art* (dated 1885); 1962 *Australian Painting: Colonial, Impressionist, Contemporary*, AGSA, AGWA, then 1963 Tate Gallery, London, National Gallery, Ottawa and Vancouver Art Gallery; 1975 *The Australian Landscape 1802-1975*; 1985-6 *Golden Summers*; 1988-89 *The Great Australian Art Exhibition 1788-1988*.

Reference: *Table Talk*, 28 November 1890, p. 5; *Argus*, 15 March 1892, p. 6; 1918 *Art in Australia*, 1st series, no. 4 (illus.); *Argus*, 21 June 1931 (Streeton's obituary of Roberts); *Argus*, 15 September p. 6 (reprinted Croll, p. 14); Croll p. 23; Badham p. 46; Hoff 1951, p. 127; Spate pp. 30, 38-9, 49, 51; B. Smith 1962, pp. 83, 94; McCulloch pp. 18, 154; Gleeson pp. 92-3; Finemore p. 99; Splatt & Bruce, pp. 34-35; Topliss no. 64; CA pp. 124, 112; GS pp. 82-83; Astbury 1989, pp. 40-42; Topliss 1992, p. 7; McQueen pp. 213-234, 241, 324-5, 460, 603-4, 674, 706, 708-9 (illus. front cover).

Provenance: c1903 Mr and Mrs Frederick McCubbin – 1920 Parliamentary Library Committee, (Commonwealth Parliament, then in Melbourne) – 1946 NLA.

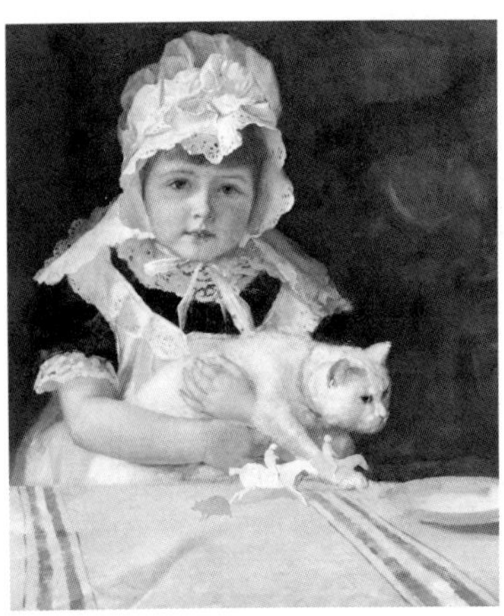

Miss Minna Simpson
1886 Melbourne
oil on canvas
59.5 x 49.5 cm
Not signed. Not dated.
Private collection, Canberra

Ten years before Roberts married Lillie Williamson he painted this portrait of one of the three daughters of Lillie's sister. Minna became a deaconess and married a clergyman named Johnson.

Exhibitions: 1886, AAA, no. 10 (illus.); 1967 *Some Interesting Australians*, George's Gallery, Melbourne, no. 1.

Reference: *Argus*, 7 September 1886, p. 7; *Table Talk*, 31 August 1888, p. 2; Topliss no. 76; McQueen pp. 165, 175.

Provenance: Mrs Simpson (Roberts's sister-in-law) – Minna Simpson (later Mrs M. Johnson) – 1930s Joshua McClelland – private collection, Melbourne – Christie's, Sydney, 14 November 1988, lot 104 – private collection, Canberra.

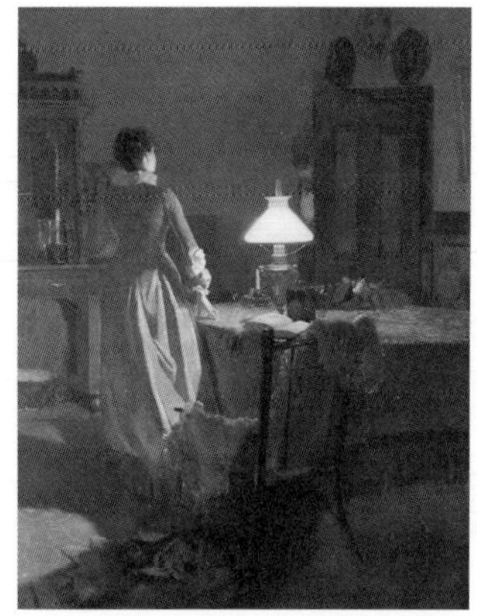

Twenty minutes past three
c1886 Melbourne
oil on canvas, mounted on composition board
100.0 x 74.3 cm (sight)
Not signed. Not dated.
Private collection, Sydney

This painting is based on a c1884 monochrome wash drawing done by Roberts in London, presumably for a possible humorous illustration in a magazine; the drawing (Topliss no. 35) is titled *1.15 a.m.*.

Exhibitions: September 1886, AAA, no. 43 (illus. in catalogue by a line drawing).

Reference: *Argus*, 7 September 1886, p. 7; Spate 1964, p. 262; Spate pp. 49, 73-74, 87; Topliss no. 65; McQueen p. 165.

Provenance: Sold at VAA 1886, original owner unknown – c1915 Fine Art Galleries, Sydney – Mr F.O. Morath – C.F. Morath.

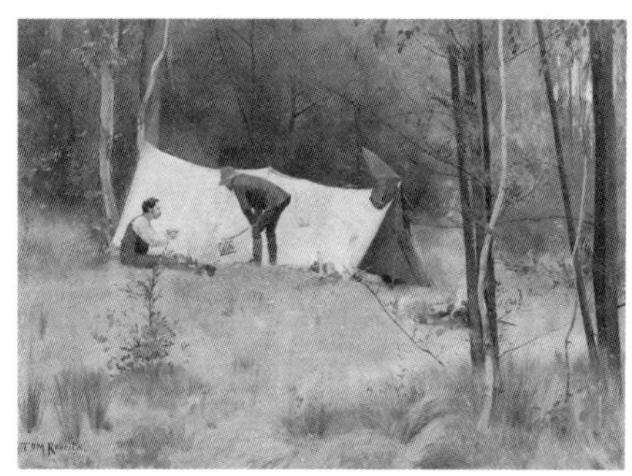

The artists' camp
1886 Melbourne
oil on canvas, 45.7 x 60.8 cm
Signed l.l., brown oil 'Tom Roberts'. Not dated.
National Gallery of Victoria, Melbourne
Felton Bequest Fund 1943

Inscribed on verso *Artists' Camp*.

This records the outdoor painting site at Houston's farm, Box Hill, where Roberts worked with Frederick McCubbin and Louis Abrahams. The seated figure is McCubbin, known as 'the Prof', and the other Louis Abrahams, known as 'the Don'. Abrahams also painted a version of this subject. Years later, in London, Roberts would burn *Eucalyptus citriodora* gum-leaves to invoke memories of this youthful period; he also kept a twig of these gum-leaves in a box of memorabilia which derived from his childhood days.

Exhibitions: September 1886, AAA, no. 34 (illustrated in catalogue); 1962 *Australian Painting: Colonial, Impressionist, Contemporary*, AGSA, AGWA, then 1963 Tate Gallery, London, National Gallery, Ottawa and Vancouver Art Gallery; 1984 *The Artists' Camps*, Monash University Gallery, Melbourne and S.H. Ervin Gallery, Sydney; 1985-86 *Golden Summers*.

Reference: *Argus*, 7 September 1886, p. 7; Hoff 1951, p. 127; Spate pp. 44, 419-50, 52; B. Smith 1962, p. 73; Finemore p. 25; Ian Burn, in Bradley & Smith, pp. 83, 94; Galbally, "Australian Artists Abroad", in Galbally & Plant, p. 61; Topliss 1984, pp. 20-22; Topliss no. 63; Topliss 1992, pp. 64-65, 68; GS pp. 60-61; Astbury 1989, pp. 74, 192; Finlay & Morgan; McQueen p. 173.

Provenance: original owner unknown – 1943 NGV.

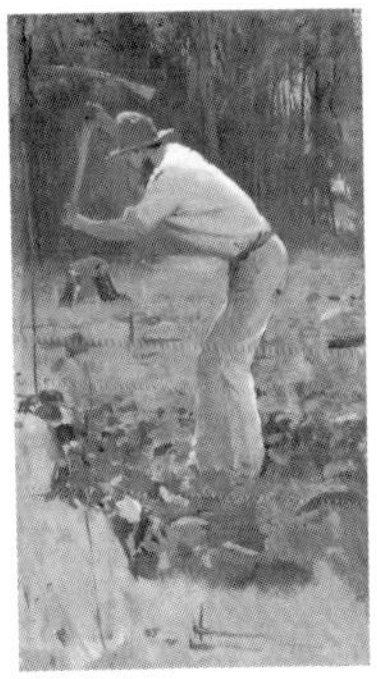

***Turning the soil* (Sketch for *Charcoal burners*)**
c1886 Melbourne
oil on panel
34.8 x 13.4 cm
Not signed. Not dated.
Art Gallery of South Australia, Adelaide
South Australian Government Grant 1982

The verso of this panel has a study of trees painted on it.

This is a study for the right-hand figure in the *Charcoal burners*. In the completed painting the two central figures are digging up soil behind the already split wood. The figure in this sketch is turning soil, presumably to make charcoal (first suggested by Ron Radford). The pose is very similar to that of *An Old Scrub-Cutter*, c1888, a very large painting; 142.0 x 79.0 cm, full title *End to a Career – An Old Scrub Cutter*, present whereabouts unknown (Topliss no. 89). In a third picture, *Twilight at Healesville*, c1886-88 (Topliss no. 88), a fire for preparing charcoal can be seen. In the latter part of the 1880s and in the early 1890s Roberts seems to have worked simultaneously on a number of subjects relating to masculine labour.

Reference: Topliss no. 87b.

Provenance: Original owner unknown – private collection, Melbourne – 1982 Deutscher Fine Art, Melbourne.

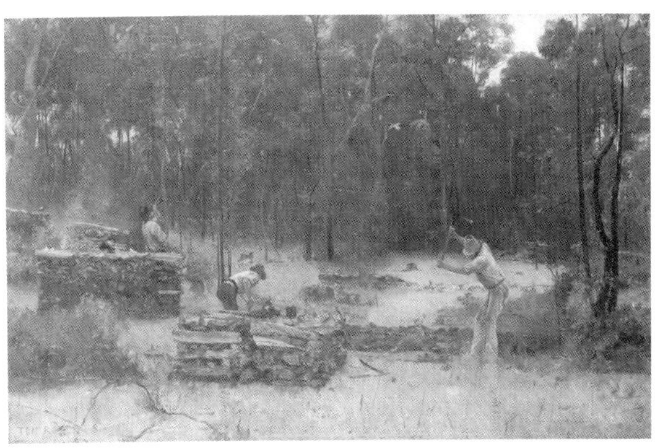

Charcoal burners
1886 Melbourne
oil on canvas, 61.4 x 92.3 cm
Signed l.l., oil 'TOM ROBERTS'. Not dated.
Ballarat Fine Art Gallery
Bequest of J.R. Hartley 1961

Previously known as *Woodsplitters*, a title given to it, within five years of its execution, by its first owner, a timber merchant. The men are not splitting wood, but working beside stacks of wood in preparation for making charcoal. Ron Radford, when Director of the BFAG and hence curatorially responsible for the painting, had proposed that this picture be titled *Charcoal burners*, an accurate description of its subject.

Exhibitions: March 1891 *Loan Exhibition*, Exhibition Buildings, Melbourne, *Woodsplitters*, no. 45 (lent by George Lush); 1985-86 *Golden Summers*.

Reference: Spate pp. 49,85, 151 (illus. front cover), plate no. 21; Topliss no. 87; Astbury 1989, p. 103*f*; GS p. 66.

Provenance: March 1891 George Lush – J.R. Harley - 1961 BFAG.

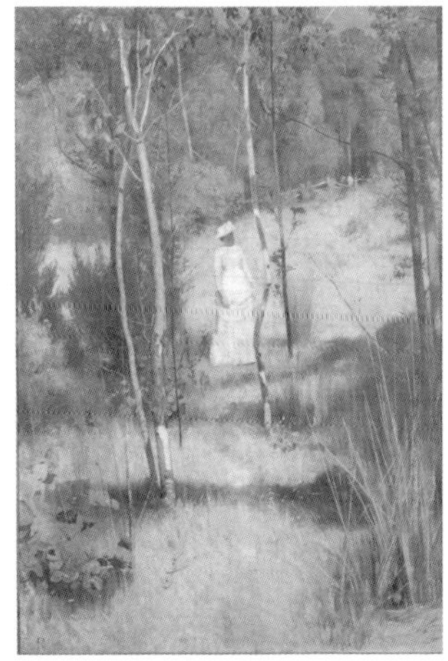

A summer morning tiff
1886 Melbourne
oil on canvas mounted on board
76.5 x 51.2 cm
Signed l.l., oil 'Tom Roberts'. Not dated.
Ballarat Fine Art Gallery
Martha K. Pinkerton Bequest Fund 1943

Painted at Houston's farm, Box Hill. It was exhibited at the AAA with a poem accompanying it in the catalogue, for which see Mary Eagle's essay in this book.

Exhibitions: September 1886, AAA no. 30; 1888 Centennial Exhibition, no. 9 (lent by David Cook); August 1893, *VAS Exhibition of Australian Art Past and Present*, NGV, no. 23 (dated 1888, lent by David Cook); November 1947-48 *Tom Roberts Retrospective Exhibition* AGNSW, NGV, AGSA; 1974-75 *Ladies in Landscapes*, no. 33; 1985-86 *Golden Summers*.

Reference: *Argus*, 7 September 1886, p. 7; Croll p. 31; *Ballarat Fine Art Public Gallery Association Bulletin*, 1946, p. 2; Hoff 1951, p. 127; Spate 1964, p. 262; Spate pp. 45, 49 52; B. Smith 1962, p. 74; McCulloch p. 22; Ron Radford, *The ninetieth anniversary exhibition of the Ballarat Fine Art Gallery: Ladies in landscapes*, BFAG, 1974; Hughes p. 57; Burn, in Bradley & Smith, p. 94; Topliss no. 66; Topliss 1992, pp. 65, 67-68; GS pp. 62-63; McQueen pp. 165, 173, 192, 204, 251, 286, 326, 454, 672.

Provenance: 1886 David Cook – 1943 BFAG.

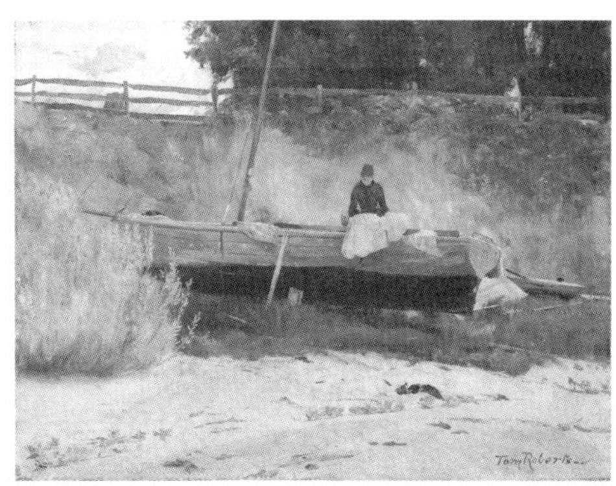

Mending the sail
1886-87 Melbourne
oil on canvas
35.4 x 46.0 cm
Signed l.r., burnt sienna oil 'Tom Roberts'
National Gallery of Australia, Canberra
Gift of W. Booth 1947

Recently retitled by Mary Eagle. Previously called *Girl sitting on a boat*. The picture is stylistically similar to *Slumbering sea, Mentone*, 1887, and could possibly have been a preliminary idea for that larger painting.

Exhibition: 1974-75 *Ladies in Landscapes* (AGNSW showing only).

Reference: Topliss no. 80.

Provenance: W. Booth – 1947 NGA.

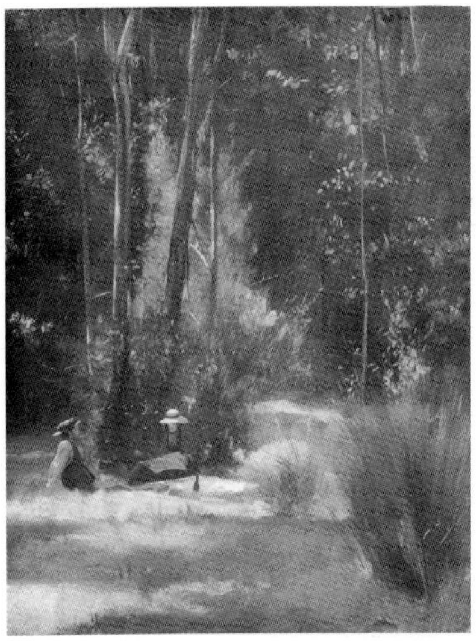

A Sunday afternoon picnic at Box Hill
c1887 Melbourne
oil on canvas
38.6 x 28.7 cm
Not signed. Not dated.
National Gallery of Australia, Canberra
Purchased 1984

The artist's original title *A Sunday afternoon* has been reinstated by Mary Eagle as a prefix to *Picnic at Box Hill*, the title by which it has been previously known. The previous owners state that this picture was given to their mother Lilian Catherine Ann Higgs on the occasion of her having played the piano at Talisman, the house built by the Robertses in 1923 at Kallista. As a young girl, Lilian Higgs had studied with Marshall-Hall at the Conservatorium in Melbourne, on the recommendation of Tom Roberts. Lilian Higgs's father, John Higgs, was a first cousin of Roberts.

Exhibitions: possibly November 1900 *Exhibition and Sale of Paintings*, Sydney, no. 53 (5 gns), *The Bush Picnic*; 1984 *The Artists' Camps*, Monash University, Melbourne and S.H. Ervin Gallery, Sydney.

Reference: Topliss 1984, p. 76; Topliss no. 69.

Provenance: Lilian Higgs 1920s – Messrs J & G. Connor (her sons) – 1984 NGA

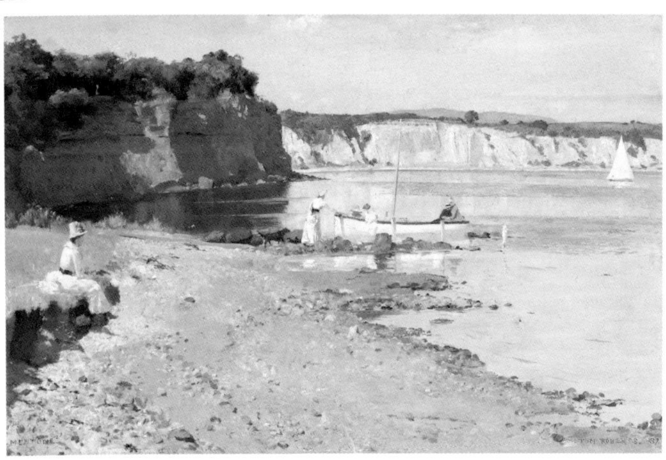

Slumbering sea, Mentone
1887 Melbourne
oil on canvas
51.0 x 76.5 cm
Signed and dated l.r., oil 'TOM ROBERTS 87'
National Gallery of Victoria, Melbourne
Purchased with the assistance of a special grant from the Government of Victoria 1979

Title inscribed l.l., oil 'MENTONE'.

Known previously as *Mentone*, the artist's original title is now reinstated. Painted at much the same time as *Mending the sail*, 1886-87, and *The Sunny South*, c1887, when Roberts, McCubbin and Abrahams held a summer camp on the coast at Ricketts Point, near Mentone. The *Argus* described *Slumbering Sea, Mentone* as "a boldly painted coast-scene full of light and warmth and local colour". The view looks west towards Mentone, so it is afternoon light.

Exhibitions: 1887, AAA, no. 23, *Slumbering Sea, Mentone*; August 1893 *VAS Exhibition of Australian Art Past and Present*, NGV, no. 158 lent by B. Sniders (see his portrait, Topliss no. 117); April 1932, *Tom Roberts, Memorial Exhibition of Paintings*, Fine Art Society, Melbourne, no. 22 (lent by F.W. Thompson); 1934 Centenary Art Exhibition, Victoria; 1974-75 *Ladies in Landscapes*, no. 31; 1975 *The Australian Landscape 1802-1975*; 1985-86 *Golden Summers*.

Reference: *Argus*, 5 March 1887, p. 14; Spate pp. 30, 50; McCulloch pp. 30, 154; Gleeson p. 94; Ron Radford, *The ninetieth anniversary exhibition of the Ballarat Fine Art Gallery: Ladies in landscapes*, BFAG, 1974; McCaughey & Manton, p. 40; Topliss 1984, pp. 31-32; Topliss no. 79; GS p. 69; Astbury 1989, p. 50; Topliss 1992, pp. 126, 128-129; McQueen p. 176.

Provenance: original owner probably B. Sniders – late 1920s F.W. Thompson – H.W.L. Thompson (his son) – Jack Manton – 1979 NGV.

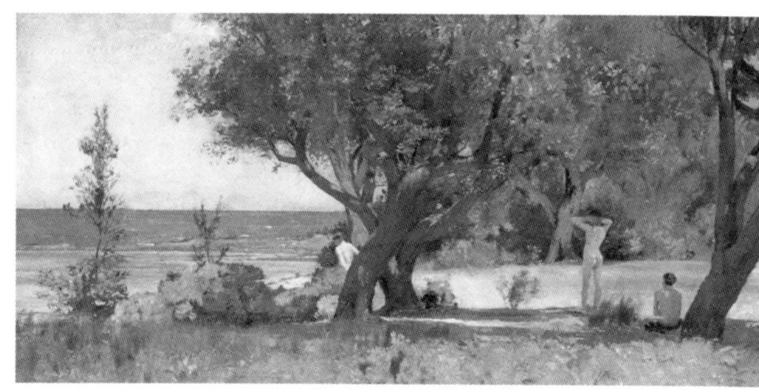

The Sunny South
c1887 Melbourne
oil on canvas
30.8 x 61.2 cm
Not signed. Not dated.
National Gallery of Victoria, Melbourne
Felton Bequest Fund 1940

The site is Ricketts Point, Beaumaris, painted in the summer of 1886-87, before its exhibition in March 1887. This picture has been known as *Boys Bathing*, but *The Sunny South* is the artist's original title, and the figures are not 'boys', but McCubbin, Abrahams and Streeton (See Mary Eagle's essay in this book).

This work now has its original frame, recently located at the Benedictine Community, New Norcia, Western Australia.

Exhibitions: March 1887, AAA, no. 9 (illus. in catalogue); 1985-86 *Golden Summers;* 1988-89 *The Great Australian Art Exhibition.*

Reference: *Argus,* 5 March 1887, p. 14; Spate pp. 12, 47, 50-2; B. Smith 1962, p. 99; McCulloch pp. 30, 154; Finemore p. 25; Topliss 1984, p. 32; Topliss no. 85; GS p. 68; CA p. 112; Astbury 1989, p. 180; Topliss 1992, pp. 3-5, 128-29.

Provenance: original owner unknown – 1949 NGV.

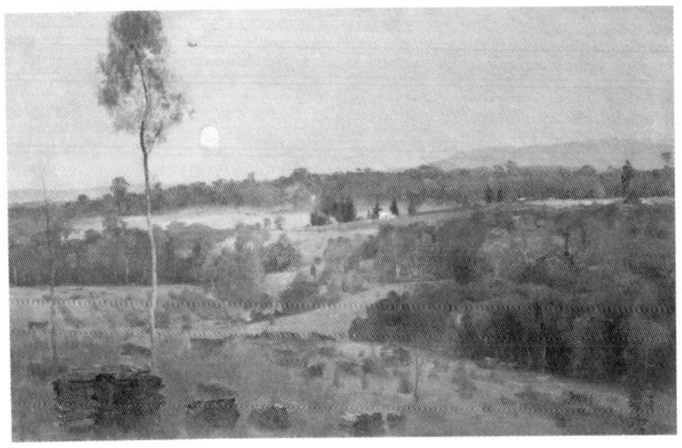

"Evening, when the quiet east flushes faintly at the sun's last look"
c1887 Melbourne
oil on canvas, 50.8 x 76.2 cm
Signed l.l., red oil 'TOM ROBERTS'. Not dated.
National Gallery of Victoria, Melbourne
W.H. Short Bequest Fund 1944

This picture was probably painted at Box Hill, its stacks of wood seen in what has become open land being a sequel to those seen in a forest clearing in *Charcoal burners*. A source for the poetic title has not been found.

Exhibitions: May 1888, VAS, no. 5; 1973, *Moonrise*, BFAG, no. 37; 1985-86 *Golden Summers.*

Reference: *Age*, 20 April 1888, p. 6; *Argus*, 30 April 1888, p.11; Spate pp. 12, 50, 54-6; Ron Radford, *Moonrise*, BFAG, 1973 (introd.); Finemore p. 40; Splatt & Bruce, pp. 40-41; Topliss 1984, pp. 25-26; Topliss no. 81; GS p. 71; Astbury 1989, p. 80-81; Topliss 1992, pp. 80, 82.

Provenance: probably Louis Abrahams until *Australian Pictures collected by the late Louis Abrahams*, Decoration & Co., Melbourne, lot 8 [18 gns], described in the *Herald* as "a charming moonrise landscape which belongs to the Box Hill period" – unknown – 1944 NGV.

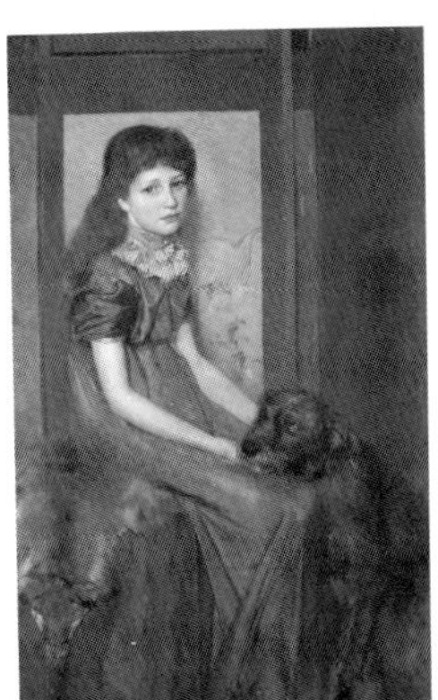

Blue Eyes and Brown
1887 Melbourne
oil on canvas
126.8 x 76.0 cm
Signed and dated l.l., black oil 'T.R. 1888' [sic].
National Gallery of Victoria, Melbourne
Purchased 1960

The signature must have been added later by Roberts, and he mistakenly dated it 1888 though it had been exhibited in March 1887. The sitter was possibly related to Professor Laurie (see his portrait, Topliss no. 91) since the picture was owned by him. It has been known as *Blue Eyes, Brown Eyes*. Here Roberts uses a Japanese screen as a studio prop.

Exhibitions: March 1887, AAA, no. 26, *Blue Eyes and Brown*; 1888 *Centennial International Exhibition*, no. 5, *Blue Eyes and Brown* (lent by Professor Laurie), 2nd Order of Merit.

Reference: *Argus* 5 March 1887, p. 14; *Argus* 19 January 1889, p. 10; Spate p. 115; Topliss no. 90; McQueen p. 341.

Provenance: c1887 Professor Laurie – Mrs E.A. Laurie – 1960 NGV.

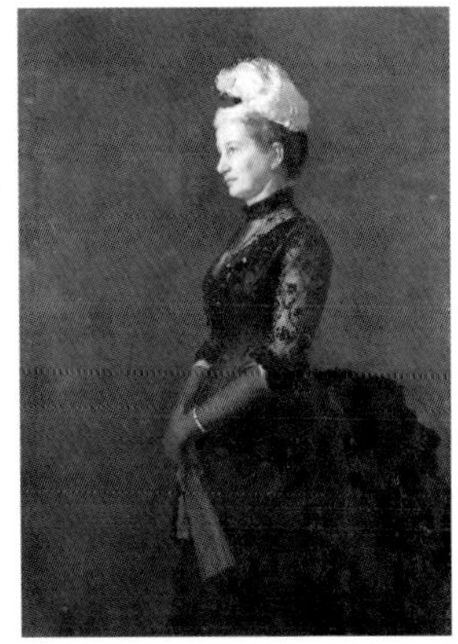

Madame Pfund
c1887 Melbourne
oil on canvas
142.2 x 98.1 cm
Not signed. Not dated.
National Gallery of Victoria, Melbourne
Purchased 1948

Madame Elise Pfund (c1833-1921) was the wife of the architect James Pfund; see his portraits Topliss nos 107, 108 and 109. The couple were early patrons of Roberts. Elise Tshaggany arrived in Australia in the 1860s and married James Pfund. Madame Pfund ran Oberwyl, a private girls' school in St Kilda.

Exhibitions: 1887, AAA, no. 46 (illustrated in catalogue); November 1947-48 *Tom Roberts Retrospective Exhibition*, (lent by Miss K.E. Loosli) AGNSW, NGV, AGSA; 1951 *Jubilee Exhibition of Australian Art*; 1985-86 *Golden Summers.*

Reference: *Table Talk*, 23 September 1887, p. 11; *Age*, 27 September 1887, p. 6; *Argus*, 7 October 1887, p. 9; *Table Talk*, 14 October 1887, p. 11; Letter from Mme Pfund to Lillie Williamson, 11 April 1896 (private collection, Melbourne); Topliss no. 92; GS p. 79; McQueen p. 187 (illus.).

Provenance: Mme Pfund – Dr Robert Loosli (her nephew) – Miss K.E. Loosli (his daughter) – 1948 NGV.

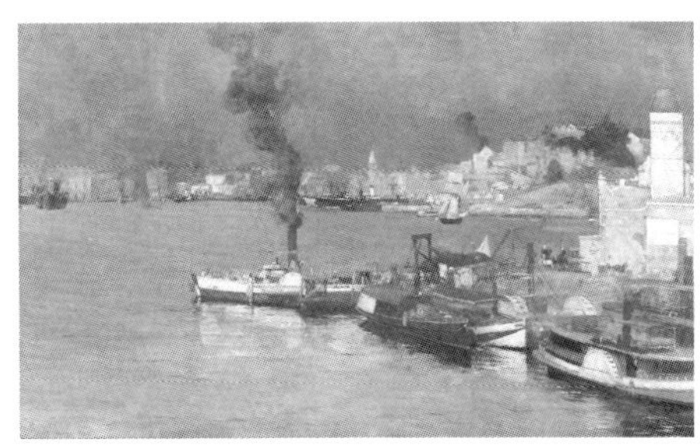

An autumn morning, Milson's Point, Sydney
1888 Sydney
oil on canvas, 45.7 x 76.2 cm
Signed and dated l.l., oil 'Tom Roberts/ Sydney. 88'.
The Art Gallery of New South Wales, Sydney
Purchased 1983

The signature is faint due to overcleaning.
Inscribed on stretcher, '22 Mortimer St [or Sq], London'.

This was painted during Roberts's nineteen-day visit to Sydney in March - April 1888. It is probably the picture referred to by the *Age* in May 1888, stating that it was painted from the horse ferry at Milson's Point: "The colouring of the buildings and ferry boats on the right, and the middle distance set off by the somewhat murky background, reminding the spectator that this is a city consuming fossil coal and not charcoal".

Exhibitions: May 1888, VAS, no. 87 (£50); 1985-86 *Golden Summers.*

Reference: *Table Talk*, 27 April 1888, p. 2; *Argus*, 30 April 1888, p. 11; *Age*, 20 April 1888, p. 6; Spate p. 39; Barry Pearce, *A Century of Australian Landscape: Mood and Moment*, Sydney: Beagle Press, 1983; Topliss no. 103; GS p. 95; Astbury 1989, p. 34; McQueen p. 242.

Provenance: Mr R.W. Knightley Goddard, London – Miss S.B. Cornock D'Oyley Goddard, London – private collection, New York – 1982 Sothebys London – March 1983, Sothebys Melbourne, lot 54.

Tom Roberts

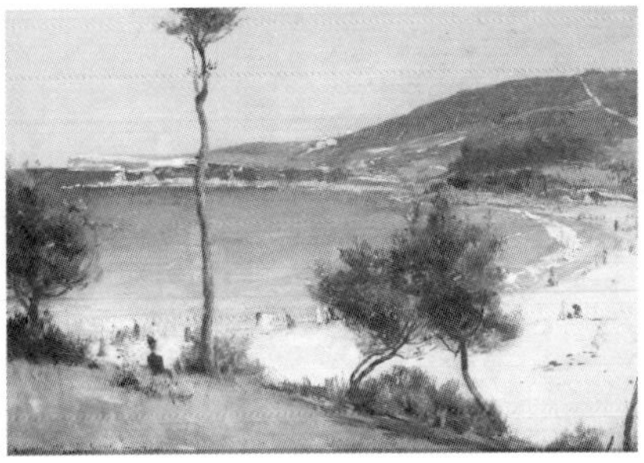

Holiday sketch at Coogee
1888 Sydney
oil on canvas, 40.3 x 55.9 cm
Signed and dated and inscribed l.l., oil 'Holiday sketch at Coogee Tom Roberts-/ April 88'.
The Art Gallery of New South Wales, Sydney
Purchased 1954

Roberts visited Sydney in the autumn of 1888 and there met Charles Conder. Both Roberts and Conder painted from the same spot at Coogee (Topliss illus. 36) and this outdoor 'Holiday Sketch' can be compared with Conder's painting of the same subject. Conder's *All on a summer's day* (AGSA), a Sydney beach scene with a woman reading, includes a tiny representation of an artist painting outdoors, standing at an easel, and holding a white umbrella; probably Roberts painting this Coogee view.

Exhibitions: March 1932 *Australian Art Exhibition*, Bulletin Building, Sydney, no. 66 (lent by Reginald Marcus Clark); 1962, *Australian Painting: Colonial, Impressionist, Contemporary*, AGSA, AGWA, then 1963 Tate Gallery, London, National Gallery, Ottawa, Vancouver Art Gallery; 1974-75 *Ladies in Landscapes*, no. 31; 1985-86 *Golden Summers.*

Reference: Croll p. 22; Croll 1946, p. 10; *Daily Telegraph* (Syd.) 8 June 1920; Spate pp. 52-4; Hoff 1969, p. 21; B. Smith 1962, pp. 75-6; Ron Radford, *The ninetieth anniversary exhibition of the Ballarat Fine Art Gallery: Ladies in landscapes*, BFAG, 1974; Ian Burn, in Bradley & Smith, p. 92; Topliss no. 104; GS p. 96; McQueen p. 241.

Provenance: c1890 Walter Barnett, photographer and friend of Roberts (see Croll 1946, p. 10) – Reginald Marcus Clark – 16 June 1954 Lawson's auction, Sydney.

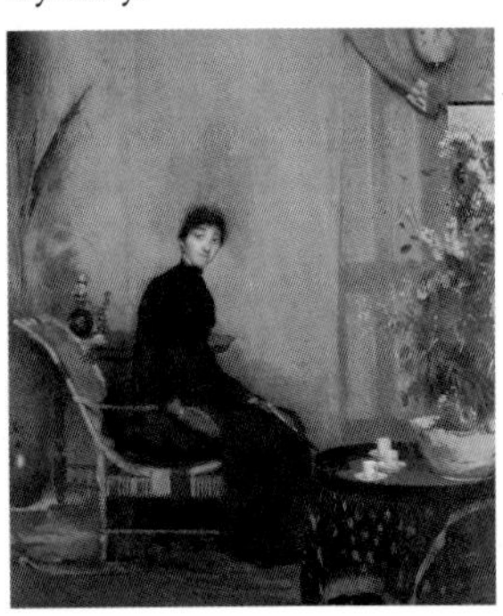

Mrs L. Abrahams
1888 Melbourne
oil on canvas
40.6 x 35.6 cm
Signed and dated l.l., black oil 'Tom Roberts 1888'.
National Gallery of Victoria, Melbourne
Purchased 1946

This has been known as *Portrait of a Lady in a Black Dress.* Mrs Abrahams (née Golda Brasch) was the wife of Louis Abrahams, a fellow painter and friend of Roberts. Louis Abrahams supplied the cigar-box-lid panels for 'The 9 by 5 Impression Exhibition' of 1889 – his family were importers of cigars. This picture was painted in Roberts's new studio at Grosvenor Chambers, Collins Street, Melbourne, into which he moved in April 1888. The interior can be compared with the only known photograph of the studio (see Topliss illus. 31) where the wicker chair in which Roberts is seated is similar to the one in this portrait. The studio props are decidedly Aesthetic: the bulrushes in a Chinese jar in the background, the arrangement of flowers in the Chinese ceramic bowl on the occasional table.

Exhibitions: November 1888 VAS, no. 31, *Mrs L. Abrahams;* 1947-48 *Tom Roberts Retrospective Exhibition,* AGNSW, NGV, AGSA; 1985-86 *Golden Summers.*

Reference: *Age*, 16 November 1888, p. 8; Spate p. 115; Finemore pp. 45-6; A. Galbally, "Aestheticism in Australia", in Bradley & Smith; Topliss no. 111; GS p. 78; Astbury 1989, pp. 34, 44; McQueen p. 341.

Provenance: presumably Mrs Louis Abrahams – her descendants – 1946 NGV.

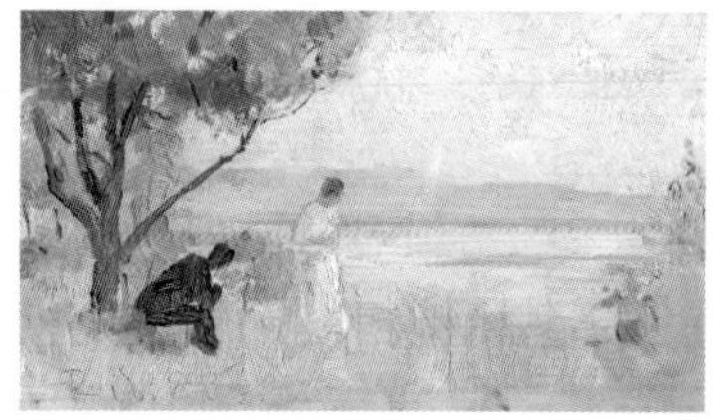

Impression
1888 Melbourne
oil on cedar panel, 11.4 x 19.0 cm
Signed with monogram and dated, incised 'R[illeg] 88'.
National Gallery of Victoria, Melbourne
Purchased 1955

Almost certainly exhibited at 'The 9 by 5 Impression Exhibition' in 1889, although it is difficult to find a precise title for it.

Exhibition: 1985-86 *Golden Summers.*

Reference: Spate 1964, p. 263; Spate pp. 66, 85; Imants Tillers, *A & A*, vol. 18, no. 3, p. 272; Topliss no. 124; GS p. 124; Astbury 1989, p. 92.

Provenance: 1955 Decoration Co. auction, Melbourne.

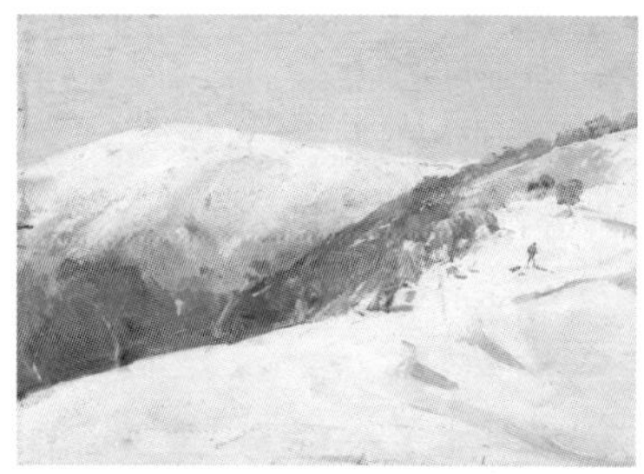

The mailman to Omeo (Snow shoes)
c1888 Melbourne
oil on cedar cigar-box lid
22.0 x 30.0 cm
Not signed. Not dated.
Private collection, Canberra

Previously known as *Snow Scene*, is surely the work of the title given here that was shown in 'The 9 by 5 Impression Exhibition'.

Exhibitions: August 1889, *The 9 by 5 Impression Exhibition*, Melbourne, no. 96 (5 gns); 1985-86 *Golden Summers.*

Reference: Topliss no. 126; GS p. 123.

Provenance: original owner unknown – 1920s Mr W.S. Reid – private collection, Melbourne.

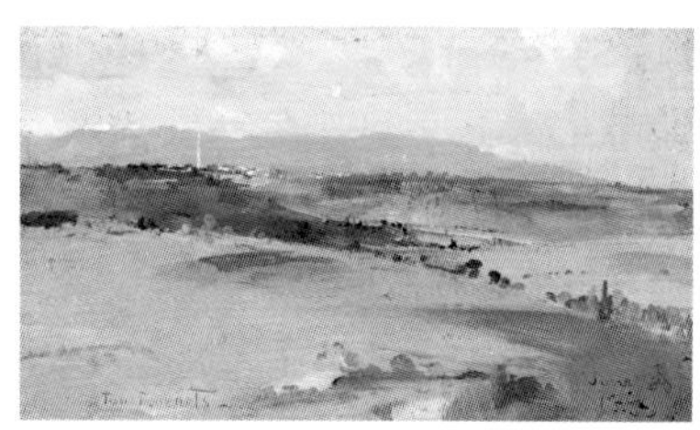

Across to the Dandenongs
1889 Melbourne
oil on cedar cigar-box lid
13.7 x 22.9 cm
Signed and dated l.l., incised 'Tom Roberts'; l.r., incised 'June 30 1889'.
National Gallery of Victoria, Melbourne
Purchased 1962

This was surely exhibited at 'The 9 by 5 Impression Exhibition', presumably as *Across to the Dandenongs*, for it depicts the view from Heidelberg to the Dandenong Ranges, and *Table Talk* noted that 'Across the Dandenong' had been bought from the exhibition by a Mr Harty, no doubt a misunderstanding of the name of the family from which the NGV acquired it as 'Across the Dandenongs'.

Exhibitions: August 1889, *The 9 by 5 Impression Exhibition*, Melbourne, possibly no. 148, *Dandenong from Heidelberg* (1 gn.) but probably no. 167, *Across to the Dandenongs* (2gns); 1984 *The Artists' Camps*, Monash University, Melbourne and S.H. Ervin Gallery, Sydney; 1985-86 *Golden Summers.*

Reference: Topliss no. 129; GS p. 126.

Provenance: Mr B.W. Harting – 1962 NGV.

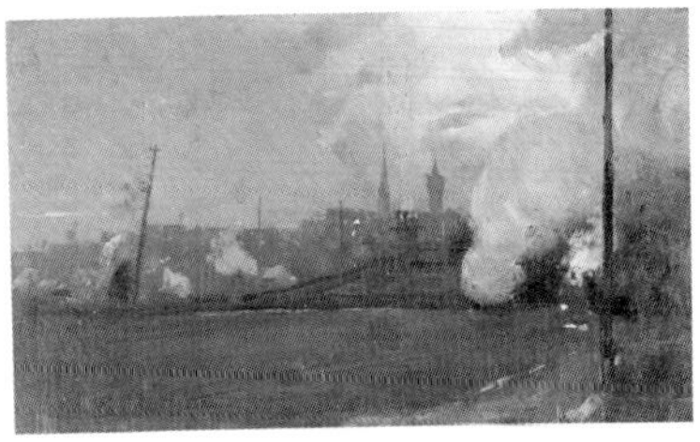

Evening train to Hawthorn
c1889 Melbourne
oil on cedar panel, 14.0 x 22. 6 cm
Not signed. Not dated.
The Art Gallery of New South Wales, Sydney
Stinson Bequest Fund 1991

On verso, label from AGNSW: 'Miss Sylvia Purves/ Title – Spencer St Station'.
Previously known as *Evening, Princes Bridge*. It was exhibited at 'The 9 by 5 Impression Exhibition'. This picture was painted from the Yarra Bank facing the Scots and Independent church spires, the latter seen in the centre of the painting.
Exhibitions: August 1889, *The 9 by 5 Impression Exhibition*, Melbourne, no. 77, *Evening Train to Hawthorn* (1 gn); 1947-48, *Tom Roberts Retrospective Exhibition, Evening, Princes Bridge* (lent by Miss Sylvia Purves) AGNSW, NGV, AGSA; 1985-86 *Golden Summers.*
Reference: Topliss no. 127; GS p. 121.
Provenance: Miss Sylvia Purves (Roberts's niece) – Ellenden's auction, Sydney, May 1976 as 'Spencer St. Station – 1977 Deutscher Fine Art, Melbourne – Mr and Mrs Rob Andrew, – private collection, Sydney.

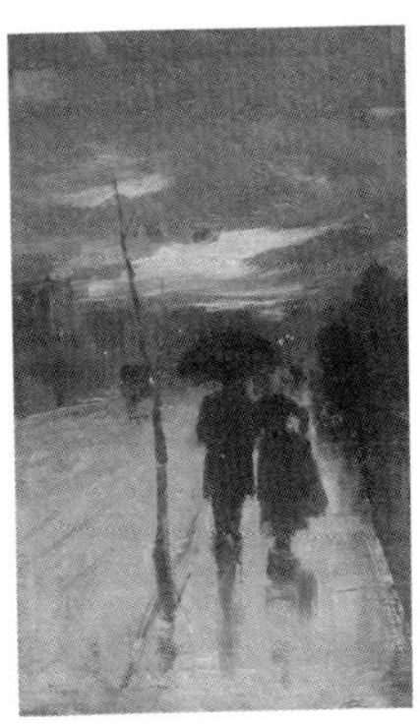

Going home
c1889 Melbourne
oil on cedar cigar-box lid
23.2 x 13.5 cm
Signed l.l., blue oil 'Tom Roberts'. Not dated.
National Gallery of Australia, Canberra
Purchased 1976
Inscribed on verso support top c., ink 'Impressionist Exhibition' Melbourne.

Exhibitions: August 1889, *The 9 by 5 Impression Exhibition*, Melbourne, no. 14 (2 gns).
Reference: Topliss no. 119.
Provenance: Sylvia Purves – 1976 Christies, Sydney, lot 311.

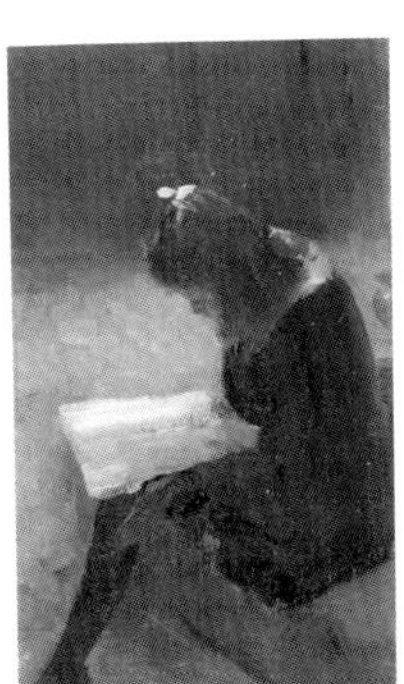

Harper's Weekly
c1889 Melbourne
oil on cedar panel, 23.8 x 14.2 cm
Not signed. Not dated.
National Gallery of Victoria, Melbourne
Purchased 1958

On verso: 'Bought from Tom Roberts/ NINE by FIVE Impression Exhibition/ Aug. 1889/ J.W. Springthorpe.'; and printed stamp '500/ Claro Colorado'. Previously known as *Quiet Study*.

Exhibitions: August 1889, *The 9 by 5 Impression Exhibition*, no. 139 (3 gns); 1985-86 *Golden Summers*.
Reference: Topliss no. 138; GS p. 122; Astbury 1989, p. 92.
Provenance: 1889 purchased by Dr J.W. Springthorpe – possibly sold as *Girl Reading*, May 1934 Joel's, Melbourne, lot 61.

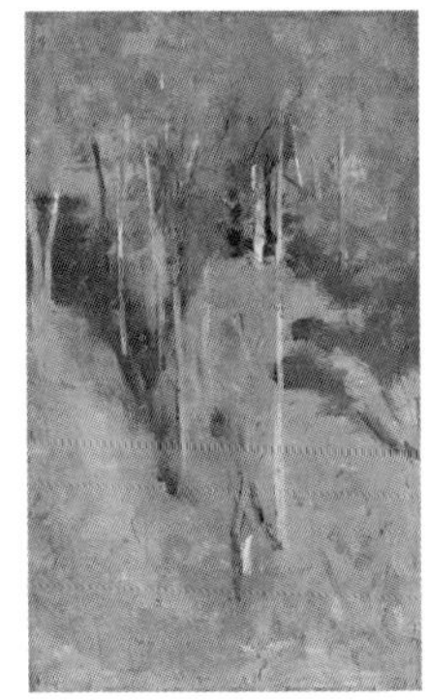

Saplings
c1889 Melbourne
oil on cedar cigar-box lid
14.5 x 34.5 cm
Not signed. Not dated.
Art Gallery of South Australia, Adelaide
Morgan Thomas Bequest Fund 1927

Bore signature lower right 'Chas. Conder 89' when bought by AGSA; this signature was later than the painting and has been removed. Ron Radford in 1980 reattributed the painting to Roberts. The subject has some resemblance to the landscape background of *Bailed up*, 1895, but the handling is not characteristic of that time and nor is the cigar-box-lid panel; rougher and larger panels were used for the occasional outdoor oil-sketches of the mid 1890s. *Saplings* could have been in the 9 by 5 exhibition of 1889 but cannot easily be identified with any of the titles listed in the catalogue.
Exhibitions: 1988-89 *The Great Australian Art Exhibition;* 1995 *Australian Colonial Art 1800-1900.*
Reference: Topliss no. 70; Radford & Hylton pp. 149, 157.
Provenance: Sedon Galleries, Melbourne

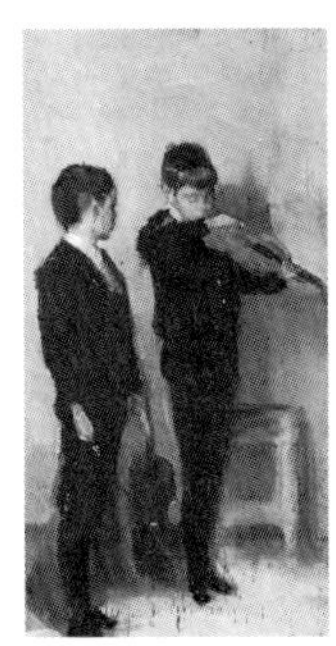

The violin lesson
c1889 Melbourne
oil on cedar panel
23.0 x 13.0 cm
Not signed. Not dated.
Private collection, Melbourne

The two boys are the sons Henry and William of Professor (of Moral Philosophy) Laurie, whose portrait is Topliss no. 91. This work is in its original frame. The frames for 'The 9 by 5 Impression Exhibition' were made of kauri wood and were constructed en masse at a local timber yard.
Exhibitions: August 1889, *The 9 by 5 Impression Exhibition*, no. 95 (3 gns).
Reference: Spate pp. 66, 67; Topliss no. 142.
Provenance: Commissioned by Mrs Laurie (wife of Professor Laurie).

Tom Roberts

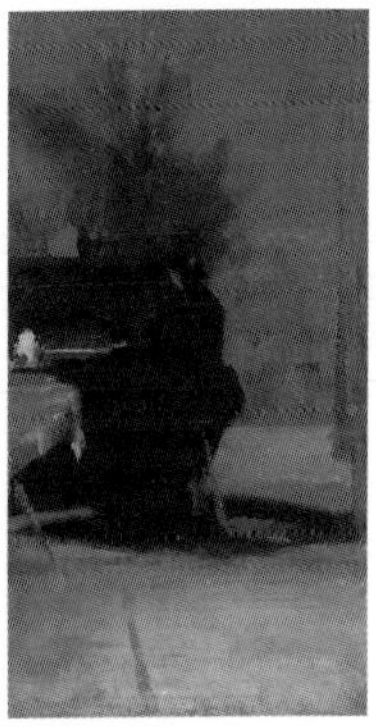

Woman at the piano
c1889 Melbourne
oil on cedar panel
26.0 x 13.1 cm
Not signed. Not dated.
Art Gallery of South Australia, Adelaide
M.J.M. Carter Collection

It is possible that like Topliss no. 111 the background represents Roberts's studio. It is probable that this work was exhibited at 'The 9 by 5 Impression Exhibition' but it is difficult to ascribe a title for it from that catalogue. It is possibly a sketch for *Whatever shall I play?*

Exhibitions: 1985-86 *Golden Summers;* 1993, 29 September – 12 December, *The M.J.M Carter Collection: A Private View of Australian Colonial Art*, AGSA; 1995 *Australian Colonial Art 1800-1900.*

Reference: Topliss no. 93a; GS p. 126; Radford 1993 pp. 55, 62; Radford & Hylton pp. 139, 148, 157.

Provenance: original owner unknown – private collection, Melbourne – 1982 Deutscher Fine Art, Melbourne.

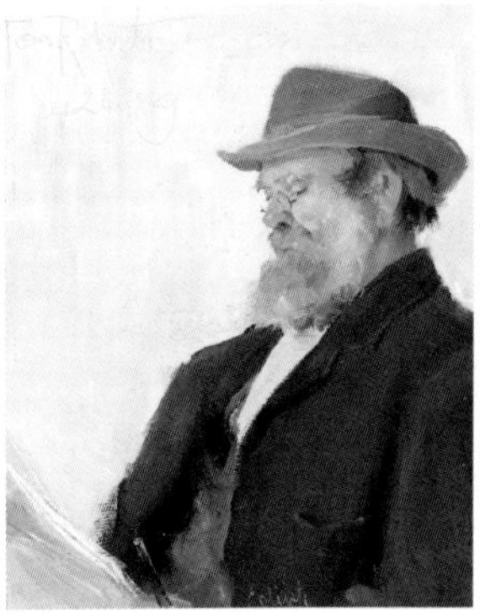

Alexander Augustus Anderson (snr)
1889 Brocklesby Station, Corowa, NSW
oil on canvas
24.1 x 19.0 cm
Signed and dated u.l., 'Tom Roberts/ Sep 24th 1889'.
Castlemaine Art Gallery and Historical Museum
Purchased with the assistance of the Caltex Victoria Art Fund and Public Appeal 1979

Alexander Anderson was a close friend of Roberts and the principal resident owner of Brocklesby Station at Corowa, where Roberts painted *Shearing the Rams*, 1888-90.

Exhibition: 1985-86 *Golden Summers.*

Reference: Terry Smith, "The divided meaning of *Shearing the rams*", in Bradley & Smith, pp. 116, 244; Topliss no. 154; GS p. 131.

Provenance: Charles Anderson (son of Alexander Anderson) – Misses I.M. and W.M. Anderson (his daughters) – Miss F.M. Anderson (his granddaughter).

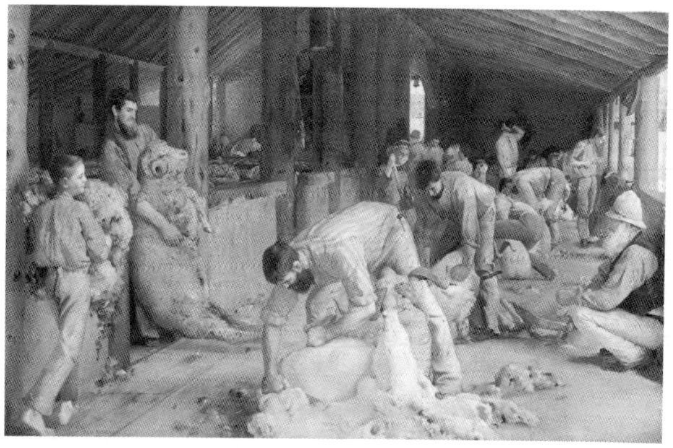

Shearing the rams
1888-90 Brocklesby Station, Corowa, NSW, and Melbourne
oil on canvas mounted on board , 121.9 x 182.6 cm
Signed and dated l.l., red oil 'TOM ROBERTS/ 1890'.
National Gallery of Victoria, Melbourne
Felton Bequest Fund 1932

This was painted in the shearing shed at Brocklesby Station, Corowa, New South Wales, and completed in Melbourne. The station was owned by Alexander Anderson, his brother Charles, and James King. Roberts first visited Brocklesby in December 1886 to attend the wedding of one of his cousins to A.A. Anderson's daughter.

Roberts began observing and working studies in late spring 1888, started work on the canvas during another long spell at Brocklesby during the next shearing season (when a portrait of A. A. Anderson was painted on 24 September) and he completed it in May 1890, when it was displayed in his Collins Street studio. In 1900 prints were made of the picture by Robertson & Moffat (100 signed artist's proofs at 3 gns and a number of prints at one guinea.

Exhibitions: May 1890, Roberts's studio, Grosvenor Chambers, Melbourne; 20 December 1890, VAS and Trustees of the NGV, no. 19 (lent by Edw Trenchard and Co.); June 1897 *Diamond Jubilee Loan Exhibition*, NGV, no. 126; 1925 *Loan Exhibition*, NGV, no. 77; April 1932, Tom Roberts, Fine Art Society, Melbourne; 1947-48 *Tom Roberts Retrospective Exhibition*, AGNSW, NGV, AGSA; 1962 *Australian Painting: Colonial, Impressionist, Contemporary*, AGSA, AGWA, then 1963 Tate Gallery, London, National Gallery, Ottawa and Vancouver Art Gallery; 1985-86 *Golden Summers*; 1988-89 *The Great Australian Art Exhibition.*

Reference: *Corowa Free Press*, 29 November 1889; *Argus*, 31 May 1890, p. 4; *Argus*, 24 June 1890, p. 6; 26 June 1890, p. 9; 28 June 1890, pp. 8, l0; 4 July 1890, p. 10 (Roberts's letter); 9 July 1890, p.5; *Age*, 30 May 1890, p. 7; 20 December 1890, p. 11; *Table Talk*,16 May 1890, p. 8; 30 May 1890, p. 7; 18 July 1890, p. 10; Conder letters to Roberts, 7 February. and 20 August 1890 (ML A247 p., V. 2); *Argus*, 30 March 1920, p. 8; Croll, pp. 33-4; Spate 1964, p. 262; Hoff 1951, p. 129; Spate pp. 19, 69, 85-8, 93; B. Smith 1962, pp. 88, 90, 120; McCulloch pp. 52, 54, 154; Gleeson p. 94; Hughes pp. 57-8; Finemore pp. 25-26, 40; Splatt & Bruce, pp. 66-67; Leigh Astbury, "Shearing the Rams: The hidden tradition", *Art Bulletin of Victoria* (NGV), no. 19, 1978, p. 68; Terry Smith, in Bradley & Smith, pp. 99-123; Ian Burn, in Bradley & Smith, p. 94; Nigel Lendon, in Bradley & Smith, pp. 73-74, 78; Jaffe; Topliss no. 149; Topliss in Donaldsons, p. 113; Astbury 1985, pp. 7, 100, 106-113, 120; Topliss 1992, pp. 3-4, 53-54; GS pp. 132 -34; CA p. 122; Astbury 1989, p. 194; McQueen chapter 14, pp. 195, 203, 326, 395, 455-46, 471, 517, 616, 709, 711, 721-23 (illus.).

Provenance: July 1890 purchased by Edw. Trenchard and Co. (see his portraits, Topliss nos 167 and 371).

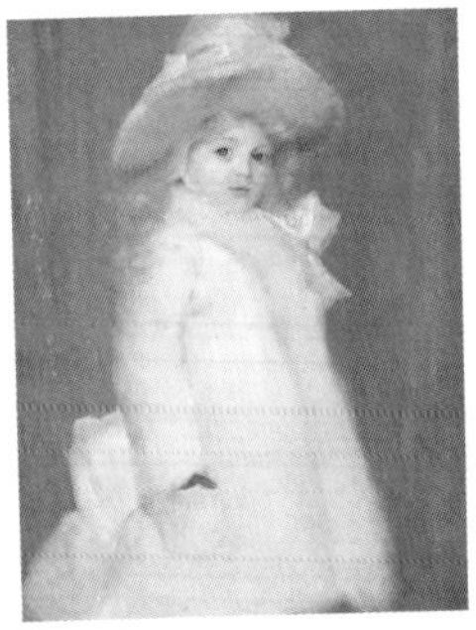

Lily Stirling
c1890 Melbourne
oil on canvas
85.5 x 65.5 cm
Not signed. Not dated.
National Gallery of Victoria, Melbourne
Purchased through the Art Foundation of Victoria with the assistance of the Chase Manhattan Overseas Corporation, Fellow, 1981

According to the sitter's brother, Alfred Stirling (letter 7 August 1977), Roberts was a friend of Lily's father, a doctor, who commissioned the portrait in Melbourne in c1892. However Terence Lane has ascribed a slightly earlier date to this work, considering the sitter's birth date of 1884 (died 1929), her extreme clothes consciousness which would have been rather out of fashion in 1892, and the fact that in 1892 Roberts was living in Sydney, not Melbourne.

Exhibitions: August 1893, *VAS Exhibition of Australian Art Past and Present*, no. 103 *A Portrait* (lent by Dr Stirling); 1947-48 *Tom Roberts Retrospective Exhibition*, no. 52 (lent by Miss E. Tatchell), AGNSW, NGV, AGSA; 1956 *Australian and Commonwealth Art Exhibition*, Norwich, England; 1985-86 *Golden Summers*.

Reference: McCaughey & Manton, p. 42; Topliss no. 195; GS p. 154.

Provenance: Dr Stirling – Miss E. Tatchell – Rev. Ian H. St Clair, Melbourne (his wife, a second cousin of Lily) – 1970 Christies, Sydney, lot 52 – Jack Manton.

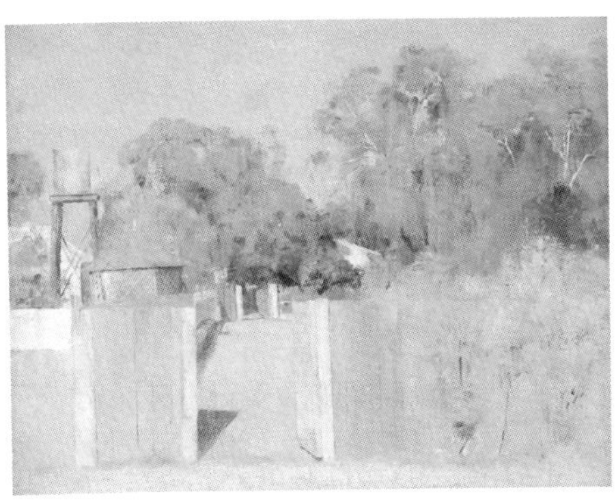

The old barracks at Collendina
c1891 Collendina Station, Corowa, NSW.
oil on canvas
40.0 x 51.5 cm (sight)
Not signed. Not dated.
Private collection, Adelaide

Roberts painted these workmen's and shearers' barracks while staying with Henry Hay at Collendina (see his portrait, Topliss no. 163, and no. 162 a portrait of his father William Hay). Roberts gave this painting and a sketchbook to Henry Hay (see Topliss no. III), perhaps not only in return for his hospitality but also because the landscape setting for *A break away!* was on Collendina, which adjoined Brocklesby to the west.

Exhibited: 10 May – 23 June 1991, *A century away! 1891-1991* ***A break away! by*** *Tom Roberts*, AGSA.

Reference: Topliss no. 164.

Provenance: Henry Hay – Mrs M. Synnot (his daughter).

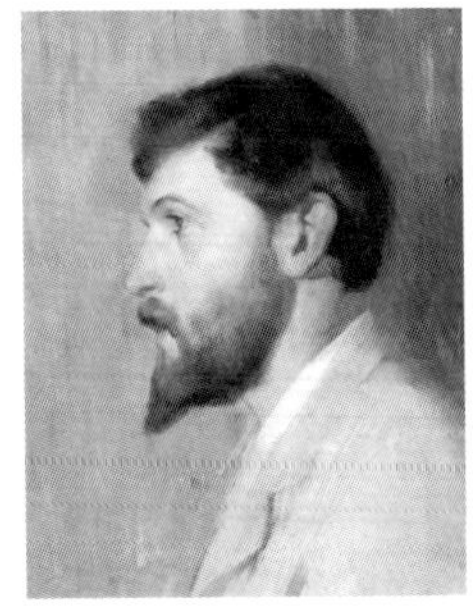

Smike Streeton age 24
1891 Sydney
oil on canvas
45.7 x 35.7 cm
Signed and dated l.l., incised 'Tom Roberts 91'.
The Art Gallery of New South Wales, Sydney
Purchased 1945

Title incised u.r., 'SMIKE/ STREETON/ AGE 24'.

This picture remained in Roberts's possession at his death and was clearly prized by him as a memento of his and Streeton's heyday. The portrait has the same delicate use of paint and transitions of colour as most of Roberts's portraits of women. The youthfulness of the sitter is emphasised; Streeton turned twenty-four on 8 April 1891, a time when he was using Roberts's studio while Roberts was at Corowa working on *A break away!*. They sailed to Sydney together in September 1891.

Exhibitions: April 1932, Tom Roberts, Fine Art Society, Melbourne, no. 45 (lent by Mrs Roberts); 1947-48 *Tom Roberts Retrospective Exhibition*, no. 13, *Sir Arthur Streeton* AGNSW, NGV, AGSA; 25 September 1953 *Retrospective Exhibition of Australian Painting*, AGNSW; 1962, *Australian Painting: Colonial, Impressionist, Contemporary*, AGSA, AGWA, then 1963 Tate Gallery, London, National Gallery, Ottawa and Vancouver Art Gallery; 1984 *The Artists' Camps*, Monash University Gallery and S.H. Ervin Gallery; 1985-86 *Golden Summers*.

Reference: McCulloch p. 61; Spate p. 117; Topliss no. 173; Topliss 1992, p. 58; GS p. 154; Astbury 1989, p. 10; McQueen pp. 345-6.

Provenance: 1931 Mrs Roberts (Roberts's second wife née Jean Boyes) – Miss Helen W. Boyes.

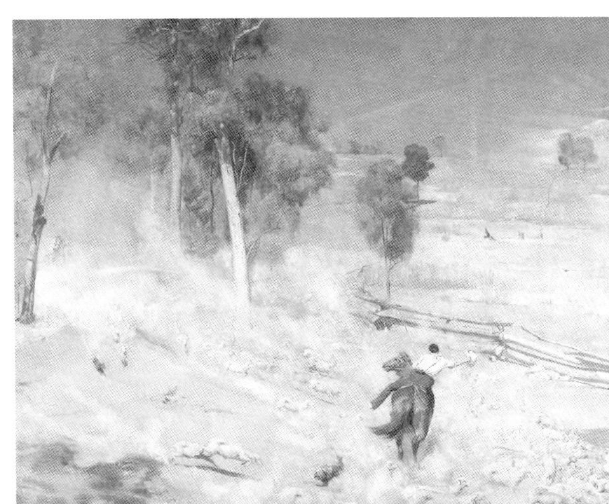

A break away!
1891 Corowa, NSW and Melbourne
oil on canvas
137.3 x 167.8cm
Signed l.l. corner, red oil 'Tom Roberts'. Not dated.
Art Gallery of South Australia, Adelaide
Elder Bequest Fund 1899

Title used at first press viewings July 1891 was reinstated in January 1988 prior to 'The Great Australian Art Exhibition'; after the first viewings it was variously *The Break Away*, *A Breakaway* or, at the Grafton Galleries, London, 1898, *A Break Away*.

Roberts was at Corowa from February to May 1891. 'Titian Redde' (A.G. Stephens) in his article on Roberts in *The Bookfellow* claimed that the £275 Roberts earned from '*Shearing at Newstead*' (but as this was painted in 1894 Stephens must have confused it with *Shearing the rams*) enabled Roberts to spend a year in the country where he painted *A break away!*. A contemporary article on Roberts describes his studio as being the Brocklesby woolshed (reprinted Croll pp. 36-37). The landscape setting was close to the woolshed, but across the boundary on the neighbouring Collendina Station. Roberts kept a photograph of this picture in his scrap-book (ML, S 24b).

Exhibitions: May 1892, VAS, no. 198 (illus. in catalogue, £300); September 1893, ASNSW, no. 176 (illus. in catalogue, £265); April 1898 *Exhibition of Australian Art*, Grafton Galleries, London, no. 40; 1899 *Second Federal Exhibition*, South Australian Society of Arts, Adelaide; 1934 *Centenary Art Exhibition*, Melbourne; 1938 *150 Years of Australian Art*, AGNSW; 1947-48 *Tom Roberts Retrospective Exhibition*, AGNSW, NGV, AGSA; 1951 *Jubilee Exhibition of Australian Art;* 1962 *Australian Painting: Colonial, Impressionist, Contemporary*, AGSA, AGWA, then 1963 Tate Gallery, London, National Gallery, Ottawa and Vancouver Art Gallery; 1985-86 *Golden Summers*; 1988-89 *The Great Australian Art Exhibition 1788-1988*, AGSA; 10 May - 23 June 1991 *A century away! 1891-1991* ***A break away!*** *by Tom Roberts*, AGSA; 1995 *Australian Colonial Art 1800-1900.*

Reference: *Table Talk*, 17 July 1891, p. 16; 27 May 1892, p. 2; *Sydney Morning Herald*, 1 September 1893, p. 6; 2 September 1893, p. 6; Croll pp. 35-37 (reprints a contemporary press account "A 'Bush' Studio"); *Magazine of Art* (London), 1898, pp. 376, 383 (illus.); *Daily Telegraph* (Syd.) 5 May 1898, p. 6; 12 May 1898 (summary of English reviews of Grafton Galleries Exhibition); *The Bookfellow*, 29 April 1899 (reprinted Croll, p. 57); *Australasian Art Review*, December 1899, p. 29; *Art in Australia*, 3rd series, no. 70 March 1938; *Bulletin of the National Gallery of South Australia*, no. 2 AGBSA, June 1939; *The Australian Artist* (Melb.) vol. 1, no. 3, 1948, p. 33; *National Gallery of South Australia Picture Book*, Adelaide: AGBSA, 1960; *Antipodean Vision*, Melbourne: Cheshire, 1962; Hoff 1951, pp. 127, 129-130; Spate pp. 86, 90-92, 97; B. Smith 1962, pp. 88, 90, 119, 122; McCulloch pp. 58, 60, 158; *Picture Book: Selected works from the collections of the Art Gallery of South Australia*, Adelaide: AGBSA, 1972; Gleeson p. 94; Hughes p. 57; Finemore pp. 25-27; Splatt & Bruce, pp. 68-69; Leigh Astbury, "The Breakaway Myth and History", *Bulletin of the Art Gallery of South Australia*, vol. 38, 1980, p. 2; Nigel Lendon, in Bradley & Smith, p. 73; Ian Burn, in Bradley & Smith, pp. 89, 94; Topliss no. 170; Astbury 1985, pp. 7, 113-121; GS pp. 128, 136 -37; CA pp. 120-21; Astbury 1989, pp. 177, 196; *Selected Works*, Adelaide: AGBSA, p. 56, 1991; *Tom Roberts, A break away! 1891*, Adelaide: AGBSA, 1991; Radford & Hylton, pp. 12, 94, 133, 142, 160, 177-178, 179,186; McQueen pp. 204, 330*ff*, 336-7, 433, 449*ff*, 605, 608-9, 645, 706, 715, 724 (illus.).

Provenance: 1899 purchased from the *Second Federal Exhibition*, South Australian Society of Arts, Adelaide.

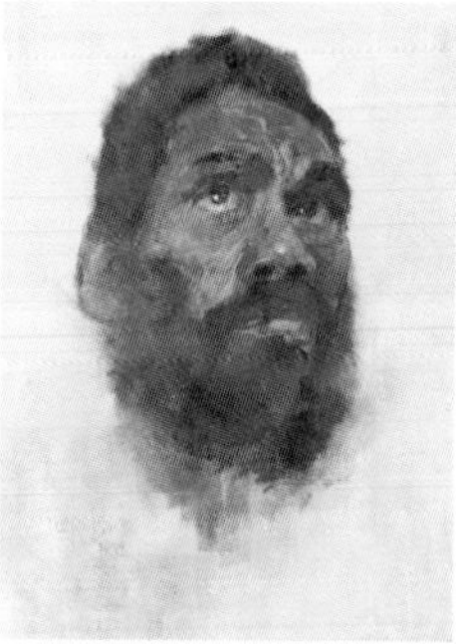

Aboriginal head (Charlie Turner)
1892? Sydney
oil on canvas on paperboard
39.4 x 29.8 cm
Signed and dated l.l., red oil 'Tom Roberts 1892'.
The Art Gallery of New South Wales, Sydney
Purchased 1892

This portrait was probably painted during Roberts's stay at Corowa in 1890 and dated 1892 when first exhibited. The *Argus* in April 1890 mentions that Roberts was making studies of the "blacks of Corowa". There is no record of Roberts having visited Corowa in 1892, although it is possible that he painted this from a sketch done in 1890. It was particularly admired by the *Sydney Morning Herald*, which said it was painted with strength and fidelity, and stated "that its value will grow year by year with the gradual disappearance from our midst of the original possessor of the soil".

Exhibitions: September 1892, ASNSW, no. 78, *Aboriginal head*; 1893, Chicago Exposition; May 1898 *Exhibition of Australian Art*, Grafton Galleries, London, no. 41; 1947-48 *Tom Roberts Retrospective Exhibition*, AGNSW, NGV, AGSA; 1985-86 *Golden Summers*.

Reference: *Argus*, 5 April 1890, p. 6; *Sydney Morning Herald* , 2 September 1892, p. 2; *Australasian Art Review*, 1 August 1899, p. 23; McCulloch pp. 60, 158; Geoffrey Dutton, *White on Black: The Australian Aborigine portrayed in art*, South Melbourne & Adelaide: Macmillan & AGBSA, p. 59; Topliss no. 183; Topliss in Donaldsons, pp. 113-114; GS p. 153.

Provenance: September 1892, purchased from Art Society of NSW.

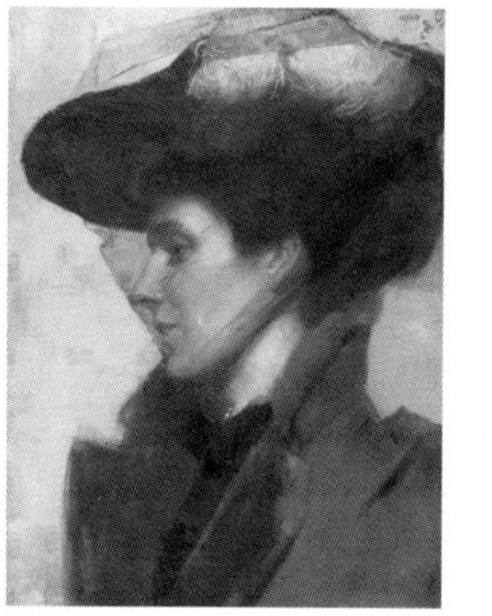

Eileen
1892 Sydney
oil on canvas
49.0 x 36.0 cm
Signed and dated l.l., brown oil 'Tom Roberts 92'.
The Art Gallery of New South Wales, Sydney
Purchased 1892

Inscribed u.r., brown oil 'EILEEN'.

The subject is Mrs Eileen Tooker (née Aird, born in Sligo, northern Ireland). Eileen met John Tooker in Cork, where they married but she also lived in Sydney. They left Ireland for Rockhampton where Tooker owned a property with his brother. Roberts placed a photograph of the portrait in his scrap-book (ML, S 42).

Exhibitions: Spring 1892, ASNSW, no. 54; 1893, Chicago Exposition; March 1920 Athenæum Hall, Melbourne, *Souvenir Exhibition*, no. 71; 1938 *One Hundred and Fifty Years of Australian Art*, AGNSW; 1947-48 *Tom Roberts Retrospective Exhibition*, AGNSW, NGV, AGSA; September 1953 *Retrospective Exhibition of Australian Painting*, AGNSW; 1976-77 *Aspects of Australian Art*, AGNSW Travelling Art Exhibition; 1985-86 *Golden Summers*.

Reference: *Sydney Morning Herald*, 2 September 1892, p. 2; *Australasian Art Review*, August 1899, p. 23; Croll p. 45; McCulloch pp. 60, 158; *Aspects of Australian Art*, Sydney AGNSW, 1976; Spate p. 117; Hughes p. 61; Topliss no. 187; GS p. 155.

Provenance: September 1892, purchased from Art Society of NSW.

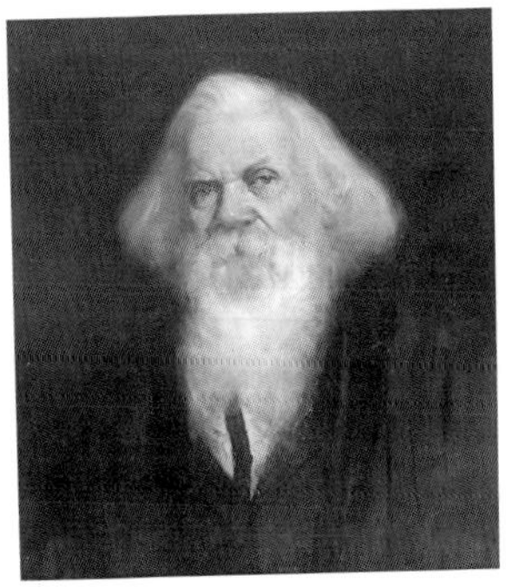

Sir Henry Parkes
1892 Sydney
oil on canvas
66.0 x 56.0 cm
Signed l.l., black oil 'Tom Roberts'. Not dated.
Art Gallery of South Australia, Adelaide
Elder Bequest Fund 1901

This is a companion picture to Roberts's portraits of Sir William Windeyer and Cardinal Moran, the three forming a triptych of 'Church, State and the Law', exhibited in September 1892 at the ASNSW, Sydney (see Topliss nos 192-4). Parkes (1815-1896) was an eminent NSW politician and journalist, born in England and emigrated in 1839. He was a spokesman for universal suffrage in 1849. In 1850 he became editor proprietor of the *Empire*, a liberal magazine. He entered the colonial parliament in 1854 and was a zealous campaigner for Federation from 1889. Alfred Deakin described him as "though not rich or versatile, his personality was massive, durable and imposing, resting upon elementary qualities of human nature elevated by a strong mind". Roberts painted another portrait of him in 1894 (AGNSW). Judging by letters written by Roberts to Parkes, they were friends (ML, CY A903 v. 33). Roberts placed a photo of this portrait in his scrap-book (ML, S 41b).

Exhibitions: September 1892, ASNSW, no 5; 1893, Royal Academy, London; November 1900 *Exhibition and Sale of Paintings*, Sydney, no. 79; 1901 *Victorian Gold Jubilee Exhibition*, Bendigo, Victoria.

Reference: *Sydney Morning Herald*, 2 September 1892, p. 2; *Antipodean*, 1894, p.81; Letter to John Plummer, 5 December 1895 (ML, Ar. 48); *Review of Reviews*, 20 November 1896, p. 517; ADB, vol. 5, pp. 399-406; Spate p. 115; Topliss no. 193; McQueen pp. 384, 422, 460, 467.

Provenance: 1901 purchased from the Victorian Gold Jubilee Exhibition, Bendigo.

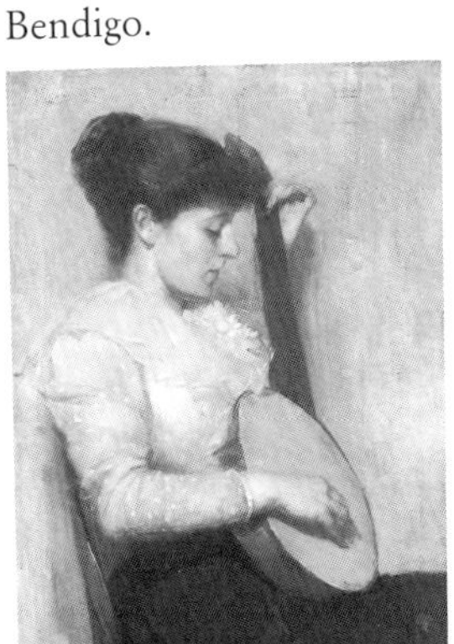

Plink-a-plong
1893 Sydney
oil on canvas
68.5 x 50.8 cm
Signed and dated l.l., brown oil 'Tom Roberts/ 1893'.
Art Gallery of South Australia, Adelaide
Elder Bequest Fund 1948

This work was previously known as *Girl playing a banjo*, retitled by Ron Radford in 1984 to its original, *Plink-a-plong*. The sitter is probably Lena Brasch, of whom there is an identified sketch portrait, Topliss no. 211. The Brasch brothers were fellow campers at Mosman Bay with Roberts and Streeton; Reuben Brasch was 'father' of the camp.
Exhibitions: 1947-48 *Tom Roberts Retrospective Exhibition* (lent by Mrs M.R. Charlton) then AGNSW, NGV, AGSA; 1995 *Australian Colonial Art 1800-1900.*
Reference: *Bulletin of the National Gallery of South Australia*, vol. 10, no. 2, AGBSA, October 1948; Topliss no. 210; Radford & Hylton pp. 14, 162, 163.
Provenance: Mrs M. R. Charlton – 1948 AGSA.

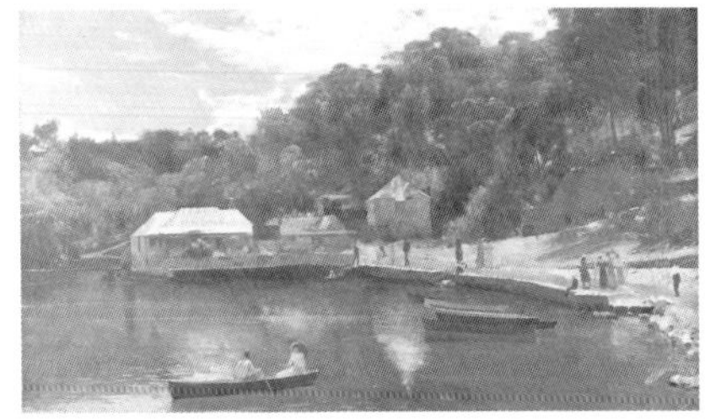

Mosman's Bay
1894 Sydney
oil on canvas , 63.5 x l06.2cm
Signed and dated l.l., oil 'Tom Roberts 94'
New England Regional Art Museum, Armidale, NSW
Gift of Howard Hinton 1933. The Howard Hinton Collection.

This was painted while Roberts and Streeton were living on the shore of Sydney Harbour at Curlew Camp, Little Sirius Cove, the next inlet east of Mosman's Bay. The building in the background is Lewis's Refreshment Rooms; Saunders' boat house is outside the picture on the right, presumably the vantage point from which Roberts was painting this picture (see Topliss illus. 50-54). The landscape background has been retouched and is more heavily painted than the buildings or the foreground. In later years, Roberts repainted a number of pictures that remained unsold.
Exhibitions: 1963 *Sydney Harbour: 175th Anniversary of Australia*, AGNSW; 1980 *Focus on the Hinton Collection*; 1985-86 *Golden Summers*; 1991, 6 June - 25 August, *Bohemians in the Bush: The artists' camps of Mosman*, AGNSW.
Reference: *Art in Australia*, 3rd series, no. 56, 1934 August (illus.); *A Memorial Volume to Howard Hinton*, Sydney, 1951; Spate p. 70; Topliss no. 222; GS pp. 160-61; Astbury 1989, p. 115; Topliss 1992, p. 136; Pearce & Slutzkin; McQueen p. 385 (illus.).
Provenance: Original owner unknown – Howard Hinton.

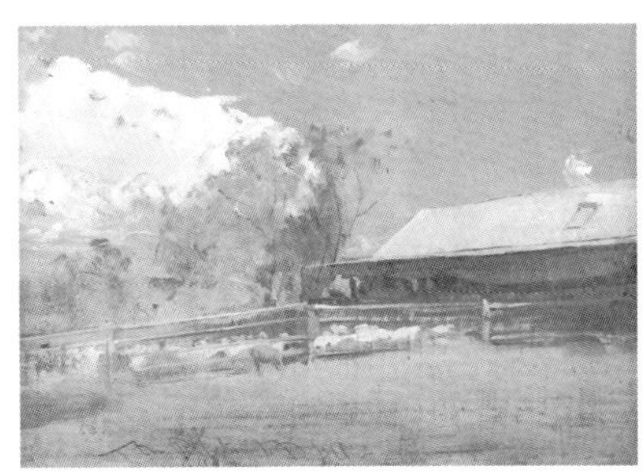

Shearing shed, Newstead
c1894 Newstead North, Elsmore, NSW
oil on wood panel, 23.5 x 35.6 cm
Signed and inscribed l.c., 'Tom Roberts to DSA [followed by an ideogram of a bulldog]'. Not dated.
Private collection, Sydney

Roberts arrived at Newstead North on 23 December 1893, for Christmas and New Year; this panel was a gift to his host ("DSA" is Duncan Sinclair Anderson) from the artist guest (the bulldog ideogram refers to Roberts's nickname). The woolshed, here seen from the north, had been built by Anderson's parents in 1868 for a larger Newstead, divided in two in 1883, since when Duncan Anderson had lived in the original homestead, one kilometre to the east. The interior of this shed became the setting for Roberts's *The Golden Fleece*, which he said he began painting in February 1894; the dusty yards seen from indoors on the left of the large canvas are the sheep yards in the foreground of this sketch. In the sketch hessian blinds shade the shearing board more thoroughly than in the large painting, where artistic licence must have raised them so that the painting could show the action in the yards. This high-summer sketch might have been given to Anderson in the festive season, and it was probably made in the course of studying a new subject. Its date therefore is likely to be December 1893 or January 1894. See Topliss no. 225 for a panel portrait of Duncan Anderson playing his cornet, painted in October 1894 on another visit to Newstead.
Exhibitions: November 1900 *Tom Roberts Exhibition and Sale of Paintings*, Sydney, no. 3 (3 gns.); 1985-86 *Golden Summers.*
Reference: Topliss no. 217; GS p. 142.
Provenance: Duncan Anderson – Alick Anderson (his son).

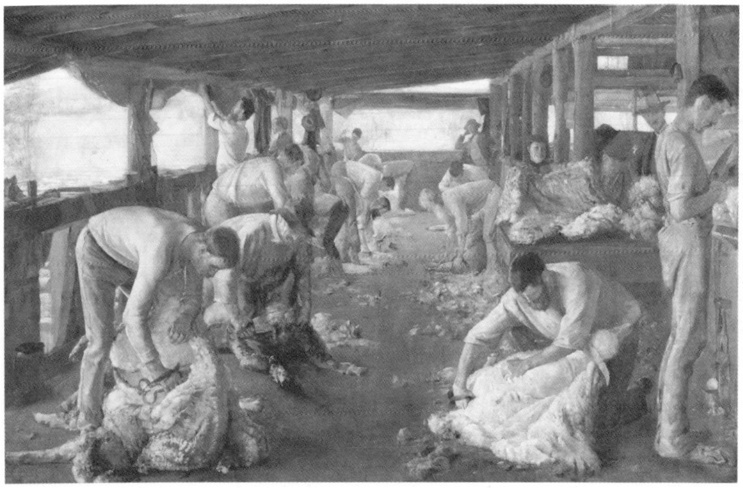

The Golden Fleece
1894 Newstead North, Elsmore, NSW, and Sydney
oil on canvas, 104.0 x 158.7 cm
Signed l.r., oil 'TOM ROBERTS', dated l.l., red oil '... 94'.
The Art Gallery of New South Wales, Sydney
Purchased 1894

Painted in the woolshed at Newstead North, begun February 1894 according to the artist, presumably worked on until May, when he was back in Sydney, where it was finished. Exhibited in Sydney at the ASNSW, 28 September, it was bought by AGNSW for £275, Roberts's first major work to enter a public collection. In the Art Society exhibition catalogue it is titled *Shearing at Newstead*, but it was reviewed in the press as *The Golden Fleece*, and was received into the Gallery's collection as *The Golden Fleece*. Perhaps a label went up in the exhibition, giving the revised title. It is likely that the title was negotiated with Duncan Anderson, the owner of Newstead North: perhaps he decided the specific place-name might compromise his privacy, or that it was prosaic, or perhaps he had to be persuaded that the reference to the archaic Greek myth, despite its ambiguous implication of a wealthy owner of a particular sheep station, was best because it was most resonant and poetic. Duncan Anderson looks over the shoulder of the foreground-right standing shearer; he holds a fleece in a hand unconnected to his own body. His presence is awkward, and seems to be a makeshift afterthought.

Exhibitions: 1894, ASNSW, no. 300, *Shearing at Newstead* (illus. in catalogue); April 1898, Grafton Galleries, London, *Exhibition of Australian Art*, no. 102, *The Golden Fleece*; 1915, San Francisco *Panama Pacific Exhibition*; 1918 April, AGNSW *Loan Exhibition of Australian Art;* April 1932, Tom Roberts Fine Art Society, Melbourne, no. 4; 1938 *150 Years of Australian Art*, AGNSW; 1947-48 *Tom Roberts Retrospective Exhibition*, no. 19, *The Golden Fleece, Newstead* AGNSW, NGV, AGSA; 1951 Geneva International Labor Organisation, *Art and Work Exhibition*; 1953, 25 September *Retrospective Exhibition of Australian Painting*, AGNSW; 1962, *Australian Painting: Colonial, Impressionist, Contemporary*, AGSA, AGWA, then 1963 Tate Gallery, London, National Gallery, Ottawa and Vancouver Art Gallery; June – August 1992 *Australian Icons*, Hyde Park Barracks, Sydney; November 1994 – May 1995, *Wool in the Australian Imagination*, Hyde Park Barracks, Sydney.

Reference: *Antipodean*, 1894, p. 81; *Argus*, 28 September 1894, p.3; *Sydney Morning Herald*, 28 September 1894, p. 3; *Review of Reviews*, 20 November 1896, p. 517; *The Graphic* (London), 16 April 1898; *Daily Telegraph* (Syd.), 5 May 1898, p. 6 (summary of English reviews of Grafton Galleries Exhibition), 12 May 1898, p. 6; *Magazine of Art* (London), 1898, p. 383; *The Bookfellow*, 29 April 1899, p. 28; *Australasian Art Review*, 1 August 1899, p. 23; Croll p. 165 (recollections of Alick Anderson, son of Duncan Anderson); 1938 March *Art in Australia*, 3rd series, no. 70 (illus.); B. Smith 1962, pp. 88, 119; Spate pp. 93-94; McCulloch pp. 62, 158; Gleeson p. 94; Hughes p. 57; Splatt & Bruce, p. 75; Nigel Lendon, in Bradley & Smith, pp. 78-79, 82; Astbury 1985, pp. 8, 121-125; Topliss no. 216; Topliss in Donaldsons, pp. 112-114; McQueen pp. 298, 382-3, 388, 394, 432-4, 471, 603, 605, 664, 707, 723.

Provenance: September 1894 purchased from Art Society of NSW.

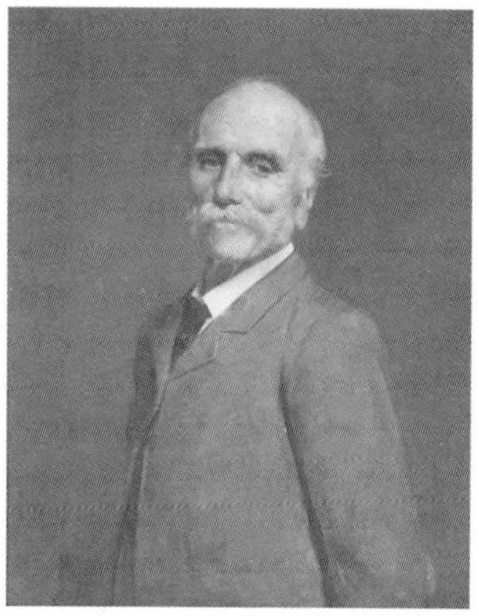

Edward Ogilvie
1895 Yulgilbar, NSW
oil on canvas, 73.5 x 58.5 cm
Signed and dated l.r., oil 'Tom Roberts 1895'
Mitchell Library, State Library of New South Wales, Sydney
Presented by Mrs G. Carson to the Mitchell Library 1972
Inscribed l.l. corner, oil 'Yulgilbar'.
Inscribed u.l. to r., oil 'Edward D. S. Ogilvie In his 81st Year'.

Ogilvie (1814-1896) was born in England and came to Sydney in 1825. In 1840 he was the first settler to explore the Clarence River, where he took up Yulgilbar, well up-river from Grafton. Ogilvie learnt the local Aboriginal dialect by kidnapping an Aboriginal boy called Pundoon, whom he returned to his people in 1842. He then made a treaty with the Aborigines, telling them that he only wanted grazing rights on the land and that they could have complete hunting rights. When Ogilvie lost his station hands to the goldfields he replaced them with Aborigines. He designed his own mansion, which was completed in 1866. Ogilvie had visited Europe in 1854 and lived in Florence and the picture frame for Roberts's portrait is characteristic of Florentine wood-carving. In a letter from Yulgilbar, dated 16 January 1895, Roberts provided a sketch of Ogilvie in his courtyard (see Topliss illus. 62) with the following description: "the chief aged 80 with no sign of mental failure, military type, in mind and physique. I got along first rate with him, disagreeing at nearly every point. Painted him in the interior court (Spanish) of the house. They are delighted it's more solid than anything I've done" (ML, MSS 1367/2 no. 8). While Roberts was at Yulgilbar a photograph (reproduced in George Farwell's biography of Ogilvie) was taken of him on his horse, Black Bess. Roberts also painted a portrait of Ogilvie's granddaughter, which he gave to Alick Anderson in 1920 (Croll p. 170). Roberts placed a photo of Ogilvie's portrait in his scrap-book (ML, S 35).

Exhibition: September 1896, SA, no. 27.

Reference: Edward Ogilvie, in *Sydney Morning Herald*, 8 July 1842; Tom Roberts's letter to S.W. Pring, 16 January 1895 (ML, MSS 1367/2 no. 8); ADB, vol. 5, pp. 358-59. George Farwell, *Squatter's Castle*, Melbourne: Lansdowne, 1973, p. 323; Topliss no. 241; Topliss in Donaldsons, pp. 126-129; McQueen pp. 392, 422 (illus.).

Provenance: Edward Ogilvie – his family – E.D. Ogilvie (his grandson) – on loan to Clarence River Historical Society, Grafton – Mrs G. Carson.

Two-column page: left column

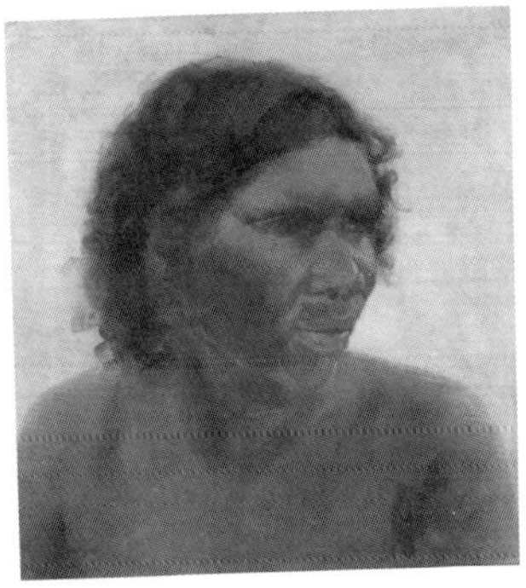

Portrait of an Aboriginal woman (Maria Yulgilbar)
1895 Yulgilbar, NSW
oil on canvas, 38.0 x 34.5 cm
Signed l.l., red oil 'Tom Roberts'. Not dated.
Dixson Galleries, State Library of New South Wales, Sydney
Presented by Sir William Dixson, March 1943
Title inscribed on verso 'Portrait of an Aboriginal Woman'.

This portrait was probably painted while Roberts was visiting Yulgilbar in 1895, where he was commissioned to paint *Edward Ogilvie* and where he also made studies of Aborigines. In a letter dated 16 January 1895 (ML) Roberts described going to Ogilvie's property to paint Aborigines: "only did one head of a native". This portrait is probably *Maria Yulgilbar* exhibited at the SA in September 1895. An 1890s photograph of an Aboriginal woman called 'Maria Charlie', from the archives of the Clarence River Historical Society, Grafton, is very close to this painting. Two drawings exist for this portrait in a Mitchell Library sketch-book (see Topliss nos 230a and 230b), the latter having Aboriginal words inscribed on it in the Bundjalung dialect of the Casino region.

Exhibitions: Probably September 1895, SA (Inaugural Exhibition), no. 31 *Maria Yulgilbar* (£21); probably November 1900 *Tom Roberts Exhibition and Sale of Paintings*, Sydney, no. 17, *Chief's Sister Yulgilbar* (8 gns.).

Reference: Tom Roberts letter to S.W. Pring, 16 January 1895 (ML, MSS 1367/2 No 8); Topliss in Donaldson, pp. 132-135; Topliss nos 230, 230a and 230b.

Provenance: Sir William Dixson, Sydney.

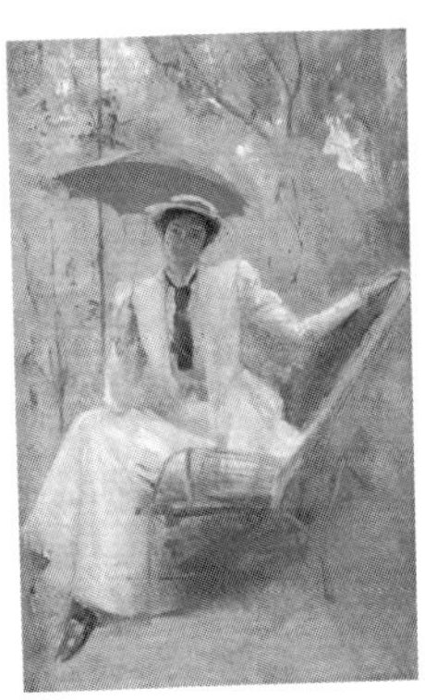

Lady with a parasol
early 1890s Sydney
oil on canvas mounted on board
45.7 x 28.2 cm
Not signed. Not dated.
Private collection, Sydney

On verso on frame 'a painting – Tom Roberts. Its O.K. H. McC'.

The front facing pose and the bush setting would seem to suggest this was painted in the early 1890s, as does the handling of the bright background landscape.

Exhibited: 1986 *Australian Works of Art*, Lauraine Diggins Gallery, Melbourne; 1988, *The Australian Impressionists: Their origins & influences*, Lauraine Diggins.

Reference: Spate 1964; Topliss no. 67; *Australian Works of Art*, Melbourne: Lauraine Diggins Gallery, 1986; Jane Clark, *The Australian Impressionists: Their origins & influences*, Melbourne: Lauraine Diggins, 1988.

Provenance: Tom Lambert (?) – c1964 private collection, Melbourne – Neville Healy, Melbourne – private collection, Melbourne.

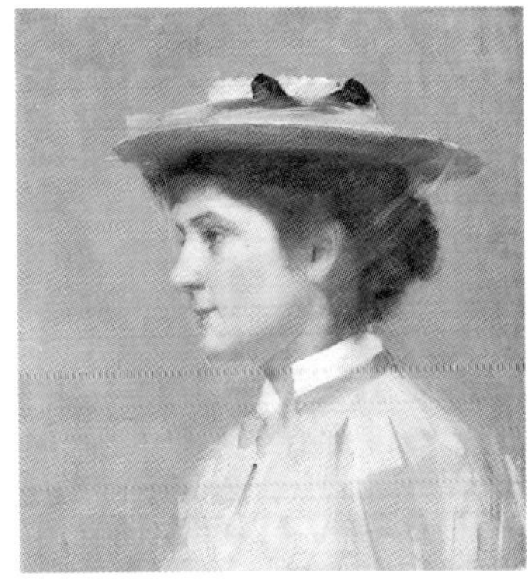

Miss Isobel McDonald
1895 Sydney
oil on canvas
46.3 x 41.3 cm
Signed and dated l.l., incised 'Tom Roberts/ Dec. 5/ 95'.
National Gallery of Victoria, Melbourne
Purchased 1957

Roberts was at his studio in Commercial Chambers, Bathurst Street, Sydney at this date. Previously titled *Profile portrait of a young girl in a straw hat*, but identified in *Golden Summers* 1985. The sitter is Miss Isobel Agnes McDonald (1871-1926), niece of the 9 by 5 exhibitor Herbert Daly and herself an art student in Melbourne, though her family lived in Queensland. She seems to have frequently visited Sydney and Melbourne.
Exhibition: 1985-86 *Golden Summers*.
Reference: Topliss no. 243; GS p. 165.
Provenance: original owner unknown – c1928 Lawson's auction, Sydney – Mrs B.E. Mendell's father – Mrs B.E. Mendell, Sydney.

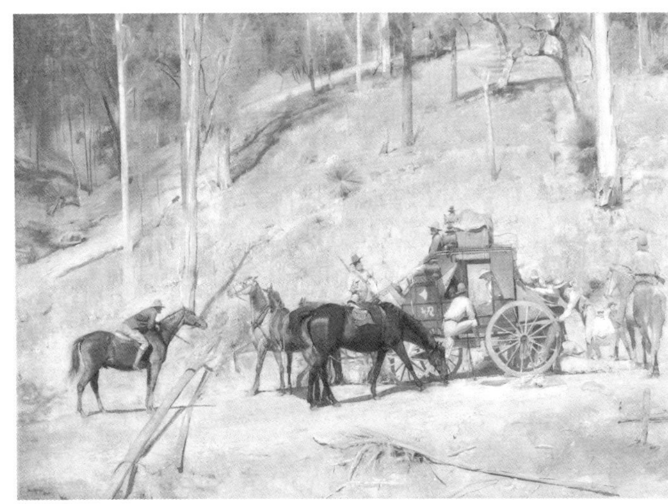

Bailed up
1895 Newstead and Inverell, NSW, and Sydney
1927 Kallista, Victoria
oil on canvas, 134.5 x 182.8 cm
Signed and dated l.l., oil 'Tom Roberts/ 95 – 27'.
The Art Gallery of New South Wales, Sydney
Purchased 1933

An imaginary event, its quiet mood is based on an account of an 1860s "stick-up" given to Roberts by "Silent Bob Bates", who in 1893-95 was the driver of the Cobb & Co. coach running between Glen Innes and Inverell.

An oil-sketch composition study (Topliss no. 234a), dated "Dec. 31 1893" was painted at Duncan Anderson's Newstead North station, apparently after Roberts was told, over dinner, how bushrangers would have robbed a coach. An appropriate site for the landscape setting might have been identified in

December 1893 – January 1894 (when Roberts was preparing to paint *The Golden Fleece* in the shearing shed at Newstead), for Anderson and Roberts often walked by road further into the hills for afternoon tea with the Anderson's cousin Russell Hughes at the neighbouring Paradise station, and the site was found on that road. *Bailed up* was begun early in 1895. Roberts was based again at Newstead, having ridden across the Great Dividing Range from Yulgilbar and Reek's gold-mining claim on the Timbarra River. In February he moved to Paradise, to begin the canvas with its landscape background, painted in the open at a site which was a shorter walk from Paradise than Newstead. In April the canvas was taken in to Inverell where a studio was established in the Oxford Hall, behind the Oxford Hotel. There the coach, its driver Bob Bates, and some of the horses were added. He left Inverell at the end of July, after going out to Newstead "to get in one important figure"; other horses and figures had apparently been painted there. Possibly there were minor adjustments in Sydney before the canvas was exhibited on 28 September, priced £275. It remained unsold for over thirty years, and the landscape background was substantially re-worked in Roberts's studio at Kallista in 1927.

The signature and dates were added by Roberts in 1928 after the picture had been purchased at the Macquarie Galleries, Sydney, by J.W. Maund, who lent it to the Art Gallery of New South Wales. When it was displayed there Roberts's friend Mrs Reay (née Anna Fraser) noticed that it was unsigned and it was through her suggestion to the Director, G.V.F. Mann, that Roberts signed it (Croll p. 129). Roberts referred to this picture in a letter to Sir Henry Parkes written from Newstead, 14 June 1895 (ML). In a letter to Rodney Cherry, 27 July 1928 (private collection, Sydney), Roberts wrote that "the show [Macquarie Galleries] went well" and mentions his "six-footer of a 'sticking up' beg. 30 yrs ago and which I put a lot of wk. on during last year".

Exhibitions: 28 September 1895, SA, no. 29 (illus. in catalogue, £275); October 1896, VAS, no. 41 (£275); November 1900 *Tom Roberts Exhibition and Sale of Paintings*, Sydney, no. 20 (70 gns); 1901-2 *Victorian Gold Jubilee Exhibition*, Bendigo, Victoria, no. 52; June 1928, Tom Roberts, Macquarie Galleries (500 gns); 1938 *150 Years of Australian Art*, AGNSW; 1941 *Art of Australia 1788 - 1941*; , National Gallery of Art, Washington, Metropolitan Museum of Art, N.Y., National Gallery of Canada, Ottawa and elsewhere in U.S. and Canada; November 1944-45, *Art of the United Nations Exhibition*, Chicago (illus. in catalogue); 1947-48 *Tom Roberts Retrospective Exhibition*, AGNSW, NGV, AGSA; 1951 *Commonwealth Jubilee Exhibition of Australian Art*, no. 111; 1953, 25 September *Retrospective Exhibition of Australian Painting*, AGNSW; 1956 *Fine Art Exhibition*, Olympic Games, Melbourne; 1962 *Australian Painting: Colonial, Impressionist, Contemporary*, AGSA, AGWA, then 1963 Tate Gallery, London, National Gallery, Ottawa and Vancouver Art Gallery; 1985-86 *Golden Summers.*

Reference: *Daily Telegraph* (Syd.), 27 September 1895, p. 6; *Argus* , 23 October 1896, p. 6; *Age*, 24 October 1896, p. 11; *Sydney Morning Herald*, 14 November 1900, p. 5; 2 March 1928, p. 13; 28 June 1928, p. 8; 14 July 1928, p. 11; *Art in Australia*, 3rd series, no. 70, March 1938 (illus.); 10 November 1947, p. 7; Unidentified press cutting Roberts Papers; Moore p. 128; Croll pp. 38, 128-129, 167-168; B. Smith 1945, pp. 116, 132, 157; Badham p. 46; Hoff 1951, p. 130; Spate 1964 p. 263; Spate pp. 73, 92, 94-5; B. Smith 1962, p. 90; McCulloch pp. 62, 64, 158; Hughes p. 57; Gleeson p. 94; Splatt & Bruce, pp. 76-77; Ian Burn, in Bradley & Smith, p. 89; Topliss no. 234; Astbury 1985, pp. 125-129; GS pp. 144-45; Astbury 1989, pp. 122, 197; McQueen pp. 396, 405, 410-11, 422-3, 460, 654, 681, 689-91, 706, 710, 719, 721, 724.

Provenance: 1928 Macquarie Galleries – Mr J.W. Maund.

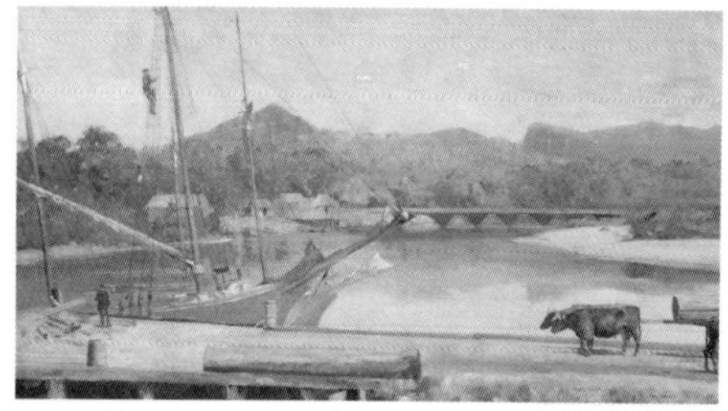

Ulverstone
1890s Tasmania
oil on canvas
40.6 x 68.7 cm
Signed l.r., black oil 'Tom Roberts'. Not dated.
Private collection, Melbourne

The small, neat signature and the painting's realist detail and crisp touches of pigment relate it to the work Roberts was doing in the early 1890s. It is somewhat flat in its handling and does not have the heavy impasto of the 1920s Tasmanian works. It also has the variety in colour and overall blond tonality of the New South Wales pictures of the 1890s, such as *Lumbering*, c1893-96 and *The Bullock Team* (Topliss nos 232, 233). Roberts was in Tasmania from late March to early May 1890 and in December 1890 at Gemmell & Tuckett, Melbourne, exhibited two Ulverstone subjects, one of them *Summer holiday at Ulverstone.* Although sunny enough, even if painted in autumn, this lacks the holiday mood that an Ulverstone beach scene could have offered. This is a view of the forested Dial Range, a railway bridge across the Leven River, and a wharf to which bullocks are delivering logs. The Robertses two-week Tasmanian honeymoon in May 1896 was spent partly at Penguin, very close to Ulverstone.

Reference: Topliss no. 165.

Provenance: George Page-Cooper – Julian Stirling – November 1967 Barr Smith – June 1976, Joel's auction, Melbourne.

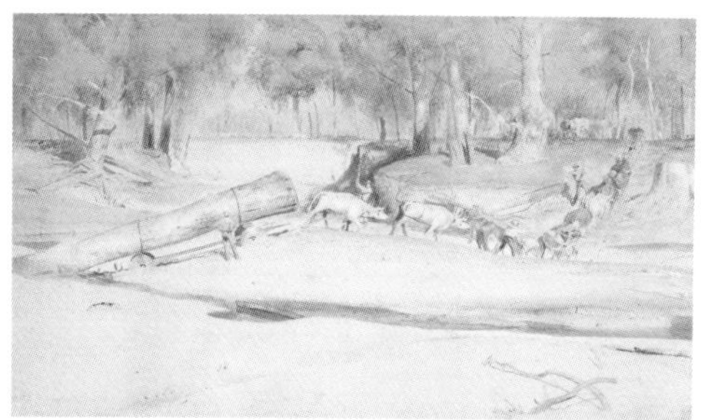

Lumbering
c1893-96 New South Wales
watercolour on paper
59.7 x 99.5 cm
Not signed. Not dated.
National Gallery of Australia, Canberra
Purchased 1978

Recently retitled by Mary Eagle, previously known as *Lumbering bullock team.* This and its companion, Topliss no. 233, were probably executed by Roberts while he was working on his subject pictures such as *Bailed up*, *A break away!*, and *On the Timbarra*, exhibited 1896 (Topliss no. 219). These two watercolours have the same warm but bright tonality of the early 1890s pastoral pictures. If it is to be identified with *Log-hauling, Murray Flats*, exhibited 1900, it could be a subject from near Brocklesby or Collendina, which had frontages onto the Murray River.

Exhibitions: possibly November 1900 *Tom Roberts Exhibition and Sale of Paintings*, Sydney, no. 32, *Log-Hauling, Murray Flats* (10 gns.); possibly April 1918, AGNSW *Loan Exhibition of Australian Art* , as *The Bullock Team.*

Reference: Topliss no. 232; McQueen p. 603.

Provenance: possibly H.M. Armytage – 1914 his sale at Decoration Pty Ltd, Melbourne, no. 304 as *Timber Hauling* – Mr D. W. Madden, Brisbane – Autumn 1978 Joseph Brown Gallery.

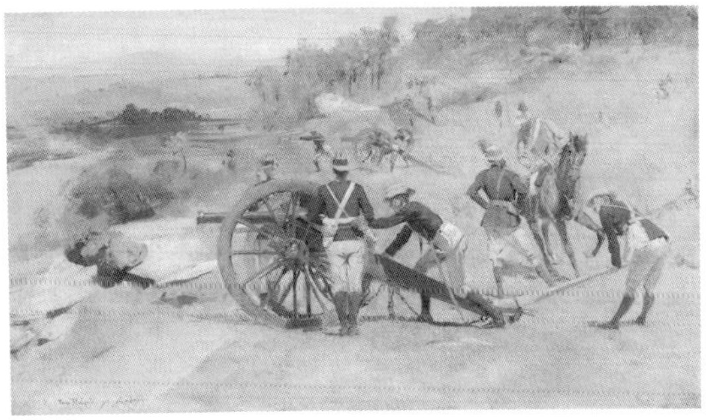

"A" Battery Field Artillery, New South Wales
1896 Sydney
oil on canvas
30.7 x 50.9 cm
Signed and dated l.l., oil 'Tom Roberts 96 Sydney'.
Australian War Memorial, Canberra
Acquired 1951

This was painted at Mosman where there were large military reserves above Little Sirius Cove, Roberts's bachelor home in Sydney. Roberts's panel portraits of Major-General Edward Hutton, commandant of the NSW Military Forces, and of two soldiers were also painted in 1896 (see Topliss nos 262-64). For contemporary photos of the site see Topliss illus. 50-53. Some sketches in the Mitchell Library sketch-books were done in preparation for this painting (Topliss nos VII and VIII).

Reference: Topliss no. 265; Astbury 1989, p. 122; McQueen p. 414 (illus.).

Provenance: Mr Cyril Staal, London.

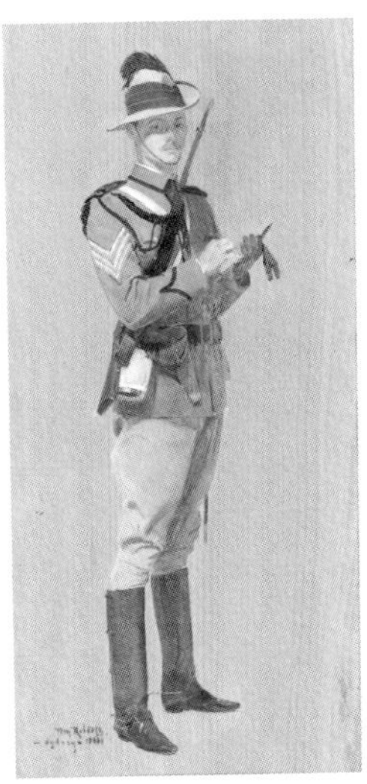

Sergeant R.D. Fraser, Mounted Rifles
1896 Sydney
oil on oak panel
62.2 x 28.3 cm
Signed and dated l.l. brown oil, 'Tom Roberts/ – Sydney 1896'.
Australian War Memorial, Canberra
Acquired 1974

Title inscribed on reverse with ink. Inscribed on verso in pencil in Roberts's hand: "If the oil still shows round the paint it [can?] be removed in England with Ink-Eraser. Frame very Dark Oak or Walnut without any gold". These instructions would seem to suggest that Roberts painted this panel portrait and its companions as mementoes for Major-General Hutton before his departure to England in 1896. They were painted at Victoria Barracks, Paddington, Sydney.

Reference: Topliss no. 264; McQueen p. 414.

Provenance: Mr Cyril Staal, London.

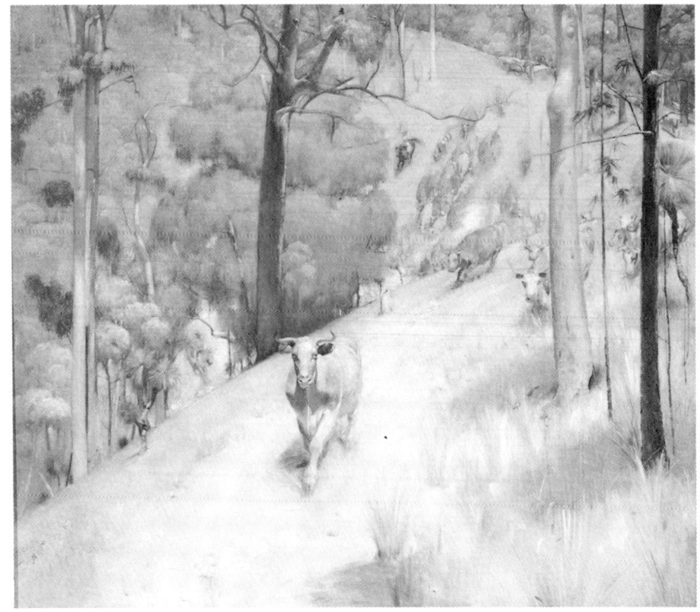

A mountain muster
1897 Newbold, NSW, and Sydney
1910s? England
oil on canvas, 129.5 x 147.3 cm
Not signed. Not dated.
National Gallery of Victoria, Melbourne
Purchased with the assistance of Central Equity Limited and Westfield Holdings, and through The Art Foundationof Victoria with the assistance of The Joe White Bequest 1995

In January and February 1897 Roberts was working on this painting at Newbold cattle station, beyond Copmanhurst, on the Clarence River about 64 kilometres up from Grafton, about half way to the more isolated Yulgilbar. Newbold belonged to W.A.B. Greaves and already in 1894 it had been visited by Roberts, with the painter A.H. Fulwood. Mrs Greaves's portrait (Topliss no. 317) was painted by Roberts in 1899; two portraits of their daughter Florence, in oil and pastel, the latter dated 1898, were also made by Roberts (Topliss nos 292 and 293). Two sketch-books (ML) contain a number of pencil studies for *A Mountain Muster* (Topliss nos IX and XI). Roberts's letter to S.W. Pring from Newbold, 16 January 1897 (ML), included a sketch of cattle drovers, and described the country: "On the hills, and valleys green, a land of richness. The ranges hung with woods, the she-oaks and pine, grey and red and cream of stem. To ride all day and camp at intervals and boil the quart and sleep at night and lay by the banks of a new big river and back over fresh to the home station and to think if one could only express it all, make others feel what beauty there is in it. Australia hasn't been fairly touched yet ...". For the catalogue of his 1920 exhibition Roberts recalled that he converted an Aboriginal 'mia mia' into a studio, and presumably also an overnight storage-place for the canvas, and that every day he rode the five miles to the scene of his labour. The painting was sketched in an undated letter to McCubbin (LT), with mention of "the London Show", i.e. the 'Exhibition of Australian Art in London', at the Grafton Galleries, April - May 1898, where *A mountain muster* and *The Golden Fleece* and *A break away!* were the big paintings amoung thirteen by Roberts. Unsold at Roberts's death, the cattle and the horsemen had been reworked, possibly in London before the exhibition in Melbourne in 1920.

Exhibitions: 2 April 1898 *Exhibition of Australian Art*, Grafton Galleries, London, no. 90; November 1900 *Tom Roberts Exhibition and Sale of Paintings*, Sydney, no. 8 (70 gns); January 1900 SA *Commonwealth Exhibition of Australian Art*, no. 61 (70 gns); 30 March 1920, *Souvenir Exhibition of Paintings by Tom Roberts*, Athenæum Hall Melbourne, no. 7 (identified in catalogue as "WRA", suggesting it must have been exhibited at a Royal Academy winter exhibition in London); 16 August 1920, Anthony Hordern, Sydney, no. 1 (400 gns); April 1932, *Tom Roberts, Memorial exhibition of Paintings*, Fine Art Society, Melbourne (250 gns); 1947-48 *Tom Roberts Retrospective Exhibition*, (lent by Sir Keith Murdoch) AGNSW, NGV, AGSA.

Reference: *Daily Telegraph* (Syd.), 5 May 1898 (summary of Grafton Galleries *Exhibition of Australian Art* reviews); *Sydney Morning Herald*, 14 November 1900; Letter to Frederick McCubbin, undated (c1898, MS 8187 Box 596/4, LT); Letter to S.W. Pring (MSS 1367/2, no. 18, ML); *Argus*, 30 March 1920, p. 8; 19 April 1932, p. 5; Spate pp. 92, 97, 98; B. Smith 1962, p. 121; McCulloch p. 158; Topliss no. 274; *The Australian*, 8 December 1995; McQueen pp. 424, 459, 625, 681, 708.

Provenance: 1931 Miss H. Boyes (Mrs Roberts's sister) – 1944 Sir Keith Murdoch – September 1953, Decoration Co., Melbourne, lot 64 – Mr H.O. Vary – 1969 Barry Stern Gallery, Sydney – 1969 Christies auction, Sydney – private collection, Perth – 27-28 November 1995, Sothebys, Melbourne, lot 49.

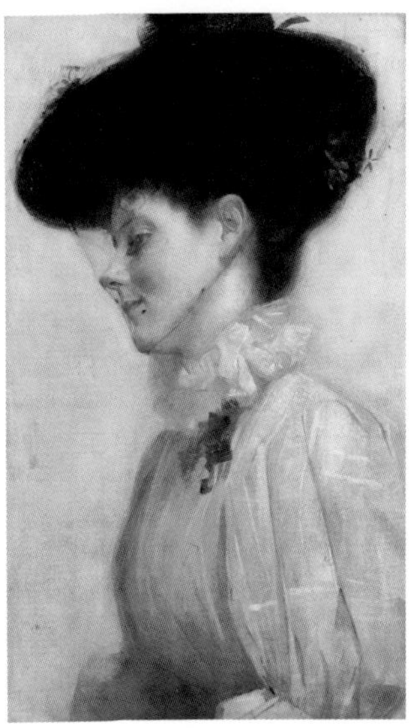

Florence Greaves
c1898 Sydney
oil on canvas
63.3 x 37.9 cm
Not signed. Not dated.
The Art Gallery New South Wales, Sydney
Bequest of Florence Turner Blake 1959

Florence Greaves (1873-1959) eventually bequeathed this, and the pastel portrait of her by Roberts, to AGNSW in her married name of Florence Turner Blake. She was a painter who exhibited with the SA, Sydney, and daughter of W.A.B. Greaves, at whose cattle station, Newbold, Roberts painted *A mountain muster*. There are two pen & ink sketches for this portrait, on one sheet (Topliss 292a).

Exhibitions: 1901, SA; 1953 *Retrospective Exhibition of Australian Art*, AGNSW; 1962 *Australian Painting: Colonial, Impressionist, Contemporary*, AGSA, AGWA then 1963 Tate Gallery, London, National Gallery, Ottawa and Vancouver Art Gallery.

Reference: Daniel Thomas, *AGNSW Quarterly*, vol. 10, no. 4, July 1969, p. 474; Spate p. 117; Splatt & Bruce, pp. 92-93; Topliss no. 292; Astbury 1989, p. 120.

Provenance: Florence Greaves (later Florence Turner Blake).

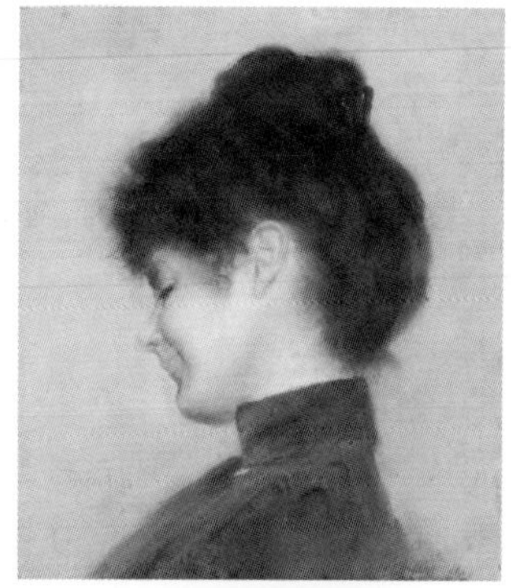

Miss Florence Greaves
1898 Sydney
pastel on paper
38.1 x 31.8 cm
Signed and dated l.l., red pastel 'Tom Roberts 1898'.
The Art Gallery of New South Wales, Sydney
Bequest of Florence Turner Blake 1959
[For exhibition in Sydney only]

Reference: Spate p. 117; Topliss no. 293.

Provenance: Florence Greaves (later Florence Turner Blake).

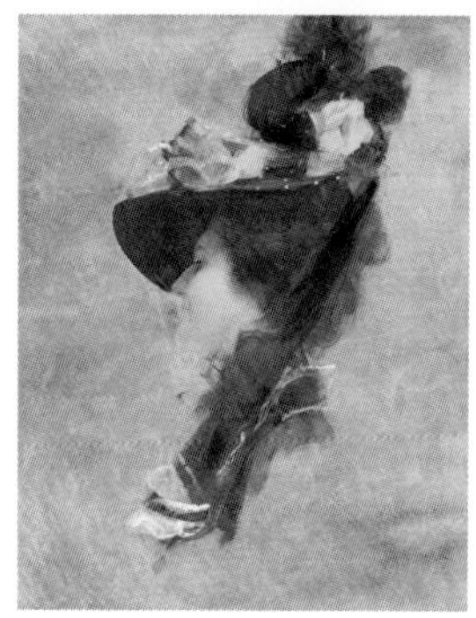

Frances Ross
c1898 Sydney
oil on wood
62.3 x 47.0 cm
Not signed. Not dated.
The Art Gallery of New South Wales, Sydney
Purchased 1954

Frances Ross (1861-1926) was an actress in the 1890s. After her marriage broke up she took up her maiden name again and went on the stage. In Sydney she joined the Bland Holt Company (information from a descendant, Mrs R.D. Bell, 1968, AGNSW Records).

Reference: Daniel Thomas, *AGNSW Quarterly*, vol. 10, no. 4, July 1969, p. 475; Splatt & Bruce, pp. 116-117; Topliss no. 306.

Provenance: J.F. Archibald – Mr D. O'Connor.

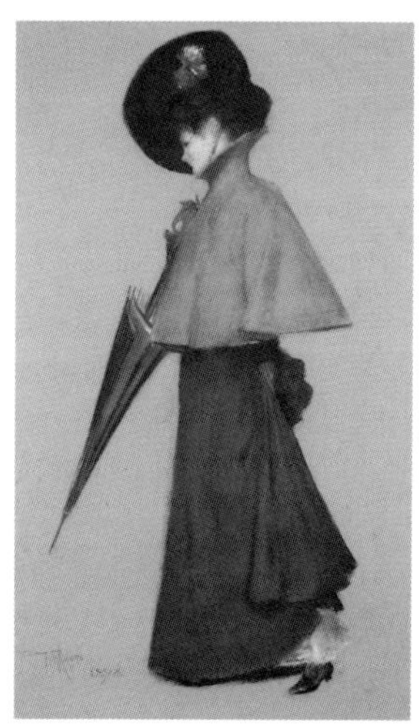

Portrait of a standing woman
c1898 Sydney
pastel on paper
85.0 x 50.0 cm (sight)
Signed and dated l.l., pencil 'Tom Roberts/ .1898'.
Private collection, Sydney

This is a full-length study of the subject dressed in hat, cape and umbrella, similar in format to the portraits of *Miss E. Giddy* (Topliss nos. 332, 332a), one a full-length study, the other a portrait bust, both in pastel.

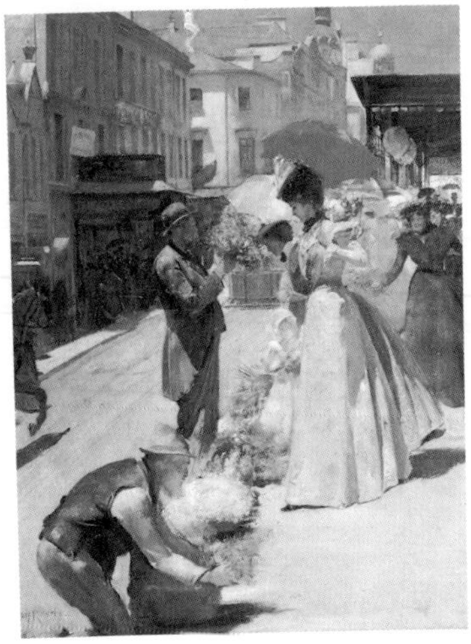

Christmas flowers and Christmas belles
c1899 Sydney
oil on canvas
52.1 x 36.2 cm
Signed l.l., oil 'Tom Roberts'. Not dated.
Manly Art Gallery & Museum, NSW
Gift of Colonel A. Spain 1940

This work was exhibited in 1918 as *Flower Sellers, King Street*. The *Sydney Mail*, Christmas number in 1899, reproduced *Christmas Flowers and Christmas Belles*, a version of this painting before obliterating a small figure of a woman and a running girl, centre left. A chromolithograph (NLA) also has the additional figures (see Topliss plate 92).

Exhibition: April 1918, AGNSW *Loan Exhibition of Australian Art*, no. 230 (lent by Col. Alfred Spain, *Flower Sellers, King Street)*.

Reference: *Sydney Mail* Supplement, 16 December 1899; Spate (as *The flower sellers*); Topliss no. 203.

Provenance: prior to 1910 Col. Alfred Spain (information from Mrs N. Russell, his daughter).

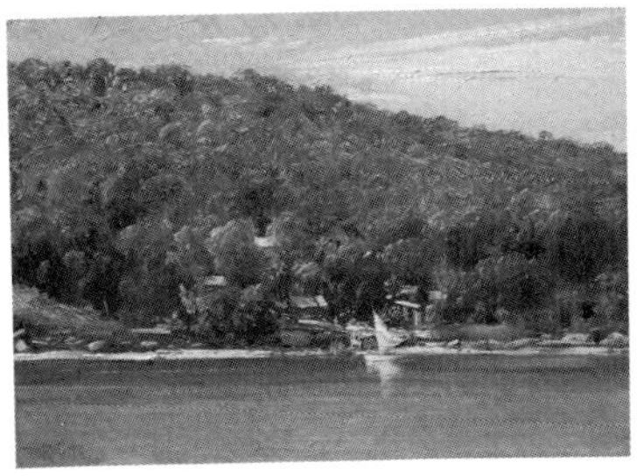

The camp, Sirius Cove
c1899 Sirius Cove, Sydney
oil on canvas on paperboard
25.4 x 34.6 cm
Signed and dated l.l., oil 'Tom Roberts/ 189[?]'.
The Art Gallery of New South Wales, Sydney
Purchased 1940

Inscribed on reverse in blue pencil framing instructions and address, given as 76 Pitt St. Also label on verso identifying the support as 'Millboard covered with oil sketching paper' and brand name 'W.C. Penfold & Co. 183 Pitt St., Sydney'. Virginia Spate dated this picture c1894. According to Sands Directory Roberts's address was '76 Pitt St' from 1898 to 1901; from 1895 to 1897 it was 80 Bathurst Street, and in 1894 it was 99a Pitt Street: Daniel Thomas therefore suggested the date 1899 since the last 9 of the inscription could be either a '4' or '9'. The heavy handling of paint seems to correspond more with the late 1890s. See the photographs of Mosman, Topliss illus. 50-54. This picture is similar to the view in Topliss illus. 51. In 1899 Roberts was married and no longer living at the camp.

Exhibitions: 1991, 6 June-26 August, *Bohemians in the Bush: The artists' camps of Mosman*, AGNSW, no. 68.

Reference: Daniel Thomas, *AGNSW Quarterly*, vol. 10, no. 4, July 1969, p. 471; Topliss no. 311; Topliss 1992, p. 137; Astbury 1989, p. 108; Pearce & Slutzkin (illus. front cover).

Provenance: Mr R. Dickinson (who had lived with Roberts at the camp at Sirius Cove) – Mrs R. Dickinson.

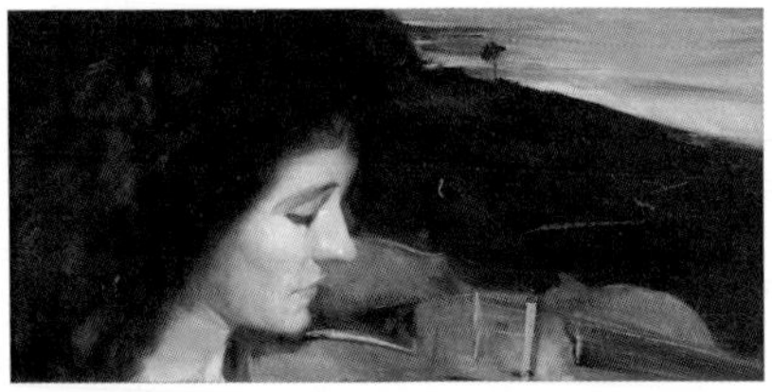

Adagio
1899 Sydney
oil on paperboard
25.6 x 51.0 cm
Signed verso, 'Tom Roberts'. Not dated.
The Art Gallery of New South Wales, Sydney
Purchased 1947

This work has been dated as 1899, the year of its first recorded exhibition, but it seems to Topliss much closer in mood, in its fluid handling and in its warm tonality to *Plink-a-plong*, 1893, and *Lena Brasch* (Topliss no. 211). However Ron Radford prefers the traditional dating to 1899. Roberts was very interested in music in the 1890s; his letters to friends contain constant references to musical soirees and to pieces of classical music. He painted a number of portraits of musicians in the mid 1890s; see Topliss nos 251, 279, 301, 318, 319, 349, 369 and the portrait of his friend Duncan Anderson playing a cornet, no. 225.
Exhibitions: August 1899, SA, no. 69 (£21.10.0); November 1900 *Exhibition and Sale of Paintings*, no. 5 *Girl with violin* (5 gns); 1947-48 *Tom Roberts Retrospective Exhibition*, (lent by Mrs C. Thomas), AGNSW, NGV, AGSA.
Reference: Spate pp. 73, 97, 99-101, 103, 117; Topliss no. 212.
Provenance: original owner unknown – April 1947 Lawson's auction, Sydney – Mrs Clarice Thomas.

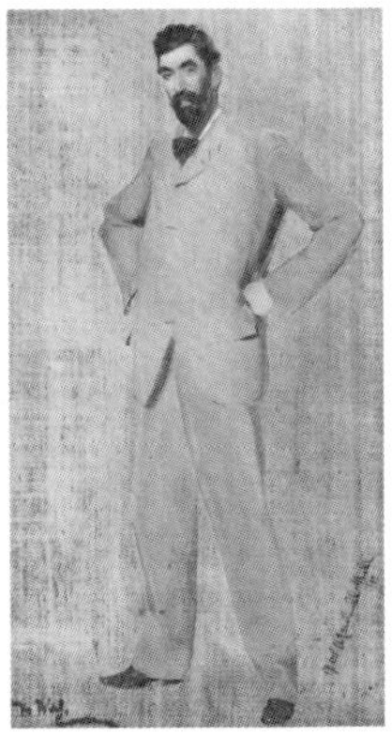

Professor G.W.L. Marshall-Hall
1899 Sydney
oil on pine panel
61.0 x 33.7 cm
Signed l.l., oil 'Tom Roberts'. Not dated.
Performing Arts Museum, Victorian Arts Centre, Melbourne
Purchased 1980

Autograph inscribed l.r. 'Prof. Marshall-Hall/ 99'.

Marshall-Hall (1862-1915), arrived in Melbourne in 1891 to take up the University's new chair of music; he established the Marshall-Hall Orchestra and the Melbourne University Conservatorium, the latter housed for a while in the Victorian Artists' Society premises. Atheist, socialist, poet and passionate bohemian as well as a Wagnerite composer, he quickly became friends with Streeton and other artists, and on visits to Sydney would stay with Streeton and Roberts in their Harbour camp at Little Sirius Cove. This 1899 portrait, aged thirty-seven, shows the Professor in his most controversial phase: the previous year, after publishing poems titled, blasphemously, *Hymns Ancient and Modern*, the Melbourne press had attached his morals (lewdness, animalism, lasciviousness and anti-clericalism) and asked why he should be permitted to "lecture to the young, especially the young women, of Victoria"; in 1900 his tenure was not renewed, and Roberts was commissioned by the students of the conservatorium to paint a second portrait, a dark profile head on canvas (Topliss no. 360). This bright pine panel was the climax to Roberts's series of small panel portraits of Australian celebrities, exhibited as a group of twenty-three in November 1900.

Exhibitions: November 1900, see Topliss no. 244; 19 July 1901, VAS, no. 42; 1964, 20 October, Joshua McClelland, Melbourne, *Nine Portraits by Frederick McCubbin and Tom Roberts* .
Reference: Croll 1946, pp. 17, 30, 37, 42, 59-61 (letters from Marshall-Hall to Roberts); Spate p. 117; Viola Tait, *A Family of Brothers,* Melbourne: Heinemann, 1971; S. Sadie, *The New Grove Dictionary of Music and Musicians,* London, 1980, vol. 11, p. 708; Topliss no. 319; McQueen pp. 456-8, 469 (illus.).
Provenance: one of the Tait brothers – private collection, Melbourne.

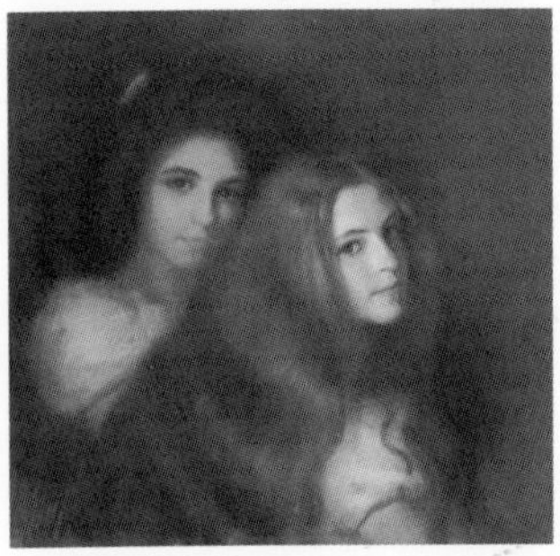

Elizabeth and Carmen Pinschof
1900 Melbourne
pastel on paper, 62. 0 x 63. 0 cm
Signed and dated l.l., pastel 'Tom Roberts 1900'.
National Gallery of Victoria, Melbourne
Bequest of Caleb Roberts 1984
[For exhibition in Melbourne only]

Elizabeth and Carmen were the daughters of Mme and Herr Pinschof and sisters of Louise (see Topliss nos 318, 371n, 348). This portrait was commissioned by Mme Pinschof as a surprise for her husband's birthday. According to Elizabeth Finley (née Pinschof) it was finished on the day of the Relief of Mafeking, 17 May 1900. In a letter to Virginia Spate, Mrs Finley wrote, "he threw down his crayons and jumped through the window and headed for town". The portrait of their sister Louise was then commissioned by Mme Goode, who thought it a shame that Roberts had only painted the two elder sisters. Roberts placed a photo of this double portrait in his scrap-book. (ML, S 45)
Reference: Croll p. 156; Spate p. 111; Topliss no. 347; McQueen p. 447.
Provenance: Mme and Herr Pinschof – Carmen Pinschof (their daughter) – Mr Monty Morris, London – private collection, Melbourne.

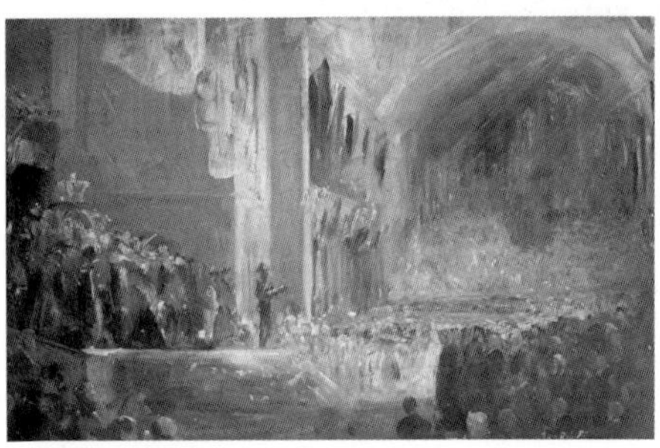

Sketch for the Opening of the First Parliament
1901 Melbourne
oil on wood panel, 30.5 x 45.8 cm
Signed l.r. incised 'Tom Roberts'. Not dated.
National Library of Australia, Canberra
Purchased 1920

This sketch was painted at the ceremony in the Exhibition Building, Melbourne, on 9 May 1901 (Croll pp. 77 and 138). "Roberts told Mr Kenneth Binns, then Commonwealth Librarian, in 1920 when the painting was purchased, how he carefully selected the location in the Melbourne Exhibition Building and planned his picture, then how he worked rapidly during the ceremony" (letter from Mr Kenneth Binns to Virginia Spate, 30 October 1960). It was purchased by the Commonwealth for 30 guineas, on the recommendation of Mr Binns, from Roberts's *Souvenir Exhibition* the Athenaeum Hall (although it is not listed in the catalogue). Roberts presented to the Commonwealth two large parchment sheets with autographs of all the participants (see Roberts's letter to the Historic Memorials Committee, 31 March 1920, Bavin papers 1487/47, NLA). There are photographs of the artist at work on the canvas in the Exhibition Building, in his Mitchell Library scrap-book (Topliss illus. 65-66). The final painting, size 304.5 x 509.2 cm, titled *Opening of the First Parliament of the Commonwealth of Australia by H.R.H. The Duke of Cornwall and York (later H.M. King George V), May 9, 1901* was completed in March 1903 and was exhibited at the Royal Academy, London, 1904.

Exhibition: 1920, 30 March-17 April, *Souvenir Exhibition of Paintings by Tom Roberts*, Athenæum Hall, Melbourne; 1985-86 *Golden Summers.*

Reference: Spate p. 112; Topliss no. 371a; GS p. 196; Astbury 1989 pp. 205-06; McQueen pp. 464, 616.

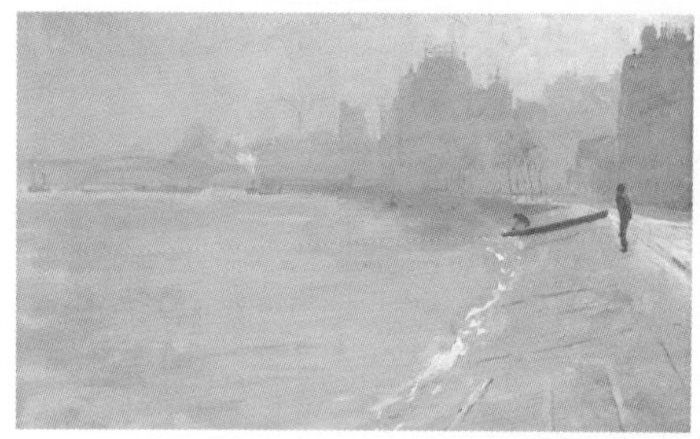

The towpath, Putney
1904 London
oil on board
24.2 x 39.5 cm
Not signed. Not dated.
ICI Collection of Australian Art, Melbourne

The title and date are inscribed on the verso by Caleb Roberts. Roberts lived at 44 Kenilworth Court, Putney, when he arrived in London with his family. This is the right bank of the Thames, looking downstream.

Reference: Topliss no. 383.

Provenance: Caleb Roberts (the artist's son) – private collection, Melbourne.

Putney Bridge, London
c1905-c1908 London
oil on canvas on cardboard
34.5 x 44.0 cm
Not signed. Not dated.
Art Gallery of South Australia, Adelaide
M.J.M. Carter Collection

Inscribed on verso in 1956 by Caleb Roberts ' "Putney Bridge", London. By Tom Roberts. Roberts was living at 44 Kenilworth Court, Putney. Not thought much of by him apparently about 1905'.

Exhibition: 1993 *The M.J.M. Carter Collection: A Private View of Australian Colonial Art*, AGSA; 1995 *Australian Colonial Art 1800-1900.*

Reference: Letter to S.W. Pring, 5 October 1905 (ML, MSS 1367/2 no. 34); Topliss no. 385; McQueen pp. 496, 497.

Provenance: artist's estate 1932 – Caleb Roberts (the artist's son) – private collection, Melbourne.

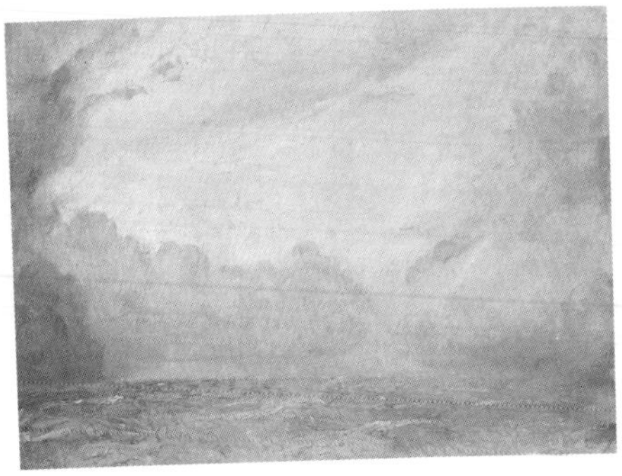

Storm at sea
1907 Mundesley-on-Sea, Norfolk
oil on canvas on plywood
35.3 x 44.5 cm
Not signed. Not dated.
The Art Gallery of New South Wales, Sydney
Purchased 1946

Title inscribed on verso.

Roberts spent some time at Mundesley-on-Sea in the early autumn of 1907. Mc Cubbin visited him there.

Reference: Topliss no. 411; McQueen p. 524.

Provenance: Miss H.W. Boyes (sister of Roberts's second wife Jean) – Mr W.G. Buckle, Sydney.

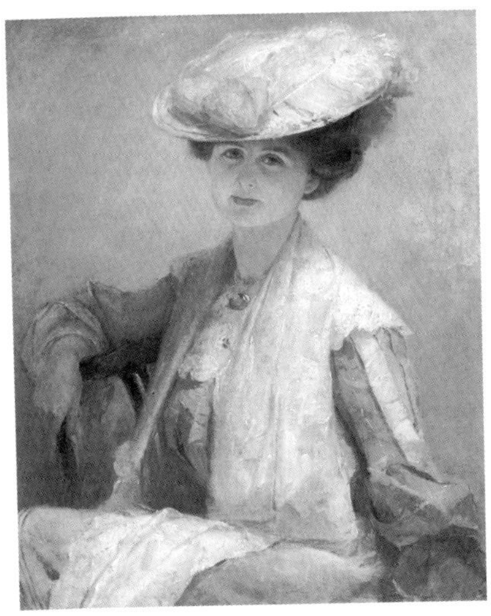

Grey Lady (Mrs Ince)
c1910-12 London
oil on canvas on paperboard
76.1 x 63.3 cm
Not signed. Not dated.
The Art Gallery of New South Wales, Sydney
Purchased 1946

This portrait was identified by Caleb Roberts (the artist's son) as being of Mrs Ince. It has the heavy impasto and dry-looking pigment of works from the second decade of the century. The canvas has been re-lined. Roberts owned a photo of the subject in a theatrical costume.

Reference: *Sydney Morning Herald*, 23 February 1946, p. 4; Spate p. 124; Topliss no. 422.

Provenance: Mr W.G. Buckle – 1946 AGNSW.

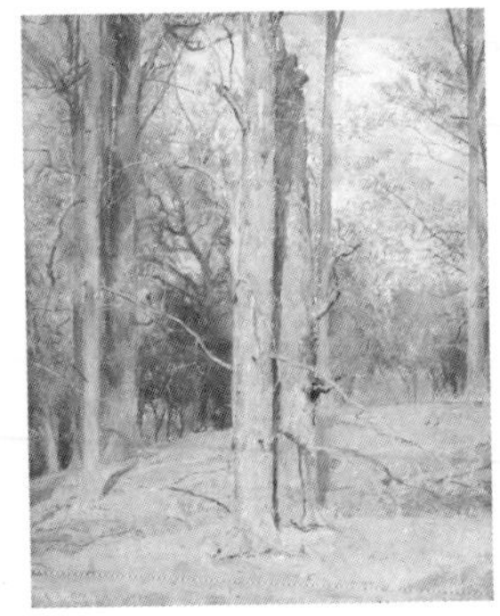

Winter, England
c1920 London
oil on board
48.0 x 38.8 cm
Signed l.l., oil 'Tom Roberts'. Not dated.
Private collection, Melbourne

Supposedly purchased by the original owner at Roberts's Athenæum Hall exhibition in Melbourne in 1920. The previous title, *Autumn England,* was probably given to it by the owner as it does not correspond with any title in the catalogue of that exhibition. The painting portrays a winter scene rather than autumn one and might be *Ham Common* (no. 11 in the Athenaeum catalogue), since its measurements correspond (18 x 14 inches, i.e. 46.0 x 36.0 cm).

Exhibition: possibly 1920 *Souvenir Exhibition of Paintings by Tom Roberts*, Athenæum Hall, Melbourne.

Reference: Topliss no. 512.

Provenance: 1920 Mr and Mrs Oswald Syme – private collection, Melbourne.

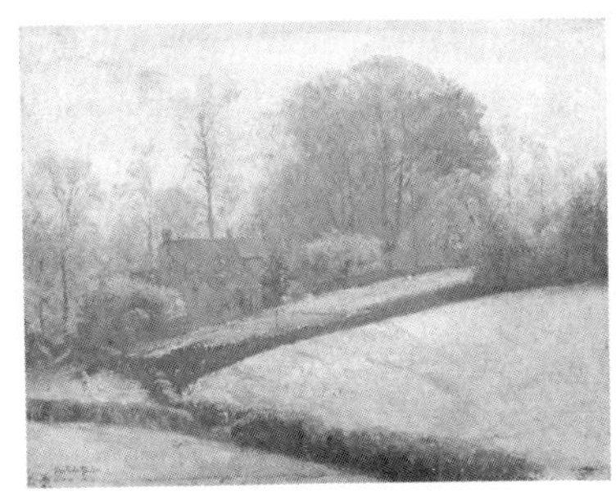

Springtime in Sussex
1921 England
oil on canvas on plywood
35.4 x 45.3 cm
Signed and dated l.r., red oil 'Tom Roberts/21-'.
The Art Gallery of New South Wales, Sydney
Purchased 1932

Roberts painted an earlier painting with a similar title, see Topliss no. 418.

Exhibitions: possibly solo exhibition September 1924, Fine Art Society, Melbourne, no. 17, *Sussex in Spring* (15 gns); or June 1926, Anthony Hordern, Sydney, no. 5 (40 gns); 1938 *150 Years of Australian Art*, AGNSW.

Reference: *Australian Studio*, 2 June 1926; Spate pp. 126-27; Topliss no. 528.

Provenance: W. Rubery Bennet – 1932 AGNSW.

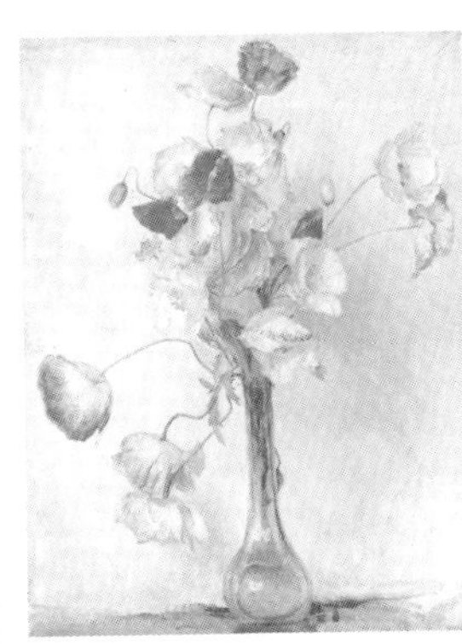

Poppies
1921 London
oil on canvas
46.0 x 33.0 cm
Not signed. Dated u.l., grey oil '21 M [illeg] 21'.
Private collection, Canberra

Reference: Topliss no. 535.

Provenance: possibly 1930s, Gayfield Shaw's Gallery, Sydney – Professor E.G. Waterhouse, Sydney.

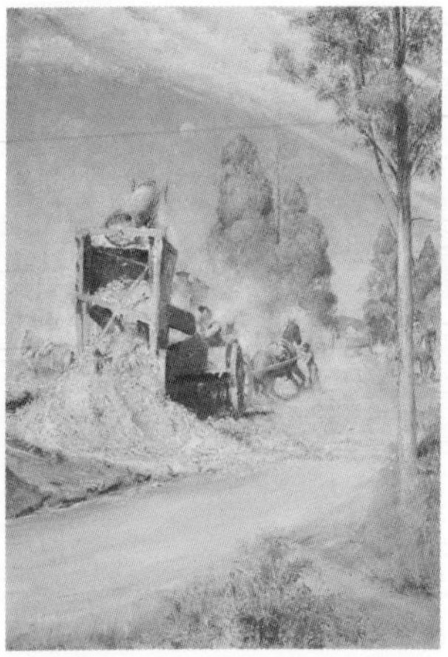

Country road makers
1923 Kallista, Victoria
oil on canvas
72.5 x 50.3 cm
Signed and dated l.l., white oil
'Tom Roberts 23'
Private collection, Sydney

Inscribed on verso 'Country Road Makers Patch Road at Cook's Corner, Kallista, Vic.'.

Exhibitions: October 1925, VAS; June 1926, solo exhibition, Anthony Hordern, Sydney, no. 12 (140 gns); c1954, Ferntree Gully Art Society Exhibition, VAS.

Reference: *Sydney Morning Herald*, 14 June 1926; Topliss no. 573.

Provenance: Mr C.G. Roberts – Mrs Norah Roberts (his wife) – Spring 1975, Joseph Brown Gallery, Melbourne.

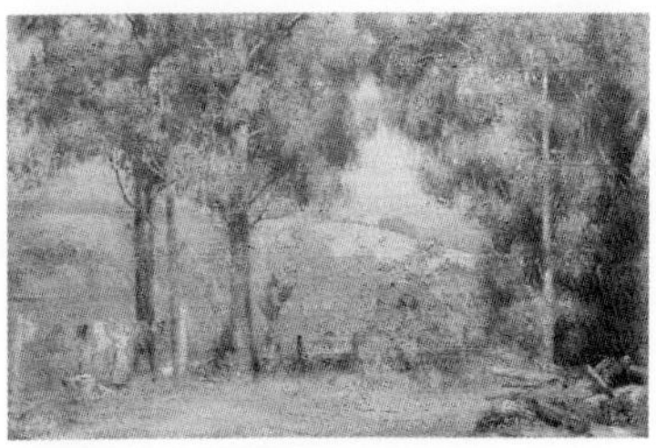

Washing day, Kallista
c1923-25 Kallista, Victoria
oil on canvas on composition board, 35.5 x 52.3 cm
Not signed. Not dated.
The Art Gallery of New South Wales, Sydney
Gift of Mrs W.G. Buckle 1947

Reference: Topliss no. 607.
Provenance: Mr W.G. Buckle – Mrs Buckle.

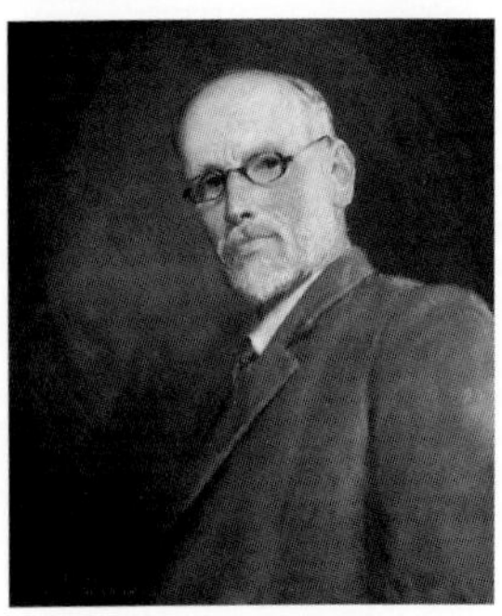

Self-portrait
1924 Kallista, Victoria
oil on canvas
61.2 x 51.0 cm
Signed and dated l.l., red oil 'Tom Roberts 24'.
The Art Gallery of New South Wales, Sydney
Gift of the artist 1924

Inscribed by the artist, following the signature, 'To the Trustees Sydney National Gallery'.

The gift was solicited by AGNSW, as were other artists' self-portraits, the best known being Margaret Preston's modernist half-length with wild flowers.

Exhibitions: April 1932, *Tom Roberts, Memorial Exhibition of Paintings*, Fine Art Society, Melbourne, no. 5; 1954-55 *Artists by Artists Exhibition*, AGNSW.

Reference: Topliss no. 595; McQueen (illus.).

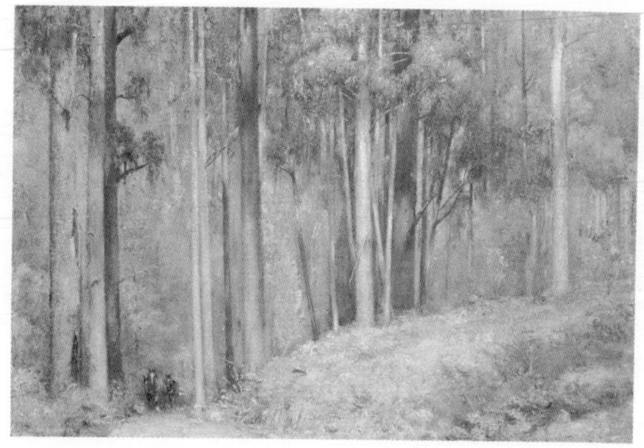

Sherbrooke Forest
1924 Dandenong Ranges, Victoria
oil on canvas on paperboard
48.0 x 68.4 cm
Signed and dated l.l., white oil 'Tom Roberts 24'.
The Art Gallery of New South Wales, Sydney
Purchased 1946

Exhibitions: possibly solo exhibition, June 1926, Anthony Hordern, Sydney, no. 15, *In the Forest* (30 gns); 1947-48, *Tom Roberts Retrospective Exhibition*, AGNSW, NGV, AGSA; 1976-77 *Aspects of Australian Art*, Sydney: AGNSW Travelling Art Exhibition.

Reference: *Sydney Morning Herald*, 23 February 1946, p. 4; Spate pp. 128-29; *Aspects of Australian Art*, AGNSW, 1976-77 (illus.); Topliss no. 585.

Provenance: c1926 Mr W.G. Buckle – 1946 AGNSW.

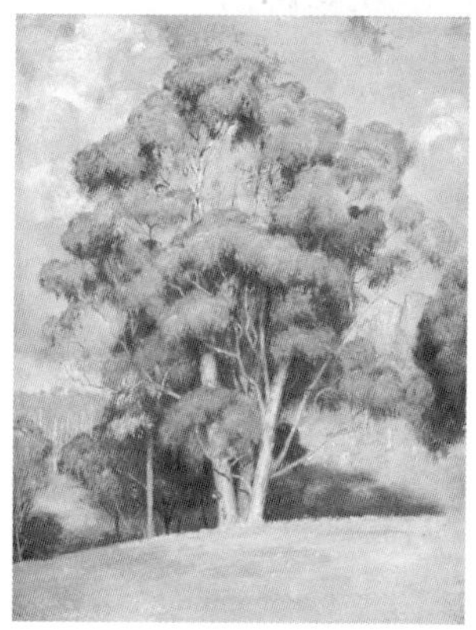

A Queen of gums
1926 near Ben Lomond, Tasmania
oil on canvas
45.0 x 35.5 cm
Signed and dated l.l., yellow oil 'Tom Roberts 26'.
Private collection, Melbourne

Given to Thomas Roberts as a wedding present by his great uncle, Tom Roberts.
Exhibitions: March 1928, solo exhibition, Fine Art Society, Melbourne (25 gns).
Reference: Topliss no. 612.
Provenance: 1928 Mr Thomas Roberts (the artist's great-nephew) – private collection, Melbourne.

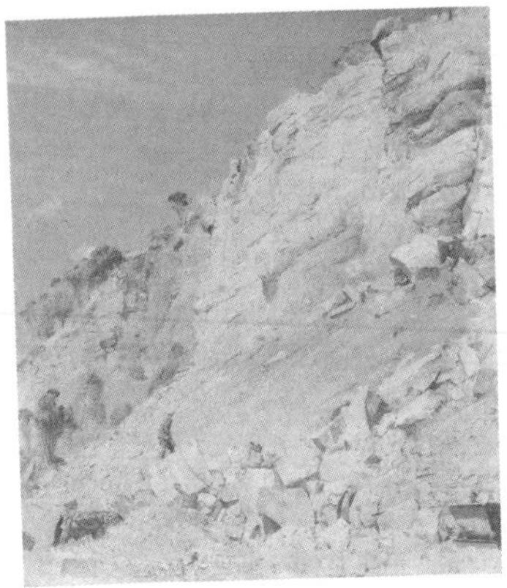

The quarry, Maria Island
1926 Tasmania
oil on canvas
60.3 x 50.2 cm
Signed and dated l.l., white oil 'Tom Roberts 26'.
National Gallery of Australia, Canberra
Bequest of Henriette von Dallwitz and of Richard Paul in honour of his father Dr Oscar Paul 1965

Exhibitions: June 1926, solo exhibition Anthony Hordern, Sydney (130 gns); September 1950, *110 Years of Australian Art.*, Farmer's Blaxland Galleries, Sydney.

Reference: *Australian Studio*, 2 June 1926; *Sydney Morning Herald*, 14 June 1926; Topliss no. 619.

Provenance: 1926 Dr R.A.O. Paul – Richard Paul (his son) – on loan Sydney University Union.

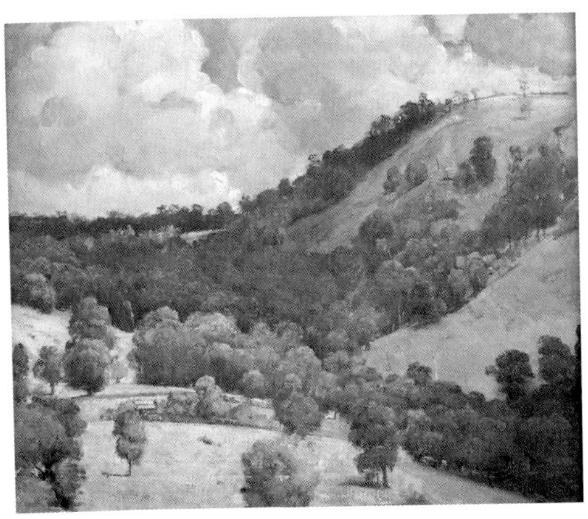

Hillside
1927 Trawool, Victoria
oil on canvas
45.7 x 53.0 cm
Signed and dated l.l., orange oil 'Tom Roberts /27-'.
Art Gallery of South Australia, Adelaide
Elder Bequest Fund 1943

One of several landscapes of the Goulbourn River Valley painted while staying at Trawool.

Reference: *Bulletin of the National Gallery of South Australia*, vol. 5 no. 3, January 1949, AGBSA; Topliss no. 638.

Provenance: original owner unknown – 1943 Sedon Galleries, Melbourne.

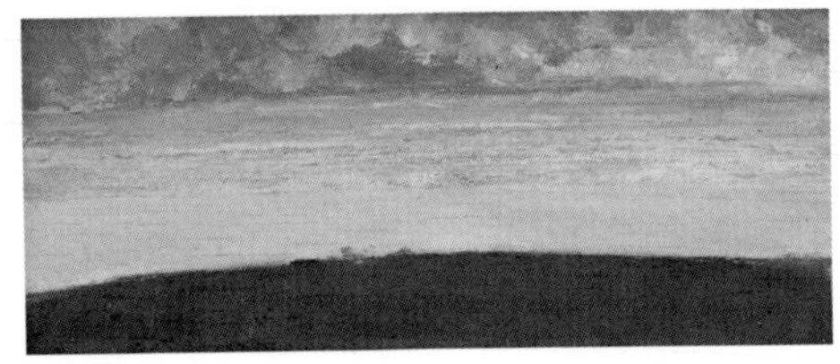

Sunrise
c1929
oil on panel
10.0 x 24.5 cm
Not signed. Not dated.
Art Gallery of South Australia, Adelaide
Gift of the Friends of the Art Gallery of South Australia 1996

This panel is believed to be one of the oil sketches remaining in his studio at the end of his life. It was probably painted in the late 1920s. Some of his oil sketches are particularly equivocal, and nearly always undated and often unsigned. Topliss illustrates several small, dark and stormy landscape panels, among them *Storm cloud*, 1929, no. 660 and *After storm*, 1930, no 677. However there remains the possibility that it was executed about 1900. Simple composition and more vivid colours would support this.

Provenance: private collection, Sydney – 1995 Masterpiece Fine Art Gallery and Antiques, Hobart.

End notes

The Fortunes of Tom Roberts
Humphrey McQueen pp. 20-37

1. *Evening Standard* (Melb.), 17 August 1889, p. 1; *Australian Life (Tit-Bits)* (Melb.), 22 August 1889, p. 15; *cf.* 4 July 1889, p. 3, 1 August 1889, p. 15, and 26 September 1889, p. 14.

2. *Australian Musical Times and Magazine of Art* (Syd.), 6 November 1897, p. 32, *cf.* p. 30.

3. *Australian Life (Tit-Bits)*, 9 June 1887, p. 2.

4. Roberts letter to Mrs Pring, 21 March 1931, MSS 1367/2/215-7, ML.

5. *Australian Life (Tit-Bits)*, 3 March 1887, p. 14 and 13 October 1887, p. 14

6. Linda Gill (ed.), *Letters of Frances Hodgkins*, Auckland: Auckland University Press, 1993, pp. 71-4.

7. *The Australian* (Syd.), 31 July 1978, p. 2.

8. *Australian Life (Tit-Bits)*, 16 September 1886, p. 3.

9. Roberts letter to Pring, 24 April 1895, MSS 1367/2/45-6, ML.

10. *Table Talk* (Melb.), 19 December 1901, p. 16.

11. *Australian Musical Times and Magazine of Art* (Syd.), 10 December 1897, p. 34.

12. *Sunday Times* (Syd.), 20 June 1926, p. 4.

13. *Australian Life (Tit-Bits)*, 19 May 1887, p. 2.

14. Sigmund Freud, *Art and Literature*, The Pelican Freud Library, vol. 14, Harmondsworth: Penguin, 1978, p. 470.

15. *Australian Musical Times and Magazine of Art*, 10 December 1897, p. 34.

16. *World* (London), reprinted *Australian Musical Times and Magazine of Art*, 2 June 1898, p. 15. Six portraits were among the thirteen paintings by Roberts in the exhibition of Australian art at Grafton Galleries.

17. Deakin letter to Roberts, 31 October 1904, MS A2480/ 192, ML.

18. *Sunday Times* (Syd.), undated cutting in MSS 4586/ 1X, ML.

A Painter Making Himself
Mary Eagle pp. 38-61

1. *Australasian Critic* (Melb.), 1 July 1891, p. 240.

2. *Argus* (Melb.), 9 October 1886, p. 11. Smith was on the National Gallery Committee which had to face the challenge. Roberts and a number of other artists declared that the ban had not existed in the European academies in which they had trained.

3. Tom Roberts wrote about 'The Loan Collection of Victorian Artists', *Argus*, 30 September 1893, p. 14, in response to Smith's article on the same subject, *Argus*, 10 August 1893, p. 7.

4. He exhibited in the Victorian Academy of Arts' black & white exhibition which opened on 12 October 1885, and monochrome illustrations in a small exhibition of watercolour and black & white work in George Ashton's studio, c20 October. From 3 December some (or all) of his paintings for the Colonial for and Indian Exhibition were on were on view with other exhibits at the Exhibition Buildings.

5. Helen Topliss noted that Alphington "was included in the *Guide for Excursionists from Melbourne* in 1869, where the view from the bridge at Darebin Creek was especially recommended", Helen Topliss, *Plein Air Painting in Melbourne 1885-1898*, Clayton, Vic.: Monash University Gallery, 1985, p. 23.

6. Streeton, quoted in Croll p. 140.

7. Streeton, handwritten text for a lecture given in 1920 or 1924, notebook, Streeton family papers. Streeton included himself in this group which is misleading since his association with Roberts began later.

8. Roberts had not seen Whistler's oil painting (produced at the Whistler/Ruskin trial in 1878), the *Nocturne: Blue and Gold – Old Battersea Bridge*, c1875 (Tate Gallery), which was in a private collection through the early 1880s and was first reproduced (as an engraving) in Theodore Child, "American Artists at the Paris Exhibition", *Harper's New Monthly Magazine* (N.Y.), vol. LXXIX, September 1889, p. 594. On the other hand Whistler was a cult figure to Roberts and his circle of London friends, and Roberts had been introduced to Whistler's prints early. Mortimer Menpes, one of Whistler's studio assistants, who in 1881-82 began helping him to print etchings, was an Australian and in 1882 a fellow student of Roberts in London.

9. *Argus*, 3 September 1889, p. 7.

10. J.S. MacDonald, *The Art of Frederick McCubbin*, Melbourne: Lothian, 1916, p. 57.

11. *Argus*, 30 April 1888, p. 11.

12. *Argus*, 11 September 1888, Supplement p. 1.

13. *Magazine of Art* (London), 1886, p. 400.

14. John Buxton Knight letter to Roberts, 8 May 1887, Roberts papers A2480, ML.

15. E. Phillips Fox letter to Roberts, 30 July 1887, Roberts papers A2480, ML.

16. Roberts letter to Lillie Williamson, 5 April 1886, Roberts family papers.

17. Manuscript poem in a volume of papers relating to the Buonarotti Club belonging to Alice Cherry (née Brotherton), private collection, Melbourne. At my suggestion, the owners deposited copies with the La Trobe Library, State Library of Victoria, Melbourne, to augment the other papers relating to that Club.

18. Streeton letter to Roberts, posted 12 October 1892, Roberts papers, A2478, ML.

19. Streeton, Notes for memoirs, Streeton family papers.

20. *Argus*, 30 April 1888, p. 11.

21. *Ibid.*

22. Jane Clark in *Golden Summers*, 1985, p. 71.

23. McCubbin letter to Roberts, 26 March 1891, Roberts papers A2480, ML.

24. McCubbin letter to Roberts, 3 July 1892, Roberts papers A2480, ML.

25. The exhibition catalogue cover was drawn by Conder and incorporates the title 'The 9 by 5 Impression Exhibition'. A variant title, '9 x 5 Exhibition of Impressions', heads page one of the catalogue, which lists 182 works, most by Roberts, Conder and Streeton and a few by R.E. Falls, C.D. Richardson, Herbert Daly and Frederick McCubbin.

26. *Melbourne Punch*, 9 May 1889, p. 300.

27. *Argus*, 3 September 1889, p. 7.

28. See Robert L. Herbert, *Impressionism: Art, leisure and Parisian society*, New Haven: Yale University Press, 1988, for an enlightening discussion about the attitude of the flâneur in French nineteenth-century painting.

29. Roberts letter to the *Argus*, 30 September 1893, p. 14.

30. McCubbin letter to Roberts, 8 December 1910, Roberts papers A2479, ML.

31. Streeton letter to Roberts, 19 December 1906, Roberts papers A2478, ML. The present-day address of Ricketts Point is Beaumaris though its postal address in the 1880s was Sandringham. McCubbin remembered the "Tea tree at Sandringham" on an evening when he, Abrahams and Roberts were together (he does not remember Streeton); *The Sunny South* was described in the *Argus*, 5 March 1887, as "... representing some bathers, who are about to emerge from the shadows of the ti-tree to plunge into the sunshine and the sea". But Streeton's memory of a painting of "the row of large Banksias (Honeysuckle)" was better. Although tea tree grows in association with banksia on the shores of Port Phillip Bay, and may indeed be present in the background of *The Sunny South*, its three human figures shelter among mature specimens of *Banksia integrifolia*, commonly known as Coast Banksia, or White Honeysuckle Banksia. Two slender, juvenile specimens of this banksia are silhouetted against the sea and sky. The botanical identification was provided 26 July 1996 by Terence Lane, Senior Curator, Australian Art to 1900, NGV.

Where The Sun Never Set. Tom Roberts and The British Empire
Virginia Spate pp. 62-95

1. Tom Roberts, reminiscences written for his son Caleb, in Croll; letter to his wife, at sea between Fremantle and Adelaide, 6 December 1919, cited Croll p. 114.

2. Roberts, letter to the *Argus*, 4 July 1890. Humphrey McQueen's *Tom Roberts* contains superabundant material on Roberts's Britishness. Unfortunately his book was published too recently for me to make proper use of it.

3. Roberts, letter 23 May 1887, Tom Roberts Papers, III, 34, ML.

4. Topliss no. 192. The portrait of Cardinal Moran has not been located. It is curious that Roberts (nominally an Anglican) used a Catholic rather than a member of the Church of England to represent the Church, since the Catholic Church was not securely a part of the British establishment.

5. I use the word 'Realism' as a generic term to indicate a commitment to truth to the external world and to contemporary life, rather than the more specific 'Naturalism'. There is no Realist 'style', but today 'Naturalism' tends to be used of the more 'photographic' forms of Realism. This would accord with some, but not all of Roberts's works. The terms Realism and Naturalism were almost interchangeable from the 1860s onwards, and are still unstable. For their connections with Imperialism, see Terry Smith, "The Divided Meaning of *Shearing the rams*: Artists and Nationalism", in Bradley & Smith, pp. 120-121

6. Topliss nos 156, 179; *Sydney Morning Herald*, 2 Sept 1892; *Daily Telegraph* (Syd.), 6 June 1926.

7. Tom Roberts letter to Alfred Deakin 4 Feb 1904.

8. Indirect quotation by Roberts's son Caleb; in Croll p. 4.

9. See my "The Sunny South: Australian Impressionism", in *World Impressionism: The international movement 1860-1920*, ed. Norma Broude, New York 1990.

10. Bernard Smith, *European Vision and the South Pacific*, Oxford University Press, 1960 (and subsequent edns); William Eisler, *The Furthest Shore: Images of Terra Australis from the Middle Ages to Captain Cook*, Cambridge University Press, 1995. See also W.J.T. Mitchell, "Imperial Landscape", in *Landscape and Power*, Chicago University Press, 1994.

11. The local organisers requested that the VAA select works which "convey a graphic picture of the resources and development of Victoria, as well as the social and material conditions of the people", cited McQueen p. 156.

12. Letter to the editor, *Argus*, 20 March 1883; see Spate, "The Sunny South", p. 120, *op. cit.* note 9 above.

13. James Smith, *Argus*, 7 Sept 1886.

14. See Ian Burn, "Beating about the Bush: The landscapes of the Heidelberg School" in *Australian Art and Architecture*, pp. 82-98, for a brilliant analysis of this and related paintings.

15. Arthur Streeton, letter to Roberts, 1908, in *Smike to Bulldog: Letters from Sir Arthur Streeton to Tom Roberts*, ed. R.H. Croll, Sydney 1946, p. 121.

16. Arthur Streeton, cited in Croll p. 16.

17. *Age*, 20 April 1888.

18. *Table Talk*, 12, 27 April 1888; *Argus*, 13 April 1889, 31 September 1891, 30 September 1893; *Age*, 13 April 1891.

19. *Table Talk*, 30 August 1889. The painting was not sent overseas since it was sold to a prominent stock & station agent in 1890.

20. Terry Smith, "The Divided Meaning of *Shearing the Rams*", pp. 111-19.

21. Nigel Lendon, "Ashton, Roberts and Bayliss: Some relationships between illustration, painting and photography in the late nineteenth century", in *Australian Art and Architecture*, pp. 78-79; Terry Smith, "The Divided Meaning of *Shearing the rams*", pp. 108, 114-15.

22. *Argus*, 4 July 1890.

23. *Table Talk*, 16, 23 August 1889.

24. *The Bookfellow*, 29 April 1899, pp. 28-33.

25. Unidentified newspaper, 1891, cited in Croll pp. 36-37.

26. Informal conversation at the Newstead woolshed, on the occasion of the Tom Roberts Festival at Inverell, NSW, 1996.

27. Cited Topliss no. 190.

28. *Argus*, 12, 19 November, 3, 4 December 1892; in Croll p. 211.

29. Roberts, letter to S.W. Pring, 16 January 1895. See Topliss nos 229-30.

30. For details on Ogilvie see Topliss.

31. The notion of failure is implied in my *Tom Roberts*, Melbourne 1972, and explicit in McQueen, *Tom Roberts*.

32. Quoted in an interview, c1913-14, in Croll p. 99.

33. Roberts, letter to McCubbin, 14 November 1913, *La Trobe Library Journal*, April 1971, p. 74.

34. See Burn, "Beating about the Bush", pp. 92-94, on the symbolism of the young gum-tree in the 1880s works.

Shearing the rams, 1888-90. The Golden Fleece, 1894.
Daniel Thomas pp. 96-107

1. John Russell letter to Roberts, undated, 1885, Roberts papers, vol. III, p.12, ML; cited in Spate 1990, p. 120.

2. *Shearing the rams* was probably intended, if it had not sold to a private owner, for London or Paris, like Streeton's sheep-haunted *Golden Summer, Eaglemont*, 1889, which went – as *Golden Summer, Australia* – to the Royal Academy 1891 and Paris Salon 1892. *Shearing the rams* was eventually bought, reluctantly, by NGV in 1932. *The Golden Fleece* was bought by AGNSW in 1894.

3. Roger Moncrieff, Tasmania, occasional shearer, 1995. Robert Anderson, woolgrower turned cattleman, Mullaley, NSW, 1994. Mr Anderson, grandson of Duncan Anderson, also provided information about classical education at Harrow, and the cartoon by Souter.

4. Christine McCormack, artist, Adelaide, 1996.

5. Phil Hynd, Department of Animal Science, Waite Campus, University of Adelaide, gave information about the sheep depicted, and about shearing practice; see also Daniel Thomas, "The Golden Fleece: Wool in Australian art", in *Wool in the Australian Imagination*, Sydney: Historic Houses Trust of NSW, 1994.

6. Dorothy Ambrose, Corowa, grand-daughter of Susan Bourne, the tar-girl who looks out from the centre of *Shearing the rams*, in 1996 gave information about the men figuring in the painting. Muriel Bryan, Inverell Family History Group, provided identifications for the men in *The Golden Fleece*. This complex subject deserves full discussion elsewhere.

7. *Argus* (Melb.), 28 June 1890.

8. Phil Hynd, see note 5 above; also McQueen, pp. 307-8.

9. *Illustrated Sydney News*, 2 August 1890, cited in GS.

10. *Bulletin* (Syd.), 6 October 1894.

11. Godfrey Rivers, *A woolshed*, 1890, oil on canvas 92 x 112 cm, QAG, gift of the artist 1895; colour repr. in Astbury 1989.

12. Virginia Spate, "No Sweat", in CA, p. 124.

13. *Corowa Free Press*, 29 November 1889.

14. "First sketch for Shearing ...", NGV, repr. GS, p. 131.

15. *Table Talk* (Melb.), 30 May 1890, cited in GS.

16. Jaffe.

17. The Brocklesby shed was burnt down in 1973, but its orientation was confirmed, August 1996, by Mr Richard Molesworth, who once lived at Killeneen, Redlands, the site of the shed.

A break away!, 1891
Jane Hylton pp. 108-115

1. The few exceptions are noted in the catalogue.

2. 'Titian Redde' [A.G. Stephens], *The Bookfellow* (Syd.), 29 April 1899; reprinted in Croll, p. 57. See also Leigh Astbury "An Australian Incident': Explosive action, still heat", in Daniel Thomas (ed.), *Creating Australia*, Sydney & Adelaide: International Cultural Corporation of Australia & AGBSA, 1988.

3. *Table Talk*, (Melb.) 17 July 1891; cited in *Golden Summers* p. 136.

4. Croll p. 37, from "A 'BUSH' STUDIO; And The Picture In It".

5. McQueen p. 335.

6. *Table Talk, loc. cit.*

7. Topliss no. 170a.

8. Croll pp. 35-37, 164.

9. Long after Roberts's death Lionel Lindsay said (1951 'Jubilee Exhibition of Australian Art') that the artist had spent six weeks with drovers before painting *A break away!*. Humphrey McQueen doubts this, and suggests a confusion with a possible later tour from Newstead, west from Inverell.

10. Ron Radford, "A National Picture for a National Gallery", in *Tom Roberts: A break away! 1891* (exhibition brochure), Adelaide: AGBSA, 1991. See also Croll *Smike to Bulldog*, p. 136.

11. McQueen pp. 449-453; South Australian State Records Office, GRG 19/2.

Bailed up, 1895/1927
Barry Pearce pp. 116-123

1. According to information given by Duncan Anderson's son Alick to R.H. Croll for his 1935 biography of Roberts (pp. 165-171), only the landscape was painted at 'The Perch', the coach was painted at Inverell, the bushrangers mainly from station hands at Newstead, and the horses from various sources. Topliss (vol. 1, p. 136) notes an unidentified newspaper clipping in which Bob Bates's son Jack claimed that the woman in the coach was a Mrs Caldow, wife of the then proprietor of the Swan Vale Hotel. During the Tom Roberts Festival at Inverell in April 1996 there was considerable dispute about the identities of figures in *Bailed up*. However the only confirmed subject of significance is the coach-driver Bob Bates, of whom the Art Gallery of New South Wales has a separate portrait study on a wood panel. At the 1996 Tom Roberts Festival it was assumed that Roberts had painted the coach *inside* the Oxford Hall, a large and splendid community hall which then stood behind the Oxford Hotel, Inverell. (Information from Bobbie Miller, Inverell Shire Library.)

2. The 1893 oil study for *Bailed up* (Topliss no. 234a) poses some intriguing questions, assuming that the building of the 'perch' at Paradise Creek, and the painting of *Bailed up* there, and at Inverell and Newstead, all happened in 1895. For in spite of its rough execution this study contains remarkably precise placement of figures and horses in accordance with the main painting. Even the tree-trunks in the background landscape bear resemblance to the final composition, although there is only a vague suggestion of the rounded slope which leads to a shallow gully at the left. Yet following his inscription dedicating this study to Mrs Anderson, Roberts has clearly dated it "Dec. 31 1893", just a few days after his arrival at Newstead, and more than one year before commencing the main painting. Presuming the accuracy of this date there are two possible explanations. Firstly, that some time between his arrival at Newstead on 23 December 1893 and the end of the month Roberts found the roadway location for his subject on the Newstead side of Paradise Creek, elevating himself, perhaps by climbing a tree, to ascertain the viewpoint he wanted (the oil study appears to be consistent in this respect), and looked at models for horses, figures and coach to begin fleshing out his idea; all within the space of about seven days. The

alternative and more plausible explanation is that the oil study for *Bailed up* is largely conceptual. Roberts may well have seen the Paradise Creek location in December 1893 and made direct sketches of it, but worked out the bushranging incident with exactitude in his mind long before he began to paint from models, simply posing them in 1895 to fit in with his already well-defined conception of a road-block log accompanied by the appropriate coach and figures. A third, but remote, possibility is that Roberts misdated the work and that he should have written 1894 not 1893. This is unlikely however, since it appears from correspondence cited by Topliss (vol. 1, p. 72) that Roberts was at Yulgilbar from late 1894 until the beginning of January 1895, when he painted Edward Ogilvie's portrait (dated 1895) before riding 270 kilometres to Newstead, preparing himself no doubt to embark upon the main painting of *Bailed up*. Even more remote is an artist's mis-date of 1895. On 31 December of that year Roberts left for Port Macquarie and the Hastings River, completing his travels on 26 January and returning to Newstead where he stayed for the rest of summer. A re-dating to 1895 would mean that the oil study was intended as a memento of *Bailed up*, completed by Roberts for Mrs Anderson either at Newstead the day of his departure, or in Sydney with the intention of giving it to her after his trip.

3. *Age* (Melb.), 24 October 1896; cited in *Golden Summers*, 1985, p. 144.

4. *In a corner on the Macintyre*, NGA, was first shown in September 1895 in the same exhibition as *Bailed up*. Although much smaller – 73.4 x 88 cm to *Bailed up*'s 134.5 x 182.8 cm – it seems intended to complement the better-known picture: a bushranger cornered by armed police, instead of honest citizens bailed up by armed bushrangers; a rock-face in a hidden river chasm receiving the full glare of the northern sun, instead of a shadowy, forested hillside facing southwards; a noisy, angular, composition echoing with gunshot, instead of mysterious pause and stately calm; camouflaged and hidden figures among the at-first-sight uninhabited rocks, instead of the suddenly lined-up crowd in a forest clearing. The rock-face casts the depicted shadows into the Macintyre River exactly at noon. The hidden site, at the confluence of the Macintyre and Paradise Creek, is one kilometre from the roadside setting of *Bailed up*. (Site inspections by Daniel Thomas 1983 and 1995 and Bobbie Miller, Inverell Shire Public Library, August 1996 who says that the south-west-facing slope which she and Thomas recognise, is not unanimously agreed to and that a second possibility faces west.)

5. In comparing the frieze-like, mythologising narrative of both *Bailed up* and *In a corner on the Macintyre* with the paintings of Puvis de Chavannes (1824-98), who was much admired by Roberts, it is interesting to consider Roberts's painting *The sculptor's studio*, 1885, depicting a sculptor at work on a classical frieze.

6. In 1996 *Bailed up* underwent x-ray photography by the Conservation Department of the Art Gallery of New South Wales, but no detailed conclusion can be made until combined with infra-red photography and paint-section analysis. X-ray revealed a portion of post-and-rail fence at the bottom left of the picture and in front of the legs of the far left horse, in accordance with the small oil study (Topliss no. 234a), but likely to have been painted out in the early stages of the work. Spate (1972, note 47, p. 141) suggests that Roberts is unlikely to have been able to change the background of *Bailed up* extensively in his late years, partly due to the fact that he was forced because of gout to paint with his left hand. However the current examination suggests, along with Roberts's own dated inscription, that the repainting in 1927 was quite substantial. The repainting of *Bailed up* and its restoration history are the subject of a paper in preparation at the Art Gallery of New South Wales. Meanwhile, Mary Eagle has suggested that study of *In a corner on the Macintyre* may give some idea how *Bailed up* may have originally looked in terms of paint handling.

7. The formal landscape properties of *Bailed up* especially had an influence on Fred Williams (1927-82). See Craig McGregor *et al.*, *In the making*, Melbourne: Thomas Nelson Australia, 1969, p. 103, which illustrates *Bailed up* with Williams's *My garden*, 1965-67, and Robert Jacks's *Red painting*, 1967, accompanied by quotes from Williams: "I repaint other people's paintings. See that there? That's *Bailed up*. You know, Tom Roberts. I've just taken the figures out and repainted the background. Now Robert Jacks has repainted my picture; he was around here the other night and had a good look at it". "I repaint other pictures all the time. With this one I even made sure mine had the same measurements as Tom Roberts's. Oh no, I'm not going to be outdone by any of those fellows ...". In fact Williams's canvas, 152.6 x 183.3cm, was bigger than *Bailed up*, 134.5 x 182.8. His subject, however, the back hill on his two acres in the Dandenong Ranges at Upwey, was steep and forested with gum trees and tree ferns, resembling the steep hillside with gum trees and grass trees in *Bailed up*. He made conscious use of Roberts's skyless precedent for the 'suspended' subject. Jacks's Minimalist *Red painting*, 175 x 237.5 cm, was not derived in any way from *My garden* or *Bailed up*, although he does remember being impressed by the large size of *My garden*. (Information given to Daniel Thomas by Lyn Williams and Robert Jacks 15 July 1996).

Masculinity and Modernity
Leigh Astbury pp. 124-147

Acknowledgements: I would like to thank Linda Sproul for helping me to re-think Roberts and Andrew Sayers for his assistance, and Daniel Thomas for his understanding.

1. D. H. Souter, "Tom Roberts, Painter", *Art and Architecture* (Syd.), vol. 3, no. 4, July – August, 1906, p. 137.

2. McQueen p. 719.

3. McQueen p. 153.

4. See Topliss nos. 33, 34, 36, 41 and 42.

5. Frederick Wedmore, "Modern Life in Modern Art", *The Magazine of Art* (London), vol. 11, 1887-88, pp. 78 and 80.

6. Sidney Dickinson, "What Should Australian Artists Paint?", *Australasian Critic* (Melb.), 1 October 1890, p. 22; Dickinson's article is reprinted in Bernard Smith (ed.), *Documents on Art and Taste in Australia: The colonial period 1770-1914*, Melbourne: Oxford University Press, 1975, pp. 247-51.

7. See Robert Dixon, *Writing the Colonial Adventure: Race, gender and nation in Anglo-Australian popular fiction, 1875-1914*, Oakleigh, Vic.: Cambridge University Press, 1995. Dixon's argument focuses on Australia's relation to Britain and the Empire, but it is more generally applicable to the relationship between Old World and New World countries during the period.

8. Moore, vol. I, p. 74. John Rothenstein, *The Life and Death of Conder*, London: Dent, 1938, p. 29.

9. William Gay, *Walt Whitman: His relation to science and philosophy*, Melbourne: Mason, Firth, McCutcheon, 1895; cited by A. L. McLeod (ed.), *Walt Whitman in Australia and New Zealand: A record of his reception*, Sydney: Wentworth Press, 1964, p. 15.

10. John Le Gay Brereton, "Hints on Walt Whitman's 'Leaves of Grass'", *Hermes* (University of Sydney), 14 August 1894, pp. 8-9, cited by A.L. McLeod, *op. cit.*, pp. 67 and 70. For Le Gay Brereton's acquaintance with Roberts in 1894, see McQueen p. 391.

11. Richard Twopeny, *Town Life in Australia*, London: Elliot Stock, 1883, p. 4.

12. See Graeme Davison, *The Rise and Fall of Marvellous Melbourne*, Carlton, Vic.: Melbourne University Press, 1978, pp. 21-22, 25 and *passim*.

13. *Argus* (Melb.), 30 September 1893, cited by McQueen p. 220.

14. Twopeny, *op. cit.*, pp. 12, 21, 74-5, 199-200. See Margaret Maynard, *Fashioned From Penury: Dress as cultural practice in colonial Australia*, Oakleigh, Vic.: Cambridge University Press, 1994, pp. 86-7.

15. Charles Baudelaire, *The Painter of Modern Life and Other Essays*, translated and edited by Jonathan Mayne, London: Phaidon, 1964, pp. 32-33.

16. For *At the Melbourne Cup* see Topliss no. 712. *Promenade, Queenscliff* appeared in the *Illustrated Australian News* (Melb.), 18 December 1886 and is reproduced in Leigh Astbury, *City Bushmen: The Heidelberg School and the rural mythology*, Melbourne: Oxford University Press, 1985, p. 59, fig. 64.

17. James Abbott McNeill Whistler, *The Gentle Art of Making Enemies* (1885), New York: Dover, 1967, p. 144.

18. Maggie Indian, "Formalisation of Urban Leisure: Melbourne 1880-1900", in Richard Cashman & Michael McKernan (eds), *Sport, Money, Morality and the Media*, Sydney: University of New South Wales Press, 1981, p. 286 and *passim*.

19. Marshall Berman, *All that is Solid Melts into Air: The experience of modernity*, New York: Verso, 1983, p. 152.

20. *Table Talk* (Melb.), 30 August 1889, cited by Spate, p. 86.

21. Andrew Garran (ed.), *The Picturesque Atlas of Australasia*, Sydney: The Picturesque Atlas Publishing Company, 1886-1889 (?), vol. 1, p. 225.

22. *Ibid.* See McQueen, p. 217, who alludes to the treatment of the theme of the arrival of the overseas mail at the Melbourne Post Office in the work of colonial artists such as Nicholas Chevalier and S.T. Gill.

23. Twopeny, *op.cit.*, pp. 74-5 and 79-80; Twopeny conjectured that the French *modistes* manufactured a hybrid style of dresses for Australian taste, "a compound of the *cocotte* and the American". This reflects interestingly on the combination of Old World and New World elements in Roberts's *Allegro con brio, Bourke Street west.* Marion Fletcher, *Costume in Australia 1788-1901*, Melbourne: Oxford University Press, 1984, pp. 120, 147-8, 159 and p. 176. Margaret Maynard, *op. cit.*, p. 84.

24. Charles Baudelaire, *Art in Paris 1845-1862: Salons and Other Exhibitions*, translated and edited by Jonathan Mayne, London: Phaidon, 1965, p. 118.

25. Chris McConville, "Imagining the Slum", in Penny Web (ed.), *Imagining the City*, Melbourne: Centre for Design at RMIT, [1992], p. 60. See more generally, Graeme Davison, David Dunstan & Chris McConville (eds), *The Outcasts of Melbourne: Essays in social history*, North Sydney: Allen & Unwin, 1985.

26. E. E. Morris (ed.), *Cassell's Picturesque Australasia*, Melbourne: Cassell, vol. 1 (1887), pp. 80-81 and 83. For a feminist critique of the male gendering of the spaces of the city and the role of the *flâneur*, see Griselda Pollock's essay, "Modernity and the Spaces of Femininity", in her *Vision and Difference: Femininity, feminism and the histories of art*, London: Routledge, 1988, especially pp. 66-75. For a discussion of the portrayal of 'women of the night' in an Australian context and Roberts's illustrations on the theme of marriage, see Juliet Peers, "The tribe of Mary Jane Hicks: Imaging women through the Mount Rennie rape case 1886", *Australian Cultural History* (Faculty of Humanities, Deakin University, Geelong, Vic.), no. 12, 1993, pp. 139-141.

27. Twopeny, *op.cit.*, p. 16.

28. Baudelaire, *The Painter of Modern Life*, pp. 24-25; Marshall Berman, *op. cit.*, p. 137.

29. Joseph A. Kestner, *Masculinities in Victorian Painting*, Aldershot, U.K.: Scolar Press, 1995, p. 157; R. W. Connell, *Masculinities*, St Leonards, NSW: Allen & Unwin, 1995, p. 187; Robert Dixon, *op. cit.*, p. 3 and *passim*; McQueen p. 348.

30. Croll *Smike to Bulldog* pp. 64-5; Robert Dixon, *op. cit.*, p. 5.

31. Souter, *loc. cit.*, p. 138.

32. See Jeffrey Richards, " 'Passing the love of women' : Manly love and Victorian society", in J. A. Mangan & James Walvin (eds), *Manliness and Morality: Middle-class masculinity in Britain and America*, Manchester: Manchester University Press, 1987. The trial and conviction of Oscar Wilde in 1895 created a marked change in public attitudes towards homosexuality so that close male friendships were liable to carry the possible taint of homosexuality. McQueen, p. 177, notes that McCubbin and Roberts had nicknamed Streeton 'Smike' after the lad in Charles Dickens's *Nicholas Nickleby* who was a devoted follower.

33. See, for example, Richard Waterhouse, *Private Pleasures, Public Leisure: A history of Australian popular culture since 1788*, South Melbourne: Longmans, 1995, section 2, "Modern Cities Modern Culture", pp. 53-154.

34. See Topliss nos. 246 and 292 for Roberts's portraits of Ada Furlong and Florence Greaves and no. 185 for *The Paris hat.* For Eileen Tooker's costume see Margaret Maynard, "Julian Ashton's *Spring*: A case for Australian dress studies", *Australian Journal of Art* (Art Association of Australia), vol. IV, 1985, pp. 55 and 62.

35. Linda Sproul, Lecture in Contemporary Visual Culture course, Department of Visual Arts, Monash University, 28 March 1996.

36. McQueen pp. 87 and 200. See Joseph A. Kestner, *op. cit.*, p. 42.

37. Topliss no. 26.

38. Elaine Showalter, *Sexual Anarchy: Gender and culture at the fin de siècle*, London: Virago, 1992, chapter 8, "The Veiled Woman", especially pp. 144-5 and 148. See Robert Dixon, *op. cit.*, pp. 84-85.

39. Mary Eagle, "Between the Bush and the Boudoir", *Artonview* (National Gallery of Australia, Canberra), no. 6, winter 1996, pp. 11-12. In terms of the imperialist connotations of the subject, we need to take into account the background of British imperialist activities in Africa, including the occupation of Egypt in the early 1880s.

40. J. G. 'DeLibra', "The Poetry of our Painting", *Australasian Art Review* (Syd.), vol. 1, no. 7, 1 September, 1899, p. 8; Topliss no. 315.

Portraiture and Nationalism
Helen Topliss pp. 148-167

1. Alfred Deakin, "*And Be One People*": *Alfred Deakin's Federal Story*, Melbourne: Melbourne University Press, 1995.

2. Foreword, *Exhibition and Sale of Paintings Prior to Leaving Australia*, Sydney: Society of Artists, 1900. (The commission for the big Parliament picture changed Roberts's intentions about leaving Australia in 1900).

3. Mihaly Szegedy-Maszak, " The Idea of National Character: A Romantic heritage", in P. Boerner (ed.), *Concepts of National Identity: An interdisciplinary dialogue*, Baden-Baden: Nomos Verlagsgesellschaft, 1986, p. 45.

4. For the influence of literature and poetry on Roberts's work see Topliss, *A catalogue raisonné*, pp. 16-18; also Helen Topliss, *The Artists' Camps: Plein air painting in Australia*, Melbourne: David Hedley, 1992, pp. 81-89, 96-99; and Leigh Astbury, "Poetic Impulse in Australian Landscape Painting: The Heidelberg School reconsidered", *Meridian: The La Trobe University English Review* (Melb.), vol. 4, no. 2, October 1985.

5. Helen Topliss, "Tom Roberts' Aboriginal Portraits", in Ian & Tamsin Donaldson (eds), *Seeing the First Australians*, Sydney: Allen & Unwin, 1984.

6. Croll p. 33

7. Tom Roberts, *Argus* (Melb.), 4 July 1890, p. 10. James Smith's critique was in the *Argus*, 28 June 1890, p. 10.

8. Roberts letter to Alfred Deakin, 17 November 1903, reprinted by R.M. Crawford, "Tom Roberts and Alfred Deakin", in Franz Philipp & June Stewart (eds), *In Honour of Daryl Lindsay*, Melbourne: Oxford University Press, 1964, letter 5, p. 163.

9. Tom Roberts, *The British Australian* (London), 30 August 1906.

10. The panel portraits are illustrated in Topliss, nos. 225, 244-264, 279 and 319.

11. D.J. Quinn, "Artists and Artistic Taste in Australia", *Review of Reviews* (Syd.), 20 November 1896.

12. Roberts letter to McCubbin, 1912, MS 8187, LT.

13. Croll p. 88.

14. Jane Price, Memoir of Roberts, reprinted Croll pp. 150 ff.

15. A.G. Stephens, *The Bookfellow* (Syd.), 29 April 1899, p. 31.

16. John McPhee, *Australian Decorative Arts*, Canberra: Australian National Gallery, 1982, p. 40.

17. The Mr Panton referred to by Prenzel was Joseph Anderson Panton, a high-ranking public servant and an amateur artist who had trained in Paris. See Douglas Pike (ed.), *Australian Dictionary of Biography*, vol. 5 (1851-1890), Melbourne: Melbourne University Press, 1974, p. 396.

18. "The Artist: Some Words with Prenzel", *Triad* (Melb.), 10 May 1923.

19. *Sydney Morning Herald*, 21 October 1895, p. 3.

20. Tom Roberts letters to Alfred Deakin, in Franz Philipp & June Stewart, *op. cit.*, p. 173.

21. Alfred Deakin, *op. cit.*, p. 3 (see above, note 1).

22. *Ibid.*, p. 169.

23. See McCubbin's 1916 account of the development of Australian art, reprinted in Bernard Smith, *Documents on Art and Taste in Australia*, Melbourne: Oxford University Press, 1975, p. 269-279.

Reflections on the late work
Barry Pearce pp. 168-181

1. *Penelope*, 1919, was purchased in 1920 by NGV from the artist's solo exhibition at Athenæum Hall.

2. Frederick McCubbin (1855-1917) made his only visit overseas for about six months in 1907, spending most of his time in England.

3. Arthur Streeton (1867-1943) left Australia in 1897, travelling to Europe via Egypt. He came back to Australia intermittently to hold successful exhibitions and travelled also to Canada and the United States. He returned to Australia permanently in 1923, settling in Victoria.

4. Charles Conder (1868-1909) left Australia in 1890 to live in France and London, never to return.

5. Roberts letter to McCubbin, 30 June 1912, MS8187/596/4 (6), LT; cited McQueen p. 555.

6. James Quinn (1871-1951), Melbourne-born and -trained, at the National Gallery School, studied for eight years in Paris from 1893 and later settled in London. In 1909 Roberts wrote to McCubbin that Quinn had suggested the restricted colour range so that the eye "isn't deceived by the brilliance of the pigment". Roberts letter to McCubbin, MS8187/596/4 (4), LT; cited Topliss, vol. 1, p. 75.

7. The portrait *Mme Hartl*, c1909, NGA; Topliss no. 406.

8. Duncan Anderson, owner of Newstead station when Roberts painted *The Golden Fleece* and *Bailed up*, had sold his Australian property and retired in 1905 to London where he remained a constant friend.

9. Humphrey McQueen, *Tom Roberts*, Sydney: Macmillan, 1996.

10. *Argus* (Melb.), 4 July 1890, p. 10.

11. Roberts letter to his wife Lillie, 6 December 1919, MS 2/2150a, Fryer Library, State Library of Queensland, Brisbane; cited McQueen p. 608.

12. Based on Topliss catalogue raisonné.

13. Talisman still stands; media reports in July 1996 that it had been felled by a falling tree during a storm were mistaken. The damaged house, the subject of Roberts's painting *The pink cottage*, 1923, faced Talisman across the beginning of Royle Avenue and was often locally confused with Talisman, perhaps because it is an older house, and conspicuous, whereas Talisman, on the western side, is almost completely hidden. The street leading to 'the pink cottage' and Talisman, formerly McIntosh Road, was re-named Tom Roberts Road following a campaign by Colonel Donovan Joynt when he owned Talisman; the new name was unofficially in use in the 1960s and formally approved by the Shire of Sherbrooke on 3 September 1973. Information from Dorothy Williams and Robert Coleman, Monbulk Historical Society, and from Sandra Steggard, Yarra Ranges Shire, July-August 1996.

14. McQueen p. 565.

15. Elioth Gruner is an interesting case in point. The late John Brackenreg, a close friend of the artist during the 1920s and 1930s, told the writer that during the first half of his career Gruner had a stronger admiration for Streeton. By the beginning of the 1920s he had become disillusioned with Streeton's commercialism but "never failed", according to Brackenreg, "to doff his hat respectfully to Roberts".

16. Based on informal discussions between the writer and Lloyd Rees, 18 February 1985, concerning the artist's paintings of the late 1930s; writer's personal diary.

17. Roberts letter to Major de Bertodano, 20 November 1924, Tom Roberts biographical file, The Art Gallery of New South Wales Library, Sydney.

18. Roberts letter to Barnett, 14 December 1926, MSS 285/14/59, ML.; cited McQueen p. 680.

19. The contemporary Queensland painter William Robinson (born 1936) is descended from the family of Tom Roberts's mother. Information from Ray Hughes, Sydney, 14 June 1996.

Tom Roberts, Etcher
Roger Butler pp. 182-185

1. Topliss also includes *Untitled. Construction site* as no. 767 in her catalogue raisonné. That etching is by Jessie Traill, most likely her *Concreting Tower – Yallourn. Sketch*, 1924.

2. *Age* (Melb.), 19 January 1886, p. 6.

3. Topliss, illustrates (no. 714) an 1889 invitation printed from a process block. Charles Conder also produced artistic invitations (Campbell Dodgson catalogue, nos 34-37).

4. This is collaborated by Croll who noted, p. 22, that "For a time following his return from the old country, he dabbled in the difficult art of etching. A few prints are extant, one being a plate done at Phillip Island in 1886, and another from one of a Chinese cafe in Melbourne, etched in 1888 [*sic*]".

5. Mason had presented a lecture on printmaking, entitled "The multiplying art", at the Technological Museum, Melbourne, in May 1871. On 17 April 1886 Roberts exhibited an etching at the Buonarotti Club, Melbourne (Buonarotti Club papers, Castlemaine Art Gallery, Victoria; photocopy, La Trobe Library, State Library of Victoria, Melbourne). Mary Eagle kindly supplied this reference.

6. Buxton Knight letter to Tom Roberts, 2 August 1887, MS A2480/89, ML. Roberts may also have seen etchings by Jules Bastien-Lepage which had been published in *L'Eau-Forte* (Paris) in 1878 and 1879.

7. Croll p. 22.

8. Catalogued by Topliss, no. 762, as *Untitled. Camp fire scene.*

9. James Lindo-Webb letter to Mrs Roberts, 29 November 1933: "... at the end of 1889 ... He was doing some etchings at this time, and I greatly prize a single proof – with a dedication to myself – of a sombre scene on 'Fisherman's Bend' on the Yarra" (Croll p. 144).

10. N. Shiels, "The Art of Etching", *Sydney Quarterly Magazine*, 1892, p. 318.

11. *Sun* (Melb.), vol. VI, no.16, 21 April 1893, p. 6.

12. Particularly *La Danse sous les arbres* (Mannocci 19). A portfolio of etchings by Claude Lorrain and Karel Dujardin was accepted from Roberts's estate by the Trustees of the AGNSW, 27 November 1931. This portfolio was drawn to my attention by the late Nicholas Draffin.

13. The NGA impression of the etching, Topliss no. 766, is signed and dated '93 (and inscribed with the title *Springtime*); another is recorded as inscribed, not by the artist, "Ring o' Roses,/ at Cremorne Point/ Sydney Harbour/ 1895 ...". A small oil painting of the landscape setting, Topliss no. 221, is signed and dated 94. The painting that was developed from the etching is signed and dated 1931 though it was painted in London in 1904-5 and reworked in Australia in 1931; titled *Ring a Ring a Roses* in Topliss (no. 690) the NGA has now reinstated its original title *Australian Pastoral* (information from Mary Eagle 8 August 1996).

14. J.W. Beattie had impressions taken from Benjamin Duterrau's plates (Clifford Craig, *The Engravers of Van Diemen's Land*, Hobart: Tasmanian Historical Research Association, 1961, p. 56). Victor Cobb reprinted Lionel Lindsay's 'Pirate Series' c1919. Angus & Robertson in 1918 republished seven etchings by Julian Ashton in editions of fourteen.

15. The plate was in the possession of Cyril Dillon in 1920 when Roberts revisited Australia. Dillon pulled proofs at that time (Croll p. 22). An impression of *A Chinese cook shop* inscribed "Printed by Cyril Dillon" is noted by Topliss. Dillon was at that time in partnership with Daryl Lindsay. They printed (and reprinted) etchings for many artists. Etched plates by Will Dyson and Harold Herbert were still in Dillon's possession at his death.

16. On 1 March 1946 Jessie Traill wrote to Mrs Croll: "Yes, I remember the plate of old Buvelot – Think I have it in my studio ... I used to keep a lot of plates in a box under the press all wraped [*sic*] in newspaper written on outside what they were ... Or on the shelf under the table [or] shelf at the window" (Croll papers, MS 8910 1211/2(d), State Library of Victoria).The Buvelot plate is now in the possession of the NGV (date of gift unknown). Most impressions of this plate are wiped in the 'artistic manner' favoured by Traill. Traill also lent an impression of *At Phillip Island* to 'A memorial exhibition of paintings by the late Tom Roberts', The Fine Art Society's Gallery, Melbourne, 1932.

Contributing Authors

Ron Radford, Director, Art Gallery of South Australia, Adelaide.

Jane Hylton, Curator of Australian Art, Art Gallery of South Australia, Adelaide.

Humphrey McQueen, Freelance historian whose biography *Tom Roberts* was published in 1996 by Macmillan.

Mary Eagle, Senior Curator of Australian Art and Curator of Australian Painting & Sculpture, National Gallery of Australia, Canberra. Author of the forthcoming *The Oil Paintings of Charles Conder, E. Phillips Fox and Tom Roberts in the National Gallery of Australia*.

Virginia Spate, Professor of Fine Arts, University of Sydney, New South Wales, and author of Tom Roberts, 1972, the first critical study.

Leigh Astbury, Senior Lecturer in Visual Art, Monash University, Melbourne, and author of *City Bushmen*, 1985, and *Sunlight and Shadow*, 1989, both on late-nineteenth-century Australian painting.

Daniel Thomas, Emeritus Director, Art Gallery of South Australia, Adelaide.

Barry Pearce, Senior Curator of Australian Art, Art Gallery of New South Wales, Sydney.

Helen Topliss, Post-Doctoral Fellow at the Humanities Research Centre, Australian National University, Canberra. Author of *Tom Roberts 1856-1931: A catalogue raisonné* published in 1985 by Oxford University Press.

Roger Butler, Curator of Australian Prints, National Gallery of Australia, Canberra.

Select Bibliography

Astbury, Leigh. *City Bushmen: The Heidelberg School and the rural mythology*, Melbourne: OUP, 1985.

Astbury, Leigh. *Sunlight and Shadow: Australian impressionist painters 1880-1900*, Kensington, NSW: Bay Books, 1989.

Badham, Herbert. *A Study of Australian Art*, Sydney: Currawong, 1949.

Bonyhady, Tim. *Images in Opposition: Australian landscape painting 1801-1890*, Melbourne: OUP, 1985.

Bradley, Anthony & Smith, Terry. *Australian Art and Architecture: Essays presented to Bernard Smith*, Melbourne: OUP, 1980.

Campbell, Robert. *Paintings of Tom Roberts*, Adelaide: Rigby, 1963.

Clark, Jane & Whitelaw, Bridget. *Golden Summers: Heidelberg and beyond*, Sydney: International Cultural Corporation of Australia, 1985 (for an exhibition organised by the National Gallery of Victoria, Melbourne).

Croll, R.H. *Tom Roberts: Father of Australian landscape painting*, Melbourne: Robertson & Mullens, 1935.

Croll, R.H. (ed.). *Smike to Bulldog: Letters from Sir Arthur Streeton to Tom Roberts*, Sydney: Ure Smith, 1946.

Eagle, Mary. *The Oil Paintings of Arthur Streeton in the National Gallery of Australia*, Canberra: NGA, 1994.

Eagle, Mary. *The Oil Paintings of Charles Conder, E. Phillips Fox and Tom Roberts in the National Gallery of Australia*, Canberra: NGA, forthcoming 1997.

Finemore, Brian. *Freedom from Prejudice: An introduction to the Australian collection in the National Gallery of Victoria*, Melbourne: NGV, 1977.

Finlay, Eleanor & Morgan, Marjorie. *Prelude to Heidelberg: The artists' camps at Box Hill*, Burwood, Vic.: Victoria College Press, 1991.

Galbally, Ann & Plant, Margaret (eds). *Studies in Australian Art*, Melbourne: Department of Fine Arts, University of Melbourne, 1978.

Galbally, Ann. *Frederick McCubbin*, Richmond,Vic.: Hutchinson, 1981.

Galbally, Ann & Gray, Anne (eds). *Letters from Smike: The letters of Arthur Streeton 1890-1943*, South Melbourne: OUP, 1989.

Gleeson, James. *Impressionist Painters 1881-1930*, Melbourne: Lansdowne, 1971.

Hoff, Ursula. "Reflections on the Heidelberg School", *Meanjin* (Melb.), vol. 10, no. 2, 1951.

Hoff, Ursula. *Charles Conder*, Melbourne: Lansdowne, 1969.

Hughes, Robert. *The Art of Australia*, Harmondsworth, Middlesex: Penguin, 1970 (and later editions).

Jaffe, David. "Cutting the dags from Shearing the rams", *Bowyang* (University of Sydney), no. 7, March 1982.

McCulloch, Alan. *The Golden Age of Australian Painting: Impressionism and the Heidelberg School*, Melbourne: Lansdowne, 1969.

McCaughey, Patrick & Manton, Jack. *Australian Painters of the Heidelberg School: The Jack Manton Collection*, Melbourne: OUP, 1979.

McQueen, Humphrey. *Tom Roberts*, Sydney: Macmillan, 1996.

Moore, William. *The Story of Australian Art* (2 vols), Sydney: Angus & Robertson, 1934.

Pearce, Barry & Slutzkin, Linda (eds). *Bohemians of the Bush: The artists' camps of Mosman*, Sydney: AGNSW, 1991 (for an exhibition).

Radford, Ron. *Moonrise*, Ballarat: BFAG, 1973 (for an exhibition).

Radford, Ron. *Ladies in Landscapes*, Ballarat: BFAG 1974 (for an exhibition).

Radford, Ron. *19th-Century Australian Art: M.J.M. Carter Collection, Art Gallery of South Australia*, Adelaide: AGBSA, 1993.

Radford, Ron & Hylton, Jane. *Australian Colonial Art 1800-1900*, Adelaide: AGBSA, 1995.

Smith, Bernard. *Place, Taste and Tradition: A study of Australian art since 1788*, Sydney: Ure Smith, 1945.

Smith, Bernard. *Australian Painting 1788-1960*, Melbourne: OUP, 1962 (and later expanded editions).

Smith, Geoffrey. *Arthur Streeton 1867-1943*, Melbourne: NGV, 1995 (for an exhibition).

Spate, Virginia. "Tom Roberts", *Art and Australia* (Syd.), vol. 1, no. 4, 1964.

Spate, Virginia. *Tom Roberts*, Melbourne: Lansdowne, 1972.

Spate, Virginia. "The Sunny South", in Norma Broude (ed.), *World Impressionism: The international movement, 1860-1920*, New York: Abrams, 1990.

Splatt, William & Bruce, Susan. *Australian Impressionist Painters: A pictorial history of the Heidelberg School*, Melbourne: Currey O'Neil, 1981.

Thomas, Daniel. *Outlines of Australian Art: The Joseph Brown Collection*, South Melbourne: Macmillan, 1973 (and expanded editions 1980, 1989).

Thomas, Daniel (ed.) & Radford, Ron (curator). *Creating Australia: 200 years of art 1788-1988*, Sydney & Adelaide: International Cultural Corporation of Australia & AGBSA, 1988 (for the Australian Bicentennial Authority's The Great Australian Art Exhibition 1788-1988).

Topliss, Helen, in Donaldson, Ian & Tamsin (eds). "Tom Roberts' Aboriginal Portraits", in *Seeing the First Australians*, Sydney: Allen & Unwin, 1984.

Topliss, Helen. *The Artists' Camps: Plein air painting in Melbourne 1885-1898*, Clayton, Vic.: Monash University Gallery, 1984 (for an exhibition).

Topliss, Helen. *Tom Roberts 1856-1931: A catalogue raisonné* (2 vols), Melbourne: OUP, 1985.

Topliss, Helen. *The Artists' Camps: 'Plein air' painting in Australia*, Alphington, Melbourne: Hedley, 1992.

Whitelaw, Bridget. *The Art of Frederick McCubbin*, Melbourne: NGV, 1991 (for an exhibition).